National Parks

Teton Range and Snake River. *Courtesy of the National Archives, Ansel Adams photograph*

National Parks

❧

The American Experience

Fourth Edition

ALFRED RUNTE

TAYLOR TRADE PUBLISHING

Lanham · New York · Boulder · Toronto · Plymouth, UK

Published by Taylor Trade Publishing
An imprint of The Rowman & Littlefield Publishing Group, Inc.
4501 Forbes Boulevard, Suite 200, Lanham, Maryland 20706
http://www.rlpgtrade.com

Estover Road, Plymouth PL6 7PY, United Kingdom

Distributed by National Book Network

British Library Cataloguing in Publication Information Available

Library of Congress Cataloging-in-Publication Data
Runte, Alfred, 1947–
National parks : the American experience / Alfred Runte. — 4th ed.
p.   cm.
Includes bibliographical references and index.
ISBN 978-1-58979-473-3 (cloth : alk. paper) — ISBN 978-1-58979-475-7 (pbk. :
alk. paper) — ISBN 978-1-58979-474-0 (electronic)
1. National parks and reserves—United States—History. I. Title.
E160.R78 2010
973—dc22
2009043910

Printed in the United States of America

In Memory of My Mother and Father

CONTENTS

CONTENTS

ILLUSTRATIONS

ILLUSTRATIONS

PREFACE

I T is said that the national parks are our best idea—that their idealism defines America. Surely, just having parks elevated conservation above simple common sense. Once Americans believed in saving beauty, the land itself became inspirational. To the founders of national parks in the nineteenth century, that meant the natural wonders of the West. In time, the national park idea was variously modified and applied to other chosen landscapes, including a multitude of recreation areas, urban preserves, military parks, and historic sites. The original label is nonetheless indelibly associated with inspiring scenery and expansive nature. When Americans hear the term "national park," they think instantly of magnificent landscapes.

That achievement—and its contradictions—remain the focus of this book. Beyond people, events, and legislation, this is the story of the national park idea. In America's perception of landscape as a cultural icon lies the enduring explanation for national parks. The purpose of this edition is to reaffirm that the parks are indeed a living subject. Much has been written over the past 30 years that needs again to be placed in proper sequence. Nor does anything like a rewrite help retrieve missed opportunities. The extent of those revisions aside, I of course stand by my original work.

To be sure, the national *idea* has not materially changed since the first edition of this book in 1979. Rather, the difference today is in the times. Fifty years ago, still beloved by the World War II generation, national parks were an American rite of passage. Like millions of American families in the 1950s, mine discovered the parks by car. In 1958 my father, Paul, died of a heart attack. A German veteran, wounded in the trenches during World War I, he had aged before his time. Although my mother, Erika, little wanted the role of a single parent, she found herself free to pursue a dream. In a national magazine, probably the *Saturday Evening Post*, she had read an article about the Teton Mountains and Jackson Hole. We should go there, she decided, before my brother, August, and I were grown. In the spring of 1959, she bought a tent, three sleeping bags with air mattresses, and a small green Coleman stove. She bought retreads for our 1954 Chevrolet station wagon, the only tires she could afford. As soon as school let out, we headed west. The road maps were our responsibility. August and I were to choose routes and give her directions so she could concentrate on the driving. For the next six weeks, on a trip covering 10,000 miles, she rarely made a turn without consulting us.

It was the experience of a lifetime made all the more meaningful by the public lands. Although our home in Binghamton, New York, lay near a state park, it hardly compared with the federal lands of the West. In South Dakota, a stopover to explore our family history first brought the importance of those lands into focus. Because the entire West began as public land, everything unwanted or unusable for settlement might later be preserved. Erika's father had originally settled in Marshall County, in the northeastern corner of the state. A German immigrant (probably fleeing conscription), he arrived in the United States through New York City in 1891. Advised to find work in the logging camps, he soon headed for upper Michigan and Minnesota. From there, he found his way to South Dakota and the bluestem prairies lying west of the timber belt.

Marshall County, we learned from the official atlas, had been settled largely in the 1880s. Following the standard process of government survey, the county had first been divided into townships. Each township contained 36 square miles, consecutively numbered and known as sections. The Homestead Act of 1862 then applied. Most claimants were entitled to a quarter section, or 160 acres. If showing improvements within five years, the land was awarded free. The first people to settle in Marshall County had obviously come away with the choicest tracts. Grandfather was left to purchase a homestead in Waverly Township, including 120 acres in the southeastern quarter of section 10. However, because the remaining 40 acres in that quarter section still belonged to the government, he was able to obtain those under the Homestead Act.

Meanwhile, still devoutly Old Country, he had found and married a German wife. Her death during childbirth in 1908 motivated grandfather's return to Germany, as no eligible women (i.e., German) remained in Marshall County. Allegedly, the moment he stepped off the ship, he headed for his hometown newspaper to place an ad. Wanted: Wife willing to live in South Dakota, Waverly Township, USA.

Although grandmother answered the ad and agreed to marry him, she had no idea what that meant. If grandfather carried pictures of the homestead, they showed the truth—not a tree in sight. Did they really have to settle *here*, grandmother asked—and the nearest neighbor a mile away? In 1914, grandfather relented and sold the homestead, using the proceeds to buy a dairy farm in upstate New York. Three of four children were born in the farmhouse, my mother in 1918. Home at last among the wooded hills, grandmother raised her family to love trees and flowers. However, Sunday was grandfather's day with the children and for story time in the parlor. Always he carried them back to South Dakota and the prairies he had also loved.

My mother's urge to see the West thus involved more than my father's death. Regardless, none of us was prepared for the awe-inspiring emptiness beyond Marshall County—the West of the public lands. By the time we reached Badlands National Monument, I knew what grandfather had missed. It seemed you could see forever, dream forever. The first idealists fulfilled by that discovery had obviously then thought of us. Before the entire West was claimed and settled, something of its wonder should be preserved. Carved into Mount Rushmore we saw the face of Theodore Roosevelt, one of those idealists, we soon discovered. At our next stop, Devils Tower, Wyoming, a ranger explained why it was called a national monument, adding that Theodore Roosevelt, securing a new reputation for presidential initiative, had proclaimed this monument as the nation's first.

The point is that by the time we arrived at Yellowstone, we were in love with the national parks. With her new friends at West Thumb campground, mother agreed it was the best investment she had ever made. August still remembers the one-armed man who took him fishing along the shore of Yellowstone Lake. Every morning, wandering the pathways above the Fishing Cone, I delighted in having the hot pools to myself. Not even the crowd and traffic jam at Old Faithful Geyser could dissuade us from the magic of such a place. The Grand Canyon of the Yellowstone then sealed the magic. Obviously, Yellowstone would always be drawing crowds.

It was on our entrance to Jackson Hole that we sensed a different kind of park. The Teton Mountains, filling the sky to the west, dwarfed our campground on Jackson Lake. For a park still open to cars and so close to Yellowstone, Grand Teton seemed gloriously undeveloped. Even though it was developed and fully accessible, somehow a sense of wilderness had not been lost. Surely, this was the national park experience Mother had read about and what the founders had meant by "unimpaired."

Ahead lay Crater Lake, Yosemite, Grand Canyon, and the anticlimactic push for home. In Yosemite, Mother drove August through the base of the Wawona Tunnel Tree while I raced around it to get a picture. I never did go through. My privilege was later to understand the moment as the lost naïveté of a golden age. On my return to the parks after college, I realized how special the summer of 1959 had been. In just 10 years, the environmental battles of the 1960s had forged a new ambivalence about whether to have great parks at all. In California, Congress talked seriously about cutting the redwoods beyond another protected grove or two. Dams were also planned for the Grand Canyon. Although the canyon was spared and a redwood national park begun, the original dream—unimpaired—seemed everywhere in jeopardy.

The few serious studies of the national parks were disappointing, at best a political history. The parks so obviously owed their establishment to American culture—to America's perception of itself. I determined to write that history as the focus of my PhD. Roderick Frazier Nash of the University of California, Santa Barbara, agreed to be my adviser. His recent *Wilderness and the American Mind* brilliantly pointed the way to what the national parks deserved. Richard Oglesby, also of the Department of History, and Harold Kirker, its cultural historian, similarly lent generously of their time and energy to the completion of my dissertation and ultimately to this book.

To my good fortune, what some have referred to as the University of the Wilderness proved to be widespread. The staffs of numerous libraries, including the Bancroft Library, William Penn Memorial Museum, Library of Congress, Yosemite Research Library, and National Archives, also gave generously of their time and facilities. A dissertation fellowship from Resources for the Future, in Washington, D.C., provided funding for an entire year. For all editions, the National Park Service, now through the Harpers Ferry Center, allowed me special access to its pictorial archives in the interest of meeting my publishing deadlines. In 2004, the Fundação O Boticário de Proteção à Natureza, Brazil (Boticário Foundation for the Protection of Nature), lent special incentive to this

edition, first inviting me to serve on the editorial board of *Natureza &
Conservação*. There followed an amazing opportunity, an invitation to
give the opening plenary address at the Fourth Brazilian Congress on
Parks and Protected Areas in Curitiba.

Encouragement also came from unexpected and unexpectedly meaningful quarters. Yellowstone often remains the trip of a lifetime for those
first experiencing national parks—at whatever age. Even as this fourth
edition was in progress, I toured the Yellowstone inspirations of my youth
with dear friend Jeffrey Duban and his 19-year-old son Paul Petrek-
Duban, a life-altering experience by both their accounts. The concluding
work in this volume was subsequently aided by a contribution from the
Petrek-Duban Family Fund, in memory of Jeanne A. Petrek, MD (1948–
2005). Jeanne was a distinguished surgical oncologist at Memorial Sloan–
Kettering Cancer Center, New York City, for over 20 years at the time of
her tragically foreshortened life. During her career, she saved, guided,
and comforted thousands of lives. In April 2006, I attended the scattering
of Jeanne's ashes at Keys View, Joshua Tree National Park, in southern
California. The location had been one of her favorites. Thus did an inspirational woman regain eternity, at an inspirational entry point, the facing mountains ranked in tribute.

Coincidentally, my mother went to Memorial Sloan–Kettering in
1987 for a second opinion about her cancer. I would like to think she
met Jeanne, even if only to say hello. In an instant, their signature smiles
would have proved them kindred spirits in whom creation had found
true advocates. A city, Mother always said, is just a city. Earth alone renewed her hope. No matter the genius of our civilization, the national
parks remind us of our greater destiny.

Because their defenders have thus persevered, the parks continue to
exist. The moment we think otherwise, they and the land will be gone. Is
that worth our constant narcissism about what is or is not "cutting edge"?
The best writing on behalf of any subject always comes from the heart.
As late historians of the national parks, Robin W. Winks, Grant W.
Sharpe, Morgan Sherwood, and Robert Cahn never feared giving me
that advice. Each was indeed a special friend. Further memorialized by
the national parks, Paul Shepard, Ansel Adams, David Brower, Wallace
Stegner, T. H. Watkins, Edward Abbey, and Hal K. Rothman are also
greatly missed.

Although it is tempting to believe that we control the earth, undoubtedly the pendulum will swing again. As I write, the national parks are to

be featured in a major series on public television by Dayton Duncan and Ken Burns. I am proud to have been among their advisers. Perhaps the series—and again this volume—will deepen the nation's interest. For never doubting the value of my efforts, I further thank my wife, Christine. On her own travels to Egypt and with me to Brazil and Europe, she has seen what parks also mean to the world.

For the United States and now nearly 200 countries, the answer to civilization is public parks. What some see as a simple choice between preservation and development is in fact history's most difficult choice— restraint. Out of the excesses of a country in the making grew the conviction of national parks. Before changing the land, Americans ought to know it in the original. Never would such beauty come again. Only if "We the People" pledged government to the protection of nature might the gift of the land prevail.

Voyageurs NP

Isle Royale NP

Apostle Islands NL

Pictured Rocks NL

Acadia NP

Sudbury, Assabet, and Concord National Wild and Scenic River

Saint Croix NSR

Cape Cod NS

Sleeping Bear Dunes NL

Mississippi NRRA

Mounds NM

Upper Delaware S&RR

Fire Island NS

Gateway NRA

Indiana Dunes NL

Cuyahoga Valley NP

Delaware Water Gap NRA

Assateague Island NS

Gauley River NRA

Shenandoah NP

New River Gorge NR

Bluestone NSR

Ozark NSR

Mammoth Cave NP

Cape Hatteras NS

Big South Fork NRRA

Obed WSR

Great Smoky Mountains NP

Cape Lookout NS

Buffalo NR

Hot Springs NP

Congaree NP

Little River Canyon N PRES

Chattahoochee River NRA

Cumberland Island NS

Timucuan Ecological and Historic Preserve

Big Thicket N PRES

Canaveral NS

Gulf Islands NS

Big Cypress N PRES

Biscayne NP

Everglades NP

Dry Tortugas NP

Key to Abbreviations

NL: National Lakeshore
NM: National Monument
NP: National Park
N PRES: National Preserve
NR: National River
NRA: National Recreation Area
NRR: National Rec River
NRRA: National River and
          Recreation Area
NS: National Seashore
NSR: National Scenic River
S&RR: Scenic and Rec River
WSR: Wild and Scenic River

Primary Units with Natural Values of the National Park System

Boundaries and Scales Approximate

0   200   400   MILES
0   200   400   600 KILOMETERS

© 2009 J. David Thorpe

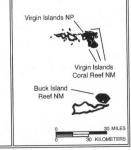

Virgin Islands NP

Virgin Islands Coral Reef NM

Buck Island Reef NM

0   30 MILES
0   30 KILOMETERS

Before the opening of the West, America's grand attraction was Niagara Falls. Originally wrapped in a wilderness setting, Niagara impressed even skeptical Europeans as great scenery. As the nineteenth century progressed, so did the raids on Niagara's beauty, until its reputation for sublime nature had been destroyed. In this winter photograph of the American Falls, c. 1900, an observation tower awaits the return of summer tourists, who will still see smokestacks above the trees. *Courtesy of the American Museum of Natural History*

PROLOGUE
Paradise Lost

Happily the United States Government (warned by the results of having allowed the Falls of Niagara to become private property) determined that certain districts, discovered in various parts of the States, and noted for their exceeding beauty, should, by Act of Congress, be appropriated for evermore "for public use, resort, and recreation, and be inalienable for all time."
— LADY C. F. GORDON-CUMMING, British traveler, 1878

EGINNING in the middle of the nineteenth century, a small group of visionaries and idealists pioneered a unique experiment in landscape democracy—the national park idea. America's natural "wonders," they believed, should not fall into the hands of profiteers. Rather, as the public lands were opened to settlement, the nation should be mindful of their scenery. Indeed the very identity of the United States required that its natural wonders remain in public ownership.[1]

Gradually, perceptions of the environment changed. Ultimately, wilderness preservation and wildlife protection gained near equivalency with protecting natural wonders. To be sure, the national park idea as we know it today did not emerge in finished form. More accurately, it evolved. The debate nonetheless remains: What should the nation preserve—and how. Despite new emphases on wilderness and ecology, most visitors to the national parks still gravitate to spectacular scenery. Magnificent landscapes and natural phenomena never seem to disappoint. Even as environmentalists struggle to reverse that perception, the understanding of parks is the need for visitors. Whether and how that affects a park's ecology has been the last thing on peoples' minds.

Throughout history, a landscape fashioned into something useful has always been the easier goal to rationalize. With that conviction, ancient civilizations of the Near East fostered landscape design and management long before the birth of Christ. By 700 B.C., Assyrian nobles sharpened their hunting, riding, and combat skills in designated training reserves. These were copied by the Persian Empire, whose great hunting enclosures and royal gardens flourished throughout Asia Minor between 550 and 350 B.C. It remained for the Greeks to democratize landscape esthetics; their larger towns and cities, including Athens, provided citizens with the *agora*, a plaza for *public* assembly, relaxation, and refreshment. Logically, with its fountains and tree-shaded walkways, the agora presaged the modern city park.[2]

Inevitably, the cities of the Roman Empire copied the Greeks, until the fall of Rome erased those experiments. Centuries earlier, even the sacred landscapes of the ancients had begun falling victim to the plough and ax.[3] Medieval Europe, like Asia Minor, then reverted to the maintenance of parks exclusively for the ruling classes. In fact, the word "park" stems from hunting as the primary use of open space. Originally "parc" in Old French and Middle English, the term designated "an enclosed piece of ground stocked with beasts of the chase, held by prescription or by the King's grant."[4] Trespassers were severely punished, and poachers could be put to death.

With the possible exception of Greece and Rome, therefore, parks as we define them today are of modern origin. Only in the recent past have they come to mean both protection and public access. Beginning in Europe and soon after the United States, the rapid spread of cities, towns, and factories forced a reawakening. The social upheaval of the industrial revolution finally could not be ignored.

Weighed down by the drudgery and grime of manufacturing, people looked for avenues of escape. A first was the romantic movement. Fashionably, urban residents used art and literature to imagine themselves somewhere else — in a beautiful meadow, gazing down from a mountaintop, or reading poetry beside a woodland stream. Visiting the countryside proper, romanticists invariably preferred landscapes only suggestive of human occupation. Too much detail invited contradictions about whether people and nature could coexist. A crumbling ruin returning to nature assured the viewer that nature was still in charge. Others held that the ultimate good might be the absence of civilization altogether — so argued deists and primitivists, at least, the former because civilization allegedly obscured God's truths, the latter in the conviction that people seemed happiest in direct proportion to the absence of their creations.[5]

While romanticism encouraged an affection for landscape, the egalitarian ideals of the American and French revolutions similarly challenged historical assumptions regarding privilege. Finally, the natural preserves of European royalty gave way to greater public use. In 1852, for example, Napoleon III began the transformation of Paris's popular Bois de Boulogne—a 2,000-acre woodland on the city's western outskirts. Likewise, change was abroad in London. There, beginning in the eighteenth century, the monarchy had released open space to the needs of the general populace. By 1845, England's road to landscape democracy included Victoria Park, on London's crowded East End. As notable, it was the first park not only managed but also expressly purchased for public instead of private use. An American admirer, Frederick Law Olmsted, similarly praised its twin in Liverpool, Birkenhead Park. Henceforth, Birkenhead was also to be "entirely, unreservedly, and for ever the people's own. The poorest British peasant is as free to enjoy it in all its parts as the British queen," he wrote. "More than that, the baker of Birkenhead has the pride of an owner in it. Is it not," he concluded, "a grand good thing"?[6]

For Olmsted and public parks, it was the beginning of a long and distinguished partnership. Certainly, no American is more associated with their early advocacy and design. On his return from England in 1850, he was still just 28. The son of a prosperous Connecticut family, he fortunately had the means to pursue his passions. With urban design and horticulture heading them, he prepared himself to become America's leading visionary in the establishment of city parks.[7]

As important, the climate of opinion had already swung in the United States, ironically, propelled by concern about the dead. As cities grew, so did the number of bodies collecting in urban churchyards. Before the Civil War and the widespread use of embalming, it was a health hazard no city could ignore. In 1831, Boston won approval from the Massachusetts legislature for a "rural cemetery" on the city's outskirts. Called Mount Auburn, it surprised visitors by serving the needs of the living and the dead. Suddenly, it was Boston's most popular spot to have a picnic or take a stroll. After all, open space was open space. The ornate statuary and tombstones dripping with sentimental passages proved another enormous draw. The combination proved irresistible. Soon Brooklyn and Philadelphia, among other cities, had rushed to create rural cemeteries of their own.[8]

As the institution proved, every combination of the aesthetic with the practical ensured the growth of the park idea. In 1832, Congress established oak preserves for the navy in Florida and protected Hot Springs, Arkansas, as a federal "reservation." Although so designated for its medicinal values, Hot Springs was arguably a public park. Certainly the *idea* of parks had gained momentum. Its next evolution drew on the work of Andrew Jackson Downing, a renowned Hudson Valley horticulturalist, and William Cullen Bryant, editor of the *New York Evening Post*. Beginning in the 1840s, both called for the establishment of a large reserve within easy reach of New York City. Despite Downing's tragic death in a Hudson River steamboat accident, his insistence on a park of at least 500 acres survived intact. In 1853, the New York legislature approved Downing and Bryant's vision, purchasing a rectangular site (slightly larger than the equivalent of one square mile) just north of the city on Manhattan Island. Once the city had built up around it, it would be "central" to all things. Meanwhile, it awaited a designer's inspiration. When the city announced a competition, Frederick Law Olmsted and his partner, Calvert Vaux, handily won.[9]

The precedent was finally undeniable. In the purchase and protection of these scattered landscapes, government had recognized the public interest. Otherwise, the national park idea evolved in response to environmental perceptions of a dramatically different kind. City parks were refuges from urban living. Urbanites might want beautiful surroundings and a quieter pace but not necessarily *scenic* preservation. In a city park, the primary concern was access. A city park might always evolve, growing from even an occupied site. Portions of Central Park itself displaced the shanty communities of struggling residents and immigrant farmers.[10] Once a site had been obtained, the landscape architect undertook to make it pleasing but not necessarily to keep it true. As convenient, lakes were added and streams diverted, rocks removed, and woodlands planted. Although natural, a city park was hardly wilderness, its only requirement that beauty should prevail.

In coming years, a growing demand for racetracks, fairgrounds, and ornate statuary strained the conviction that even urban parks were meant for beauty. A tireless opponent of all such schemes, Frederick Law Olmsted argued that the line was clear. The difference between enjoying a park and simply encroaching on it was whether the addition spoke to nature. Uses purely amusing could be accommodated anywhere. Regardless, open space was forever *the* temptation. How, critics asked, could anyone harm a square-mile park by taking just a piece?[11]

Later, the placement of roads, trails, and lodgings in the national parks invited a similar range of arguments. Yet beyond the need for allowing access, the national parks were different. The city park came after the city—a response to the noise and monotony of crowded streets. In contrast, the national parks preceded settlement in an attempt to save the West. Scenery for its own sake was indeed the catalyst. Emerging from the East, explorers and pioneers found the West monumental. Cliffs and waterfalls thousands of feet high, canyons a mile deep, and mountains soaring above the timberline satisfied a cultural longing. National parks, as distinct from urban parks, called for a different set of rules. In the West, scenery alone was justification for having parks, even if their recreational value would not be realized for years or decades.

The West had one other, enormous advantage: The vast majority of it was public land. Beginning with the Ordinance of 1785, the Confederation Congress provided for the survey and disposal of the public domain. Once obtained by treaty and fully surveyed, western lands were slated to be sold. A survivor of the Constitutional Convention, the pattern lasted until 1936 (in Alaska until 1960). The point is that throughout the process, settlers consistently picked the choicest lands. Mountains and deserts where the scenery soared to perfection invariably remained in public ownership. Despite every other travail, including squatting, timber theft, and illegal entry, a great deal of land survived in government hands. Simply, the fortuitous combination of public land and spectacular scenery was a phenomenon of the West.[12]

In the East, the appreciation of scenery had largely followed settlement; in the West, the process was reversed. Whether as scenery or public lands, most of the East had already been claimed by private owners. Often, what the transcendentalists themselves described as nature was their neighbors' fields and farms. No sooner had the mountains of the East been visited by artists than loggers, too, were right behind. Even then, losing everyday landscapes was not compelling, no matter what artists and writers thought.

Simply, preservation in the East lacked a sense of urgency. The decision not only to admire nature but also to preserve it needed some irrefutable loss. For the East, indeed for the nation, that loss proved to be Niagara Falls. Then America's identifying natural wonder, every artist

In this tourist lithograph c. 1910, the conquest of Niagara Falls is complete. Factories and the city of Niagara Falls line the banks of the Niagara River. A visitor railway monopolizes the popular overlooks. Left of the arch bridge, virtually a third cataract has been formed to power a grouping of mills below the American Falls. On the Canadian side, a powerhouse commands the lower foreground. Featuring Goat Island between the American and Horseshoe falls, the 1885 Niagara Reservation, meant to protect nature from civilization, seems virtually overwhelmed. *Author's collection*

and traveler felt obliged to see it. Every European visitor felt the same. By the 1830s, all noticed the falls disappearing behind an array of fences and tacky buildings. Drawn by the surge in tourism following completion of the Erie Canal in 1825, developers battled to control the overlooks. As the railroads brought even more tourists, the competition for business did not abate. By 1850, the best overlooks had been fenced and gated and visitors forced to pay handsomely—many claimed exorbitantly—for the privilege of getting through.[13]

As a first and troubling consequence, European visitors escalated their criticism of American democracy, pointing to the commercialization of Niagara. To be sure, although half of the falls lay in Canada, rarely was that mentioned in America's defense. As often, the lines between Canada and the United States grew blurred. Because both were behaving badly, neither should be excused. Perhaps Europe's most famous critic to write in this vein was the young political scholar Alexis de Tocqueville. In 1831, during the extended visit to the United States that led to his classic work *Democracy in America*, he urged his mother to "hasten" to Niagara if she wished "to see this place in its grandeur. If you delay," he warned, "your Niagara will have been spoiled for you. Already the forest round about is being cleared. . . . I don't give the Americans ten years to establish a saw or flour mill at the base of the cataract." In a similar vein, E. T. Coke, a British journalist, wrote in 1832 of a "company of speculators" intending to erect "grist-mills, store-houses, saw-mills, and all other kinds of unornamental buildings" in the vicinity. "The die is then cast," he concluded, "and the beautiful scenery about the Falls is doomed to be destroyed."[14]

Although early by American standards, a good number of these observations concluded with a plea to protect Niagara. "'Tis a pity," Coke further wrote, "that such ground was not reserved as sacred in perpetuum; that the forest trees were not allowed to luxuriate in all their wild and savage beauty about a spot where the works of man will ever appear paltry, and can never be in accordance. For my own part, most sincerely do I congratulate myself upon having viewed the scene before such profanation had taken place." Another English traveler, Thomas Rolph, as swiftly shared Coke's lament. "I wish it were provided by law," Rolph agreed, "that no building should be erected . . . immediately adjoining the cataract." As matters stood in 1833, "another twenty years may see the whole amphitheatre filled with grog-shops, humbug museums, etc., etc.—Who knows but it may be profaned by cotton factories?"[15]

Other British writers foreseeing factories included two Congregational ministers, Andrew Reed and James Matheson. Visiting in 1834, they noted the "shabby town" of Manchester hugging the bank on the American side. "Manchester and the Falls of Niagara!" They made no effort to veil their disgust. "One has hardly the patience to record these things." Some "universal voice ought to interfere, and prevent them," they agreed with Coke and Rolph. "Niagara does not belong to [individuals]; Niagara does not belong to Canada or America. Such spots should be deemed the property of civilized mankind."[16]

If still the missing word was "park," all of a park's critical emotions were in place. To be sure, heeding Coke, Rolph, Reed, and Matheson, perhaps England, and not the United States, would now be credited for inventing the national park idea. Until Canada won its independence in 1867, England certainly had the opportunity. West to the Pacific, the Canadian provinces boasted a variety of natural wonders, many on a par with those in the United States. European countries simply lacked the provocation; Europe's identity was secure.

Meanwhile, Europe's disparaging comments—especially the published ones—went to America's heart. Was the problem a lack of pride, many asked? "By George, you would think so indeed, if you had the chance of seeing the Falls of Niagara twice in ten years," answered another British traveler, Sir Richard Henry Bonnycastle. Visiting the cataract in 1849, he confirmed the credibility of all past ridicule. Certainly, by now the fate of the falls was "a well-worn tale." Surely "so old a friend as the Falls of Niagara; for you must have read about those before you read Robinson Crusoe," deserved better than injury "by the Utilitarian mania." But "the Yankees [have] put an ugly shot tower on the brink of the Horseshoe [Fall]," he lamented, "and they are about to consummate the barbarism by throwing a wire bridge . . . over the river just below the American Fall. . . . What they will not do next in their freaks it is difficult to surmise," he wrote, then echoed his predecessors' disgust: "but it requires very little more to show that patriotism, taste, and self-esteem, are not the leading features in the character of the inhabitants of this part of the world." As "a public property," Niagara Falls "should be protected from the rapacity of private speculators," he concluded, "and not made a Greenwich fair of."[17]

In truth, many Americans had fallen in love with their continent, but again, just not enough. As early as 1765, the flora and fauna of the American Southeast excited the brilliant surveys of John and William Bartram. Even as Niagara Falls was besieged, another great naturalist, John James Audubon, labored to complete his handsome folio volumes of American birds. Lewis and Clark had long since returned from the Pacific, with their journals and drawings safely intact. The eyes of wonder and discovery America had. A leadership for preservation it did not.

Talk about redeeming Niagara Falls had come too late. Although clearly the nation's irrefutable wonder, it had succumbed entirely to private ownership. Any reprieve for nature (and the nation's reputation) finally lay across the continent. It was now up to the Rocky Mountains and Pacific slope. As the settled East became their opposite, distance further magnified their appeal. The effect was to make the East the audience to the final act of national development. Fortuitously, Americans conquered the West precisely as popular literature, art, and journalism came of age. While the last frontier passed into history, the nation watched intently, if not in person then through its dime novelists, correspondents, artists, and explorers.

As each glorified the West, the nation slowly grasped the opportunity, until the words "public" and "protection" were no longer far apart. Just as Europe retained custody of the artifacts of Western civilization, so the United States might sanctify its natural wonders. The problem again was delay; the wonders of the West would not stay public forever. At least disappointment had turned to hope. The West indeed offered a chance to redeem Niagara, if for once the nation could act in time.

From a sketch by Thomas A. Ayres, this first published view of Yosemite Valley in 1855 featured what was then known as Yo-Hamite Falls. Although frequently dry in summer, no natural wonder more rapidly assured Americans that the West was a repository of superlative scenery. *Courtesy of the Yosemite National Park Research Library*

CHAPTER 1

The American West

Eastward I go only by force, but westward I go free.
— HENRY DAVID THOREAU, 1851

The eastern half of America offers no suggestion of its western half.
— SAMUEL BOWLES, 1869

Why should we go to Switzerland to see mountains or to Iceland for geysers? Thirty years ago the attraction of America to the foreign mind was Niagara Falls. Now we have attractions which diminish Niagara into an ordinary exhibition.
— NEW YORK HERALD, 1872

A MERICA'S incentive for national parks lay in the discovery that scenery was a cultural asset. Writing his one true book, *Notes on the State of Virginia*, Thomas Jefferson set the stage. Asked to support the American Revolution, France asked in return to know its suitor. Why should France take the risk, and more, on a nation yet to prove itself? The result was Jefferson's responses, his *Notes*, begun in the fall of 1780. Just what *had* America achieved, he was also forced to ask himself. What would France—indeed the rest of Europe—admire and respect? So far, there was nothing distinctive about American architecture; the United States had few painters whom Europe envied. In truth, the country was as raw as its independence, and that independence was still much in doubt.[1]

Jefferson found himself stripped to a single argument—what the United States *might* become. As decisively, European intellectuals were bound to disagree. In Europe's view, a distinctive American culture had yet to make its mark. Jefferson's one hope was to turn creative, using an opening provided by France itself. Preceding its questions on American society, France asked about the character of the nation's topography. What were its navigable rivers and noted mountains; what important sea-ports did it claim? What natural riches—minerals, trees, fruits, and plants—distinguished the country's productivity? Did it have notable cas-cades and possibly caverns, and where might these be found?

If Jefferson the scientist answered with painstaking accuracy, as a na-tionalist he banked on pride. The Potomac River, he stated boldly, was all the proof that France should need. "The passage of the Patowmac through the Blue ridge is perhaps one of the most stupendous scenes in nature," he wrote. The site of present-day Harpers Ferry, it was hardly as he described. No matter, in Jefferson's estimation the Blue Ridge matched the Alps. "You stand on a very high point of land. On your right comes up the Shenandoah, having ranged along the foot of the moun-tain an [*sic*] hundred miles to seek a vent. On your left approaches the Patowmac, in quest of a passage also." Together, the rivers rushed the mountain, rent it asunder, and passed off to the sea. "This scene is worth a voyage across the Atlantic," he concluded, his pride finally cresting with the mountains. Americans, forsaking Europe, had all they needed in the Blue Ridge Mountains—and beyond.[2]

As a later guide for national parks, the point of Jefferson's challenge was that protected scenery should be dramatic. Mindful that eastern landscapes needed exaggeration, nationalists came to embrace the West as their reprieve. Like Jefferson, they had been right about America's vi-sual supremacy, only early, as it were. The Rocky Mountains and Sierra Nevada were still far distant. Jefferson meanwhile took note of Virginia's other fabled wonder, Natural Bridge in the Shenandoah Valley. It was in fact his property, acquired by patent in 1774. "It is impossible for the emotions, arising from the sublime, to be felt beyond what they are here: so beautiful an arch, so elevated, so light, and springing, as it were, up to heaven, the rapture of the Spectator is really indescribable!"[3]

In Jefferson's *Notes* are preserved these reminders that nationalism was the key to parks. In proving themselves to Europe, Americans neces-sarily emphasized what they had. The belittlements of the Count de Buf-fon and the Abbé Raynal rang immediately in Jefferson's ears.[4] "One must be astonished," he quoted Raynal, "that America has not yet pro-duced one good poet, one able mathematician, one man of genius in a

Writing in 1781, Thomas Jefferson declared the Potomac River at Harpers Ferry "worth a voyage across the Atlantic." Long afterward, the problem for American nationalists was convincing themselves that Harpers Ferry lived up to the claim. After all, why would Europeans find Harpers Ferry more imposing than the Rhine River or the Alps? *Courtesy of the National Park Service*

single art or a single science." Jefferson's answer came straight out of the revolution. "When we shall have existed as a people as long as the Greeks did before they produced a Homer, the Romans a Virgil, the French a Racine and Voltaire, the English a Shakespeare and Milton," he wrote, only "then might Europe honestly say: 'America has not yet produced one good poet.'" Given the same amount of centuries, Americans would do as much. Meanwhile, the United States, "though but a child of yesterday, has already given hopeful proofs of genius," he protested, among them, George Washington "in war" and Benjamin Franklin "in physics."[5] Getting the argument back to nature, the young nationalist Philip Freneau agreed with Jefferson. Monumental rivers, Freneau asserted, proved what America had and the Old World lacked. Consider the Mississippi, "this prince of rivers," he wrote, "in comparison of whom the *Nile* is but a small rivulet, and the *Danube* a ditch."[6]

The Danube of course was not a ditch. And why should Europeans risk crossing the Atlantic Ocean just to see Harpers Ferry? Certainly, Europe had the equivalent of the Potomac River in the scenery of the Rhine. America's penchant for stretching reality only helped Europe prove its point. The United States may have potential, but Europe still owned the past. Whether the ruins of ancient civilizations, great architecture, or the paintings of the masters, every recognized milepost of Western civilization still had to be found abroad.

Simply, the New World remained uncomfortably new. For every nationalist measuring cultural greatness in the hand of nature, another like Washington Irving still despaired. Where else might an American experience the cradle of civilization? Only Europe, Irving confided to his *Sketch-Book* in 1819, might satisfy that need. "I longed to wander over the scenes of renowned achievement; to tread, as it were, in the footsteps of antiquity; to loiter about the ruined castle; to mediate on the falling tower; to escape, in short, from the commonplace realities of the present, and lose myself among the shadowy grandeurs of the past." Although Irving conceded that no American need "look beyond his own country for the sublime and beautiful of natural scenery," anyone hoping for scenery imbued with history had no choice but visit Europe.[7]

By now 40 years had passed since Thomas Jefferson's *Notes on Virginia*, and still America was steeped in doubt. Indeed, it remained a cultural wasteland, confirmed another popular account. Worse, its author, a British clergyman and critic, was the acerbic Sydney Smith. "In the four quarters of the globe," he asked in 1820, "who reads an American book? or goes to an American play? or looks at an American picture or statue?"[8] His answer was readily apparent: no one that mattered; no one European. Even the most spirited followers of Thomas Jefferson could not be blind to the problem his argument faced. If America was to compensate with scenic nationalism, it had better find something truly great.

James Fenimore Cooper, writing in the 1840s, doubted that the disparity could ever be resolved, at least not before civilization in the New World had also advanced to "the highest state." Meanwhile, he agreed with Washington Irving: America must "concede to Europe much the noblest scenery . . . in all those effects which depend on time and association." Always "the great distinction between American and European scenery" had been America's "want of finish." Cooper recalled again "the greater superfluity of works of art in the old world than in the new"—majestic cathedrals, walled castles and cities, and similar "picturesque and striking collections of human habitations." Although nature had "certainly made some differences" between Europe and North America, still no American could deny the Old World's superiority in landscapes blessed with "the impress of the past."[9]

Printed in *The Nation* and later in *The Home-Book of the Picturesque*, Cooper's essay was widely read. An important anthology, *The Home-Book* further included essays by Washington Irving, William Cullen Bryant, and Nathaniel Parker Willis. However, even the volume's still rising authors had received critical acclaim, among them Cooper's daughter Susan. Describing a northeastern landscape (probably her home around Otsego Lake, New York), she echoed her father's misgivings. One "soft, hazy morning," she began, "we were sitting upon the trunk of a fallen pine, near a projecting cliff which overlooked the country for some fifteen miles or more; the lake, the rural town, and the farms and valleys beyond, lying at our feet like a beautiful map." Suddenly, the taverns and shops below reminded her of the "comparatively slight and furtive character of American architecture." Unlike Europe, there was "no blending of the old and new in this country; there is nothing old among us." Even if the United States were "endowed with ruins"—her bitterness grew—"we should not preserve them"; rather, "they would be pulled down to make way for some novelty." She was left to imagine some transformation—the village miraculously reconstructed into an Old World hamlet. At last, she saw the bridge she wanted—"of massive stone, narrow, and highly arched." She imagined an "ancient watch-tower" rising above the trees. She smiled down on thatched-roof cottages sprinkled among country estates. Unfortunately, it was just a spell, after all. In an instant, "the country resumed its every-day aspect." America had reverted to its raw and blemished self.[10]

As the Coopers reconfirmed, using nature as a basis for cultural superiority had clearly been problematical. All their best rhetoric aside, leading American writers and intellectuals had failed to convince themselves that the argument really worked. Against the claim of a distinctive landscape stood the realities of geography. Until the middle of the nineteenth century, the United States lay principally east of the Rocky Mountains. Outside of a scattering of natural wonders, most notably Niagara Falls, few Americans considered their country extraordinary—certainly with nothing comparable to the Alps. Added James Fenimore Cooper, "As a whole, it must be admitted that Europe offers to the senses sublimer viewers and certainly grander, than are to be found within our own borders, unless we resort to the Rocky Mountains, and the ranges in California and New Mexico."[11]

So far, the most visible thread of disagreement had come from the nation's artists and in literature the transcendentalists. Beginning in the 1820s, artists of the Hudson River School looked beyond geography to deeper interpretations of the natural world. As the intricacies of creation, rocks, trees, and flowers were held to be the word of God. Undeniably, Europe would always represent the best of the human past; the point about America was its purity. As God's original Bible, nature in America was new to art. Europe's altered landscapes, however historic, revealed only the muddled word of God.[12]

America's dilemma was that its new catechism could not escape constant changes in the landscape, too. In his noted speech and essay "Walking," Henry David Thoreau wished again for a compensating geography. Like James Fenimore Cooper, he laid his emphasis on the West. "I must walk toward Oregon, and not toward Europe," Thoreau wrote. "We go eastward to realize history and study the works of art and literature, retracing the steps of the race; we go westward as into the future, with a spirit of enterprise and adventure." The West of which he spoke was "but another name for the Wild; and what I have been preparing to say is this, that in Wildness is the preservation of the World."[13]

Still the problem, as Thoreau himself implied, was that eastern landscapes were being changed. Finally, even Niagara Falls humbled American artists into taking license, as if the development strangling its beauty did not exist. Confirming the penalty to American culture, in 1857 Frederic Edwin Church completed his masterpiece of the cataract, simply named *Niagara*. Never before, critics agreed, had a painting so captured Niagara's soul—"so vast a multiplicity of water effects," wrote one, "foam, flash, rush, dark depth, turbidity, clearness, curling, lashing, shattering, and a hundred more."[14] The point was that just as an American artist had finally mastered those details, the edge of the falls screamed the opposite. Applied to the riverbank and observation points, the same accuracy resplendent in the water would have invited critics to loath the painting. Consistently mindful that the sublimity of Niagara required its surrounding landscape, Frederick Law Olmsted concluded that the falls had indeed succumbed, now to be just another "rope-walking, diving, brass bands, fire-works" display.[15]

By the 1850s, even the most ardent champions of eastern scenery were taking cultural refuge in the West. As easterners, all dutifully visited Niagara Falls and other scenic highpoints close to home. Yet there was no denying that the nation's westward march had provided new excitement. Drawn by continental events and ambitions, by 1848 the tide of expansion had reached the Pacific coast. First the Louisiana Purchase and finally war with Mexico had enlarged the country by threefold. In the Pacific Northwest, Great Britain, conceding America's power, had withdrawn peacefully into Canada. Everywhere west, Americans grew eager to know what new scenery the country owned.

A special audience, committed nationalists, had at last found their vindication. The nation's development was not to close anticlimactically, forever stinging from the commercialization of Niagara Falls. The hint of even greater scenery lay ahead. The fortunate twist in the opportunity was the presence of the public domain. Preserving each discovery—at least temporarily—was its status as government land. Until the clearance of Indian title and an official survey, these lands remained closed to sale and settlement. Because the process was taking years, Americans had time to know what they had. Simply, the shame of Niagara need not be repeated as long as the government reserved the best scenery for itself.

As fortuitous, dramatic scenery was invariably rugged and inaccessible, land settlers tended to avoid. As president, even Thomas Jefferson, instructing the Lewis and Clark Expedition, asked for a practical route to the West. There was no point getting lost in the mountains when it was river commerce the nation needed. Still the glimmer of the national park idea survived in Jefferson's description of Harpers Ferry as monumental. He could only imagine what wonders the West was hiding. Perhaps Lewis and Clark would unearth something exotic, whether animal, vegetable, or mineral. Although the expedition discovered no living fossils (one of the president's fondest hopes), it proved that the anxiety he expressed in *Notes on the State of Virginia* drove the nation's thoughts—and his.[16]

Despite crossing the Rocky Mountains twice, Lewis and Clark sidestepped every future park. From their published reports, at least, came great expectations about western scenery. A later familiarity with the region's blank spots still left the mountain men sharing anecdotes. The confirmation of a first great wonder remained for the California gold rush. In 1848, the discovery of gold in the Sierra Nevada foothills presaged the usual clashes between natives and miners. In 1851, following repeated Indian resistance, a battalion of miners marched into the mountains to drive the natives out. Suddenly, the battalion looked down into a gaping, granite valley—obviously the Indians' stronghold. On hearing the word *Yo-che-ma-te*, the miners assumed that the Indians meant the valley. The word was eventually recast and the valley named—Yosemite.[17]

As news of its discovery spread to the East, nationalists had the answer to their prayers. Indeed merely the height of Yosemite's waterfalls left every nationalist reassured. Assembling the first party of visitors in 1855, James Mason Hutchings, a miner turned promoter and journalist, confirmed that his party had been stunned. "When we come to the 'Yo-Semite Falls' proper," his guidebook later invited a comparison, "we behold an object which has no parallel anywhere in the Alps. The upper part is the highest waterfall in the world, as yet discovered, being fifteen hundred feet in height." In 1863, William H. Brewer, of the California Geological Survey, similarly could not contain himself. "[Yosemite Falls] comes over the wall on the far side of the valley," he began, "and drops 1,542 feet the first leap, then falls 1,100 more in two or three more cascades, the entire height being over 2,600 feet! I question if the world furnishes a parallel," he continued, "certainly there is none known." Even Bridal Veil Falls—only a fraction as high as Yosemite Falls—seemed "vastly finer than any waterfall in Switzerland," he concluded, "in fact finer than any in Europe."[18]

By then, the influential editor and publisher of the *New York Tribune*, Horace Greeley, had also given Yosemite's reputation a powerful boost. However, the summer visitor would be advised to forget Yosemite's waterfalls, which, arriving in the month of August, his party had found virtually dry. Yosemite Falls itself was "a humbug," he described, making no effort to hide his disappointment. That said, Yosemite the place was well worth "a fatiguing visit." Truly, "no single wonder of nature on earth" rivaled the valley as "the most unique and majestic of nature's marvels."[19]

A year later, the Reverend Thomas Starr King wrote a similar series of articles for the *Boston Evening Transcript*. Before his party "had been twenty minutes in the Yosemite Valley," they arrived "at the foot of a fall as high and more beautiful than the celebrated Staubach, the highest in Europe." Yet while not suffering Greeley's disappointment over dried-up waterfalls, King agreed that "such stupendous rock scenery" would forever remain the greater attraction. "Is there such a ride possible in any other part of the planet?" he asked. Imagine formations such as "The Sentinel," standing 4,347 feet. "Reader, do you appreciate that height?" Nowhere "among the Alps, in no pass of the Andes, and in no Cañon of the mighty Oregon range" did anything seem to approach it. Only "the awful gorges of the Himalaya," he finally conceded, perhaps rivaled the scenery of the Sierra Nevada.[20]

Best of all, its wonders were not limited to cliffs and waterfalls. Again eclipsing anything known in the East, the Sierra further included the gi-

Offering a foretaste of the West's spectacular scenery, Yosemite Valley reassured a later generation of nationalists that Thomas Jefferson had been right. If eastern landscapes failed the
claim, Yosemite certainly met Jefferson's challenge that America was "worth a voyage across
the Atlantic." *Courtesy of the National Park Service, Ralph H. Anderson photograph*

ant sequoias, or big trees, confirmed in 1852. Certainly, no one venturing
all the way to California should miss them, Horace Greeley beseeched
his readers. From Yosemite Valley, the most popular route into the giant
sequoias led south to the Mariposa Grove. "Here, the Big Trees have
been quietly nestled for I dare not say how many thousand years," he reported. Regardless, "that they were of very substantial size when David
danced before the ark, when Solomon laid the foundations of the Temple, when Theseus ruled in Athens, when Aeneas fled from the burning
wreck of vanquished Troy, when Sesostris led his victorious Egyptians
into the heart of Asia," Greeley had "no manner of doubt."[21]

Writing in 1864, the giant sequoias, agreed the explorer Clarence
King, proved a greater American antiquity. Nothing in the Old World
had their magic ability of measuring time in "green old age." With a suggestive reference to the Sphinx and the pyramids, he dismissed all of the
big trees' architectural challengers. No "fragment of human work, broken
pillar or sand-worn image half lifted over pathetic desert,—none of these

link the past and to-day with anything like the power of these monuments of living antiquity," he maintained.[22] A graduate of Yale University, King was another perfect example of those still harboring cultural doubts. At last, possessed of Yosemite Valley and the giant sequoias, educated Americans might—for the first time—believe in their own argument.

As in the East, the tide of description wanted only for proof—artists capable of bringing the descriptions alive. In the West, the limitation of the Hudson River School was its lingering commitment to detail. A more challenging topography called for artists willing to cut canvas into yards—also to sharpen mountains and deepen canyons, if such license helped the viewer to grasp immensity. Again, while the East generally voided such exaggeration, its practice in the West seemed vital. In a smaller painting given to detail, the size of the West would vanish. Feeling that power—understanding the landscape—viewers needed to believe that they were part of the painting.

Later identified as the Rocky Mountain School, it was more accurately the Hudson River School revised. In each, colors and light were objects of perfection; it was just that the West demanded that the viewer feel its scale. Thus, on entering the Rocky Mountains in 1859, Albert Bierstadt laid the foundations of his reputation as the first of its noted artists. In the company of Colonel Frederick Lander's expedition, he sketched Wyoming's Wind River range. Returning east, he moved his studio from New Bedford, Massachusetts, to New York City, where, shortly afterward, the first of his paintings went on display at the National Academy of Design. Measuring 4½ by 9 feet, *The Base of the Rocky Mountains, Laramie Peak* thrilled visitors in April 1860. In 1865, measuring 6 by 10 feet, *The Rocky Mountains, Lander's Peak* (1863) sold for $25,000, then the highest sum ever awarded an American artist. Not only had Bierstadt's reputation been assured but, again, so had the reputation of the West for stunning scenery.[23]

Pursuing the region's most publicized wonder, Bierstadt next invested in a trip to Yosemite. He arrived in August 1863 to spend the better part of two months.[24] With every stroke of his pen or brush, the reputations of Horace Greeley, the Reverend Thomas Starr King, and other journalists rose equally in the public's estimation. As an artist, Bierstadt's edge was a public hungry for a vibrant, visual record. Nor was his audience disappointed. More monster paintings followed—Yosemite's walls soaring, its waterfalls hurtling, even its sunsets brought home alive. God's perfection, a Bierstadt painting advised, must surely be found in Yosemite. His clients most certainly believed it. In 1867, *Domes of the Yosemite*, meas-

After Albert Bierstadt's acclaimed painting, *The Rocky Mountains, Lander's Peak* (1863), this contemporary lithograph (James David Smillie, engraver) demonstrates the critical process by which the popular media broadcast the grandeur of the West. *Courtesy of the Library of Congress*

uring a whopping 9½ by 15 feet, equaled the price paid for *The Rocky Mountains, Lander's Peak*—another $25,000.[25]

In those instances when the public doubted Bierstadt, there remained the simultaneous rise of landscape photography to put those doubts aside. As early as 1861, Carleton E. Watkins photographed Yosemite Valley and the giant sequoias, producing 30 mammoth plates. With fanfare similar to that reserved for Bierstadt's paintings, the photographs then toured the East. Beyond that critical note of verification, the advantages of a painting remained. More than confirming the place, the viewer, it seemed, was *there*. Allowed the powers of color and artistic license, Bierstadt fashioned Yosemite into a feeling as much as scenery. In *The Rocky Mountains, Lander's Peak*, the placement of an Indian encampment in the foreground similarly amplified the mountains. Popular with nationalists, the style was seen as bolstering the argument that American scenery also exceeded the sensations of the Alps. Not until the 1880s and a rise in America's confidence did that technique—and Bierstadt—fall out of favor. Meanwhile, if he embellished his landscapes to look more alpine— or painted stunning composites of several views—he merely gave the country what it wanted. At last, Bierstadt assured the nation, all of Europe's scenery had been eclipsed.[26]

Copied as engravings for popular distribution in newspapers and magazines, the works of Albert Bierstadt, Carleton E. Watkins, and other artists provided the visual component of cultural nationalism. To be sure, they alone did not inspire the national park idea. Yet by consistently dramatizing the nation's losses, artists contributed to the evolution of concern. It was in fact a young Pennsylvania artist, George Catlin, who suggested how failure in the future might be avoided. In 1827, he had eagerly joined the throng of painters determined to try their hand at Niagara Falls. However, as much as the water intrigued him, he soared mentally above the cataract. There ruminating on the changing face of Niagara, he produced an accurate bird's-eye view. Whether meant to assure tourists that Niagara was "civilized" or possibly to lament that fact, his 1831 series of lithographs, *Views of Niagara*, began by noting the roads, mills, fields, and farmhouses invading Niagara from every side.[27]

In 1829, Catlin headed west, now as determined to paint the Indians before their cultures were swept away. Three years later, at Fort Pierre, Dakota Territory, he observed a band of Sioux slaughtering buffalo in order to trade their hides for whiskey. Might there be an alternative? he asked the following year, writing a letter to the *New York Daily Commercial Advertiser*. Against the corrupting influences of civilization, he offered "A *nation's Park*, containing man and beast, in all the wild and freshness of their nature's beauty!" Niagara Falls must have been on his mind when he sensed how his park would redeem America. Think what "a beautiful and thrilling specimen" it would be, he concluded, "for America to preserve and hold up to the view of her refined citizens and the world, in future ages!"[28]

Certainly, Niagara was not that example. Meanwhile, if talk of saving Niagara had gained little traction, it was hardly surprising that Catlin's grander vision also stalled. Given the perceived difficulty of assimilating natives in the first place, now to suspend their cultures seemed truly radical. Indeed, not until a century later—as exemplified in 1934 with the authorization of Everglades National Park—did national park proponents recognize wilderness (let alone natives) as the equivalent of spectacular scenery. In founding the national parks, the United States would consistently prefer limiting their area, and exactly, as Catlin agonized, sweep aside all but the remnants of native America.[29] At least, the word "park" had been applied to an actual landscape and might, at the appropriate time, be resurrected farther west.

Twenty years later, a spirited exchange between American and European botanists involving the giant sequoias presaged that opportunity. Inevitably, such monumental plants needed a monumental name. Speaking for Britain, the noted botanist John Lindley offered *Wellingtonia gigantea* in honor of the Duke of Wellington. "We think that no one will differ from us in feeling that the most appropriate name to be proposed for the most gigantic tree which has been revealed to us by modern discovery is that of the greatest of modern heroes," Lindley wrote, pleading his case. "Wellington stands as high above his contemporaries as the California tree above all the surrounding foresters. Let it then bear henceforward the name WELLINGTONIA GIGANTEA."[30]

But of course, Wellington was *England's* hero, and this an *American* discovery and tree. How dare the British forget the hero of Yorktown while advancing the hero of Waterloo. The tree should be *Washingtonia gigantea* and celebrate the American Revolution, recalling Thomas Jefferson's *Notes on Virginia*, honoring "whose name will triumph over time, and will in future ages assume its just station among the most celebrated worthies of the world." Not so much as the stump of a sequoia, Americans still agreed, should honor the Duke of Wellington.[31]

In a less passionate moment—and with a slight bow to George Catlin—the giant sequoias officially became *Sequoia gigantea* after Chief Sequoyah, the inventor of the Cherokee alphabet.[32] The deeper point about this debate remains its added incentive for national parks. Already, promoters had targeted specimen sequoias for display in the East and Europe. Thus, "The Mother of the Forest," in the Calaveras Grove, was vandalized in 1854. Rather than topple the giant, a process requiring days, promoters decided to remove only the bark. Satisfied after reaching a height of 116 feet, they finally cut the shell into manageable sections and shipped everything off to New York. During its first European unveiling, the exhibit further bedazzled thousands at London's Crystal Palace.[33]

The point finally was the number of opponents. Like an earlier exhibit, the "Discovery Tree," this one was both heralded and condemned. In 1853, *Gleason's Pictorial,* a popular British journal, published a letter protesting the Discovery Tree's disfigurement as "a cruel idea, a perfect desecration." Actually a transplanted Californian, the writer noted that "such a natural production," if native to Europe, "would have been cherished and protected, if necessary, by law; but in [our] money-making, go ahead community, thirty or forty thousand dollars are paid for it and the purchaser chops it down and ships it off for a shilling show."[34] A rash of similar accusations (and lingering cries of a hoax) suggested that America had failed again. If indeed its cultural identity resided in landscape, why were the big trees being felled? Ultimately in failing to protect the sequoias, the nation had simply renewed Niagara's shame.

Making matters worse, settlers further argued for the right to claim Yosemite Valley in advance of an official survey. In 1859, a Virginia settler, James C. Lamon, claimed land in the east end of the gorge. Four years later, James Mason Hutchings returned to the valley, claiming 100 acres of its best meadow and building land. However development of the valley proceeded, it would somehow touch his property. Never had the specter of Niagara loomed so near. If title to Yosemite passed to Lamon and Hutchings, even the public lands offered no protection for scenery. Although anyone distant from the government land office had the right to settle and later secure proper title, that law—called preemption—applied only to surveyed lands. Because that official survey of the region had not occurred, any claim to Yosemite was null and void.[35]

The dilemma remained the possibility that Hutchings and Lamon might still prevail. Nothing prevented Congress from amending the law or granting them an exception.[36] Merely the threat of favoritism was enough to jeopardize Yosemite's value as a cultural icon. As Niagara proved and then the sequoias, only if America protected the valley from encroachment would the world agree that the nation cared.

The momentous convergence of these events and ideas may be traced to the winter of 1864. Finally moving on the conviction that the sequoias and Yosemite Valley were national treasures, a small group of Californians persuaded their junior U.S. senator, John Conness, to propose federal legislation for a park. Although the campaign failed to list its members, the commitment they wanted was abundantly clear. The known advocate is Israel Ward Raymond, the California state representative of the Central American Steamship Transit Company of New York. On February 20, 1864, he addressed a letter to Senator Conness, urging preservation of Yosemite Valley and the Mariposa Grove of giant sequoias "for public use, resort, and recreation." Raymond was equally insistent that both parcels be "inalienable forever."[37] Perhaps the term was his own. More likely, several people suggested the wording, including Frederick Law Olmsted, whom Raymond suggested be appointed a park commissioner. Since 1863, Olmsted had also been in California—in fact just a day's ride west of Yosemite—managing the holdings of the Mariposa Estate. Although he did not see the valley proper until August 1864, he was well aware of its fame. Either in New York or California, Raymond and Olmsted could have met several times.[38] In any case, Conness took the initiative. Requesting that the commissioner of the General Land Office prepare a bill, he forwarded Raymond's letter and repeated, "Let the grant be inalienable."[39]

That Conness agreed to the wording reflects how far America had come. The motives of preservation aside, securing Yosemite without a commitment to its permanence hardly tested the nation's resolve. With specific reference to the giant sequoias, Conness similarly reminded his Senate colleagues that their lasting duty was patriotic. In obvious reference to the Crystal Palace, he noted that the British, on first seeing a big tree, had "declared it to be a Yankee invention, made from beginning to end; that it was an utter untruth that such trees grew in the country; that it could not be." The events of the Civil War coincided perfectly with his strategy. With the conflict in its third and bloodiest year, many in Britain continued to sympathize with the South. As bad as giving aid and comfort to the enemy, they had discredited an American icon. "They would not believe us," Conness repeated. Yosemite Valley, although believed, was equally in jeopardy from private claimants. Whichever argument tipped the scales, Congress proved receptive from the start. On June 30, 1864, Abraham Lincoln signed the Yosemite Park Act into law.[40]

As presaged by a decade of description, the purpose of the park was scenic. Only Yosemite Valley and its encircling peaks—approximately 56 square miles—ultimately received protection. A similar restriction applied to the southern unit, the Mariposa Grove of giant sequoias. There, a maximum of four square miles was allowed protection.[41] Obviously, such limitations ignored the biological framework of the region, especially its major watersheds. Nationalism, not environmentalism, still explains the origins of the Yosemite grant.

To be sure, every lingering problem of interpretation hinges on why California received the grant. On the surface, it would seem that Yosemite was intended as a state park. However, Congress was not confused. The point was that Yosemite lay entirely across the country in a time of civil war. As a practical matter, Congress awarded the grant to California, whose responsibility to the nation in accepting the grant was clear: "inalienable for all time." The stipulation for "public use, resort, and recreation" also meant the *American* "public." Even as California accepted the park in 1866, writers indeed described it as a *national trust.*

The issue is best clarified in the treatment of James Hutchings and James Lamon, who immediately asked for a resolution of their claims. When the park commissioners offered them just 10-year leases, both appealed to the California legislature—and won. However, fully acknowledging the wording of the Yosemite Act, the legislature qualified that Congress must also approve. In 1868, the men won a split decision, the House voting yes and the Senate no. Senate opponents, led by George H.

Williams of Oregon, noted that Yosemite Valley had not been surveyed. The legal point remained, Williams insisted. Settlers residing on the un-surveyed public domain did so "at their peril." The government was under no obligation to sell to anyone; the mere act of squatting conveyed no rights. Hutchings and Lamon should rather have weighed their prospects by "the remarkable features of the place." So forewarned, they should have known that Yosemite Valley might "not be treated by the government like agricultural lands of an ordinary character." Yosemite Valley, "one of the wonders of the world," had been set aside as a public trust. "The government is under no equitable obligation to maintain their claims to the prejudice of the public interests."[42]

In deferring to congressional authority, the California legislature had admitted as much. If only a state park, Yosemite Valley hardly required congressional oversight whether Lamon and Hutchings deserved their claims. The legislature instead recognized the will of the nation. Although California had been given the honor of managing Yosemite, the American people remained its owners.

Looking to the future, Frederick Law Olmsted argued, the greater problem would be what to save. As a first priority, management should elevate Yosemite above the status of a "wonder or curiosity." Ideally, visitors would also learn to appreciate its "tender" aesthetic resources, notably the "foliage of noble and lovely trees and bushes, tranquil meadows, playful streams" and similar varieties "of soft and peaceful pastoral beauty."[43] In 1868, a young John Muir entered Yosemite Valley and formed the same opinion. A self-styled "poetico-trampo-geologist-bot. and ornith-natural, etc!-!-!" he wished to know all of nature. However, writing in 1875, he declared the rest of the world still "not ready for the fine banks and braes [hills] of the lower Sierra." Alleging those to be familiar landscapes, people were glad to be just passing through. "Tourists make their way through the foot-hill landscapes as if blind to all their best beauty," he lamented, "and like children seek the emphasized mountains—the big alpine capitals whitened with glaciers and adorned with conspicuous spires." Although optimistically concluding that "the world moves onward" and that one day "lowlands will be loved more than alps, and lakes and level rivers more than water-falls," he would, like Olmsted, rarely convince his contemporaries that gentle scenery mattered for *national* parks.[44]

Nineteenth-century Americans valued the West precisely because it delivered on Jefferson's promise. However the region's wonders were described, Europeans could never call them commonplace. With the conclusion of the Civil War in 1865, America's tide of description only swelled. Renewing the salvo, Samuel Bowles, as the popular publisher of the *Springfield* (Massachusetts) *Republican*, reported on his lifelong dream to see the West. "The two sides of the Continent," he began, "are sharp in contrasts of climate, of soil, of mountains, of resources, of production, of everything." In the "New West," nature had wearied "of repetitions," creating "originally, freshly, uniquely, majestically." Here was scenery "to pique the curiosity and challenge the admiration of the world."[45] Yosemite Valley "suggested the great impressiveness, the beauty and the fantastic form of the Gothic architecture." In comparison to the natural cathedrals of Yosemite, "those of Cologne and Milan are but baby-houses," Bowles instructed.[46] Accompanying his party, Albert D. Richardson of the *New York Tribune* wrote for another substantial readership, "Think of a cataract of half a mile with only a single break!" As for readers looking for the standard comparison, "Niagara itself," he confirmed, "would dwarf beside the rocks in this valley."[47]

The life-giving properties of Yosemite awaited pilgrims of another age. For the moment, Americans longed for greatness. Inevitably, the ability of the West to offer grandeur ordained it as the cradle of preservation. The "wise cession" of Yosemite, agreed Samuel Bowles, should be duplicated throughout the country.[48] Thus had Americans, in crossing the continent, come to realize that nationalism was not enough. Scenery must be preserved. If indeed American scenery was a cultural resource, it was time for nationalists to believe in parks.

Like Yosemite Valley, the wonders of Yellowstone offered the United States bragging rights as the country with the grandest scenery in the world. From the moment of their discovery, the Lower Falls and Grand Canyon of the Yellowstone inspired comparisons to European art and architecture. *Courtesy of the National Park Service, George A. Grant Collection*

CHAPTER 2

Yellowstone

As an agricultural country, I was not favorably impressed with the great Yellowstone basin, but its brimstone resources are ample for all the matchmakers of the world. . . . When, . . . by means of the Northern Pacific Railroad, the falls of the Yellowstone and the geyser basin are rendered easy of access, probably no portion of America will be more popular as a watering-place or summer resort than that which we had the pleasure of viewing, in all the glory and grandeur of its primeval solitude.

— WALTER TRUMBULL, 1871

We pass with rapid transition from one remarkable vision to another, each unique of its kind and surpassing all others in the known world. The intelligent American will one day point on the map to this remarkable district with the conscious pride that it has not its parallel on the face of the globe.

— FERDINAND VANDEVEER HAYDEN, 1872

IN 1872, the national park idea, shaped by the monumental grandeur of Yosemite Valley and the giant sequoias, was realized in name as well as in fact with the establishment of Yellowstone National Park. In marked contrast to the Yosemite grant, Yellowstone Park was huge, approximately 3,500 square miles in area. As momentous, because Yellowstone overlapped three territories, the federal government retained absolute jurisdiction. The point is that those departures from the Yosemite grant were still largely accidental. In no way had Yellowstone broken with the tradition of seeking out monumental landscapes. If anything, Yellowstone National Park reinforced tradition. Pure uncertainty explained its size; simply, no one knew how many wonders were awaiting discovery. A big expanse of territory ensured their protection until more surveys had been made. It is in hindsight that we call Yellowstone an ecosystem or, if not that definition, call it wilderness. But again, neither term was on the mind of the public in 1872. Rather, Yellowstone was becoming "wonderland." As in Yosemite, its fabled geysers, waterfalls, canyons, and other "curiosities" engrossed the nation as a cultural repository. Although Yellowstone, by far, was larger than Yosemite—and was first to be *called* a national park, its purpose was to reaffirm the ideals of 1864.[1]

To be sure, if in 1864 Yellowstone had been known and publicized, likely the two parks would have been established simultaneously. However, Yellowstone was still a rumor. Between 1806 and 1810, the mountain man John Colter may have traversed it, although his exact route—and what wonders he may have seen—is speculative. James Bridger's stories from the 1830s are more reliable; at least, his descriptions of the place ring true. As for other trappers' accounts and recollections, there remains the problem of verification. At best, Yellowstone was difficult to penetrate and off the serious explorer's path. The mountain men themselves were looking for beaver pelts, not scenery or natural wonders. Publicizing Yellowstone awaited adventurers of an entirely different bent.[2]

Northwest of Yellowstone, the discovery of gold in Virginia City, Montana Territory, ensured the arrival of those adventurers. Along with the flood of miners came the inevitable wave of politicians looking for social advancement and prestige. In 1866, an aging Jim Bridger verified his stories. Miners advancing up the rivers were finding steam vents and colorful canyons. The settlements were aroused. Just what might those distant mountains and their headwaters finally reveal?[3]

By the summer of 1869, an expedition had been organized. However, as the date of departure drew near, most of the men dropped out, ostensibly because of business conflicts but more likely in fear of Indian reprisals. Apprehension had only grown on word from Fort Ellis (Bozeman) that no military escort could be provided. With summer drawing to a close, three of the men, Charles W. Cook, David E. Folsom, and William Peterson, decided to take the risk and travel alone. On September 6, they began a circuitous journey south from Diamond City (east of Helena), entering the Yellowstone Valley on September 11.[4]

On ascending the Yellowstone River into the high country, they began finding the stories to be true. And because the men were committed publicists, finally their descriptions would endure.[5] By early October, they had seen the Grand Canyon of the Yellowstone River, Yellowstone Lake, and the thermal wonders of the Lower Geyser Basin. Again their revealing claim was to declare those wonders the equivalent of Europe's romantic past. As Charles Cook was comforted to note, a limestone formation observed on entering Yellowstone "bore a strong resemblance to an old castle" whose "rampart and bulwark were slowly yielding to the ravages of time." Regardless, "the stout old turret stood out in bold relief against the sky, with every embrasure as perfect in outline as though but a day ago it had been built by the hand of man." Granted, perhaps no other comparison fit; the formation simply looked like a castle. The point is that Cook did not stop there but rather daydreamed he *was* in Europe. Indeed, the explorers "could almost imagine," he concluded, "that it was the stronghold of some baron of feudal times, and that we were his retainers returning laden with the spoils of a successful foray."[6]

Arriving at the Grand Canyon of the Yellowstone, Cook repeated America's now popular claim. Again, "it required no stretch of the imagination to picture," deep inside the canyon, "fortresses, castles, watchtowers, and other ancient structures, of every conceivable shape." The inventory continued near Yellowstone Lake, where the men found new "objects of interest and wonder," among them "stone monuments" formed "by the slow process of precipitation, through the countless lapse of ages."[7] As in Yosemite, any natural force, if suitably directed, might itself be compared to human initiative. Salvaging a past need not be difficult as long as nature cooperated—and the world believed.

Having covered Yellowstone over 36 days, Charles Cook and David Folsom were prepared to do their part. Back in Montana, they collaborated on a diary of their descriptions that appeared in the July 1870 issue of *Western Monthly Magazine*.[8] By then, a second expedition of 19 men was making its final plans and preparations. Its nominal leader, Henry Dana Washburn, had just parlayed two terms as an Indiana congressman into an appointment as the surveyor general of Montana Territory. His arrival allowed him a fortuitous opportunity to join in further exploration of the Yellowstone. Other key participants included Nathaniel Pitt Langford, a native of New York State, and Cornelius Hedges, a young lawyer with a degree from Yale. Walter Trumbull, formerly a reporter for the *New York Sun*, offered a prestigious link with the U.S. Congress; his father, Lyman Trumbull, was the senior senator from Illinois. Another New York native, Lieutenant Gustavus C. Doane, commanded the military escort of six men.[9] These brief biographies remain instructive that the West was being perceived by easterners. The East would continue to look most favorably on those explorers who confirmed Yellowstone's wonders as unsurpassed.

With the Washburn-Langford-Doane Expedition, any lingering doubts were put to rest.[10] After departing Fort Ellis on August 22, 1870, the men retraced the previous year's expedition by ascending the Yellowstone River into the mountains. Inside Yellowstone proper, they, too, marveled at the Grand Canyon of the Yellowstone and its spectacular upper and lower falls, over 100 and 300 feet high, respectively. "A grander scene than the lower cataract of the Yellowstone was never witnessed by mortal eyes," Langford stated. "It is a sheer, compact, solid, perpendicular sheet, faultless in all the elements of grandeur and picturesque beauties."[11] On September 1, the men resumed their march south toward Yellowstone Lake, stopping to examine the Mud Volcano. After sighting the lake on September 3, they decided to follow its southern shore, only to exhaust themselves trying to penetrate a seemingly endless jungle of tumbled pines. The maze had soon claimed one member of the party, Truman C. Everts, who found himself hopelessly lost. Nor could his companions, on dropping their search, be confident he had survived. Badly weakened and emaciated, he would be found 37 days later crawling along a mountainside, still trying to make his way back to the settlements. At least, his account of the ordeal brought him fame, while the expedition basked in the sharpened publicity of having its descriptions tinged with drama.[12]

With the abandonment of their search for Everts, the explorers, understandably subdued, continued westward to the headwaters of the Firehole River. Here their spirits lifted with the sighting of the Upper Geyser Basin, which Cook and his party had missed the previous year. To the Washburn Expedition went the honor of locating and naming the basin's renowned attractions. Among them, Old Faithful Geyser endures as the most recognized symbol of America's national parks. The point is that whatever the public perceives today, those first publicists welcomed another opportunity to elevate the United States at the world's expense. "To do justice to the subject would require a volume," Lieutenant Doane wrote in his report to Congress. "The geysers of Iceland sink to insignificance beside them; they are above the reach of comparison." Similarly, Nathaniel Langford proclaimed Yellowstone's geysers the "new and, perhaps, most remarkable feature in our scenery and physical history." Again, there was nothing like them in the world. "It is found in no other countries but Iceland and Tibet," he maintained. "Taken as an aggregate," Lieutenant Doane added, "the Firehole Basin surpasses all other great wonders of the continent."[13] It followed that the Rocky Mountains, as earlier the Sierra Nevada, might lead the country out of its cultural doldrums. The geyser was America's alone—at least with respect to Europe—to the delight of every nationalist concerned.

To be sure, Yellowstone was soon the talk of the popular press. No sooner had the Washburn Expedition returned to Montana than several of the men, including Washburn, Langford, and Hedges, composed a series of descriptive articles for the *Helena Daily Herald*.[14] Within days, those accounts had spread to the East. On October 14, for example, the *New York Times* carried a lengthy editorial praising Washburn's report. "Accounts of travel are often rather uninteresting," the *Times* began, "partly because of the lack of interest in the places visited and partly through the defective way in which they are described." In contrast, Yellowstone, as portrayed by the surveyor general of Montana, struck the reader "like the realization of a child's fairy tale." The expedition had everywhere encountered formations "that constantly suggested some mighty effort at human architecture." For instance, one stream coursed "between a procession of sharp pinnacles, looking like some noble old castle, dismantled and shivered with years, but still erect and defiant."[15] And "beautiful" hardly seemed "the word for the Lower Falls of the Yellowstone. Here the height more than doubles Niagara." Such a revelation, the *Times* concluded, in addition to "geysers of mud and steam that must exceed the size and power of those in Iceland," explained why Washburn's writings were "so gilded with true romance."[16]

Publicity of that caliber inevitably led to other important invitations. Even before the venture, Jay Cooke of the Northern Pacific Railroad had contracted with Nathaniel Langford to give winter lectures in the East. In Washington, D.C., Langford's audience included Dr. Ferdinand Vandeveer Hayden, a professor of geology at the University of Pennsylvania and, of significance for Yellowstone's future, the director of the U.S. Geological and Geographical Survey of the Territories. Langford's speech—added to the many similar reports by Cornelius Hedges, Lieutenant Doane, General Washburn, and others—convinced Hayden to change his plans. That coming summer of 1871, he had intended to operate in Dakota and Nebraska. Suddenly, he could not wait to survey Yellowstone.[17]

Congress sealed its approval with $40,000, a sum that enabled the Hayden Survey to pursue more than new descriptions. In marked contrast to the Cook and Washburn forays, Hayden's team included entomologists, topographers, a zoologist, a mineralogist, a meteorologist, and a physician.[18] Secure in his cadre of scientists, Hayden returned to the necessity of good publicity. Thomas Moran, the artist, and William Henry Jackson, a popular frontier photographer, were invited to provide the all-important visual record.[19] In Moran's case, the Northern Pacific Railroad had again intervened, first writing Hayden with the suggestion and further providing the artist a loan to pay expenses. With Jackson's photographs as validation, Moran took brilliant artistic license, culminating in what many believe to be his best painting, *The Grand Canyon of the Yellowstone* (1872). Although completed after the establishment of Yellowstone Park, Congress itself validated the painting's influence by purchasing it to hang in the Senate lobby. At 7 by 12 feet and commanding $10,000 from the nation's taxpayers, the canvas firmly established Thomas Moran as Albert Bierstadt's principal rival in the West.[20]

Departing Fort Ellis on July 15, the Hayden Survey constituted the third major investigation of Yellowstone in as many years. Yet a fourth expedition, a military reconnaissance commanded by one Captain John W. Barlow and Captain David P. Heap, entered Yellowstone with the Hayden party but, for obvious reasons, never achieved the same distinction. Meanwhile, fortune smiled on both expeditions as they ascended the Yellowstone River, where they were greeted by the steaming terraces of Mammoth Hot Springs.[21] Previously, the Cook and Washburn parties had missed the wonder, having chosen a slightly different route. Finding much of fascination and interest, the Hayden Survey lingered in the area two days, then resumed its march southward to the Grand Canyon of the Yellowstone.[22]

Again, no landscape provided greater assurance that European architecture had been eclipsed. Immediately, the precipitous cliffs and kaleidoscopic colors inspired the creativity of Thomas Moran, inviting the monumental imagery earlier popularized by Albert Bierstadt. Now it was Moran's opportunity to shape the nation's vision. Within a year, his watercolor sketches had evolved into *The Grand Canyon of the Yellowstone*. In the middle distance, the Lower Falls leaps into the canyon, partially shrouded in a rising mist. To the right, great pinnacles of rock suggest a wilderness equivalent of European castles and cathedrals. To Ferdinand V. Hayden, the formations indeed stood out like "Gothic columns . . . with greater variety and more striking colors than ever adorned a work of human art."[23] Equally compelling in black and white, William H. Jackson's large-format photographs confirmed for the public the canyon's charms. As Americans had found in Yosemite, so they had come to find in Yellowstone. In architecture, the divine hand of God was America's unrivaled builder and Yellowstone Canyon His latest discovered masterpiece.

On the evening of July 28, the Hayden Survey arrived at Yellowstone Lake. Three days later the men split up. Those mapping the shoreline would stay behind while the others, including Hayden, W. H. Jackson, and Thomas Moran, pushed over the continental divide to the Firehole River. After sighting the Lower Geyser Basin on August 3, they investigated the Upper Geyser Basin beginning on August 6, where the main attraction, Old Faithful Geyser, continued to gush on cue. Soon afterward, it was time for the men to return to their comrades finishing their mapping of Yellowstone Lake. For yet another week the men made separate forays, principally to see what lay to the west and south. All then regrouped for the march north and home. On August 27, with the survey safely back in Montana, Hayden officially closed his season in the field.[24]

Like the discovery of Yosemite Valley and the giant sequoias, the revelation of Yellowstone to the world offered the United States another opportunity for cultural redemption. The protection of Yellowstone as a further outgrowth of cultural nationalism has simply been lost in other debates. Because Yellowstone was first to be *called* a national park, the claim persists that Yosemite was largely irrelevant.[25]

This line of reasoning begins with the diary of Nathaniel Pitt Langford, in particular his entry dated September 20, 1870. "Last night," that entry opens, "and also this morning in camp, the entire party had a rather unusual discussion. The proposition was made by some member that we utilize the result of our exploration by taking up quarter sections of land at the most prominent points of interest," specifically those that "would eventually become a source of great profit to the owners." However, following that proposal and several others, Cornelius Hedges had disagreed, declaring "that he did not approve of any of these plans—that there ought to be no private ownership of any portion of that region, but that the whole of it ought to be set aside as a great National Park, and that each one of us ought to make an effort to have this accomplished." According to Langford, the proposal then "met with an instantaneous and favorable response from all—except one—of the members of our party, and each hour since the matter was first broached, our enthusiasm has increased." Indeed, Langford concluded, "I lay awake half of last night thinking about it;—and if my wakefulness deprived my bed-fellow (Hedges) of any sleep, he has only himself and his disturbing National Park proposition to answer for it."[26]

Marking the site, an official monument at the junction of the Firehole and Gibbon rivers testifies to the popularity of Langford's account. But that the explorers discussed a *national* park at this time is doubtful. Suspicions have been cast on Langford's diary itself. Edited and revised for publication in 1905, it appeared 35 years after the event. The explorers' immediate publications also failed to mention the term "national park," a surprising omission if the proposal had been adopted by all but one of their group. More likely, as the national park idea grew in popularity, so Langford could not resist the embellishment. What the Washburn Expedition probably discussed the night of September 19, 1870, if in fact the men were in agreement *then*, was something similar to the Yosemite grant, which preserved Yosemite Valley and the Mariposa Redwood Grove in two distinct sections. Yellowstone's wonders needed only a similar arrangement; in either case, only as the men later clarified their objectives and announced their resolve in public did the term "national park" sporadically appear. However, even then it appeared nowhere in the enabling act itself; the term *"public* park" was consistently used.[27]

The chronology remains what it is, with Yosemite the model for Yellowstone and not the other way around. Ultimately, the debate has persisted on the observation that Yellowstone was by far the larger park. Yellowstone sounded altruistic and splendidly looked the part, encompassing a swath of territory. Future Americans might imagine anything on that landscape, even wilderness and a refuge for wildlife. Regardless, that population of Yellowstone with new ideas was still to come. For the moment, its size did nothing to mask its parallel intent with Yosemite — the preservation of natural wonders.

Beyond admitting that Yellowstone was "picturesque," its explorers looked for *cultural* reassurance. A preserved wilderness was the least of their aims. Nathaniel Langford's own vision for Yellowstone Lake was closer to Lake Como or the French Riviera. "How can I sum up its wonderful attraction!" he exclaimed. "It is dotted with islands of great beauty, as yet unvisited by man, but which at no remote period will be adorned with villas and the ornaments of civilized life." Certainly, he confided to his diary, Yellowstone Lake "possesses adaptabilities for the highest display of artificial culture, amid the greatest wonders of Nature that the world affords." The country need not wait long, he predicted, "before the march of civil improvements will reclaim this delightful solitude, and garnish it with all the attractions of cultivated taste and refinement."[28]

His dream would be realized, at least partially, in the construction of Yellowstone's grand hotels. The point is that our hindsight was not consistently the explorers' foresight, at least not in 1871. If today we also value Yellowstone because of its ecology, they were constantly on the lookout for natural wonders. Complementing Langford's description of Yellowstone Lake, the Upper Falls of the Yellowstone River provided Cornelius Hedges with a vision more appropriate for his future. "I fancied I could see in the dim distance of a few seasons an iron swing bridge," he declared in the pages of the *Helena Daily Herald*, "with bright, happy eyes gazing wondrously upon this beauty of nature in water colors." In the meantime, a "convenient ledge, with a surface accommodation for 20 persons," provided the necessary access.[29]

Such descriptions were in keeping with the explorers' urge to lend their exploits cultural as well as historical significance. As vindicated provincials, they freely joined Langford in further dismissing European culture with their newly discovered "spires of protruding rocks," "pillars of basalt," and other forms of the "majestic display of natural architecture." Nor did Langford hesitate to mention the crater of a geyser that seemed to him "a miniature model of the Coliseum."[30] Even if his comparison remained predictable—what other "models" did Langford have?—the point remained to secure America's present as better than anything in Europe's past.[31]

It followed that as in the case of Yosemite Valley, the threatened confiscation of Yellowstone could not be ignored. Even as the explorers confirmed its natural phenomena, the best had come under local scrutiny. Entering the geyser basins in 1871, the Hayden Survey observed two claimants cutting poles in anticipation of fencing off portions of the Firehole River. Supposedly, the Washburn Expedition had discussed—and rejected—a similar scheme the previous year. The point was how quickly others had mounted the threat. If the nation was finally serious about protecting Yellowstone, the decision could no longer be postponed.[32]

By the fall of 1871, a sense of urgency had built among the interested parties, aided again by precedent. Ever since its establishment in 1864, the Yosemite grant had remained perennially in the public eye. In 1868, a new label, "National public park," had found its way into a major guidebook.[33] As suddenly, the Yosemite land claims were in the spotlight. Rebuffed by Congress in 1868 and again in the winter of 1871, James M. Hutchings had taken his case to the U.S. Supreme Court.[34] As if anyone needed proof of the threat to Yellowstone, citizens need only read in the popular press that their "national public park" was still under siege.

To be sure, despite the details lacking in the Yellowstone Park campaign, motive is not among them. Nathaniel P. Langford's diary aside, other interests wanted Yellowstone protected, among them his own benefactor, the Northern Pacific Railroad. On October 27, 1871, the railroad wrote again to Ferdinand V. Hayden. Having initially requested that Thomas Moran be allowed to accompany the Hayden Survey, A. B. Nettleton, Jay Cooke's chief assistant, now requested another favor. Would

Hayden further support this suggestion: "Let Congress pass a bill reserving the Great Geyser Basin as a public park forever, just as it has reserved that far inferior wonder the Yosemite Valley and big trees. If you approve this," Nettleton asked, "would such a recommendation be appropriate in your official report?"[35]

The slight to Yosemite was a predictable response from a railroad that would never be going there. Nettleton's intervention is key for other reasons, namely, how it helped advance park legislation. Once the bill had been drafted and introduced, the Northern Pacific diplomatically stayed out of the limelight, watching confidently as the House and Senate consulted with the explorers. As Nettleton had foreseen, Ferdinand V. Hayden proved especially influential. Cited repeatedly on the Senate floor, he further prepared a report for the House Committee on the Public Lands. This the committee then released as its own report. The need for a park, Hayden reworked a century of cultural anxiety, was to head off private claimants intending to rob Yellowstone of its character. Already, those entering the geyser basins intended "to fence in these rare wonders so as to charge visitors a fee, as is now done at Niagara Falls, for the sight of that which ought to be as free as the air or water." The failure of Congress to intervene, he concluded, would doom "decorations more beautiful than human art ever conceived" to be, "in a single season," despoiled "beyond recovery."[36]

A final push by the explorers ensured that Congress would "see" Yellowstone before passing judgment on the bill. In the Capitol rotunda, Hayden arranged for a major exhibit, including geological specimens from his survey. Thomas Moran's sketches and William Henry Jackson's photographs were also prominently displayed. A copy of Langford's two-part article in *Scribner's Monthly* (May and June 1871) found its way to every House and Senate desk. Similarly, Hayden, Langford, and Delegate William Clagett of Montana claimed to have lobbied every member. In Clagett's words, "There was not a single member of Congress in either House who was not fully posted by one or the other of us in personal interviews."[37] News that Moran had begun his magnificent painting of Yellowstone Canyon further tinged the campaign with hope and romance.[38]

Certainly, the depth and sophistication of that campaign boldly contradict any reference to Yellowstone as "accidental." The problem in Yosemite Valley was constantly referenced on the floor of Congress, proof that the decision makers knew full well what they were doing. As Senator Samuel Pomeroy of Kansas expressed the opportunity, it was a chance to correct that first mistake. "We found when we set aside the Yosemite valley that there were one or two persons who had made claims there," he noted, "and there has been a contest, and it has finally gone to the Supreme Court to decide whether persons who settle on unsurveyed lands before the Government takes possession of them . . . have rights as against the Government." At best, Yellowstone would attract only speculators wishing to control its features. "There is the wonderful Yosemite valley," Senator Lyman Trumbull of Illinois agreed, "which one or two persons are now claiming by virtue of a preemption." His prestige enhanced by the reports of his son Walter, a member of the Washburn Expedition, Trumbull was no less convinced than Pomeroy. Even though farming in Yellowstone seemed out of the question, "it is possible that some person may go there and plant himself right across the only path that leads to these wonders, and charge every man that passes along between the gorges of these mountains a fee of a dollar or five dollars." Although Niagara Falls better matched that analogy, Trumbull stayed with Pomeroy's example. "We did set apart the region of country on which the mammoth trees grow in California, and the Yosemite valley also we have undertaken to reserve, but there is a dispute about it. Now, before there is any dispute as to this wonderful country, I hope we shall except it from the general disposition of the public lands, and reserve it to the Government."[39] With Yosemite as its object lesson, Congress swiftly approved the bill, and on March 1, 1872, President Ulysses S. Grant signed the Yellowstone Park Act into law.[40]

Everything unknown about the campaign remains inconsequential, such as who authored the initial bill. A leading candidate for the honor would be Representative Henry L. Dawes of Massachusetts. A distinguished supporter of the Hayden Survey, he was equally acquainted with Frederick Law Olmsted and the Yosemite grant. Delegate William Clagett of Montana Territory has also been widely credited. The more significant point remains: Yosemite was Yellowstone's model. Similar to Yosemite Valley and the Mariposa Redwood Grove, Yellowstone was "dedicated and set apart as a public park or pleasuring ground for the benefit and enjoyment of the people."[41] Until enough people found the means and the time, Yellowstone would survive just as its explorers had presented it, like Yosemite, as another repository of national pride.

As authorized, the secretary of the interior was to prepare regulations providing "for the preservation from injury or spoliation, of all timber, mineral deposits, natural curiosities, or wonders within said park," which

Yet to grasp the meaning of wilderness, the American public originally welcomed Yellow-stone as a repository of natural marvels. These tourists, dressed in their Sunday finery and visiting a thermal basin in the early 1900s, certainly confirm the enduring perception of Yellowstone as a wonderland resort. *Courtesy of the National Park Service, E. B. Thompson Negative Collection*

were to be retained "in their natural condition." Yellowstone's dramatic departure from Yosemite—enduring size—was in fact an extension of that mandate. The key official again was Hayden. When it came time to determine Yellowstone's boundaries, he remained the obvious choice. In his view, the nation should be generous and those boundaries spacious. After all, Yellowstone had barely been touched by scientists. Pending an exact survey of its remaining "decorations," Congress should err on the side of caution.[42] Absent that uncertainty, Yellowstone itself probably would have been established in scattered parcels, each limited to a specific wonder.

Rarely indeed would national parks in the future be as large or as inclusive. The great paradox of "earth monuments" was not to require the protection of their surroundings. Because Yellowstone seemed to have honored that greater mandate, we ignore the preconditions at the time. Even with those larger boundaries, the motive still was monumentalism. Nor had the nation ignored its pioneer heritage—on public lands truly ripe for settlement, parks would always be asked to compromise. Fortunately for the national park idea, there seemed to be enough public land for both. The only requirement when revisiting those decisions was that the parks behave as promised. All should preserve wonders—and nothing more.

Opponents of the national parks accepted rugged terrain as some measure of reassurance. Monumental or not, the glaciated peak of Mount Rainier, here reflected in the waters of Eunice Lake, said all that profit-seekers needed to know about the absence of timber and arable land. *Courtesy of the National Park Service*

CHAPTER 3
Worthless Lands

Nothing dollarable is safe, however guarded.

—JOHN MUIR, 1910

YOSEMITE and Yellowstone, as the first of their kind, would forever frame the ideal of national parks. Yet later endorsements of the idea were not unqualified, nor had either park set an unconditional precedent for preserving natural wonders. As much as Yosemite and Yellowstone excited the nation, there had been another side to their debates. Ever since the Ordinance of 1785, the public lands had been meant for sale and settlement. Now that public parks had been invented, that precondition still prevailed. The bigger the park, the more precedent demanded that Congress err on the side of caution. Either parks should exclude commercial resources at the outset or, on the finding of significant resources, the parks themselves should be redrawn. As John Conness, introducing the matter of Yosemite, reassured his colleagues in 1864, "I will state to the Senate that this bill proposes to make a grant of certain premises located in the Sierra Nevada mountains, in the state of California, that are for all public purposes worthless, but which constitute, perhaps, some of the greatest wonders of the world." However, in closing, he repeated, "It is a matter involving no appropriation whatever. The property is of no value to the Government. I make this explanation that the Senate may understand what the purpose is."[1]

Without his assurance that "purpose" and "value" were not in conflict, there would have been no public park. Conness was able to prove

The giant sequoias, first protected in the Yosemite Grant of 1864, remained a principal motivation behind subsequent national parks established in the High Sierra. Nonetheless, sequoia groves believed to encumber logging were cut indiscriminately, and individual trees were constantly felled for display. In this view, the Mark Twain Tree, the bottom portion of which was given to the American Museum of Natural History in New York, is cut from what is now Kings Canyon National Park in 1891. *Courtesy of the National Park Service*

instead that its effects on the value of the West would be strictly confined. Setting aside seven square miles in Yosemite Valley hardly disrupted the region's agriculture. Authorizing the protection of four square miles of giant sequoias made no dent in the nation's logging. The remainder of the Yosemite grant would be high and rugged—composed entirely of its bordering mountains and precipitous cliffs.

Ultimately, that very character of western scenery enabled the country to "afford" the national parks. Spectacular scenery assured a marginal landscape already devoid of other values. The expectation further imposed on national parks was that those conditions would persist. Parks forever in public trust should remain valueless for lumbering, grazing, mining, and agriculture. The Yosemite grant was merely the first to establish how preservation might in fact take precedence over use.

Beginning with Yellowstone, wherever protection seemed to call for larger parks, their proponents would not always find Congress as receptive. Consistently, in every face-off between natural wonders and the economy Congress first asked the wonders to give up territory. It remains the great paradox of America's national parks that they evolved from compromise as much as pride. Even beyond parks, the concept of useless scenery has virtually determined what landmarks the nation has agreed to protect and how it has protected them.[2]

Beginning in 1868, Congress on several occasions had seriously revisited the issue of settlers' claims in Yosemite Valley (chapter 2). In sudden receipt of a similar bill to establish a "public park" in Yellowstone, Congress reaffirmed that it needed to know the region's value. In the Senate, the bill came up for final debate on January 30, 1872; the House debated the measure February 27. While many in Congress sympathized with the legislation and had voted to deny Yosemite's settlers, Yellowstone's own approval hinged on absolute assurance that no repeat of Yosemite's claims was possible.

Still Congress's principal source of information was Ferdinand V. Hayden. The congressional debates in particular mirror Hayden's report to the House Committee on the Public Lands. On the floor, the principal speeches began or ended with his assurance that Yellowstone was only scenic. "The entire area comprised within the limits of the reservation contemplated in this bill is not susceptible of cultivation with any degree of certainty," he advised, "and the winters would be too severe for stock-raising." Because Yellowstone averaged well above 6,000 feet in altitude, settlement itself would be "problematical unless there are valuable mines to attract the people." Yet even that seemed a remote possibility in light of the region's "volcanic origins." Thus, it was "not probable that any mines or minerals of value will ever be found there." Nor did agricultural interests stand to profit. "Even if the altitude and the climate would permit the country to be made available, not over fifty square miles of the entire area could ever be settled," Hayden noted. "The valleys are all narrow, hemmed in by high volcanic mountains like gigantic walls." Even in summer, he repeated for emphasis, "the thermometer frequently sinks as low as 26°. There is frost every month of the year."[3]

These were also undoubtedly Hayden's high points as he and others personally lobbied Congress. Certainly, all of the bill's proponents were quoting him. In the Senate, George Edmunds of Vermont advanced the final debate with a similar declaration. "I have taken some pains to make myself acquainted with the history of this most interesting region. It is so far elevated above the sea that it cannot be used for private occupation at all, but it is probably one of the most wonderful regions in that space of territory which the globe exhibits anywhere, and therefore we are doing no harm to the material interests of the people in endeavoring to preserve it." His immediate protagonist, Senator Cornelius Cole of California, still believed that Yellowstone's case had been overstated. "I have grave doubts about the propriety of passing this bill," he began. Although he supposed "there is very little timber on this tract of land," surely it was not, as claimed, off limits to grazing and agriculture. No harm should come to the geysers if their environs reverted to private control, he maintained. Besides, there was an "abundance of public park ground in the Rocky Mountains" that never would be occupied at all. Perhaps Yellowstone, however, was a place "where persons can and would go and settle and improve and cultivate the grounds, if there be ground fit for cultivation." Further guarantees by Senator Edmunds that Yellowstone was "north of latitude forty" and "over seven thousand feet above the level of the sea" failed to quiet Cole's objections. "Ground of a greater height than that has been cultivated and occupied," he retorted; then he asked, "But if it cannot be occupied and cultivated, why should we make a public park of it? If it cannot be occupied by man, why protect it from occupation? I see no reason in that."[4]

Cole need only look at home, Senator Lyman Trumbull of Illinois reminded him. "I think our experience with the wonderful natural curiosity, if I may so call it, in the Senator's own State, should admonish us of the propriety of passing such a bill as this." Trumbull of course meant Yosemite Valley, just as his son Walter, a member of the Washburn Expedition, remained a personal source for his views. However, neither family ties nor impeccable science precluded Trumbull's close. "At some future time, if we desire to do so, we can repeal this law if it is in anybody's way; but now I think it a very appropriate bill to pass."[5] Still the key to understanding the limitations of parks remains that sentence—his declaration that Congress was always free to change its mind.

In the House, a similar declaration fell to Henry L. Dawes as sponsor of the bill. The bill's existing "analogy," the Massachusetts congressman reconfirmed, was "Yosemite valley and the 'big tree country.'" His legislation had the distinction of avoiding that dispute. "This bill reserves the control over the land, and preserves the control over it to the United States, so that at any time when it shall appear that it will be better to devote it to any other purpose it will be perfectly within the control of the United States to do it." Again, the bridge past Dawes's altruism was Trumbull's reminder that the economy of the West came first. There, the topography was great reassurance, Dawes himself observed. "It is a region of country seven thousand feet above the level of the sea, where there is frost every month in the year, and where nobody can dwell upon

it for the purpose of agriculture," he said, his clarification now firmly established. However, it did contain "the most sublime scenery in the
United States except the Yosemite valley, and the most wonderful geysers ever found in the country." As to whether those qualities should prevail, that was the advantage of making a park in Yellowstone. "It is rocky,
mountainous, full or gorges, and . . . is unfit for agricultural purposes,"
he repeated. Where a rugged terrain allowed nothing else, altruism
could prevail.[6]

The paradox in the history of the national parks is that altruism has
rarely survived the qualification. It is always present, and always forceful,
no matter what Congress in fact sets aside. Dawes himself more than reassured his colleagues; rather, the qualification became his argument.
As a practical matter, "if upon a more minute survey" Yellowstone was
found "useful for settlers, and not depredators," the bill properly could
be repealed. "This bill treads upon no rights of the settler, infringes
upon no permanent prospect of the settlement of that Territory," he
maintained. "We part with no control; we put no obstacle in the way of
any other disposition of it; we but interfere with [those] who are going
there to plunder this wonderful manifestation of nature." Still looking
for the perfect close, he found it. Even "the Indians," he forcefully concluded, "can no more live there than they can upon the precipitous
sides of the Yosemite valley."[7]

Presaging the future of national parks, Dawes's double standard
would endure as the nation's own. The sin of exploitation was not the
pursuit of personal gain but rather abusing a cultural resource. If Yellowstone was to be compromised, restitution to the economy must exceed
the loss. Congress again had done nothing deliberate to make a large
park; rather, the circumstances remained fortuitous. No one could say
with confidence what *might* be there. However, if along with new wonders the nation found valuable resources, Congress had provided the
means to reduce the park.

Proof of that lingering vulnerability was soon to come. Itself distracted
as the country slipped into economic depression, Congress literally ignored the park for the next five years. When funding was approved, in
1877, the amount was lost in other headlines. Pursued by the army on
their infamous flight to Canada, Chief Joseph and his Nez Perce band
crossed the heart of Yellowstone from west to east. Tourist encounters
with the Indians led to several casualties. A calmer round of newspaper
stories next proclaimed the advance of the Northern Pacific Railroad, including a branch line up the Paradise Valley to Cinnabar, three miles

north of the park. As of 1883, easterners could finally visit Yellowstone entirely by railroad, except for the required staging inside the park.[8]

As an unforeseen consequence of the Northern Pacific's arrival, promoters looked to extend the railroad across the park. The most serious proposal envisaged a branch line east to Cooke City, Montana, where gold had been discovered. But although Congress steadfastly refused the project, the reason was the mines and not the park. Despite the glowing predictions of their boosters, few of the mines had met expectations. Lacking incontrovertible reason to side with the miners, Congress continued to side with the park. But that Congress even considered the so-called Cinnabar and Clark's Fork Railway and, on more than one occasion, confirmed that promoters eyeing the national parks for their resources might not always come up empty-handed.[9]

To be sure, there had been no turning point in congressional attitudes toward scenic preservation. With each renewal of the public's interest in parks, Congress reaffirmed the precedents of 1864 and 1872. Invariably, park boundaries conformed to economic rather than ecological dictates. Even later awareness about wilderness, wildlife, and biological conservation did not change the primary criterion of preservation. Whether at the time of their establishment or in the future, national parks should be restricted to worthless lands.

Following Yellowstone, the nation took a long respite from national parks. A small national park in Lake Huron, Mackinac Island, was set aside in 1875. However, its later transfer to Michigan to become a state park was far more appropriate to the site.[10] The true resurgence of the national park idea awaited the renewal of cultural anxiety. Presaging the Census Report of 1890, a growing number of journalists and government officials predicted the close of the American frontier. For the first time in nearly 300 years, the Census confirmed, the nation no longer possessed a distinct boundary between the settled and unsettled West. While islands of uninhabited land remained, most were mountains or desert expanses of little economic use. The point of despair among knowledgeable Americans was how suddenly their country had reached middle age. Since the first English settlements along the Atlantic coast and the dawn of westward expansion, the frontier had symbolized the essence of personal and economic freedom. It followed that the land base of the United States was no longer by itself unique. Like Europe, suddenly the New World faced the prospect of growing older and more complacent. Despite having rushed to fill the country, few Americans relished the thought of their coming confinement.[11]

The prospect seemed all the more objectionable when viewed against the rise of urban America. By 1890, the largest metropolitan areas of the eastern seaboard were close to or well past a million inhabitants; just 30 years later, one of every two Americans would live in an urban community of 2,500 or above.[12] Just when nature was coming to be appreciated, whether inside cities or on the public lands, it seemed that the nation faced losing livability to the increasing pressures on open space.

Intellectuals increasingly asked whether the United States could maintain its strength and patriotism solely as an urban nation. Charles Eliot Norton, the Harvard scholar and former editor of the *North American Review*, was among those who answered pessimistically. "Men in cities and towns feel much less relation with their neighbors than of old," he lamented to a close friend in 1882. Urban life threatened instead to sap the nation of its "civic patriotism" and "sense of spiritual and moral community."[13] Thus, the Census Bureau only confirmed what Norton and many others already feared—the twentieth century would find the United States a very different nation indeed.

Throughout the Northeast, a similar fear of urban consequences breathed new life into the movement for public parks. Turning despair into opportunity, Charles Eliot Norton partnered with Frederick Law Olmsted in a new campaign for the protection of Niagara Falls. A critical breakthrough was achieved in 1885 with the dedication of the Niagara Falls Reservation. Established by New York State, it preserved only the American side of the falls; at least, a beginning had been made. At long last, the billboards, fences, shops, gatehouses, stables, mills, and hotels were slated for removal. In their place would rise a magnificent public park, in Frederick Law Olmsted's words, safe from "all the trees cut away, quarries opened in the ledges, the banks packed with hotels and factories, and every chance-open space occupied by a circus tent." His closest allies, among them Norton and Frederic E. Church, shared his feeling of triumph. Despite the loss of Niagara's wilderness, some of its gentler charms still remained. All might applaud that New York State had come to recognize the importance of Niagara's "adjoining scenery."[14]

For the moment, Olmsted might forgive the qualifications brought about by decades of delay. Regardless, much development and unsettled claims remained. The restoration of nature was largely cosmetic, a last gasp against wholesale development. The actual park was a mere 400 acres, fully three-fourths of them underwater. Hydroelectric interests, denied access to the brink of the falls, next retaliated with proposals to divert their flow. The river could just as easily be made to bypass the falls and dropped over the cliffs downstream. At least, additionally buttressed by Canada's park, dedicated in 1888, visitors could expect a reduction in the visual pollution, along with an end to the exorbitant fees for access to the popular overlooks.[15]

In another conservation milestone, New York State further proceeded in 1885 to establish the Adirondack Forest Preserve. Of immediate concern was the protection of watersheds vital to the emerging cities of the Mohawk and Hudson River valleys. Although extensive settlement had bypassed the Adirondacks, widespread logging had been a mainstay. Consequently, the Adirondack Forest Preserve was best described as a patchwork. Necessarily composed of cutover lands, most of its original 681,000 acres were acquired piecemeal as penalties for unpaid taxes due on abandonment of the logging sites. Ensuring the forest's recovery, the new state constitution, ratified in 1894, declared the preserve "forever wild." Regardless, the original wilderness had been sacrificed. Niagara Falls and the Adirondack Forest Preserve, as part of the settled, industrialized Northeast, graphically portrayed the difficulty of campaigning for larger parks in areas already claimed by development.[16]

Still the best hope for parks or wilderness lay on the public lands of the West. As late as 1875, John Muir described the Sierra Nevada as "almost wholly unexplored," even its limited explorers "nervous" raiders who preferred staying close to trails. Within a decade, his confidence—and that of the nation—had been eroded once again. In the wake of long-awaited government surveys, speculators had spread their tentacles across Muir's "vast wilderness of mountains," finally to threaten the watersheds of Yosemite itself. His immediate concern was unrestricted grazing. So many sheep were being driven into the high country that even their steepest slopes had been stripped of vegetation. Wildflowers everywhere had been forced to become "wallflowers," he lamented, "not only in Yosemite Valley, but to a great extent throughout the length and breadth of the Sierra."[17]

Yosemite Valley, supposedly protected from defacement, had also become the victim of its popularity. Much as Frederick Law Olmsted had predicted in 1865, tourists welcomed the proliferation of roads and buildings that catered to their wants. Hemmed in by the narrowness of the valley, any development was quickly magnified. Sheds, stables, and fences for the accommodation of tourists necessitated the clearance of woodlands and undergrowth. Livestock supplying transportation and produce sacrificed the meadows, stream banks, and wildflowers. The park commissioners, many of them political appointees, simply ignored the damage. Still the obvious comparison was Niagara Falls. Josiah Dwight Whitney, as director of the California Geological Survey, had already drawn the comparison in 1868. Yosemite Valley, rather than being "a joy forever," faced instead the prospect of becoming a swindle "like Niagara Falls, a gigantic institution for fleecing the public. The screws will be put on," he warned, "just as fast as the public can be educated into bearing the pressure."[18]

The giant sequoias proved equal incentive to heed the warning. By the 1870s, botanists understood that the big trees were confined to the Sierra Nevada along principally the western slope of the mountains for approximately 200 miles. Undeterred, lumbermen and curiosity seekers continued to penetrate and vandalize the larger groves. As in the 1850s, the cutting seemed unjustified. Except as a curiosity, the size of the big trees had proved misleading. As distinct from their redwood cousins along the California coast, giant sequoias often shattered as they hit the ground. In the end, the brittleness of the wood made it virtually useless for all but grape stakes and cabin shingles. If further interspersed among merchantable timber, such as sugar pine, the sequoias were considered a nuisance. Wishing to economize, loggers grew in the habit of felling both.[19]

In protest of the waste and with the Yosemite grant as their example, in 1878 several prominent Californians organized to protect additional sequoia groves. Among them was George W. Stewart, editor of the *Visalia Delta*. His stinging editorials proved just what the movement needed to help alert the national press. Support continued to build among many groups, including the American Association for the Advancement of Science and the California Academy of Sciences. By 1885, Stewart and his associates had focused their campaign on the headwaters of the Kaweah River, whose North Fork included the Giant Forest and the General Sherman Tree. Approximately 10 miles to the northwest, another significant grove, containing the General Grant Tree, also appeared in jeopardy.[20]

As in 1864, the combination of Yosemite-like scenery and vulnerable sequoias reawakened the nation's interest in the High Sierra. The perennial doubt was whether Congress would support additional parks. As a continuing source of motivation, newspapers and magazines remained influential in alerting the public to the wonders of the West. A new generation of writers included Robert Underwood Johnson, associate editor of *Century Magazine*. A resident of New York City, Johnson reflected the growing interest in preservation initially fostered by eastern journalists such as Samuel Bowles and Horace Greeley. Every year, the pages of his popular literary monthly included important articles about conservation, the best of them linked to Johnson. In 1889, visiting San Francisco, he made it a priority to meet John Muir, who in turn agreed to accompany him on a two-week tour of the High Sierra in and about Yosemite Valley. Inevitably, their evenings around the campfire and rambles through the backcountry sparked endless discussions about its future. As proved by the management failures in Yosemite Valley, that smaller park was incomplete. Unless its scope of protection could be enlarged, the high country itself would be destroyed. Muir's immortalization of sheep as "hoofed locusts" convinced Johnson of that greater need. "Obviously the thing to do is to make a Yosemite National Park around the Valley on the plan of the Yellowstone," he suggested to Muir. Allegedly, Johnson overcame Muir's initial skepticism by asking him to write two articles for the *Century*. "We would illustrate them with pictures of the wonderful natural features of the Government lands proposed to be taken for the park," Johnson recalled, "and with these pictures and the proofs of Muir's articles I would go to Congress," there to advocate the park's "establishment before the committees on Public Lands."[21]

For the moment, it seemed advisable not to confront California by demanding that the valley be returned. However, that later object was abundantly clear in Muir's articles linking everything with the original park. "For the branching canyons and valleys of the basins of the streams that pour into Yosemite are as closely related to it as are the fingers to the palm of the hand," Muir wrote, "as the branches, foliage, and flowers of a tree to the trunk." Another graphic definition, "fountain region," spoke to his larger purpose. Everything "above Yosemite," he continued, "with its peaks, canyons, snow fields, glaciers, forests and streams, should be included in the park to make it a harmonious unit instead of a fragment, great though the fragment may be."[22] Only those generous boundaries would protect Yosemite's watersheds and "the fineness of its wildness." This too was a worthy objective, he insisted, especially to the "lover of wilderness pure and simple."[23]

Yet it was Muir's practical example—protecting watersheds—that aided his cause in Congress. George W. Stewart's parallel campaign for the giant sequoias aside, California irrigators were especially concerned about the overall health of the High Sierra. Farming was pointless on lands that perennially flooded because the mountain forests upstream had been destroyed. The Southern Pacific Railroad, with substantial interests in the San Joaquin Valley, was of an identical mind. Armed with data, Daniel K. Zumwalt, an important land agent for the railroad, arrived in Washington, D.C., to lobby Congress. If California's farms could be secured with parks, which themselves would attract thousands of tourists, the railroad was not about to slight either benefit and in fact vigorously campaigned for both.[24]

This constant reliance on practical arguments proves the limitations imposed on parks. Still the economy of the West should not be made to suffer because of park development. When a first Yosemite bill proposed only a limited park, John Muir himself advanced his greater park by arguing for it as worthless lands. "As I have urged over and over again," he began in a letter to Robert Underwood Johnson, "the Yosemite Reservation ought to include all the Yosemite fountains." For although they were "glorious scenery," none was "valuable for any other use than the use of beauty." Only the summits of the mountains "are possibly gold bearing," he continued—in language highly reminiscent of F. V. Hayden's 1872 Yellowstone report—"and not a single valuable mine has yet been discovered in them." The watershed was best described as "a mass of solid granite that will never be valuable for agriculture," although "its forests ought to be preserved."[25]

As further reason to recognize the giant sequoias, Muir's argument also held in the southern Sierra. On September 8, 1890, a bill providing for Sequoia and General Grant national parks passed Congress with no debate. Three weeks later, on September 30, Congress approved the Yosemite bill, which simultaneously enlarged Sequoia National Park from 75 to 250 square miles. Behind that enlargement and the Yosemite bill itself lay a critical change in terminology. In their original enabling acts, Sequoia and General Grant were to be "public parks," each distinctly limited to its big tree groves. In the final Yosemite bill—which included the expansion of Sequoia and the official establishment of General Grant—the term "public park" was dropped. The language substituted, "reserved forest lands," was critical to achieving the expansive units, in Yosemite's case a reserve five times the size of the park originally introduced in Congress. Although John Muir was obviously pleased, the new wording better matched the aims of farmers and irrigators—and the powerful Southern Pacific Railroad. The hand of its land agent, Daniel K. Zumwalt, could be detected in every version of the bill. Convinced by the railroad and by Zumwalt, Congress allowed Yosemite a great rectangle of territory containing 1,512 square miles. General Grant, with only four squares miles, and even Sequoia after its enlargement still advised the limitations imposed on scenery in the presence of natural resources.[26]

The irony of the national park idea is how long it ignored the prairies, where in 1832 the artist George Catlin first envisioned "A *nation's Park.*" Shown in this photograph, the proposed Prairie National Park in Pottawatomie County, Kansas, is also headed for failure (1961). Land ideal for grazing, opponents charged, should never be used for public parks. Finally established in Chase County, Kansas, in 1996, a Tallgrass Prairie National Preserve of 10,894 acres authorized a public-private partnership requiring only 180 acres of federal land. *Courtesy of the National Park Service*

The pivotal decision to manage all three areas as national parks belonged to John W. Noble as secretary of the interior. Certainly Congress, it appeared to Noble, expected him to protect their natural features. Following the turn of the century, when "national forests" became synonymous with the controlled exploitation of natural resources (as opposed to strict preservation), the significance of his interpretation stood out.[27]

Much as Yellowstone owed its size to confusion, Yosemite National Park had been the beneficiary of important supportive goals. Finally backed by a railroad looking for commerce and tourism, Yosemite had enjoyed every political advantage of the times. "Even the soulless Southern Pacific R.R. Co.," Muir later acknowledged, "never counted on for anything good, helped nobly in pushing the bill for this park through Congress."[28] Otherwise molded in the worship of the great or near great in landscapes, the national park idea moved into the twentieth century little changed from the standards and limitations of 1864 and 1872. The issue of worthless lands, it followed, must also be dealt with again.

Heading off the loss of scientific and native objects on the public lands, Congress authorized
the president to take the initiative in protecting endangered sites as "national monuments."
Devils Tower, Wyoming, proclaimed by President Theodore Roosevelt in September 1906,
was the nation's first. *Courtesy of the National Park Service, George A. Grant Collection*

CHAPTER 4

The March of Monumentalism

Be it enacted by the Senate and House of Representatives of the United States of America in Congress assembled, That any person who shall appropriate, excavate, injure, or destroy any historic or prehistoric ruin or monument, or any object of antiquity, situated on lands owned or controlled by the Government of the United States, . . . shall, upon conviction, be fined . . . or be imprisoned . . . or shall suffer both fine and imprisonment, in the discretion of the court.

—ANTIQUITIES ACT, 1906

L ED by Yellowstone, Yosemite, Sequoia, and General Grant national parks, the United States in the 1890s found itself with the beginnings of a national park *system.* The absence of direction and, often management, in no way diminished what its units meant. The nation knew perfectly well what it had accomplished and why it wanted those parks to exist. Just by running the gauntlet of a skeptical Congress, each had proved the depth of public sentiment. Further, in 1886, beginning with Yellowstone, the U.S. Cavalry agreed to protect the parks. By all contemporary accounts and later the admission of the National Park Service, the troopers performed their tasks superbly. Beyond management, the more serious qualification weighing on the future was the precedent of "worthless" lands. Only where scenic nationalism did not conflict with materialism could the national park idea hope to expand.

A companion question, whether expansive parks were necessary, was itself soon in the spotlight. In 1891, responding to the fear of timber famine, Congress passed legislation afterward known as the Forest Reserve Act. Full authority resided with the president to choose—and proclaim—

what portions of the public domain should be retained as forests. By implication, parks like Yosemite, encompassing timbered watersheds, could be readjusted for a single role. Henceforth, parks strictly for scenery and forest reserves providing timber could separately coexist. Offering a more hopeful reassessment, an act of 1894 for the protection of Yellowstone's wildlife reminded the nation that scenery itself was more than landscape. Still the point about replicating Yellowstone or even approximating it in size required overcoming the strictures imposed by worthless lands.

In its final gesture for national parks in the nineteenth century, the nation next turned its eyes to Washington State's Mount Rainier. Rising majestically above the Pacific Forest Reserve, proclaimed in 1893, the great volcano invited the cultural fantasies so prevalent during the opening of the West. "I could have summoned back the whole antique world of mythology and domiciled it upon this greater and grander Olympus," wrote one hopeful preservationist. Before Mount Rainier, "the mild glories of the Alps and Apennines grow anemic and dull," he declared, while from its summit "the tower of Babel would have been hardly more visible than one of the church spires of a Puget Sound city." Yet only as a national park, he cautioned in conclusion, would "its fame widen with the years" and "our great army of tourists gain a new pleasure, a larger artistic sense, and a higher inspiration from the contemplation of the grandeur and beauty of this St. Peter's of the skies."[1]

It remained for John Muir to remind the nation why that description was incomplete. From experience, the park was likely to include just the mountain, leaving its encircling forests entirely vulnerable. "The icy dome needs none of man's care," he maintained, "but unless the [forest] reserve is guarded the flower bloom will soon be killed, and nothing of the forests will be left but black stump monuments."[2]

Seeming to agree with Muir, President Grover Cleveland added significantly to the nation's forest reserves on February 22, 1897. Included were major additions to the Pacific Forest Reserve, to be renamed Mount Rainier. Regardless, preservationists still wanted the mountain proper to be designated and managed as a national park. The problem, as Muir had agonized, was that such a park would include little else. Now in the Cascade Range, as in the Rockies and Sierra Nevada, Congress remained bound by the belief that parks should be restricted to their focal "wonders." As written and passed in 1899, the Mount Rainier National Park Act failed to preserve the lowland environments Muir had also singled out for preservation. Nor had Congress anywhere relaxed its caution. Just in case even the experts had been misled and Mount Rainier proved to have gold deposits, Congress allowed mineral exploration to continue.

And that was merely the surface of the intrigue. Largely shielded from public view, Congress allowed the Northern Pacific Railway to rid itself of worthless lands. Inside every railroad land grant lay mountainous territory no railroad could hope to use. The Geological Society of America, in favoring the park for scenery, also said it best for the Northern Pacific: "The boundaries of the proposed national park have been so drawn as to exclude from its area all lands upon which coal, gold, or other valuable minerals are supposed to occur, and they conform to the purpose that the park shall include all features of peculiar scenic beauty without encroaching on the interests of miners or settlers."[3] Simply, the Northern Pacific's holdings on Mount Rainier were virtually useless, a circumstance the railroad and its shareholders hoped to correct.

The practice of distributing railroad land grants in a so-called checkerboard (square-mile sections alternated between railroad and government ownership) meant that even some of the largest forest reserves were just 50 percent government land. If a railroad land grant had preceded the forest proclamation—as most land grants had—the railroad had already been awarded its share of sections. The actual "forest" left to the government was only its half of the remaining checkerboard—now further interlocked by the railroad's squares. At this point, the Northern Pacific sensed a magnificent opportunity to use the practice to its advantage. If allowed to exchange its holdings on Mount Rainier—and if allowed to exchange them section for section—it could scoop up a square mile of valuable timber for every worthless square mile of rock and ice. In that respect, the bill for a Mount Rainier national park became a front— effectively written by the Northern Pacific Railway and its supporters so that those exchanges could occur.[4]

Half of the bill, sections 3 and 4, dealt entirely with the railroad's wishes. In another telling display of favoritism, Congress extended the privilege of making exchanges to the entirety of the surrounding Mount Rainier Forest Reserve. The railroad might also select from the rich timberlands of Oregon on the basis of a minor spur. A final benefit changed land law itself. In choosing what lands it wanted, the railroad might select from the *unsurveyed* public domain. Claiming the same right in Yosemite Valley, James Lamon and James M. Hutchings had been denied (chapter 1). Suddenly, having identified the richest timberland in the West, Congress opened it only to the Northern Pacific Railway. It alone need not wait for the government surveyors and, indeed, enjoyed rights ahead of any settler.[5]

Beyond any of its famous predecessors, Mount Rainier National Park had proved the influence of materialism over preservation. Big business and frontier individualism still listened intently to hear a park called worthless lands. Thus, three years later, the term and the reassurance were again mandatory in the discussions leading to the protection of Oregon's brilliant Crater Lake. Originally the crest of ancient Mount Mazama, Crater Lake, like Mount Rainier, was once among the active volcanoes of the Cascade Range. Around 5900 B.C., a violent eruption capsized the summit and left the huge cavity in its stead. Over the centuries, rain and melting snows washed into the crater, filling it to a depth of nearly 2,000 feet. In such instances, natural resources were obviously limited, and again preservationists embraced the wonderland as strictly monumental. Speaking in that vein, its most famous publicist was William Gladstone Steel, the Portland judge whose dedication and persistence led to park status in 1902. "To those living in New York City"—he said, offering the standard form of description—"I would say, Crater Lake is large enough to have Manhattan, Randall's, Wards and Blackwell's Island dropped into it, side by side without touching the walls, or, Chicago and Washington City might do the same." At Crater Lake, "all ingenuity of nature seems to have been exerted to the fullest capacity to build one grand, awe-inspiring temple" the likes of which the world had never seen.[6]

A skeptical Congress still wished to know whether such beauty hid other values. Anticipating that concern, Thomas H. Tongue of Oregon introduced the proposed Crater Lake National Park to the House of Representatives as "a very small affair—only eighteen by twenty-two miles," containing "no agricultural land of any kind." Crater Lake was simply "a mountain, a little more than 9,000 feet in altitude, whose summit [had] been destroyed by volcanic action," and was "now occupied by a gigantic caldron nearly 6 miles in diameter and 4,000 feet in depth." Although he had asked for adequate boundaries, he had insisted they be laid out "so as to include no valuable land." The object of the bill was "simply to withdraw this land from public settlement [to protect] its great beauty and great scientific value."[7]

Nonetheless, led by John H. Stephens of Texas, the bill was immediately put to the test. Might there be mineral deposits in the proposed reserve? Stephens asked. Tongue lamely reassured his colleague that "nothing of any value" was to be set aside. Yet the bill itself implied the presence of minerals by prohibiting their exploration. The restriction, Tongue clarified, was meant to keep people from entering the reserve "under the name of prospecting" when their real intent was to destroy "the natural conditions of the park and the natural objects of beauty and interest." A more likely source for minerals was the mountain range opposite Crater Lake. However, the House by then had sided with Stephens. Only after Tongue had amended the bill to allow mining would his colleagues reconsider the motion and call for a vote. The amendment unavoidably diluted wording that the national park was to be "forever." Certainly, not since the "inalienable" clause in the Yosemite Act of 1864 had the concept of perpetuity been so openly reaffirmed. Thus amended, the Crater Lake park bill cleared the House, passed the Senate without debate, and received President Theodore Roosevelt's signature on May 23, 1902.[8]

As demonstrated by the restriction of Mount Rainier and Crater Lake national parks to their focal wonders, the national park idea entered the twentieth century as a visual experience, little changed in 50 years. The notable exception, a wildlife bill for Yellowstone, could be laid to monumentalism in a different form. With the close of the frontier had come the decimation of the bison and the threat of their extinction. In what was often reported as their largest remnant, several hundred animals had taken refuge in Yellowstone National Park. The possibility of losing the entire herd became dramatically apparent in the winter of 1894. A single poacher, caught with 11 skins and carcasses, proved that the bison could be gone in months. Within days of the incident, emergency legislation had been introduced in Congress by John F. Lacey of Iowa. "Prompt action is necessary or this last remaining herd of buffalo will be destroyed," he concluded the House report. Further to ensure against poaching of any kind, the bill applied to all birds and animals in the park.[9]

The point about 1894, as distinct from 1872, was Lacey's sources of new support—a closing frontier, a rising anxiety about cities, and, beginning in 1887, the emergence of the Boone and Crockett Club. Beyond scenery and natural resources, the club insisted, the public lands were crucial as wildlife habitat. Whether called forest reserves or national parks, each provided a refuge for endangered animals. With that conviction, the club had helped secure several reputations in conservation, including that of its cofounder, Theodore Roosevelt. Joined by George Bird Grinnell, editor of *Forest and Stream*, Roosevelt had promoted the club to 100 founding members interested in hunting the big-game animals of North America. The pending extinction of the bison as a "monumental" species struck the public itself as catastrophic. No less than Yellowstone's canyon or geyser basins, they provided another link with America's past. On such examples, Lacey, himself a member of the Boone and Crockett Club, secured public and congressional support. In just a month his bill was law, signed May 7, 1894, by President Grover Cleveland as "An Act to Protect the Birds and Animals in Yellowstone National Park."[10]

Yellowstone's ability to make that adjustment still rested on its good fortune in 1872. Since then, little had emerged to challenge Congress's generosity in preserving 3,500 square miles of land. Drawn to protect natural wonders, Yellowstone had inadvertently protected wildlife. As an open test of that mandate, Yosemite proved a better example. By the time Congress approved the park in 1890, the High Sierra had been surveyed. Already more than 60,000 acres of the territory included in the park had fallen into private hands. Consequently, Yosemite, unlike Yellowstone, came pockmarked with numerous internal claims. Today a circular park, Yosemite was originally a spacious rectangle. To the west, great forests of sugar pine were inside the boundary; to the south and southeast, mineral claims had been included. All served the undeniable argument of the frontier—and their owners—that the park should be reduced.

The boundary "question," Congress finally agreed in 1904, needed to be resolved. A special commission, appointed by the secretary of the interior, concluded that the disputed territories should be deleted, relieving "the park of that never-ending menace to its future existence." In a first major test of its national influence, the Sierra Club proposed limiting the reductions on the west and in fact adding land to the east, but to no avail.[11] An act of February 7, 1905, removed the disputed acreage and further reopened the unclaimed lands to entry. All told, the deleted area comprised 542 square miles, fully one-third of the original Yosemite National Park. In a small gesture of compensation—and not where the Sierra Club had wanted it—Congress extended a portion of the northern boundary to encompass an additional 113 square miles of territory. Prior surveys of the addition, however, coupled with its ruggedness and high altitudes, had already established its worthlessness beyond any reasonable doubt.[12]

The specter of further adjustments to the national parks was equally compounded by the rising popularity of "utilitarian" conservation. Professional foresters, for example, argued against the entire concept of preservation. Trees rather should be grown like crops, albeit ones "harvested" at 50-, 75-, or 100-year intervals. Similarly, hydraulic engineers maintained that rivers should be dammed and their waters diverted for electricity and irrigation. Natural drainage, like preserving trees, was much too "wasteful" of the resource. Efforts to stabilize the environment called for the manipulation of natural cycles. The demand for greater industrial and agricultural "efficiency" required the sciences of intervention. Only then would civilization's historical dependence on the whims of nature be overcome.[13]

The persuasiveness of utilitarian conservation, as distinct from preservation, lay in its obvious link with the pioneer ethic. After all, to use resources wisely was still to *use* them. It followed that parks remained at a disadvantage. Without greater visitation, preservationists had no recognized "use" of their own to counter the objections of resource interests. And still the nation's geography was against preservation. Although nine-tenths of the population lived in the eastern half of the country, every park was still in the West. On a positive note, the number of rail passengers to the parks had annually increased. However, not until the 1920s, when mass production of the automobile democratized long-distance travel, were the parks economically within reach of the middle class.[14]

Upheld by the Forest Reserve Act of 1891, utilitarian conservation compelled the public by promising to reverse perceived shortages of timber, water, and arable land. Before leaving office in March 1893, President Benjamin Harrison designated 17,564,800 acres of government forests—far eclipsing the national parks. Subsequent proclamations by presidents Grover Cleveland and William McKinley swelled the system to 47,191,389 acres. Here the figure stood in September 1901, when Theodore Roosevelt assumed the presidency in the wake of McKinley's assassination in Buffalo, New York.[15]

Personally committed to the nation's forests, Roosevelt equally delighted preservationists with his affectionate grasp of parks. The public lands in his estimation were for beauty and production both. A New York City birth and upbringing provided important clues. Born in 1858—the same year Central Park was dedicated—Roosevelt had the further advantage of wealthy parents who encouraged his aesthetic interests at home and abroad. Time in the country was also a family pastime. "While still a small boy," he recalled in his autobiography, "I began to take an interest in natural history." A home museum, featuring mounted birds and animal skeletons, consumed his attention for days on end. "I was fond of walking and climbing," he later added. By his early twenties, he had hiked extensively in the Adirondacks and canoed the north woods of Maine.[16] Entering Harvard University in 1876, he took every course in natural history he could find. "I fully intended to make science my life-work," he admitted, but "did not, for the simple reason that at that time

Harvard, and I supposed our other colleges, utterly ignored the possibilities of the faunal naturalist, the outdoor naturalist and observer of nature." He explored a political career instead, winning election to the New York Assembly. The tragic deaths of his mother, wife, and father—his wife and mother on the same day—temporarily soured him on politics. Grieving creatively with new pursuits, he spent two years in North Dakota as the owner and operator of a sprawling ranch. "It was still the Wild West in those days," he wrote, noting the significance of its passing.[17] Twenty years later, with his rise to the presidency completed, it was the lesson still uppermost on his mind.

In the future, whatever remained of the West—remained of wilderness—would need to survive on the public lands. As if personally born for the task of saving them, Roosevelt repeatedly invoked his presidential powers on behalf of forests and parks. By March 1909 and the end of his administration, he had more than tripled the forest reserves alone—to 151,000,000 acres. Now known as the national forests, the system had never been in more sympathetic hands. A Reclamation Service, established in 1902, further directed irrigation projects large and small. Henceforth, the example of forests protecting watersheds—and dams to hold their waters back—served the argument that all utilitarian agencies were innately scientific and cooperative.[18]

What dismayed preservationists was the tendency of Roosevelt's lieutenants to deny categorically the need for parks. The point about Roosevelt—and forever his redeeming feature—was that he obviously believed in parks himself. A much-anticipated trip in the spring of 1903 took him to all the major parks. Outside Yellowstone, before a crowd of thousands, he dedicated the cornerstone of the new Gardiner Gateway arch. In Yosemite, eschewing crowds, he camped in the open with John Muir. At Grand Canyon, still not a national park, he reminded onlookers that the designation was overdue. "I want to ask you to do one thing in connection with it," he began, addressing the canyon's future. "In your own interest and the interest of all the country keep this great wonder of nature as it now is." Beyond the people of Arizona, his wider audience was abundantly clear. "You cannot improve upon it," he concluded, directing his words to the national press. "The ages have been at work on it, and man can only mar it. Keep it for your children and your children's children and all who come after you as one of the great sights for Americans to see."[19]

The ambivalence of his administration lay in his many advisers who remained committed to a utilitarian bent. By far the most influential, Gifford Pinchot, summed up his philosophy in a single sentence: "The first duty of the human race is to control the earth it lives upon." However, until Roosevelt's presidency and, in fact, his reelection, Pinchot's hands had been largely tied. His government home, the Bureau of Forestry in the Department of Agriculture, had virtually no authority. The General Land Office in the Department of the Interior actually managed the forest reserves—or mismanaged them, as Pinchot repeatedly charged. First securing the president's trust and friendship, he determined to have the forests transferred. Approved February 1, 1905, the act of transfer assigned Pinchot's Bureau of Forestry, shortly renamed the U.S. Forest Service, with all of the nation's forests but not its parks. No matter, Pinchot relished that the matter of forest preservation had been laid to rest. Rather than preserve the forests, he was free to manage them—leasing their minerals, developing sites for waterpower, and, most important, ensuring that all mature timber was sold and cut.[20]

Even the national parks might harbor important resources, Pinchot still argued. Supportive of that philosophy, the bill transferring the forest reserves—and that reducing Yosemite National Park—passed only a week apart. Forced to recognize Pinchot's growing power, preservationists stressed the "utility" of promoting tourism. And therein remained the problem. Before the argument could be effective, tourists in greater numbers in fact needed to visit the national parks.

In the absence of greater patronage, their survival continued to hinge on their appeal as cultural mileposts. Bolstered by the assurance that new parks could be restricted and older parks reduced, a fledgling national park system had been allowed to grow. By the opening of the twentieth century, a last exploration of the American Southwest reaffirmed the resilience of the parks' cultural origins. Adding to the region's scenery, the discovery of native ruins further suggested vanished civilizations comparable to those of Europe. That the ruins were actual instead of fanciful added a powerful note of authenticity. Real people had lived in these castles, if not the nobility of the Middle Ages. Simply, in the search for an American identity, a new source of antiquity had been found.

Meanwhile, the ruins themselves confirmed the dilemma of protecting anything deemed commercially useful. Even the remotest sites had been repeatedly vandalized in the search for salable relics. Reputable museums were further complicit in excavating for pottery, tools, and skeletons. A final source for souvenir hunters included the relics of the public domain itself. From prehistoric fossils to petrified wood, new markets had rapidly appeared for wealthy collectors determined to own the nation's heritage.

Informed of those latest losses, Americans were again ready to be aroused. In Congress, the campaign fell naturally to John F. Lacey as chairman of the House Committee on Public Lands. The principal architect of the 1894 bill to protect Yellowstone's birds and wildlife, he still motivated preservationists to think of the national parks in broader terms. In 1900, his bid to prohibit interstate commerce in wildlife had also ended in success. A 1903 visit to the Southwest inspired his next campaign—historical sites and antiquities. "Practically every civilized government in the world," he noted, "has enacted laws for the preservation of the remains of the historic past, and has provided that excavations and explorations shall be conducted in some systematic and practical way so as not to needlessly destroy buildings and other objects of interest."[21]

The problem for Congress was acting decisively the moment a threat appeared. Rather than waste time belaboring each threat, Lacey proposed legislation modeled on the Forest Reserve Act of 1891. Similar authority, his bill read, should reside in the president to select from the "objects of historic or scientific interest that are situated upon the lands owned or controlled by the Government of the United States." Allowed the speed of the president's signature, threatened objects might escape destructive delays. The bill's obvious departure from the national parks was Lacey's emphasis on artifacts as distinct from scenery. Still, his identical motivation was clear in the provision that the new sites be called *national monuments*.[22]

The continuing influence of cultural nationalism also stood out in the title of the bill: "An Act for the Preservation of American Antiquities." It followed, from that moment on, why the bill's best friend would be Theodore Roosevelt. Among his many talents, he was an accomplished historian, with a specialty in the American West. On the question of antiquities, if not the preservation of forests, his break with the utilitarian leanings of his administration was complete. Within weeks of the bill's passage, he had interpreted the word "scientific" to include geological (hence scenic) wonders—the western landscape he had learned to love. Thus, Devils Tower, an imposing monolith of igneous rock rising 1,267 feet above the plains of northeastern Wyoming, became the first national monument on September 24, 1906.[23] Three additional sites followed in December—Petrified Forest and Montezuma Castle, both in Arizona, and El Morro, New Mexico, also known as Inscription Rock.

Along with native images, the names and carvings of Spanish explorers and American adventurers qualified El Morro as an antiquity. Montezuma Castle—a five-story cliff dwelling—also qualified as a historic structure.[24] In contrast, Petrified Forest—like Devils Tower—compelled a

scientific rationale. Over the eons, great prehistoric trees from the Meso-
zoic era had crystallized into dazzling minerals. Proclaimed to thwart
collectors and vandals, the monument came in the nick of time.[25] The
important subtlety in Roosevelt's proclamations was that every antiquity
was also scenery. If worthy scenery could not be saved for its own sake,
the president need only find a way to proclaim it an antiquity.

Congress itself extended the terminology in the establishment of
Mesa Verde National Park, Colorado. Spanish for "green table," the region was believed to contain hundreds of pre-Columbian cliff dwellings,
all of them endangered. A logical follow-up to the Antiquities Act, which
preceded it by just three weeks, Mesa Verde anticipated the future status
of national monuments once Congress recognized their qualifications as
national parks. Meanwhile, under either designation, Mesa Verde promised to end decades of illegal pot hunting and still not threaten the economy of the West.[26] It remained that latter challenge cautioning Roosevelt
to plan carefully using the Antiquities Act for scenery. After declaring
Lassen Peak and Cinder Cone, California, an "object," in January 1908
he was ready. Upholding his 1903 speech at Grand Canyon, he declared
it an "object," too—by his proclamation to be known as Grand Canyon
National Monument, perhaps the greatest "antiquity" of all time.[27]

Indeed, true to his earlier request of Arizona, "keep this great wonder
of nature as it now is," the monument embraced more than 800,000
acres. His ultimate willingness to fit the Antiquities Act to that amount of
land remains the hallmark of his fame. In a creative update to his description, Grand Canyon was suddenly "an object of unusual scientific
interest, being the greatest eroded canyon within the United States."
Thus had the Antiquities Act become decisive in setting aside landscapes,
not merely threatened "objects." Undaunted to the last, just before leaving office, on March 3, 1909, he provided equivalent protection for
600,000 acres encircling Mount Olympus in Washington State. Again,
his obligatory bow to the Antiquities Act identified "objects of unusual
scientific interest," namely, the "numerous glaciers" on the mountain's
flanks. A second object, "the summer range and breeding grounds of the
Olympic elk," should also be preserved.[28] All of it was vintage Roosevelt.
Antiquities should be boldly declared, he reasoned, now to include glaciers and wildlife habitat, "because they add to the beauty of living and
therefore the joy of life."[29]

In neither case, the Grand Canyon or Mount Olympus, had he adhered
to expected guidelines. In "all instances," the Antiquities Act declared, each
monument should be "confined to the smallest area compatible with the

proper care and management of the objects to be protected." Their scientific worth aside, the Grand Canyon and Mount Olympus were hardly "objects." The lack of organized opposition, at least immediately, lay in the character of the sites themselves. Although mineral deposits had been found in Grand Canyon, few prospectors had seriously attempted to bring them out. The monument itself excluded major forests on both the north and the south rim. Similarly, Mount Olympus National Monument, although heavily forested, lay on the remote Olympic Peninsula. In 1915, after loggers had in fact assessed the monument, President Woodrow Wilson, succumbing to their demands, reduced the "object" by its timbered half.[30]

The lasting significance of the Antiquities Act was its usefulness for bypassing a deadlocked or hostile Congress. Preservationists need only convince an individual—the president—to initiate a national monument.[31] Although easier said than done, it generally happened just that way. Meanwhile, even Theodore Roosevelt at times puzzled preservationists, both signing the bill to reduce Yosemite National Park while increasing the prestige of the Antiquities Act. In an important gesture of solidarity, California agreed in 1905 to return Yosemite Valley to federal control; Congress accepted the recession the following year.[32] Still the question about retaining parks or turning monuments into parks was whether Congress would insist that they remain worthless lands.

New proposals for a park in northwestern Montana assured the revival of that debate. A telling description of what is now Glacier National Park, "the walled-in lakes," followed the 1885 explorations of George Bird Grinnell.[33] Heading a commission to remove Indian title, he returned in 1895. With the Blackfeet absent and the hopes of miners fading, he repeated his hopes for the region in 1901. "Here are cañons deeper and narrower than those of the Yellowstone, mountains higher than those of the Yosemite," he wrote in *Century Magazine*. Headed by those natural wonders, "the crown of the continent" should be preserved.[34] Like John Muir and Robert Underwood Johnson, it helped that Grinnell had a national name. Initially recognized for his defense of Yellowstone, he was among those whose drive for better management brought the cavalry to its rescue in 1886.[35] Then the editor of *Forest and Stream* and soon afterward cofounder of the Boone and Crockett Club with Theodore Roosevelt, he had learned that the American public, in assessing preservation, believed foremost that every park should be unique.

"Here is a land of striking scenery," he reaffirmed that uniqueness. A skeptical Congress still demanded that Glacier be scrutinized, ensuring that scenery was its only worth. Local opposition, led by the Kalispell Chamber of Commerce, helped defeat the bill in 1908 and 1909. "This is rough and frozen country," George Bird Grinnell wrote, continuing to take solace in the facts. "The mountains included in this area are for the most part covered with timber, much of it small, and all of it far from a market." Surely the bill would be reintroduced.[36] That successful version, sponsored by senators Thomas H. Carter and Joseph M. Dixon of Montana, reached the Senate floor in January 1910. Rising in support, Senator Boies Penrose of Pennsylvania opened with the critical and by-now-familiar claim. "I have hunted and traveled over almost every inch of the [Glacier] country," he began. It "is one of the grandest scenic sections in the United States, absolutely unfit for cultivation or habitation, and as far as I know not possessing any mineral resources." Only then did he pronounce the region "admirably adapted for a park." The Senate still chose to postpone. When debate resumed in February, Senator Dixon defended Penrose. As promised, Glacier's lack of natural resources had been proved. "This is an area," Dixon reminded his colleagues, "of about 1,400 square miles of mountains piled on top of each other." Such rugged territory was not easily exploited. "There is no agricultural land whatever," he confirmed. "Nothing is taken from anyone. The rights of [its] few settlers and mineral entrymen are protected in the bill."[37] A delighted George Bird Grinnell, reporting in *Forest in Stream*, noted that the Senate then finally approved. "Let everyone," he concluded, "now put his shoulder to the wheel and push."[38]

In fact, discussion in the House was surprisingly brief. However, its amended version of the bill required a conference with the Senate before a final version could be approved. "It is where the mountains are piled on top of each other," Senator Dixon repeated for the conferees. "I do not think there is a ranch within its confines. All of it is now a forest reserve. So there will not be a great deal of difference in its future status from its present."[39] In the unlikely event that valuable mines were discovered, the bill provided for their use. Reclamation and sustained-yield forestry were similarly allowed. Section 1, for example, empowered the Reclamation Service to "enter upon and utilize for flowage or other purposes any area within said park which may be necessary for the development and maintenance of a government reclamation project." A similar concession to the Forest Service authorized the secretary of the interior to "sell and permit the removal of such matured, or dead or down timbers as he may deem necessary or advisable for the protection or improvement of the park." Again the obvious contradiction, how logging might "protect" or "improve" the park, was not spelled out. In reality, Congress had handed both resource agencies another blank check. Thus constrained, the bill for Glacier National Park went to the president, who approved it on May 11, 1910.[40]

A now jubilant Grinnell might finally report to his readers: "This is the third in size of our national parks, being exceeded only by the Yellowstone and the Yosemite parks. It is the fifth of the larger reservations of this character." If lacking Yellowstone's "attractions," namely, its "hot springs, sprouting geysers, and tremendous waterfalls," Glacier expressed its uniqueness in other ways, including "a fauna distinctly its own and different in many respects from that of the Yellowstone."[41]

Grinnell again emphasized what preservationists hoped. In truth, Congress had already announced a different direction for Yosemite—warning that its contradictory language would apply. In 1905, Yosemite's best timber and lowland environments had been excised from the park. Now an even greater vulnerability, its prized sources of freshwater, had similarly sparked a national controversy. As early as 1882, the city of San Francisco had looked to the canyons of the High Sierra for a permanent freshwater supply. Eight years later, however, the city's ideal site for a dam and reservoir, the Hetch Hetchy Valley, became part of Yosemite National Park. The potential for conflict only sharpened as preservationists began to appreciate what Hetch Hetchy in fact possessed. Although half the size of Yosemite Valley, its cliffs and waterfalls were strikingly identical. Completing the resemblance, the Tuolumne River split the floor of Hetch Hetchy, much as the Merced River divides Yosemite. Hetch Hetchy's distinction was still to look like a park. Sacrificed to tourism in Yosemite Valley, its wildflowers had virtually disappeared. Its meadows and woodlands, laced with roads and structures, consistently appeared overrun. Imagine a second Yosemite, preservationists asked, whose natural charms were still intact. Imagine Yosemite Valley itself restored on the model of its unblemished glacial twin.[42]

San Francisco, however, was adamant. If hailed as a second chance for preservation, Hetch Hetchy remained the perfect site for a dam. Nothing technical stood in the way of the project; its one major obstacle, outside of the aesthetic loss, was its location within a national park.[43]

In 1901, the city completed its engineering study and formally applied for the dam. As secretary of the interior and the petition's recipient, Ethan Allen Hitchcock denied it in 1903. Jubilant preservationists, led by California's Sierra Club, cheered his opinion that the project was "not in keeping with the public interest." Hitchcock further turned back the city's appeal. Increasingly overconfident, preservationists believed the proposal dead. San Francisco simply waited for a more opportune moment—and a different secretary. The city, after all, looking to the future, realized that every such project was long term.[44]

And indeed, on Hitchcock's resignation four years later, San Francisco filed a new request. By then, events had also conspired against preservationists, notably, the great earthquake of 1906. In less than a minute, the city was handed an argument virtually impossible to refute. Hetch Hetchy water might have made the difference putting out the fires and aiding victims. Although any water mains would have ruptured, the new interior secretary, James A. Garfield, was free to frame his decision as one of necessity. A known admirer of Chief Forester Gifford Pinchot, Garfield indeed alluded to that response. In 1908, San Francisco had what it wanted—the Interior Department's permission to dam Hetch Hetchy.[45]

Approval of the permit set the stage for the greatest cause célèbre in the early history of the national parks. The stakes for preservationists could not have been higher. Prior reductions to the national parks, principally Yosemite, had been limited to their borders. Their focal wonders had remained secure. Preservationists themselves had often differed whether common topography belonged in national parks. Hetch Hetchy invited no such spirit of compromise. The battle was not over the fringes of a national park but rather the heart of one. The outcome conceivably would be universal. If even Yosemite's inner sanctum could not be protected in perpetuity, no national park, then or in the future, could be considered safe from exploitation.

The Hetch Hetchy controversy was indeed a struggle over precedent. Both before Congress and in the popular press, preservationists justified their crusade as an effort to forestall the inevitable dismantling of national parks. Thus, the decision of Congress, in the closing months of 1913, struck preservationists as a major setback. By wide margins in both houses, the Garfield permit of 1908 was upheld and San Francisco allowed to construct its reservoir.[46]

In retrospect, preservationists had always been at a disadvantage. Weighed against the needs of a major city, the argument that 2,000 or 3,000 campers enjoyed Hetch Hetchy Valley seemed a bit extreme. Similarly, contending that Hetch Hetchy was another Yosemite in effect admitted that the valley was not unique. Opponents were quick to ask that if the nation already had one Yosemite Valley, why did it need two? "The question [is] whether the preservation of a scenic gem is of more consequence than the needs of a great and growing community," wrote John P.

Fulfilling its promise to reconsider national parks that proved valuable for commercial uses, in 1913 Congress authorized the city of San Francisco to build a reservoir in Yosemite's Hetch Hetchy Valley. *Top*: A Sierra Club photograph shows the valley before being flooded. *Bottom*: In this official Park Service photograph, the Hetch Hetchy reservoir has been in place for 50 years. *Top: Courtesy of the National Park Service, Joseph LeConte photograph. Bottom: Courtesy of the National Park Service, Ralph H. Anderson*

Young, managing editor of the *San Francisco Chronicle*. Besides, Hetch Hetchy was about to become what preservationists wanted—a scenic wonder in its own right. Although its meadows and trees "would be submerged," the immensity of the "reservoir created would substitute in their place a vastly more attractive feature" and "a far more powerful attraction to persons in search of inspiring scenery than the eliminated beauties of the past." The lake would "still be enclosed by towering peaks and massive walls, and the falls of the Hetch Hetchy [would] still tumble." However, all would be mirrored "in the waters of the new creation." Simply, the reservoir would double the monumental beauty of Hetch Hetchy. Granted, some of the "present adornments will disappear," Young admitted, but "in their place will be substituted that which will make Hetch-Hetchy incomparable and cause it to rank as one of the world's great scenic wonders."[47]

A retouched photograph, commissioned by the city, illustrated the claim for Congress and the national press. Not a ripple stirred the "lake"; its surface instead reflected the cliffs and waterfalls in exact detail.[48] Preservationists challenged the photograph as contrived and absurd. Whenever water levels fell, the reservoir in reality would be edged with mudflats and a bleached-out ring of rocks. "Under conditions of nature lakes occur," stated J. Horace McFarland, one of the project's leading opponents, while "under conditions brought about by men ponds are created. Flooding the Hetch Hetchy will make a valley of unmatched beauty simply a pond, a reservoir, and nothing else."[49]

Nonetheless, the contrivance in the photograph symbolized the dilemma the dam's opponents faced. Except for the movement's occasional prophets, notably Frederick Law Olmsted and John Muir, preservationists for half a century, like San Francisco's "ghost" photographer, had won converts by highlighting monumental scenery. The national parks were promoted largely as nature's best displays. The emphasis on wonders at last had backfired. Hetch Hetchy's other values, especially its wildness, needed years of subtle argument to convey. But time had run out. On December 19, 1913, President Woodrow Wilson signed the legislation granting San Francisco all rights to the gorge.[50]

Ultimately, the city had proved Hetch Hetchy more useful than the sum of its scenic parts. It was not worthless lands after all. Somehow preservationists must identify and publicize incontrovertible methods by which the parks could pay the same dividends to the national purse. The need for haste was also evident. Surely if Hetch Hetchy betokened the future, similar and even greater threats to the national parks were right behind.

No true American, nationalists insisted, would visit Europe before seeing the United States. Acknowledging Switzerland as their chief competitor, the railroads of the West eagerly joined in promoting new national parks. Dressed to re-create Switzerland in the Montana wilderness, these waitresses at Glacier National Park in 1933 colorfully suggest the durability of the See America First campaign. *Courtesy of the National Park Service, George A. Grant Collection*

CHAPTER 5

See America First

See Europe if You Will, but See America First.
— SOO RAILROAD BROCHURE, c. 1910

War with Switzerland!
— MARK DANIELS, 1915

The influence of [the national parks] is far beyond what is usually esteemed or usually considered. It has a relation to efficiency—the working efficiency of the people, to their health, and particularly to their patriotism—which would make the parks worth while, if there were not a cent of revenue in it, and if every visitor to the parks meant that the Government would have to pay a tax of $1 simply to get him there.
— J. HORACE MCFARLAND, 1916

NOT since Niagara had there been a catalyst like Hetch Hetchy to force the issue of national parks. Even John Muir instructed his followers on the wisdom of being practical. "Thousands of tired, nerve-shaken, over-civilized people are beginning to find out that going to the mountains is going home," he wrote, "that wildness is a necessity, and that mountain parks and reservations are useful not only as fountains of timber and irrigating rivers, but as fountains of life." Although a softer use of utilitarian terminology, it was indeed the same defense. The wise use of scenery, not just natural resources, was critical to the advancement of human "efficiency." But if "we must consider [the national parks] from the commercial standpoint," Allen Chamberlain, a New England preservationist, immediately added, "let it not be forgotten that Switzerland regards its scenery as a money-producing asset to the extent of some two hundred million dollars annually."[1]

As the railroads had insisted for decades, greater tourism might be an asset. Parks capable of increasing railroad revenues were obviously a business in their own right. As for preservationists, it hardly mattered how parks stayed protected as long as another Hetch Hetchy was avoided. The rewards of this "pragmatic alliance"[2] were soon confirmed by railroad support for a bureau of national parks. As envisioned by preservationists, the agency would be distinguished by the principles of aesthetic as opposed to utilitarian conservation. Such were the foundations of the National Park Service, signed into law by President Woodrow Wilson on August 25, 1916.

As an outgrowth of the West, the national park idea finally competed directly with the forces of wise use. In the last decade of the nineteenth century, touted similarities between national parks and forest reservations encouraged the perception they were identical. As proof, preservationists cited the clause "reserved forest lands" in the Yosemite Park Act itself.[3] It followed that if Yosemite's forests were meant as scenery, so was scenery the purpose of every forest reserve. Only as resource professionals disagreed did preservationists realize that their assumption was mistaken. By then, foresters and hydrologists had mounted their own campaign to extend utilitarian management even to the national parks.[4]

The key to protecting the parks, preservationists finally conceded, was to forge an alliance with the railroads. Although a form of exploitation, tourism at least protected the principal scenery of the national parks. Building on those essentials, preservation itself had finally become a movement. From an initial scattering of national interest groups, notably the Appalachian Mountain Club (1876), Boone and Crockett Club (1888), and Sierra Club (1892), by 1910 at least 20 recognizable organizations advocated scenic protection.[5] To these could be added a host of garden clubs, women's clubs, horticultural societies, and other sympathetic coalitions. Much like the artists of the Hudson River School 75 years earlier, all sought to promote a bucolic landscape. The worst effects of cities and industry should forever be muted by providing parks and beautification. New suburban neighborhoods might offer a pleasing transition between city streets and open space. As long as nature flourished somewhere in the urban environment, a sense of the bucolic might be sustained.[6]

Here again, the stern directives of resource scientists seemed remote and unappealing. Rather, as they had for the national parks, urban professionals logically swelled the ranks of preservationists. For them, the term "back to nature" still meant to reaffirm Jefferson's concept that beauty was a national asset. Meanwhile, in their renewed emphasis on nearby beauty, preservationists had not deserted the monumental West. The point is that neither had they subscribed to the notion that utilitarian values might save threatened landscapes close to home.

An important new leadership energized with this viewpoint included J. Horace McFarland of the American Civic Association. The association itself was the merger of two progressive groups: the American League for Civic Improvement and the American Park and Outdoor Society. Following the merger in 1904, McFarland was elected president. In the realm of parks and urban welfare, no one better epitomized the concerns of civic leaders at the height of the Progressive movement. In his other life a successful printer, publisher, and horticulturist from Harrisburg, Pennsylvania, McFarland moved the American Civic Association into the forefront of scenic preservation. This continued to mean a deep appreciation of the public lands but, more to the point, also a deep appreciation of the land itself. No less important were those everyday landscapes where people lived and worked. A successful city could be measured only by its number of parks and gardens. As contrasting evidence, the spread of billboards became McFarland's nemesis, proving all that had gone wrong with urban life. Blight allowed under the guise of providing information was no less "offensive" and "in bad taste." Billboards and flowers (his horticultural specialty was roses) simply did not mix. "Let the traveler indulge in no hope that the awe-inspiring grandeur of Niagara will daunt the vandals," McFarland added, "for he sees the Falls with Coca Cola on the side, while Mennen's Toilet Powder hangs over the great gorge." If again the nation would deface Niagara, there was no denying America's resignation to ugliness as a fact of daily life.[7]

McFarland was determined to change that. It was initially the second campaign to save Niagara Falls that brought him national notoriety. Within months after becoming president of the American Civic Association, he had marshaled its forces against the latest scheme to harness Niagara, this time for the production of hydroelectric power on a truly massive scale. The developers, thwarted by protection of the falls proper as a state park in 1885, had since retaliated with plans to divert the river simply by capturing it above the cataract.

Thanks largely to McFarland, the diversion controversy had soon attracted the attention of the national press. In a constant stream of private letters, he began by alerting scores of government, civic, and business leaders to the pending tragedy of a waterless Niagara. The springboard for his public campaign was the *Ladies' Home Journal*, already a leading women's magazine. As of 1904, he was in fact a regular columnist under the banner "Beautiful America." "Shall We Make a Coal-Pile of Niagara?" he asked in September 1905, making the question the column's headline. "Every American—nay, every world citizen," he began, "should see Niagara many times, for the welfare of his soul and the perpetual memory of a great work of God." Yet "the engineers calmly agree that Niagara Falls will, in a very few years, be but a memory. A memory of what? Of grandeur, beauty and natural majesty unexcelled anywhere on earth, sacrificed unnecessarily for the gain of a few!" Projects already in place or recently approved threatened nearly a quarter of the river's flow. At 36 percent, the planned total, McFarland warned, the diversions would spell the ruination of the falls themselves, effectively negating the original campaign to save Niagara and its environs from industrial and tourist blight. Before and after illustrations suggested the result: "The words might well be emblazoned," McFarland concluded, "in letters of fire across the shamelessly-uncovered bluff of the American Fall: 'The Monument of America's Shame and Greed.'"[8]

Worse, a legitimate economy was being destroyed. As a tourist mecca alone, he noted, the loss of Niagara was "folly unbounded. To the railroads of the country and to the town of Niagara Falls visitors from all the world pay upward of twenty million dollars each year—a sure annual dividend upon Nature's freely-bestowed capital of wonders, which, valued commercially, would thus stand at over three hundred million dollars," he estimated. "All this will be wiped out, for who will care to see a bare cliff and a mass of factories, a maze of wires and tunnels and wheels and generators?"[9]

As McFarland and others despaired, it seemed finally that Niagara was beyond redemption. In that case, still the enduring lesson in losing the falls to development was to suggest the critical need for national parks. Notably on the West Coast, McFarland's denouncement of waterpower interests caught the eye of William E. Colby, secretary of the Sierra Club. Faced with a similar struggle to protect Hetch Hetchy, the Sierra Club had anxiously begun searching for allies of its own. The American Civic Association, McFarland confirmed, would gladly close ranks on the Hetch Hetchy issue in exchange for the club's willingness to speak out on Niagara. Colby had similarly contacted the Appalachian Mountain Club in Boston, then pushing for legislation to protect the forests of the East. From these initial accords sprang a formal alliance called the Society for the

Preservation of National Parks. On its letterhead appeared the declaration, "To preserve from destructive invasion our National Parks—Nature's Wonderlands." John Muir agreed to serve as president; Allen Chamberlain, director of exploration for the Appalachian Mountain Club, Robert Underwood Johnson of *Century Magazine,* and J. Horace McFarland, among others, joined the Advisory Council.[10]

Noticeably absent from the roster were the names of respected resource conservationists. A known supporter of the Hetch Hetchy reservoir, Gifford Pinchot predictably headed the list of people whom the society wished to convert. Certainly, no critic of preservation enjoyed greater influence with Congress and the president. From past experience, Pinchot's stance on the Hetch Hetchy controversy might well determine its outcome. "We had counted on you for support in this fight," Colby wrote, hoping to rattle the forester's conscience. "Does it not give you pause when you stop to consider that such men as John Muir . . . and the leaders of the Appalachian [Club] and the American Civic Association, and other kindred organizations—all of them men who have stood in the fore front of your fight for the preservation of our forests and who helped create public sentiment for you in your noble work, . . . should now be standing shoulder to shoulder in most earnest opposition to this attempt to enter and desecrate one of our most magnificent National Parks? We need you as a friend in this cause," Colby pleaded in conclusion, "and call upon you to assist us."[11]

Although Pinchot was not likely to bend, preservationists might indeed capture his rhetoric. The terms "waste" and "inefficiency," they learned from persistence, could just as easily be applied to people. Thus, conservation, McFarland wrote Pinchot in November 1909, meant also the wise use of *human* resources. "I feel that the conservation movement is now weak," McFarland noted, "because it has failed to join hands with the preservation of scenery, with the provision of agreeable working conditions, and with that suggestion which is the first thing to produce patriotism." He appeared determined to perfect his argument. "I want to say that somehow we must get you to see that the man whose efforts we want to conserve produces the best effort and more effort in agreeable surroundings; that the preservation of forests, water powers, minerals and other items of national prosperity in a sane way must be associated with the pleasure to the eye and the mind and the regeneration of the spirit of man."[12]

If not one of McFarland's eloquent moments, his equation of parks with national productivity proved both forceful and creative. His historical conundrum was how much the response also relied on exploitation.

If, as alleged, the national parks increased human efficiency, it followed that parks lacking people—lacking exploitation—were themselves inefficient. Heading off purely utilitarian aims, the concept of parks—and later of wilderness—required that people still experience parks and spread the word. As late as 1908, barely 13,000 tourists enjoyed Yosemite National Park as a scenic wonderland let alone as one of Muir's "fountains of life." Among those visitors, only a few hundred hiked into the Tuolumne River watershed and Hetch Hetchy Valley. The dilemma for preservationists was painfully obvious. While San Francisco demonstrated a current need for freshwater—and that among 500,000 users—preservationists could appeal only to the future, when the floor of Hetch Hetchy *might* be needed. In the meantime, the city easily portrayed preservationists as "nature cranks" and "elitists."[13] John Muir personally refuted the charge by agreeing to the construction of a road into the valley. Others called for a large hotel.[14] As reminders that Hetch Hetchy lacked for visitors, both concessions came far too late. Having failed to produce the actual visitors, preservationists conceded to San Francisco the stronger argument.

J. Horace McFarland had meanwhile returned to the popular press to suggest what losing natural beauty actually cost the nation. "Are we to so proceed with the conservation of all our God-given resources but the beauty which has created our love of country," he asked in the March 1909 issue of *The Outlook*, "that the generation to come will increasingly spend, in beauty travel to wiser Europe, the millions they have accumulated here, being driven away from what was once a very Eden of loveliness by our careless disregard for appearance?" Within days, he received a detailed reply from Allen Chamberlain of the Appalachian Mountain Club. "Your article on 'Ugly Conservation' in a recent *Outlook* is the right sort," Chamberlain wrote enthusiastically. There was no question that preservation as much as patriotism contributed to the economic well-being of the country. "Our friends the conservationists, that is the professionals, are exceedingly loath to recognize this point of view." Chamberlain wrote to suggest that the argument be made more specific, especially in light of the Hetch Hetchy debate. "It seems to me that we should try in this connection to stimulate public interest in the National Parks by talking more about their possibilities as vacation resorts," he remarked, similarly emphasizing visitation over wilderness. Indeed, only "if the public could be induced to visit these scenic treasurehouses," he concluded, "would they soon come to appreciate their value and stand firmly in their defense."[15]

Supported by McFarland with the same enthusiasm, Chamberlain wrote his own article for *The Outlook*. Under the title "Scenery as a National Asset," it appeared May 28, 1910. In keeping with his suggestions to McFarland, Chamberlain focused on the national parks and national monuments. "Here are some of the world's sublimest scenes," he noted, not to mention "many wonderful records of past ages" and "relics of the prehistoric occupants of portions of our land." Unfortunately, because many were "so remote from railways," the public was "just beginning to realize" that the parks existed. Within the parks, the lack of visitor facilities further hampered public awareness. "Take the Yosemite Park as an example," Chamberlain observed. "Everyone is herded into the great valley, and little is done to encourage people to go into the magnificent country farther back in the mountains." As a result, two equally beautiful attractions, the Hetch Hetchy Valley and Tuolumne Meadows, were effectively off limits to visitors. "The extension of the present road for nine miles will open the former," he said, alluding to John Muir's ideal compromise to save the valley, while "the latter can be reached by repairing the old Tioga road." Following those improvements, "hotels, or boarding camps at the very least, would undoubtedly be established at both of these points if opened."[16]

The widespread belief that some development must be allowed in the parks continues to explain why most preservationists, including Chamberlain, did not make direct reference to Hetch Hetchy's wilderness attributes.[17] To save the valley, indeed the entire park system, seemed to hinge on greater visitation, hardly less. Simply, given a choice in 1910, preservationists preferred roads, trails, and new hotels to reservoirs, power lines, and conduits. "In short," Chamberlain concluded, "the nation has in these parks a natural resource of enormous value to its people, but it is not being developed and utilized as it might be." As dramatized instead by Hetch Hetchy, "selfish interests are likely to steal an important part of our birthright."[18]

There, the railroads of the West, by promoting travel, offered preservationists their best support. Suggesting a definition, Richard B. Watrous, as secretary of the American Civic Association, termed travel the "dignified exploitation of our national parks." All preservationists, he urged during the summer of 1911, needed to publicize "the direct material returns that will accrue to the railroads, to the concessionaires, and to the various sections of the country that will benefit by increased travel." Among those interests, consistently the railroads, as the principal agents of transport, were preservation's "essential" allies, and obviously, Watrous concluded for emphasis, "one of those practical phases of making the aesthetic possible."[19]

STAY AWAY

FROM

EUROPE

THIS

YEAR

AND GO

TO THE

West from Golden Gate.

YELLOWSTONE

PARK

BE PATRIOTIC—

BE AN AMERICAN!

"*Lives there the man with soul so dead,*
Who never to himself hath said
'*THIS IS MY OWN, MY NATIVE LAND'?*"

The scene above is of one of the beautiful spots in the YELLOWSTONE PARK. As the tourist leaves the GOLDEN GATE he enters a lovely mountain valley; in the distance are rugged mountains, in the foreground a tiny lake—behind, a land of grim rocks and cliffs. Send to CHAS. S. FEE, Gen'l Pass. and Ticket Agent of the Northern Pacific Railroad, St. Paul, six cents in stamps and receive the new tourist booklet **INDIANLAND AND WONDERLAND** and read all about the PARK.

In perhaps the earliest advertisement of its type, in *Harper's New Monthly Magazine*, April 1894, the Northern Pacific Railroad had already perfected the See America First argument, advising travelers to take a "patriotic" vacation in Yellowstone National Park. *Author's collection*

In fact, the association's efforts in 1911 anticipated a major milestone, the first government conference on national parks. Gathering in September at Yellowstone's Old Faithful Inn, the two-day conference, called by Interior Secretary Walter L. Fisher, sought to identify common management and access problems. So far, the railroads had done the most to publicize and develop the national parks. "We know that costs them money, and although the inducement is a financial return to the railroads, it is an enlightened selfishness which is entitled to our grateful recognition." Without the railroads, the parks would be isolated. "In other words, the way to start this conference is with the question of how we are going to get to the parks."[20]

Led by Louis W. Hill of the Great Northern Railway, the railroads returned Fisher's praise. All would continue to assist the government in upgrading park hotels, roads, and trails. Next, the conference turned to J. Horace McFarland, who agreed that the railroads were not the problem. "I think the transportation at the present time is admirable," he testified, confirming the campaign of the American Civic Association. "All I have to say is that the railroads are in advance of the Government in the treatment of these national parks and that it is up to the general public, including the railroad men, to bestir themselves to see that the national parks are put in such shape and under such management as will bring about the conditions they themselves want."[21]

Looking outside the conference, the establishment of Glacier National Park the previous year had proved the value of the railroads. Although Glacier's apparent lack of resources had secured the bill (chapter 4), supporters had strengthened their cause with a railroad term, "See America First." "Two hundred million dollars of the good money of the people of the United States are paid out annually by Americans who visit the mountains of Switzerland and other parts of Europe," reasserted Senator Thomas H. Carter of Montana, for example. "I would say that our own people might direct their course to our own grand mountains, where scenery equal to that to be found anywhere on this globe may be seen and enjoyed." By 1915, with consideration of the Rocky Mountain national park bill, the amount that Americans spent overseas on scenic travel supposedly had soared to an estimated $500 million yearly, a "considerable portion" of which, agreed Representative Edward T. Taylor of Colorado, "goes to see scenery that in no way compares with our own." Indeed, he continued, "the American people have never yet capitalized our scenery and climate, as we should. It is one of our most valuable assets, and these great assets should be realized upon to the fullest extent."[22]

More than cultural nationalism with an economic boost, the boost itself had become an argument. Generally attributed to the Great Northern Railway, the See America First campaign had gripped the nation with the economic possibilities of the national parks. "We receive comparatively nothing for [our scenery]," Congressman Taylor elaborated in 1915, "while Switzerland derives from $10,000 to $40,000 per square mile per year from scenery that is not equal to ours. But Switzerland knows that the public is ready and willing to pay for scenery, and they have developed it for selling purposes." A failure to profit from Switzerland's prudence, he concluded, especially with the outbreak of war "closing European resorts to American travel this year," would cost the United

The See America First campaign promoted wilderness while promising visitor comforts, led by new railroad lodges and park hotels. This Glacier National Park advertisement from 1915 assures prospective travelers that no one needs to rough it. *Author's collection*

States a golden opportunity for teaching its "citizens to visit and appreciate our own parks."[23]

The last hurdle between his argument and Rocky Mountain National Park remained the assurance of worthless lands. As Taylor confirmed, the projected park had already been reduced by two-thirds to appease mining and grazing interests. Apparently satisfied, the Senate held no formal discussion, but there was a spirited debate in the House, where Taylor again elevated the uselessness of Rocky Mountain National Park into a convincing economic dividend. Located just 60 miles northwest of Denver, the park would be "marvelously beautiful," surpassing "Switzerland in the varied glory of its magnificence." The needed assurances were right behind. Mountains that rugged supported "comparatively little timber of merchantable value" and the altitude was much "too great for practical farming." The territory simply had "no value for anything but scenery." That was not only his opinion, he added, but also the consensus of "thousands [of people] from all over the world." An obligatory list of amendments still held Taylor to his word. Those exempted from preservation and allowed entry included prospectors and the Reclamation Service—just in case, in arguing "See America First," he had forgotten the West's true owners.[24]

It was another reminder why preservationists had come to see their alternative—hotels and railroads—as the key to every park's survival. By 1910, famous railroad hotels included Old Faithful Inn in Yellowstone (Northern Pacific) and El Tovar on the South Rim of Grand Canyon (Santa Fe). Meanwhile, Louis W. Hill and the Great Northern Railway planned two major hotels for Glacier National Park. For horseback riders and avid hikers, a series of Swiss-style chalets scattered through the high country would fill in the gaps a day apart. Visiting the completed buildings in 1915, the novelist Mary Roberts Rinehart summed up her impressions for *Collier's Magazine*: "Were it not for the Great Northern Railway, travel through Glacier Park would be practically impossible." The terrain itself was visibly daunting. "If the Government had not preserved it, it would have preserved itself. No homesteader would ever have invaded its rugged magnificence and dared its winter snows. But you and I would not have seen it," she reminded her readers. Because of the Great Northern Railway, Glacier National Park might actually be enjoyed.[25]

A perceived need to define enjoyment itself as something practical reflected the new reality of national parks. Led by J. Horace McFarland, preservationists continually refined the argument that parks were eminently practical for social and cultural needs. The combination of mounting world tensions and urban expansion provided another creative if somewhat improbable platform—military preparedness. In that vein, Robert Bradford Marshall, chief topographer of the U.S. Geological Survey, linked the protection of scenery with national defense. "I come now to a hobby of mine—our national parks," he said in a March 1911 speech before the Canadian Campers Club in New York City. "Now, you may think I am a national park crank, but I am going to prove to you that a fine, generous national park system is absolutely essential to the proper handling of an American war Fleet in case of a great war, or to the establishment and maintenance of an army which, in the event of such a catastrophe shall be invincible against the armed hosts of the world." Speeded by America's rapidly developing cities, the increase in urban inhabitants had been unforeseen. Thus, while "city soldiers in the past have made good," he observed, as urban areas became "more and more congested," the "physical status" of boys and men "deteriorated" and would "continue to deteriorate." Hanging "from the straps of crowded [street] cars," working men "forget they have legs." What prescription might restore their physical vitality? "Give them national parks," places "where they can go every year or so and forget something of the rush and jam and scramble of the modern life . . . and build up their bodies by being next to nature. Then, should there be a call to arms, the dwellers of the city canyons will be able to meet the physical needs of a strenuous field service."[26]

Revisiting the ideals of J. Horace McFarland, George Otis Smith, as director of the U.S. Geological Survey, concentrated on the general good of parks. "The nation that leads the world in feverish business activity requires playgrounds as well as workshops," he wrote in 1909. For the maintenance of "industrial supremacy" presupposed "conserving not only minerals but men." Thus, "arguments for scenic preservation need not be limited to aesthetic or sentimental postulates"; to the contrary, the "playgrounds of the nation are essential to its very life." Like McFarland, he took no credit for being original; indeed, perhaps John Muir had said it best, Smith admitted. Muir's definition, "fountains of life," aptly described the national parks, for only there "can be had the recreation that makes for increased and maintained efficiency." Even "the materialist" must not "turn aside from this demand of the times," Smith added, "for no greater value can be won from mountain slopes and rushing rivers than through the utilization of natural scenery in the development of [our] citizens." Robert Marshall's speech also lent itself to a reminder about the economic advantages of scenic protection: "Manage the national parks on a business basis and work for good transportation facilities to and from them," Marshall directed, "so that the multitude may visit them."[27]

Entirely traceable to the American Civic Association, the idea for a bureau of national parks had finally matured. Without permanent safeguards and a centralized authority, a broadened role for parks was pointless. Nor had existing legislation proved reassuring. Although every park had an enabling act, even the biggest parks lacked uniformity. As a primary illustration, J. Horace McFarland contrasted "the Yellowstone—having a satisfactory, definite, enabling act," with "the Yosemite—being no park at all but actually a forest reserve." The further paucity of even "general" legislation dismayed preservationists, as did what McFarland called "confused and indefinite" management procedures.[28]

The issue had been further complicated in 1906 with passage of the Antiquities Act. Again, rather than entrust the national monuments to a single, centralized agency, Congress allowed the original holder of the land to retain each unit. As a result, "of the twenty-eight national monuments created by executive action," McFarland noted in 1911, "thirteen are under the Forest Service and fifteen under the Interior Department." Inevitably, "none were being adequately controlled or logically handled."[29] The two largest monuments, Grand Canyon and Mount Olympus, offered special cause for concern. Carved from the holdings of the U.S. Forest Service, each remained with that agency. Then were they "parks" or "forests"? Inasmuch as the Forest Service perceived everything to be a resource, it seemed that the agency's utilitarian biases would prevail.

The mission of protecting the parks finalized the confusion. Beginning in 1886, the U.S. Army took over Yellowstone and later the California national parks. But although the troopers did a superb job (one historian contends they actually "saved" the reserves), military oversight of civilian visitors and private concessionaires invariably brought other problems.[30] Army engineers assigned to improve the roads in Yellowstone again answered directly to the War Department.[31]

In 1900, presaging his sponsorship of the Antiquities Act, Representative John F. Lacey of Iowa introduced legislation "to establish and administer national parks." However, even without the national monuments to consider, the measure gained little support. When the project resurfaced, in 1910, the American Civic Association was heading the effort. Bending the ear of any willing listener, J. Horace McFarland continued describing the vulnerability of the parks as a problem of unified management. Their citizen champions needed support within the government that no opponent might conveniently budge.

At McFarland's urging, Interior Secretary Richard A. Ballinger made the campaign official, endorsing a bureau of national parks in his annual report for 1910.[32] Developing his long-range strategy, McFarland then sought the advice and support of leading preservationists, notably Frederick Law Olmsted Jr. A distinguished landscape architect in his own right, Olmsted's reputation included his father's gift for language. His reply to McFarland, included in the record of the 1911 national park conference, revealed Olmsted's hopes for the bureau. Above all, its enabling act should include "some kind of legislative definition in broad but unmistakable terms of the primary purpose for which the parks and monuments are set apart, accompanied by a prohibition of any use which is directly or indirectly in conflict with that primary purpose." Other purposes not in conflict might be allowed provided that they remained in the spirit of the primary purpose.[33] Simply, before a national parks bureau could be effective, the parks themselves needed to be better defined.

The Union Pacific Railroad brought its first passengers to Yellowstone National Park in June 1908, then exhibited Yellowstone in 1915 at the Panama-Pacific International Exposition in San Francisco. Featured here on a souvenir postcard, the stunning attraction of the exhibit was a full-sized replica of Old Faithful Inn (1904, Robert C. Reamer, architect). The back of the postcard reads: "The most pronounced success at the Panama-Pacific Exposition is the four-acre exhibit contributed by the Union Pacific System. Old Faithful Inn, seating 2,000 with the Official Exposition Orchestra of eighty men, is the popular place to dine." *Author's collection*

A next major coup for the association came at its seventh annual convention, convened December 13, 1911, in Washington, D.C. None other than President William Howard Taft agreed to give the keynote address in a day devoted to the national parks. Their development, Taft confirmed, would remain inadequate "unless we have a bureau which is itself distinctly charged with the responsibility for their management and for their building up." Surely, it was "a proper expense, a necessary expense," he concluded. "Let us have the bureau." Interior Secretary Walter L. Fisher followed Taft with a report on the national park conference just held in Yellowstone. "And it was a very significant thing to me," he remarked, "as I think it will be to you, to find that the Northern Pacific Railroad Company, whose road leads to one of our principal parks, was, and is, much in favor, through its representatives, of having a National Park Bureau established." In fact, all the principal railroads endorsed it, Fisher observed, having similarly concluded "that it was for their own best interest" to improve conditions in the national parks.[34]

Among the opposition, the U.S. Forest Service—with extensive holdings in the West—feared that it stood to lose the most. In the future, new parks inevitably would come from the national forests, again at the expense of the existing agency.[35] Gifford Pinchot, recently fired as chief forester, further mined his dispute with President Taft to warn the public of this latest threat to wise use. Others objected to the term "bureau" itself, suggesting that a "bureau of national parks," as distinct from a government "service," lent the parks greater prestige than they deserved.[36]

On that point, the bureau's congressional sponsors, led by Senator Reed Smoot of Utah, were diplomatically inclined to agree.[37] Even with the name change, however, the National Park Service faced an uphill fight.[38] The Forest Service insisted on retaining its national monuments and further asked to manage its own national parks. Gifford Pinchot remained no less divisive, speaking out against any efforts to coordinate the parks unless handled "efficiently, economically, and satisfactorily by the Forest Service."[39]

The problem for the Forest Service was that Pinchot had never prepared it to talk openly of promoting tourism. In contrast, thanks to the American Civic Association and its allies, park supporters continued to reinvent the national parks. Answering the Forest Service about efficiency, there was no better example than parks that paid dividends to the national economy. Leading off testimony on the Park Service bill before the House Committee on the Public Lands, Interior Secretary Walter

Fisher reworked the theme. "For instance, we should try to make our people spend their money in this country instead of abroad, and certainly as far as spending it abroad for the scenic effect." The scenic offerings of the United States did "not have to ask any odds of any other country on earth."[40] Added J. Horace McFarland in a later hearing, "I think sometimes we fall into a misapprehension because the word 'park' in the minds of most of us suggests a place where there are flower beds . . . and things of that kind." However, "the park has passed out of this category in the United States." Beyond aesthetics, the parks met a very practical need. The "park is the direct competitor . . . of the courts, of the jail, of the cemetery, and a very efficient competitor with all of them," he elaborated. By providing rest and relaxation, parks kept "at work men who otherwise would be away from work. That is the park idea in America," he concluded, "as it has come to be the idea of service and efficiency, and not an idea of pleasure and ornamentation at all."[41]

It is here that the common story line of the National Park Service forgets the importance of national events. The unlikely event that in fact sealed the agency was the completion of the Panama Canal. In celebration, both San Diego and San Francisco had been designated to host a major world's fair in 1915. San Francisco hoped to showcase its recovery from the devastating earthquake of 1906. An added advantage was to draw attention away from Hetch Hetchy, which the city had appropriated in 1913. In both cities, invited exhibitors were asked to feature world commerce, invention, and the arts. By far the larger undertaking, sprawled over a square mile, arose beside San Francisco Bay. Engulfing the Marina District, the Panama-Pacific International Exposition opened its doors on February 20, 1915, for a nine-month run. Including new and repeat visitors, more than 18 million people officially passed through the turnstiles for an average of 65,000 a day.[42]

As a boost for the Park Service bill, still stalled in Congress, it was a classic case of perfect timing. The theme universally chosen by the transcontinental railroads was See America First. Let others celebrate the canal; they intended to feature the national parks. The actual exhibits, the railroads advised by 1914, would include all the major units. In San Francisco, the Union Pacific Railroad was modeling Yellowstone on four and a half acres of land. Aptly, the railroad's publicist described the exhibit as "titanic," the best of Yellowstone brought "true to life." Far more than a taste of its scenery, the railroad promised, "this Yellowstone reproduction is the largest exhibit ever erected at any World Fair, involving the use of two million feet of lumber and the expenditure of half a million dollars."[43]

Among the exhibit's modeled wonders, the feature attraction was Old Faithful Geyser. "At regular intervals, uniform with those of its prototype, great gushes of vast volumes of boiling water and steam are thrown high into the air." A one-acre relief map added a bird's-eye view of Yellowstone—showing all "the important geyser and other plutonic formations; hot springs, roaring mountains, lakes, falls, cascades, grottoes, government roads, trails and other outlines." The exhibit concluded with a full-size replica of Old Faithful Inn, reconfigured into a restaurant seating 2,000. An 80-piece orchestra played onstage. "Its exterior is, in size and construction, a replica of its prototype in faraway Yellowstone"—in all details "exact," promised the Union Pacific. "The hewn-log pillars, railed balconies, multi-gabled roof, and, high above all, the eight flapping pennants, are all there."[44]

Mounting a direct challenge to the Union Pacific, the Santa Fe Railway had appropriated six acres on the fairgrounds for an indoor model of Grand Canyon. During a 30-minute tour, visitors skirted the rim in "an electric observation parlor car," stopping at "seven of the grandest and most distinctive points." More than 100 miles of the canyon were on display, the railroad reported, "reproduced accurately, carefully and wrought so wonderfully that it is hard to realize that you are not actually on the rim of the Canyon itself." Pueblo Indians, occupying a village on the roof of the building, completed the Santa Fe's picture of the romantic Southwest.[45]

If not what George Catlin had envisioned for native America in his description of a "nation's Park," both the Yellowstone and the Grand Canyon exhibits reminded fairgoers that such parks did indeed exist. At the Great Northern Railway building, Blackfeet Indians met arriving visitors, shepherding them inside to find displays of Glacier National Park. Lavish exhibits at the Southern Pacific Building featured Yosemite Valley and the giant sequoias.[46] Four other railroads were sponsoring The Globe, a re-creation, through dioramas and models, of a railroad journey west. Available at the door, a souvenir brochure announced the exhibit's features. "The earth itself is on display," the text began. "The United States, with its mountains, rivers, valleys, national parks and cities, is taken in at a glance. In fact, the eye travels with tiny trains which flit across the huge miniature exactly as the trains they represent are in flight across the continent." Visitors returning home should at least make a stopover at one or more national parks. Far beyond the publicity normally provided to ticket agents, principally timetables and brochures, the Panama-Pacific International Exposition affirmed the national parks as America's greatest achievement—and destination.[47]

A mile deep, miles wide, & painted like a sunset

That's the Grand Canyon of Arizona

For art booklets of the train
and trip address
W. J. Black Pass Traffic Mgr.
A T & S F Ry System
1066 Railway Exchange Chicago

You can go there in a Pullman to the rim
at El Tovar, en route to Sunny California
on the train of luxury

The California Limited

Santa Fe All the way

Not to be outdone by its competitors, the Santa Fe Railway devoted six acres to an indoor model of the Grand Canyon at the Panama-Pacific International Exposition. Beginning in 1901, the railroad monopolized the actual canyon with a spur track to the South Rim, hoping to attract wealthy socialites on their way to California, such as this Gibson Girl from the December 1910 issue of *McClure's*. Author's collection

In retrospect, preservationists desperate to secure the national parks against invasive development could not have asked for more. That the loss of Hetch Hetchy came to overshadow the California expositions is a matter of forgetting history. In 1915, the expositions were front-page news. Virtually the entire population relied on the railroads for commerce and daily travel. As a catalyst for the National Park Service, what the railroads wanted mattered greatly. Having proved in spectacular fashion that they wanted parks, Congress and the country could not help taking notice.

At the Interior Department, reforms to accommodate the concerns of the railroads began with the presumption that a Park Service bill would be approved. Instead of relying on the office of the chief clerk, to whom the railroads had generally reported, Secretary Franklin K. Lane moved to fill a new post, that of assistant secretary. His permanent choice, Stephen T. Mather, was a self-made millionaire and friend. In Mather, the railroads would find a skilled executive rather than someone called a clerk. The industry in which Mather had made his fortune, borax mining, was also easily understood by fellow industrialists. Mather's longtime membership in the Sierra Club further added to his credibility. Drawing heavily from the San Francisco business community, the Sierra Club had never been immodest in the observation that wealth supported conservation. As a final advantage, Mather, like Lane, was an alumnus of the University of California. Centered in several university departments, including the Museum of Vertebrate Zoology, no faculty was more distinguished for its research on the national parks.[48]

On graduating from the university in 1887, Mather began a career in journalism as a reporter for the *New York Sun*. Five years later, his ambitions unsatisfied, he turned his energies to business and the borax industry. By 1914, he had made his fortune and was ready for a different challenge. A summer sojourn into the High Sierra led to an attractive opportunity. Observing that Yosemite and Sequoia national parks had been mismanaged, he wrote a letter of protest to Secretary Lane. Lane's reply remains the stuff of legend: "Dear Steve, If you don't like the way the national parks are being run, come on down to Washington and run them yourself." Mather allegedly wavered, then accepted the challenge, provided that Lane shielded him from bureaucratic hassles. Lane accommodated Mather with a shrewd assistant—and yet another Californian and Berkeley graduate—a young law student named Horace M. Albright.[49]

Where this traditional story line again fails the history is to lose sight of larger events. Lane had already considered Mather for the post and months before their purported letters. Lane's more compelling reason was taking shape in San Francisco—the Panama-Pacific International Exposition. It was no time for minor officials, however dedicated, to be directing park affairs at Interior. In 1912, a second national parks conference held in Yosemite reaffirmed the weakness of that arrangement. The railroads again were adamant: all wanted the government to improve the parks. A chorus of concessionaires added a firm amen. Yet a third conference, planned for March 1915, would coordinate with the Panama-Pacific Exposition. There, the railroads planned to be hugely visible. After opening on the campus of the University of California at Berkeley, the conference spent its final day on the fairgrounds, meeting in the auditorium of the palatial building of the Southern Pacific Railroad. The

Stephen T. Mather, as first director of the National Park Service, was instrumental in furthering a "pragmatic alliance" with the western railroads, especially the Union Pacific, which he asked to develop new parks in Utah. Mather is shown here on the observation car of the North Coast Limited, providing service to Yellowstone National Park on the Northern Pacific Railway. *Courtesy of the National Archives*

conferees then broke for lunch in "Yellowstone National Park," gathering in the Union Pacific's replica of Old Faithful Inn.[50]

This is the greater background behind the advancement of the National Park Service bill. In later years, Mather and Horace Albright memorialized the Interior Department, but it was because of the railroads that they swayed the Congress. Mather's personal campaign, featuring a two-week camping trip in the High Sierra, emphasized individuals over the broader public. The trip's carefully vetted guest list led to 15 acceptances by leaders in industry, government, and the media. Mather and Horace Albright served as hosts. Clearly Mather's biggest coup was the presence of Gilbert Grosvenor, editor of *National Geographic Magazine*. The one railroad official, Ernest O. McCormick of the Southern Pacific, was vice president of passenger operations. On July 15, 1915, the participants left Visalia, California, for Sequoia National Park. Mather was anxious that his guests see the problem of private ownership in Giant Forest, which had been claimed before the park began.[51] The venue of a tight-knit group enraptured by his overtures showed Mather at his best. His public campaign was indeed familiar. "Secretary Lane has asked me for a business administration," he wrote just four months after taking office. "This I understand to mean an administration which shall develop to the highest possible degree of efficiency the resources of the national parks both for the pleasure and the profit of their owners, the people." Well before Stephen Mather, the American Civic Association had invented that argument. "A hundred thousand people used the national parks last year," he continued. "A million Americans should play in them every summer." Again, his ending came straight from history. "Our national parks are practically lying fallow, and only await proper development to bring them into their own."[52]

The point is that no individual inspired the National Park Service. As rather the logical extension of the national park idea, it came entirely from American culture. See America First was just the latest catch-phrase of many interests asking the American public to believe in parks. All could take credit for the breakthrough that came on August 25, 1916, when President Woodrow Wilson signed the National Park Service Act into law. Here at last, preservationists congratulated themselves, was the clarity of purpose they had wanted. Section 1 provided for a director, assistant director, chief clerk, draftsman, and messenger in addition to "such other employees as the Secretary of the Interior may deem necessary." Title to all existing and future national parks passed to the Park Service; similarly, it received the national monuments in the Interior Department. There, the Forest Service, having made the monuments an issue, had successfully held the line. Its monuments were to remain with the national forests unless Congress reauthorized them as national parks.[53]

It was a disappointment but not a deal breaker. Preservationists still cheered their larger victory. For years, they had pursued legislation that would codify the management of all the national parks. Working closely with the American Civic Association, Frederick Law Olmsted Jr. had been their guide. The language was principally his. The "fundamental purpose" of the national parks, the act clarified, "is to conserve the scenery and the natural and historic objects and the wildlife therein and to provide for the enjoyment of the same in such manner and by such means as will leave them unimpaired for the enjoyment of future generations." Olmsted himself granted that the wording was imperfect. Precisely what, for example, was meant by "unimpaired"? How much would managers of the future allow projects that disrupted park ideals? Although those debates seemed potentially endless, at least a basic consensus had been achieved.[54]

It now fell to Stephen Mather to build the Park Service, for which he relied heavily on Horace Albright. Suffering from severe bouts of depression, Mather was often gone months at a time. As much as he loved the spotlight, cajoling people took its toll. His career as director of the National Park Service nonetheless proved inspired. Several months before his death (in January 1930), Horace Albright assumed the post, bent on preserving the Mather tradition even if that meant occasionally bending history. Four years later, in a reversal of Mather's career, Albright resigned to become president of the American Potash Company. By then, the legend was solidly in place—Stephen T. Mather had started it all.[55]

In January 1917, a fourth national parks conference, convened in Washington, D.C., reminded the nation otherwise. As in the previous three western conferences, the principal speakers got right to the point. Among them, Senator Reed Smoot of Utah disclosed his reasoning for having cosponsored the Park Service bill. "I think I can see in the future a great portion of the three hundred and fifty million American dollars now spent annually abroad for recreation, rest, and sightseeing diverted to American railroads, American hotel keepers, American guides, American merchants, and American farmers," he said. As chairman of the House Committee on the Public Lands, Scott Ferris of Oklahoma emphatically agreed. "The amount of money that goes abroad every year by tourists is no less than alarming. The best estimate available is that more than $500,000,000 is expended by our American people every year abroad vainly hunting for wonders and beauties only half as grand as nature has generously provided for them at home." Surely, he concluded, such overseas spending demanded "that we of the Congress and you members of the conference" find some way "to keep at least a part of that money at home where it belongs."[56]

Finally, the national parks had come full circle. None was worthless lands after all. At least, carefully gerrymandered to exclude their natural resources, they might add to the nation's economy. The downside was that in allowing the compromise, inspiration would never be good enough reason for having parks. The unanswered question, even within the National Park Service, was what values the parks were meant to serve. Perhaps See America First was the future, the one alliance capable of making business and inspiration work. If so, only time—and the ghost of Hetch Hetchy—would prove whether the National Park Service was all that its supporters had hoped.

A more inclusive look at the natural world was officially reflected in the evolution of park interpretation. Interpretive programs, inaugurated in the 1920s, led tourists off the road to such places as Mount Stanton in Glacier National Park. *Courtesy of the National Archives, Hileman photograph*

CHAPTER 6

Complete Conservation

Our national parks system is a national museum. Its purpose is to preserve forever . . . certain areas of extraordinary scenic magnificence in a condition of
primitive nature. Its recreational value is also very great, but recreation is not
distinctive of the system. The function which alone distinguishes the national
parks . . . is the museum function made possible only by the parks' complete
conservation.

—Robert Sterling Yard, 1923

It is now recognized that [national] Parks contain more than scenery.

—Harold C. Bryant, cofounder,
Yosemite Free Nature Guide Service, 1929

THE success of the "See America First" campaign reassured preservationists that the national parks would survive. Still open to question was whether they would survive as originally established.
Hetch Hetchy proved the resistance of Congress to larger parks on the order of Yellowstone, whose expanse protected (if unintentionally) other
natural values besides scenic wonders. A now visible belief that the
preservation of natural environments should be the role of national parks
only heightened the tension regarding their integrity. Americans increasingly recalled the pronouncement of the Census Bureau in 1890 that the
frontier was no more. Indeed, "it has girdled the globe," Mary Roberts
Rinehart confirmed in May 1921 for readers of the *Ladies' Home Journal*.
"And, unless we are very careful," she cautioned, "soon there will be no
reminders of the old West," including "the last national resource the

American people have withheld from commercial exploitation, their parks." That others had said as much did nothing to lessen her sense of urgency. Outside the national parks, it seemed that the West was about to be transformed. Plans to dam the Columbia River, for example, threatened the image of Lewis and Clark reaching out "on their adventurous journey into the unknown." Soon the river would "be harnessed, like Niagara, and turning a million wheels. Our wild life gone with our Indians, our waterfalls harnessed and our rivers laboring, our mountains groaning that they might bring forth power, soon all that will be left of our great past," she restated emphatically, "will be our national parks."[1]

As a catalyst of the national park idea, the search for an American past through landscape was nothing new. The difference lay in adding the insistence that all components of the American scene should be represented. Preserving a sense of history, as recalled through broad expanses of native, living landscapes, was perhaps as crucial to the identity of the United States as the protection of natural wonders. It followed that preservationists might, for the first time, draw a clear distinction between all parks and national parks. Formality of any kind, Rinehart herself believed, smacked too much of the city park experience. In the West, one came to appreciate "that a park could be more than a neat and civilized place, with green benches and public tennis courts." The word "park" itself was "misleading." "It is too small a name," she maintained, "too definitely associated with signs and asphalt and tameness."[2] In the future, preservationists should be as determined to defend the parks as a vestige of primitive America. "In this respect a national and a city park are wholly different," two vertebrate zoologists, Joseph Grinnell and Tracy Storer, agreed in 1916. "A city park is of necessity artificial . . . ; but a national park is at its inception entirely natural and is generally thereafter kept fairly immune from human interference."[3]

Notable exceptions included park lodges and even grand hotels, which, however rustic, could not seriously be considered "entirely natural." If most preservationists were not opposed to building lodges, it was in appreciation that the parks needed to attract visitors, or—as in the case of Hetch Hetchy—risk far more damaging intrusions. Besides, "the great hotels are dwarfed by the mountains around them, lost in the trees," Rinehart assured her readers. "The wilderness is there, all around them, so close that the timid wild life creeps to their very doors."[4]

The same obviously could not be said of dams and reservoirs, nor did preservationists believe that they could ever make that compromise. To be sure, hardly had the Park Service been established than ranchers and farmers in the state of Idaho proposed to tap Yellowstone Lake and the falls of the Bechler River—in the southwestern corner of Yellowstone Park—for irrigation.[5] Preservationists immediately perceived the scheme as a threat to their own proposal to extend the boundaries of the park southward to include portions of the Thorofare Basin, Jackson Hole, and the Teton Mountains. This appeared necessary if Yellowstone were to be managed along natural rather than political boundaries. Out of the plan emerged Grand Teton National Park, established in 1929 as a "roadless" preserve. Any pretext that the park had seriously broken with tradition, however, was dispelled by its failure to include the lowlands and wildlife habitat of Jackson Hole.

It remained instead for Everglades National Park, Florida, authorized in 1934, to mark the first unmistakable pledge to the protection of natural environments. The commitment seemed all the more convincing in light of the topography of the Everglades. For the first time, a major national park lacked great mountains, deep canyons, and tumbling waterfalls. The protection of native plants and animals alone seemed justification for Everglades National Park. A growing fear that its pristine character might also be sacrificed stemmed from pressures to restrict the park considerably under the ceiling approved by Congress. In the protection of natural environments, no less than natural wonders, asking for lands that nobody else seemed to want still offered the best hope for success.

The conviction that national parks were the last vestiges of primitive America proved the important catalyst for their broader management. Ever since Yosemite and Yellowstone, the overriding criterion for national parks had been the presence of natural wonders. Congress occasionally seemed aware that the parks might fill other roles; the Yellowstone Park Act, for example, provided against "the wanton destruction of the fish and game found within said park, and against their capture or destruction for the purposes of merchandise or profit."[6] However, until the act of 1894 protecting the birds and animals in Yellowstone, the discretion in the phrase was greatly abused. Even after 1894, simply to recognize that park animals were being exterminated could hardly be called game management. Both the science and public appreciation of its importance did not mature until the twentieth century.[7]

The burden of proof on a park remained primarily physical; only then might other factors boldly be advanced. "So with the Yellowstone," Stephen T. Mather agreed, writing for the *National Parks Portfolio* in 1916: "all have heard of its geysers, but few indeed of its thirty-three-hundred square miles of wilderness beauty." The inclusion of wilderness had been purely unintentional. The park "is associated in the public mind with geysers only," Robert Sterling Yard, author of the *Portfolio*, reaffirmed. "There never was a greater mistake. Were there no geysers, the Yellowstone watershed alone, with its glowing canyon, would be worth the national park." Of course, the canyon itself was a scenic wonder. But "were there also no canyon," Yard continued, "the scenic wilderness and its incomparable wealth of wild-animal life would be worth the national park."[8]

Provided free to 275,000 American leaders in politics, business, and education, the *National Parks Portfolio* hinted at the coming reappraisal of the role of national parks. "That these parks excelled in grandeur and variety the combined scenic exhibits of other principal nations moved the national pride," Yard recalled. At last, Americans were awakening to the realization that the national parks "embodied in actual reality . . . a mighty system of national museums of the primitive American wilderness." Indeed, "the national parks are much more than a playground," Mary Roberts Rinehart agreed. "They are a refuge. They bring rest to their human visitors, but they give life to uncounted numbers of wild creatures." The animals certainly were "of no less consequence than the scenery," Joseph Grinnell and Tracy Storer maintained. "To the natural charm of the landscape they add the witchery of movement." Ultimately, the advancement of science would require that park managers consider the sum total of these phenomena. "Herein lies the feature of supreme value in national parks," the biologists concluded: "they furnish samples of the earth as it was before the advent of the white man." The reserves, agreed Stephen Mather, "in addition to being ideal recreation areas, serve also as field laboratories for the study of nature." Robert Sterling Yard was even more emphatic: "In all of them wild life conditions remain untouched."[9]

In fact, that was not the case. As scientists, Grinnell and Storer had already reminded the scientific community that wildlife conditions had changed dramatically. As director of the Museum of Vertebrate Zoology at the University of California at Berkeley, Grinnell had undertaken a major research program in Yosemite. There, he found a vigorous program leading to the extermination of predatory animals. Nor did the Park Service feel it had anything to hide. To the contrary, as early as October 1920, Stephen T. Mather reported a "very gratifying increase" throughout the national park system "in deer and other species that always suffer through the depredations of mountain lion, wolves, and other 'killers.'"[10] As Grinnell observed, without a biologist's understanding, park managers remained trapped in the conviction that an animal killing other animals was "undesirable."

In the preservation of natural environments, human emotions should have no place. Advising his students privately, Grinnell urged them to enter the National Park Service, ultimately to effect the necessary changes that scientific management would require. Only inside the agency might they further advance the transformation of the national parks into public classrooms. "As the settlement of the country progresses," he remarked in his article with Tracy Storer, "and the original aspect of nature is altered, the national parks will probably be the only areas remaining unspoiled for scientific study." It followed that "every large national park" should provide for "a trained resident naturalist who, as a member of the park staff, would look after the interests of the animal life of the region and aid in making it known to the public." Techniques would include "popularly styled illustrated leaflets and newspaper articles" along with "lectures and demonstrations at central camps." All would "help awaken people to a livelier interest in wild life, and to a healthy and intelligent curiosity about things of nature." Along with years of research, the scientists included a personal observation: "Our experience has persuaded us that the average camper in the mountains is hungry for information about the animal life he encounters." A few simple suggestions for study were usually "sufficient to make him eager to acquire his natural history at first hand, with the result that the recreative value of his few days or weeks in the open is greatly enhanced."[11]

Of course, these important preambles to the preservation of natural environments did nothing to displace the original rationale for national parks. John Burroughs, for example, was another contemporary naturalist who still attained popularity using descriptions more suggestive of nineteenth-century explorers. "In the East, the earth's wounds are virtually all healed," he noted in 1911, "but in the West they are yet raw and gaping, if not bleeding." The Grand Canyon in particular did "indeed suggest a far-off, half-sacred antiquity, some greater Jerusalem, Egypt, Babylon, or India," he wrote. "We speak of it as a scene; it is more like a vision, so foreign is it to all other terrestrial spectacles, and so surpassingly beautiful."[12]

Realizing the ambitions of Theodore Roosevelt and the Santa Fe Railway, in 1919 Congress promoted Grand Canyon National Monument into Grand Canyon National Park. Also in 1919, Zion Canyon, Utah, first set aside as Mukuntuweap National Monument, became Zion National Park. Justly renowned as "the Yosemite of the Desert" by virtue of its steep, brilliantly colored sandstone cliffs, Zion itself had nearby rivals, notably

Bryce Canyon National Monument, proclaimed in 1923. Established as Utah National Park in 1924, it officially became Bryce in 1928. Yet a third regional wonder, Cedar Breaks, was proclaimed a national monument in 1933.[13]

Clustered in southern Utah and comfortably within a day of the North Rim of Grand Canyon, each of the new parks added to what Rufus Steele dubbed "the Celestial Circuit." (The region would continue to inspire monumental parks, notably Canyonlands [1964], Arches [1971], and Capitol Reef [1971].) A writer for *Sunset Magazine*, Steele indeed focused on dramatic scenery—"canyons set about with majestic peaks" and still "other canyons that are filled with cathedrals and colonnades, ramparts and rooms, terraces and temples, turrets and towers, obelisks and organs," and similar "incredible products of erosion."[14]

The problem in opening the region was isolation, however splendid its natural wonders. For the railroads, the other problem was the realization that train travel to the national parks had finally peaked. Stephen T. Mather nonetheless prevailed on the Union Pacific Railroad that developing the parks would be a good investment. "The Grand Canyon?" Union Pacific asked, advertising its four new lodges and tours by motor bus. "Nowhere on the face of the globe is there anything like it." Even Bryce Canyon, although considerably smaller, was no less worthy of a rail pilgrimage west. Its "great side walls are fluted like giant cathedral organs," the railroad insisted. "Other architectural rockforms tower upward in vast spires and minarets—marbly white and flaming pink." Royalty itself was present, "high on painted pedestals" and "startlingly real. Figures of Titans, of kings and queens!" Finally came Zion, its "tremendous temples and towers" rising "sheer four-fifths of a mile into the blue Utah sky." Surely, "every true American" would want to see these latest national parks "on an exclusive Union Pacific tour."[15]

As still the preeminent force for preservation, monumentalism further guided the establishment of new mountain national parks. Units protected in 1916 included Mount Lassen Volcanic National Park in California and Hawaii Volcanoes National Park on the islands of Hawaii and Maui. In 1917, Congress established Mount McKinley National Park in Alaska, ostensibly as a game preserve. It was among those eager to make that criterion valid that the new parks proved disappointments. Much like their predecessors, they were also rugged, limited in area, or, even allowing for the size of Mount McKinley, compromised with allowances to economic interests, led by the right to search for minerals. Prospectors might also kill game and birds. Obviously, market hunters need simply refer to themselves as prospectors, and the wildlife would be in jeopardy.[16] In either case, the alleged refuge had not been achieved without rugged scenery as its focus; Mount McKinley National Park was still a monument.

Proof that the nation was serious about wildlife protection awaited the first national park without an imposing topography. As a beginning, mountain parks in the East, where the mountains were relatively modest, would help confirm the nation's sincerity. As early as 1894, the North Carolina Press Association petitioned Congress for a national park in the state; five years later, the Appalachian National Park Association, organized at Asheville, seconded the proposal. Other preservation groups rapidly followed suit, including the Appalachian Mountain Club, the American Civic Association, and the American Association for the Advancement of Science. It still remained for Mount Desert Island, a rugged fragment of Maine seacoast, to form the nucleus of the first eastern park. This was Acadia, established in 1919. Several New England gentlemen of means inspired the project, including Charles W. Eliot, president of Harvard University, and George B. Dorr, a wealthy Bostonian. As early as 1901, they financed a program to secure portions of the island threatened by development; large contributions from other philanthropists, most notably John D. Rockefeller Jr., furthered the cause. In 1916, the group persuaded President Woodrow Wilson to proclaim the first 6,000 acres acquired a national monument. In 1918, Congress provided $10,000 to manage the monument and the following year—largely at the insistence of George Dorr and Stephen T. Mather—authorized the reserve as a national park.[17]

Along similar lines, the highlands of Virginia, Tennessee, and North Carolina continued to attract park supporters. A promising outgrowth of their efforts was the formation of the Southern Appalachian National Park Commission. In 1924, Interior Secretary Hubert Work asked the five-member commission to assess the region's suitability for representation in the national park system. "It has not been generally known that eastern parks of National size might still be acquired by our Government," the delegation advised. Its report nonetheless identified "several areas" agreed to contain "topographic features of great scenic value," each comparing "favorably with any of the existing parks of the West." In order of their ruggedness, two were preeminent—the Smoky Mountains (elevated by park supporters into the "Great" Smoky Mountains), forming the border between North Carolina and Tennessee, and the Blue Ridge Mountains of Virginia. The need for haste was therefore evident.

"All that has saved these nearby regions from spoliation for so long a time," the commissioners warned, "has been their inaccessibility and the difficulty of profitably exploiting the timber wealth that mantles the steep mountain slopes." Now those woodlands, too, were jeopardized by the "rapidly increasing shortages and mounting values of forest products." Every year, it seemed more probable "that the last remnants of [the] primeval forests will be destroyed," the commission concluded, "however remote on steep mountain side or hidden away in deep lonely cove they may be."[18]

The point about the "primeval" character of the mountains was the important indicator of coming change. In the Smoky Mountains, an appreciation of their value as a natural environment coalesced around their importance as a botanical refuge. "There are 152 varieties of trees alone," observed Isabelle F. Story, editor in chief of the National Park Service. It was indeed "impossible to describe the Great Smoky forest," agreed Robert Sterling Yard, "so rich is it in variety and beauty."[19] Neither Yard nor Story denied the importance of the forest's monumental base; the point was that if the East were to have parks, Americans needed to look beyond topography. Thinking in terms of scenery and natural environments, the Smoky Mountains and Blue Ridge combined the best of both. "It may be admitted that they are second to the West in rugged grandeur," Commissioner William C. Gregg conceded, "but they are first in beauty of woods, in thrilling fairyland glens, and in the warmth of Mother Nature's welcome." Concurred Stephen Mather, "The greater portion of the lands involved in these two park projects are wilderness areas." All that their natural environment needed was a familiar base. As Mather himself concluded, "and in the Smoky Mountains are found the greatest outstanding peaks east of the Rocky Mountains."[20]

The problem throughout the East was the absence of any significant public lands. For the East, there had been no public domain; by the Revolution, practically everything was in private hands. The establishment of a national park was no longer a matter of transferring land from one federal agency to another. As with Acadia, repurchasing the land was required. There, Congress was adamant that either the states or private donors would have to assume the financial and legal costs. To coordinate their efforts, preservationists organized the Shenandoah National Park Association of Virginia, the Great Smoky Mountains Conservation Association, and Great Smoky Mountains, Inc. Swayed by this outburst of citizen support, in May 1926 Congress authorized the secretary of the interior to accept, on behalf of the federal government, a maximum of

521,000 acres for a Shenandoah National Park and 704,000 acres for Great Smoky Mountains.[21]

The absence of federal assistance continued to delay both projects. Gradually, the cost of acquiring sufficient property in the Smokies exceeded $10 million, a goodly sum from the rural states represented. Aided by outside citizens, the residents of North Carolina and Tennessee raised half the amount. The project was finally rescued by John D. Rockefeller Jr., who made up the difference between the $5 million subscribed and the amount needed for a worthy park. A substantially smaller but no less welcome Rockefeller contribution further speeded Shenandoah National Park. Spared a truly crippling delay, in 1934 and 1935, respectively, Great Smoky Mountains and Shenandoah joined the national park system as member units in full standing.[22]

Shenandoah and Great Smoky Mountains are best seen as transition parks. While both anticipated the ecological standards of the later twentieth century, Congress required that each somehow approximate the visual standards of national parks in the West. Whatever the merits of the Great Smokies and the Blue Ridge Mountains as wilderness, wildlife, and botanical preserves, none of those features had as yet been recognized apart from its scenic base. Mountains remained the framework of protection; what lived or moved on their surfaces finally buttressed the traditional arguments, yet it was tradition that guaranteed the parks. Still unresolved—especially for the largest park proposals—was whether those devoid of geological wonders might win admittance to the national park system.

The cornerstone of that new perspective was total preservation. Its meaning was not yet fully defined; still, more Americans were coming to realize that the essential difference between all parks and national parks lay in the protection of primitive conditions. State and city parks could be said to be scenic; few but the national parks offered scenery unmodified. "Except to make way for roads, trails, hotels and camps sufficient to permit the people to live there awhile and contemplate the unaltered works of nature," Robert Sterling Yard described the distinction, "no tree, shrub or wild flower is cut, no stream or lake shore is disturbed, no bird or animal is destroyed." In short, the uniqueness of the national parks lay in "complete conservation." Nature was still best where it was modified the least.[23]

In a first major test of that new resolve, Yellowstone returned to the spotlight as the symbolic standard for national parks. Despite even its size, its boundaries had been drawn in haste and in the absence of complete knowledge about the territory. Only gradually did a later generation of preservationists fully appreciate the many worthy features left outside the park. Of these, none was considered more inspiring than the magnificent Teton Range. Sheer and glacier carved, the mountains guard the southern approach to Yellowstone on a north–south axis approximately 40 miles in length. The highest peak, Grand Teton, rises to 13,770 feet. To the east, the mountains fall off abruptly into Jackson Hole, which, at roughly 6,000 feet in elevation, is often referred to as the Tetons' "frame." Native vegetation in the valley includes a mixture of woodlands, grasslands, and sagebrush flats. Several lakes hugging the mountains, notably Jenny, Leigh, and String, majestically mirror the peaks. Jackson Lake, raised by a dam, visibly dominates the northern end of Jackson Hole. Exiting Jackson Lake, the Snake River roughly divides the remainder of Jackson Hole into an eastern and a western half.[24]

Like Yellowstone National Park immediately to the north, the ideal time to protect the region was before anyone had seriously claimed it. The nation's attention instead was fixed on Yellowstone's wonders. The opportunity to include Jackson Hole and the Tetons in the park had vanished before it was realized. By the late 1880s, Jackson Hole had been discovered. Soon the intrusions of the settled West were everywhere visible, led by ranches, farms, fences, and roads.[25]

Wildlife was first to feel the effects. For centuries, Yellowstone's southern elk herd had migrated through Jackson Hole to winter in the Green River basin, west of the Wind River Range. Other large mammals, including moose and antelope, themselves depended on "greater Yellowstone," the millions of acres surrounding the national park. With settlement of the Green River basin and then Jackson Hole, the elk were gradually squeezed off their wintering grounds by barbed-wire fencing and roads. Domestic livestock further competed for the forage previously reserved for the elk. They could not stay in Yellowstone; the snow was too deep and the cold too bitter. Every winter, thousands of the animals starved and died. Poaching considerably worsened the toll, as the hunters, lining up outside the park, knew that the animals would be forced to exit. Although legal, sport hunting led to the same result. No less than market hunters, trophy hunters sought out the specimen animals needed to maintain the herd.[26]

Even if the fate of the elk had been foreseen in 1872, it is doubtful Congress would have protected Jackson Hole. On average 2,000 feet lower than Yellowstone Park, the elevation is borderline for agriculture. Throughout the West, the mere possibility of establishing farms and ranches pre-

Horace M. Albright, as superintendent of Yellowstone National Park in the 1920s, and later the second director of the National Park Service, led the campaign to establish Grand Teton National Park, Wyoming, with an emphasis on preserving Jackson Hole. *Courtesy of the National Park Service*

empted claims to preserve the public lands. The few public officials who began pushing the Tetons and Jackson Hole as a park were themselves continually frustrated. In 1898, one notable report by Charles D. Walcott, director of the U.S. Geological Survey, and Dr. T. S. Brandegee, a San Diego botanist, called for extending Yellowstone Park southward to include the upper portion of Jackson Hole and most of the neighboring Thorofare Basin. Vested interests would not be harmed, the report noted. Most settlers had been drawn to the southern end of the valley, where the soil and grass were richer. In other words, the territory actually to be included was the poorer land and, besides, was primarily owned by the government as part of the Teton Forest Reserve.[27]

No matter, preserving access to the forest reserve was reason enough for valley residents to oppose the plan. As a concession to local needs, settlers and ranchers were allowed a broad range of access privileges, including the right to hunt, graze livestock, and cut wood for fuel and fencing. Few tenants in the valley now wanted to forgo those privileges for the sake of Yellowstone National Park. In 1902, a petition was taken up in the valley against the extension, claiming a perpetual need for those lands. It remained for the state of Wyoming, in 1905, to declare the region a game preserve and curtail the poaching of the elk. However, in the absence of a comprehensive plan to deal with existing development, even the game preserve was visibly compromised.[28]

The lines were now drawn for one of the longest and most emotional battles in the history of the national park idea. Over the next decade, the tragedy of the elk occasionally focused attention on the fate of Jackson Hole. Always on the lookout for good publicity, in July 1916 Stephen T. Mather and Horace Albright briefly visited the valley with a small party of government officials. It was this trip, Albright later recalled, that inspired him with the conviction that "this region must become a park" to protect forever its "beauty and wilderness charm."[29] The following winter, he and Mather "looked up the status of Jackson Hole lands and tried to formulate some feasible park plans." On the surface, their proposal to extend Yellowstone National Park southward into Jackson Hole was nothing new. The big change since the Walcott and Brandegee report lay within the Interior Department itself. By August 1916, the National Park Service had been approved. Mather believed in trying for a park, if with the standard concession that Jackson Hole was virtually useless. Indeed, the northern half of the valley "can never be put to any commercial use," he noted, while "every foot naturally belongs to Yellowstone Park."[30]

The problem with the worthless-lands argument in Jackson Hole was the southern half of the valley. Residents there continued looking northward for the privileges they had previously known. The Park Service agreed to maintain grazing privileges in the addition and, true to Mather's word, pursued only the inclusion of Jackson Hole's marginal, northern extremity. Regardless, on February 18, 1919, an extension bill died in the Senate, led by the opposition of John F. Nugent of Idaho. Nugent had merely raised the claim that portions of the extension would not in fact be open to grazing. As before, even the slightest proof of an existing use was all that western interests needed to kill a national park.[31]

The controversy then took a new twist. Although the skepticism of the ranchers had been foreseen, opponents of the extension suddenly had a new target—a road-building program endorsed by the National Park Service. In part to counter objections that the Yellowstone extension would affect the economy of Jackson Hole, the Park Service offered to expand and improve the valley's roads. This would include a direct link with the Cody Road (Yellowstone's east entrance) via Thorofare Basin. "In Washington we were constantly impressed by visiting callers from the West with the demand for more and better roads," Horace Albright later explained, justifying the decision. It followed that the people of Jackson Hole would think the same. Better roads make a better economy. "We even put this tentative idea on a map, believing that it was what Wyoming wanted. How many times later," he confessed, "we wished that map had never seen the light of day."[32]

It may have been a tentative proposal, as Albright noted, but there was nothing tentative about building roads in the national parks. Mather wanted them, and so did Albright, the better to attract more visitors from the middle class. The actual publication of the map in the Park Service's *Annual Report* also implied that the roads were wanted.[33] It was against this backdrop that Horace Albright, now superintendent of Yellowstone, returned to Jackson Hole in August 1919. A public meeting was to be held on the extension in which the issue of forest access might be resolved. At least that is what Albright thought. Instead, his hopes for the extension had soon evaporated in a storm of opposition. Behind the hostility, he determined, were the dude ranchers of Jackson Hole. Unlike traditional ranching interests, which by and large welcomed roads, the dude ranchers considered public works intrusive. The more roads that appeared in Jackson Hole, the more it would lose the flavor of the West. The West that the dude ranchers wanted to preserve was not the West of automobiles and tourists. Rather, they and their clients were principally eastern born and well-to-do. All had come to Jackson Hole to escape anything smacking of development and crowds. It was they, Albright reported, "who felt that park status meant modern roads, overflowing of the country with tourists, and other encroachments of civilization that would rob it of its romance and charm."[34] They even "refused to abide by the daylight-saving law," he complained to Director Mather in October. "They do not want automobiles . . . they will not have a telephone; and they insist that their mail should not be delivered more than three times a week." His veiled disgust was understandable; the National Park Service believed that the West needed to be opened to as many new visitors as possible. Without greater public support for the national parks brought about by increased visitation, all might be in jeopardy. "One must, of course, feel a certain sympathy for these people who are trying to get away from the noise and worries of city life and go as far into the wilds as possible," Albright conceded, "but they can not expect to keep such extraordinary mountain regions as the Tetons and their gem lakes . . . all for themselves."[35]

However, in view of such determined opposition, the Park Service agreed to reassess its priorities. Barely a year after Albright's run-in with valley residents, the agency's position had clearly changed. "Should the extension of the park be approved," Mather as director now wrote, "it would be the policy of this service to abstain from the construction or improvement of any more roads than now exist in the region." It was further his "firm conviction that a part of the Yellowstone country" likewise "should be maintained *as a wilderness* [emphasis added] for the ever-increasing numbers of people who prefer to walk and ride over trails in a region abounding in wild life." As if even to deny that the Park Service had encouraged a false impression about its commitment to building roads, Mather himself now claimed that any roads around Yellowstone Lake and across the Thorofare Basin "would mean the extinction of the moose." Behind his overcompensation lay the realization that the Park Service had lost the trust of the dude ranchers in Jackson Hole. "I am so sure that this view is correct," he concluded, "that I would be glad to see an actual inhibition on new road building placed in the proposed extension bill, this proviso to declare that without the prior authority of Congress no new road project in this region should be undertaken."[36]

As further testimony to his sincerity, he immediately extended the restriction to Yosemite National Park. The ban was not total; rather, new roads must not be considered until old ones proved inadequate. Still, Mather insisted, "In the Yosemite National Park, as in all of the other parks, the policy which contemplates leaving large areas of high mountain country wholly undeveloped should be forever maintained."[37]

Sequoia National Park was similarly protected. In 1926, after several years of delay and litigation, Congress enlarged Sequoia by taking in a substantial portion of the Sierra Nevada east of the Giant Forest, including Mount Whitney. Debate in the House of Representatives inevitably led to the question of developing the new section. The bill's sponsor, Henry E. Barbour of California, refused to concede the need. "It is proposed to make this a trail park and keep it a trail park," he stressed. "It is now a trail park . . . ; there are no roads contemplated into this new area at this time." The bill itself underscored the point, providing "for the preservation of said park *in a state of nature* [emphasis added] so far as is consistent with the purposes of this Act."[38] Although leaving leeway for development, the enlargement of Sequoia National Park proved that the preservation of natural environments was winning converts, especially with regard to the placement of roads.

Of course, little was sacrificed by prohibiting roads in the backcountry of the most rugged national parks. In this regard, Horace Albright conceded that the Sierra Nevada and Jackson Hole were worlds apart. "Good

Of growing concern to preservationists, the protection of wildlife from human interference guided efforts to establish parks of unquestionable biological integrity. Visitor behavior that undermined the policy was another matter, as park officials often overlooked the feeding of animals. Here, a deer begs for food from a car in Yellowstone during the summer of 1926. *Courtesy of the National Park Service*

roads for the hurrying motorist, on the one hand," he noted, discussing the issue in Jackson Hole, "and protection of the dude ranchers from invasion by automobiles, on the other, were foreseen as difficult problems soon to be faced."[39] The topography of the valley was entirely supportive of roads, even if the dude ranchers remained opposed.

Valley residents traced the year of reckoning to 1923. By then, "it seemed that road development might get entirely out of hand," Albright recalled. An influential partner of the Bar BC dude ranch, Struthers Burt, agreed. Each year, "the increasing hordes of automobile tourists" swept Jackson Hole "like locusts," he wrote. These motorists had not "the slightest perception . . . that there existed other and equally important philosophies and vital, fundamental human desires." The charge foreshadowed Burt's own change of heart toward the National Park Service. "In the beginning I was bitterly opposed to park extension, and remained so for some time," he admitted. "The advent of the automobile alone would have changed my mind."[40]

Finally convinced of Albright's sincerity, in July 1923 the dude ranchers invited him back to Jackson Hole to discuss additional options, including an outdoor museum or recreation area. Threatened projects by the U.S. Forest Service and Reclamation Service (renamed the Bureau of Reclamation) only added to the ranchers' sense of urgency. In 1916, for example, the bureau had dammed the outlet to Jackson Lake, increasing its surface area by 50 percent. As the water level rose, miles of dead trees and debris littered the shoreline. Meanwhile, irrigation interests backed the bureau's search for other reservoir sites, including the wilderness lakes edging Jackson Hole. Whether an outdoor museum could thwart the dam builders was highly questionable; who, for example, would invest in the proposal? Albright's words of encouragement still rested on the hope that the dude ranchers would eventually support a park.[41]

Three years later, in July 1926, Albright got his chance. Mr. and Mrs. John D. Rockefeller Jr. and their sons planned to vacation in Yellowstone National Park. Offering himself as their personal escort, Albright suggested that they round out their stay with a visit to Jackson Hole. Certainly, from previous trips the Rockefellers were aware of the controversy; Albright would be telling them nothing new. He simply hoped to immerse them in the array of gas stations, billboards, and dance halls adding to the visual blight of Jackson Hole. It worked. On the spot, Rockefeller requested that Albright forward him a list of the affected properties and estimates for the cost of restoring them. Late that fall, when Albright hand delivered the data to Rockefeller's New York City office, he received an even bigger surprise. The philanthropist seemed disappointed that Albright had been conservative. While his proposal called for spending approximately $250,000 to acquire only the land nearest the mountains, Rockefeller wished to invest four times that amount to purchase and restore both sides of the Snake River. Understandably jubilant, Albright quickly compiled a list of the affected property owners in Rockefeller's proposed addition.[42]

To expedite purchase offers, in 1927 Rockefeller and his staff, on advice from Albright, incorporated the Snake River Land Company out of Salt Lake City, Utah. Albright correctly reasoned that if Rockefeller's identity were known, speculation would increase. Although Rockefeller intended to pay fair prices, he further agreed that any knowledge of his interest in the valley would encourage opposition. Not until 1930, after most of the key real estate had been acquired, did Rockefeller's sponsorship of the Snake River Land Company and his intention to deed its holdings to the National Park Service become public information.[43]

All told, Rockefeller purchased approximately 35,000 acres, nearly 22 percent of that portion of Jackson Hole eventually awarded park status. As critical to his success, in February 1929 President Calvin Coolidge agreed to withdraw most of the adjoining public lands from entry. Without the withdrawals, nothing legally prevented speculators or the farmers and ranchers who had just sold to Rockefeller from simply filing a claim to another homestead and forcing him to buy that out.[44]

What he could not have imagined was Congress's refusal to accept his gift for another 20 years. The roadblock again was the issue of "uselessness." Congress chose sides in 1929, setting apart just the Teton Mountains as a national park. The protection of only rugged terrain could not seriously be considered a threat to any established economic interest. Excusing that tradition, the geologist Fritiof M. Fryxell remained pleased with the result. "The peaks—these are the climax and, after all, the raison d'etre of this park," he maintained. "For the Grand Teton National Park is preeminently the national park of mountain peaks—the Park of Matterhorns."[45] Congress itself saw no reason to make the reserve contiguous with Yellowstone; similarly, Jackson Hole was excluded. Hugging the mountains' eastern flank, Jenny, Leigh, and String lakes were about the only level land in the 150-square-mile preserve. Its western boundary further excluded major watersheds, forests, and wildlife habitat by tracing the tips of the peaks themselves. Yet even above timberline, Congress was cautious. Notably, when the U.S. Forest Service protested that asbestos deposits could be found in the northern third of the range, Congress deleted the entire area from the enabling act.[46]

Granted, the two-thirds remaining still made for a magnificent national park. However, Fritiof M. Fryxell spoke to monumentalism, not the dream of John D. Rockefeller Jr. and Horace Albright. Since 1898, the movement to extend Yellowstone southward to include Jackson Hole had been advanced in an effort to preserve the region in its greater diversity. Without Jackson Hole, the park was in fact another bow to mountain scenery and had nothing to do with natural environments.

The one concession to complete conservation in the enabling act—a clause banning new roads, permanent camps, or hotels in the park—had already been challenged and revised. As initially worded, the clause declared it to be the "intent of Congress to retain said park in its original *wilderness* character" (emphasis added). The concession was meant to satisfy the dude ranchers, who still were opposed to roads. The provision's congressional opponents simply turned the tables, charging that wilderness might actually exclude trails from the national park. As a result, all reference to "wilderness" was dropped. Even when a further amendment exempted trails, the word "wilderness" was not reinstated.[47] A term that strict might be going too far, even in the Tetons.

Of course, their ruggedness virtually guaranteed that their natural environments would prevail. The point was that without Jackson Hole in the park, the commitment had lost its meaning. A park capable of protecting itself still spoke of mountain scenery. The indigenous plants and animals outside those mountains but related to them were finally the object of preservationists' concerns. As Struthers Burt put it, until the valley itself was fully protected, there remained the distinct possibility that "the tiny Grand Teton National Park, which is merely a strip along the base of the mountains, [will be] marooned like a necklace lost in a pile of garbage."[48]

Given the failure of Grand Teton National Park to break with tradition by including the woodlands and sagebrush flats of Jackson Hole, other parks were left to confirm the nation's pledge to total preservation. A likely candidate proved Isle Royale National Park in Michigan, authorized in 1931. But although Isle Royale was advocated as a wilderness and wildlife preserve, nothing within its enabling act bound the National Park Service actually to manage it for those values. Isle Royale's supporters as often singled out the island's "boldness" and "ruggedness"—in short, its topographic as distinct from its wilderness qualities.[49]

It remained for the Everglades of southern Florida to close the final gulf between preserving scenery and natural environments. The prevailing description, then as now, properly identified the Everglades as "a river of grass." As such, it lacks a distinct channel with noticeable banks; rather, its "streambed" sprawls across the landscape an average width of 40 miles. The flow arcs southward from Lake Okeechobee—in the south-central portion of the state—to the tidal estuaries and mangrove forests of the Gulf coast and Florida Bay. Over those 100 miles, the drop in elevation is just 17 feet, barely two inches per mile. But although the current moves slowly, indeed almost imperceptibly, the lack of visible runoff is misleading. Water seeping underground recharges expansive aquifers where it may be stored for future use. Approaching the coast, the creep of water similarly buttresses the tidelands against brackish seawater, allowing freshwater flora and fauna to prevail.[50]

The cycle dates back at least 5,000 years, when glacier-fed seas last ebbed and exposed the southern Florida peninsula. During the rainy season between June and October, the flow is extensively recharged. In wet-

When Everglades National Park was proposed, even biologists, who were sympathetic that the park was intended for wildlife, complained that it failed to meet the scenic standards of the West. *Courtesy of the National Park Service, George A. Grant collection*

ter years, Lake Okeechobee generally spills, providing the Everglades an actual "source." Storms moving in off the ocean contribute additional runoff, until, by late fall, the prairie of grass (known as saw grass) fills to a depth of between one and two feet. Historically, drought and hurricanes periodically broke the rhythm but as temporary conditions did little harm to the plants and animals. The threat to their permanence awaited twentieth-century profiteers who disrupted, perhaps irreparably, the drainage pattern and wildlife sanctuary of which the Everglades had long been the crucial link.[51]

The birdlife was first to suffer. By the early twentieth century, feathered hats were the rage of women's fashion. Southern Florida, with its teeming populations of American and snowy egret, quickly became a principal source. The term "market hunting" aptly described the carnage as the rookeries were shot to pieces. To thwart the poachers, responsible sportsmen and conservationists organized the National Association of Audubon Societies, after the famed nineteenth-century naturalist John James Audubon. The murder of two Audubon wardens, the first in 1905, greatly aroused public opinion. Legislation followed to protect the birds by outlawing interstate shipments of plumes and feathers. Yet the victory was limited to birds. As quickly, the market hunters switched their targets, finally to poach alligators for shoes, luggage, and handbags. Throughout the American South, including the Everglades, the toll by 1930 had already reached 100,000 animals per year.

By then, agriculture loomed as an additional threat to the longevity of the ecosystem. Drawn by the richness of the soil immediately south of Lake Okeechobee, landowners insisted that the region be drained. After World War I, construction began on a series of canals, locks, and dams to check the lake's seasonal overflows and shunt the so-called excess to the sea. Nature itself struck back. In 1926 and again in 1928, severe hurricanes spilled Lake Okeechobee, costing at least 2,300 lives. The toll overshadowed the widespread flooding, crop, and property damage. Obviously, this was the time to conclude that the Everglades should not have been settled in the first place. The survivors instead looked on the disasters as proof of the need for even greater control over the lake. In 1929, the Florida legislature authorized the state to cooperate with the federal government on a more efficient system of holding basins and drainage canals. Over the next 30 years, the network was greatly expanded, largely under the auspices of the U.S. Army Corps of Engineers.[52]

As with Jackson Hole, the best opportunity to protect the Everglades intact had slipped away before it could be realized. Preservationists again could only hope to stem the tide of development. The point is that even to make the attempt in the Everglades marked a radical about-face for the national park idea. Devoid of topographical uniqueness, no region lent more convincing testimony to the growing popularity of complete conservation. Dr. Willard Van Name, associate curator of the American Museum of Natural History, spoke for a growing number of preservationists when he asked if the absence of "Yosemite Valleys or Yellowstone geysers in the eastern States" was all that prevented the enjoyment and protection of "such beauties of nature as we do have. National Parks have other important purposes besides preserving especially remarkable natural scenery," he stated, "notably that of preserving our rapidly vanishing wild life." In that regard, no portion of the East was a better candidate for national park status than the Everglades. "The movement to establish an Everglades National Park in Florida appeals strongly to me," Gilbert Grosvenor, president of the National Geographic Society, also testified. "Mount Desert [Acadia], Shenandoah, Great Smoky, and Everglades— what a magnificent string of Eastern Seaboard parks that would make!"[53]

The formation of the Tropic Everglades Park Association in 1928 officially launched the campaign. As chairman and founder of the association, Ernest F. Coe, a Miami activist, worked tirelessly introducing the Everglades to newspaper editors, journalists, scholars, and influential members of Congress. Ensuring the scientific credibility of the association, Coe invited Dr. David Fairchild, an internationally recognized botanist with the U.S. Department of Agriculture, to serve as president.[54] Marjory Stoneman Douglas, whose father owned the *Miami Herald*, offered numerous articles in support of the park. "A committee was formed with David Fairchild, John Oliver LaGorce of *National Geographic* magazine and other notables," she later recalled, "but really it was Mr. Coe's project and it was Mr. Coe who persevered. He never got enough recognition. There ought to be a memorial to him out there."[55]

Coe was indeed central to the protracted debate regarding the suitability of the Everglades for national park status. As he and his associates inevitably discovered, not all preservationists were agreed that the Everglades justified a national park. Some suggested that if the region warranted protection, a state park would be more than adequate. Still others advocated a botanical reserve, although not necessarily under federal jurisdiction. The outspoken dissent of William T. Hornaday added a final note of frustration. Renowned for a lifetime protecting wildlife, few conservationists were better known to the general public. Rather than support the park, he condemned it, recalling visits to the Everglades beginning in 1875. "I found mighty little that was of special interest, and absolutely nothing that was picturesque or beautiful," he asserted; "both then and now, . . . a swamp is a swamp." On a more charitable note, he conceded that "the saw-grass Everglades Swamp is not as ugly and repulsive as some other swamps that I have seen." However, his charity ended there. Surprisingly ignoring the region's birds and wildlife, he spoke only about topography. "It is yet a long ways from being fit to elevate into a national park, to put alongside the magnificent array of scenic wonderlands that the American people have elevated into that glorious class."[56]

Obviously for Hornaday, as for the American public, the national parks were still about scenic wonders. Proving him wrong, the Tropic Everglades Park Association openly encouraged a series of "special" investigations. A first, conducted by the National Park Service in February 1930, observed the requirements of a bill passed by Congress under the auspices of Senator Duncan U. Fletcher of Florida. The inspection was to be led by Horace Albright, now director of the agency. The first day out, the party circled above the proposed park in a blimp provided by the Goodyear Dirigible

Corporation. "I believe," Albright reported, "that the old idea of an Everglades with dense swamps and lagoons festooned with lianas, and miasmatic swamps full of alligators and crocodiles and venomous snakes was entirely shattered." The group instead found forests, rivers, and plains supporting "many thousands of herons and other wild waterfowl." Each member of the investigation could well imagine, he concluded, "what an exceedingly interesting educational exhibit this entire area would be if by absolute protection these birds would multiply and the now rare species come back into the picture for the enjoyment of future generations." Toward that end, the Albright committee unanimously endorsed the proposed Everglades National Park. "Before leaving I sounded out the opinion of the individual members," he assured the secretary of the interior, "and all were agreed that all standards set for national park creation would be fully justified in the establishment of this new park."[57]

Only the branch of skeptics represented by William T. Hornaday remained to be convinced. Not unusual even for scenic parks, the park bill had also stalled in Congress. The suspicion of the National Parks Association, chaired by Stephen Mather's former assistant, Robert Sterling Yard, especially frustrated Albright, Ernest F. Coe, and their associates. After all, Mather himself had been instrumental in forming the association as a private watchdog for park standards. Chosen as executive secretary in 1919, Yard was virtually Mather's pick.[58] In the Everglades, Yard took his job seriously—perhaps too seriously, Albright now believed. Noting the region's preponderance of private land, Yard found a perfect objection. Achieving the park, the value of worthless properties would be exaggerated, and real-estate speculators would benefit at public expense.[59] Further applying his purist bent, the National Parks Association would not, under any circumstances, accept preexisting man-made structures inside other new national parks. Allowing that precedent especially for dams and reservoirs, Yard reasoned, preservationists would have no standing against another Hetch Hetchy. The acceptance of existing dams would forever cripple the argument that dams never belonged in parks. Thus, along with his skepticism about the Everglades, he opposed unequivocally the enlargement of Grand Teton National Park. Beginning in 1906, Jackson Lake had been raised by a dam. Allowing Jackson Lake into the park would only say to Congress that preservationists now regretted opposing dams.[60]

The continuing flow of such opposition in part led to a second major investigation of the Everglades under the auspices of the National Parks Association. With Robert Yard's hold on the organization growing tenuous, a professional assessment seemed finally possible. The American

Civic Association, the American Society of Landscape Architects, and the National Association of Audubon Societies asked that they also be represented. As principal investigator, the National Parks Association chose Frederick Law Olmsted Jr., whose authorship of key portions of the National Park Service Act of 1916 had won the respect of preservationists nationwide. The distinguished naturalist William P. Wharton accompanied Olmsted; on January 18, 1932, following two weeks of personal exploration in the Everglades, they presented their findings to the trustees of the National Parks Association.[61]

Both the thoroughness of the report and the reputation of its senior author finally convinced the National Parks Association of the value of the Everglades. Without question, Olmsted and Wharton agreed, the region should be a national park. "What we were chiefly concerned to study in the Florida Everglades," they wrote, "was the validity or invalidity of doubts . . . as to whether the area is really characterized by qualities properly typical of our National Parks from the standpoint of scenery." The major preconception to be overcome was that scenery must in all cases be defined as landscape. And "in a good deal of the region," the men stated, revealing that prejudice within themselves, "the quality of the scenery is to the casual observer somewhat confused and monotonous." Visitors might compare the region to "other great plains," for example, whose scenic qualities were "perhaps rather subtle for the average observer in search of the spectacular." Yet even the scenery of a plains could be "bolder" in appearance. The scenery of the Everglades was better described as an emotional experience. Apart from landscape, it consisted "of beauty linked with a sense of power and vastness in nature." That indeed was scenery of the type "so different from the great scenes in our existing National Parks," they conceded. Rather, the "sheer beauty" of "the great flocks of birds, . . . the thousands upon thousands of ibis and herons flocking in at sunset," could be a sight "no less arresting, no less memorable than the impressions derived from the great mountain and canyon parks of the West."[62]

In further compensation for its lack of rugged terrain, the Everglades literally enthralled the visitor with its "sense of remoteness!" and "pristine wilderness." Foremost among the elements of the region evoking that emotion was the mangrove forest bordering the coast. "It is a monotonous forest, in the sense that the coniferous forests of the north are monotonous." Yet "it is a forest not only uninhabited and unmodified by man," they noted, "but literally trackless and uninhabitable." Ten thousand people might boat through the region every day and "leave no track upon the forest floor." Again, the average visitor might not grasp the essence of wilderness; still, even for the uninitiated traveler, the men repeated, the Everglades should "rank high among the natural spectacles of America" by virtue of its great wildlife populations alone.[63]

Admittedly, where it called attention to a *quantity* of animals, the Olmsted–Wharton report was a throwback to the past. Much as earlier Americans had compared the wonders of the West and Europe to the inch, their use of superlatives to describe the wildlife suggested lingering hints of cultural doubt. Still, finally to justify a national park exclusively on the basis of wildlife revealed a dramatic advance in preservation.

As testimony to the depth of that transformation, the Everglades National Park Act specifically called for preserving the natural environment. Although the Olmsted–Wharton report had addressed the policy in principle, setbacks including Jackson Hole underscored the difficulty of establishing the policy in the field. The defenders of the Everglades therefore insisted that an appropriate clause be drafted and included in the park's enabling act. "Such opposition as has been evidenced among organizations to the Everglades Bill," Horace Albright's successor, Arno B. Cammerer, explained in April 1934, "has been directed to the form of the bill and not to the project, and solely to the alleged insufficiency that the future wilderness character of the area was not fully provided for." On the basis of the Olmsted–Wharton report, the National Parks Association spearheaded the drive for declaring the Everglades a "wilderness" preserve. "I would not object to a restatement of this principle in an amendment to the bill," Secretary of the Interior Harold Ickes agreed, "if . . . such an amendment would not endanger its passage."[64]

Including that amendment, the bill passed Congress on May 30, 1934. The victory for natural environments finally seemed complete. Indeed, how else could the park be interpreted, asked Ernest F. Coe—"it has no mountains, its highest elevation being less than eight feet above sea level"? Rather, the "spirit" of Everglades National Park, in fact its very inspiration, he maintained, "is primarily the preservation of the primitive."[65] For the first time, an enabling act, specifically section 4, directed managers to respect the environment as the wonder. "The said area or areas shall be permanently reserved *as a wilderness*" (emphasis added). Similarly, no development of the park for visitors must "interfere with the preservation intact of the unique flora and fauna and the essential primitive conditions." That clause alone, Coe noted, marked a momentous "evolution" in the character and standards of the national parks. Everglades National Park provided clear evidence of the growing respect for "natural ecological relations," of "that interlocking balanced relation between the animate and the inanimate world." The national parks "have much of interest in bold topography and other uniqueness," Dr. John K. Small of the New York Botanical Garden agreed. "Why not also have a unique area exhilarating by its lack of topography and charming by its matchless vegetation and animal life?"[66]

Everglades National Park proved an astounding answer. Meanwhile, the hurdle was to deal with the preconditions further laid down by Congress. Most notably, as with Shenandoah, Great Smoky, Isle Royale, and similar parks outside the public domain, it remained for the state of Florida, in cooperation with private individuals, to actually buy the Everglades. Before Congress made the park official, all property had to be deeded to the federal government. As a result, Everglades National Park would not be formally dedicated until 1947. The point is that nothing during the interval affected its guiding purpose as a wilderness and wildlife preserve. Congress rather reaffirmed the precedent, first in 1937, by authorizing Cape Hatteras National Seashore, North Carolina, "as a primitive wilderness." Outside those areas best meant for recreation, no portion of the park was to be administered in a manner "incompatible with the preservation of the unique flora and fauna" or the original "physiographic conditions." As in the Everglades, nothing in the salt marshes and sand dunes of Cape Hatteras could be linked with monumentalism. The first national seashore in the United States was equally the beneficiary of the distinctions advanced under the heading of "complete conservation." At Cape Hatteras, the nation again paid formal recognition to the virtues of protecting an ecosystem for its own sake.[67] Simply, if finally the national park idea was to represent all of the American land, tradition needed to make way for ecology.

Everglades National Park was the all-important precedent. The sincerity of attempts to apply total preservation to existing national parks might still be discredited by their imposing topography. Devoid of the mileposts of cultural nationalism, the Everglades confirmed the depth of commitments to protect more than the physical environment. Granted, preservationists themselves initially doubted their break with tradition. However, by gradually closing ranks, for the first time they realized the possibilities. If any doubt remained, it was the hangover of worthless lands. Aside from the latest terms advancing preservation, if the parks thereby advanced disclosed valuable resources, could even those terms be made to stick?

When Redwood National Park was established in October 1968, the slopes above the Tall Trees Grove, although outside the park, were also forested. In this photograph taken in June 1976, only the narrow strip of parkland fronting Redwood Creek has not been cut. The fate of the "worm," as this section of the park came to be known, prompted Congress to expand Redwood National Park by 48,000 acres in 1978. By then, however, all but 9,000 acres had been logged. Preservationists, who were adamant that the ecology of the park had been deliberately undermined, used this and similar photographs to make their case. *Courtesy of the Save-the-Redwoods League, Dave Van de Mark photograph*

CHAPTER 7

Ecology Denied

A park is an artificial unit, not an independent biological unit with natural boundaries (unless it happens to be an island).

— GEORGE M. WRIGHT ET AL., 1933

The biotic associations in many of our parks are artifacts, pure and simple. They represent a complex ecologic history but they do not necessarily represent primitive America.

— LEOPOLD COMMITTEE, 1963

T HAT the preservation of natural environments was an afterthought of the twentieth century was nowhere more apparent than in the national parks. Although "complete conservation" assumed the protection of living landscapes as well as scenic wonders, the first attempts to round out the parks as biological units had been largely ineffective. Traditional opponents of scenic preservation, led by resource interests and utilitarian-minded government agencies, still believed in holding the parks to a minimum. Nor could the reluctance of Congress to expand their boundaries be laid to ignorance about the needs of wildlife. As early as 1933, the National Park Service publicized the need for broader management considerations in its precedent-breaking report *Fauna of the National Parks of the United States.* Its authors, George M. Wright, Ben H. Thompson, and Joseph S. Dixon, were experts on wildlife management, natural history, and economic mammalogy, respectively.[1] "Unfortunately," they said, setting the theme of their study, "most of our national parks are mountain-top parks," comprising but "a fringe around a mountain peak," a "patch on one slope of a mountain extending to its crest," or "but portions of one slope." Each reflected the placement of "arbitrary boundaries laid out to protect some scenic feature." Of course, park boundaries were anything but arbitrary. By removing from the parks their best timber and known mineral deposits, Congress had ensured that the parks would feature scenery. Regardless of the reasoning behind those exclusions, the disruption of living environments was no less complete. For example, the scientists concluded emphatically, "It is utterly impossible to protect animals in an area so small that they are within it only a portion of the year."[2]

Even a park the size of Yellowstone might prove a dramatic example. While Yellowstone appeared to be a wildlife refuge, its spacious boundaries in fact failed to compensate for the region's high altitude, on the average of 8,000 feet. Winter cold and snow still drove most of the large mammals, including the southern elk herd, to sheltering valleys such as Jackson Hole. Because these valleys were outside the park, protection ended at the boundary.

Addressing the problem, *Fauna of the National Parks* asked Congress to distinguish between animate and inanimate scenery. "The realization is coming that perhaps our greatest natural heritage" rather "than just scenic features . . . is nature itself, with all its complexity and its abundance of life." Even "awesome scenery" could be sterile without "the intimate details of living things, the plants, the animals that live on them, and the animals that live on those animals." In managing the parks, the enduring obstacle to sound ecological management was the prior emphasis on natural wonders. "The preponderance of unfavorable wildlife conditions," the authors continued, "is traceable to the insufficiency of park areas as self-contained biological units." In "creating the national parks a little square has been chalked across the drift of the game, and the game doesn't stay within the square." Indeed, "not one park," the report concluded, "is large enough to provide year-round sanctuary for adequate populations of all resident species."[3]

To the example of Yellowstone could be added the Florida Everglades. As we have seen, in 1934 Congress authorized its southern extremity as the first national park expressly designated for wilderness and wildlife protection. Because the reserve still failed to include the entire ecosystem, it was immediately vulnerable to outside development. Over the years, an ever-increasing proportion of the natural flow of freshwater southward to the Everglades was disrupted and diverted to factories, farms, and subdivisions. A similar failure to protect an entire watershed immediately compromised efforts to establish a Redwood national park. As loggers cut heavily into all of the best watersheds, hundreds of great trees awaiting protection were undermined by flash floods and mudslides off the logging sites. Congress again could not claim ignorance about the ecological needs of the redwoods. Rather, they, like Jackson Hole and the Everglades, were simply the latest victims of political and economic reality.

Throughout the twentieth century, parks that came easiest into the fold were still, to the best of knowledge at the time, economically valueless from the standpoint of their natural wealth. Recreation and sightseeing were beside the point. In that vein, there was little objection in 1935 to the authorization of Big Bend National Park, a spectacular wilderness in southwestern Texas. It was, after all, predominantly rugged and inaccessible and well removed from the commercial centers of the state.[4]

Any exception to that rule could still be expected to arouse significant opposition. The proposed Olympic national park in Washington State, with its prized stands of Douglas fir, red cedar, western hemlock, and Sitka spruce, was soon the leading example. Preservationists had forever chafed at the reduction of the national monument by President Woodrow Wilson in 1915. In 1933, an opportunity to restore the lost acreage emerged with the election of President Franklin D. Roosevelt. With a determination shown in the Florida Everglades, preservationists now insisted that even old-growth forests in the lowlands of the Olympic Peninsula should be included in the park.

Three outspoken preservationists carried the battle: Rosalie Edge, Irving Brant, and Willard Van Name. The moment they asked for trees below the timberline, they invited the vociferous opposition of the logging industry. Still, the object of Olympic National Park, the trio maintained, was to protect the unique rain forests at the base of the mountains, not merely, in the words of another observer, "an Alpine area [of] little or no commercial value."[5] The relentless opposition of the lumber industry and U.S. Forest Service assured that the bulk of the reserve would be comprised of mountains. However, the park as designated in 1938 provided for the study and inclusion of five major river valleys rich in timber—the Elwha, Queets, Quinault, Bogachiel, and Hoh. On January 2, 1940, President Roosevelt proclaimed those additions, totaling 187,411 acres. Among them were tens of thousands of acres of old-growth rain forests that otherwise would have fallen to the ax.[6]

No further excuse was needed for park opponents to ask consistently for reductions. The Park Service itself resented the necessity of having to defend so much timber. After the United States entered World War II, the agency prepared its own map of possible reductions. At least, the secretary of the interior should open the reserve to logging in support of the nation's war effort. When Germany and Japan surrendered, the lumber companies revived the economy as reason to log the park. The superintendent of Olympic obliged them personally, deciding to log the park on his own. Over the next 10 years, 150 million board feet of timber—most from the largest trees in the park—was secreted to the mill in Port Angeles without the public's knowledge.[7] Even the National Park Service, steeped in monumentalism, was unprepared for the responsibility of protecting timbered lands.

The proposed Kings Canyon National Park, California, lying immediately north of Sequoia National Park, contained scenery more to the agency's liking. Even then, the park was controversial. As early as 1891, John Muir had called for the protection of Kings Canyon in *Century Magazine*. The 49-year delay leading to the park reflected the continuing strength of the opposition. As with Hetch Hetchy to the north, waterpower interests maintained that Kings Canyon should be a reservoir. This time, having proved that other locations met the need, preservationists won the argument. Congress then agreed that access into Kings Canyon should be limited and the region managed to ensure its "wilderness character."[8]

The further advantage at Kings Canyon was its status as public lands. The same largely applied to Olympic National Park. Each merely required that title be transferred from the U.S. Forest Service to the National Park Service.[9] In the Everglades and Jackson Hole, there remained the problem of how to deal with substantial amounts of private land. Still, a willingness to make those purchases was undeniable proof of the nation's growing commitment to natural environments. Meanwhile, the mere mention of linking Jackson Hole to Grand Teton National Park aroused the West to a fever pitch. The valley should be developed and John D. Rockefeller Jr. confine his meddling east of the Mississippi. What preservationists called philanthropy the West called interference. Especially for Wyoming, the issue was that Rockefeller had purchased the land in secret. Worse, he fully intended to take all of it out of production by giving it back to the federal government. Homesteading in reverse was not what the West had in mind.

Finally, the Jackson Hole controversy had come to a head. Assured that Rockefeller was serious about divesting his holdings if an agreement were not reached, on March 13, 1943, President Franklin D. Roosevelt proclaimed the entire north end of Jackson Hole a national monument. As the source of his authority, the majority of the monument remained in

In the 50-year controversy over Jackson Hole, the example of Jackson Lake was key. Raised in 1916 by a dam, the expanded lake killed thousands of trees. Purists objected that Jackson Hole was therefore disqualified from inclusion in Grand Teton National Park. An existing reservoir would set a terrible precedent for all the national parks. Encouraging public acceptance of the lake, the Civilian Conservation Corps removed debris from the shoreline in the 1930s. *Courtesy of the National Park Service, George A. Grant collection*

the Teton National Forest. When further combined with Rockefeller's holdings in the Snake River Land Company, the unit came to approximately 221,000 acres.[10]

The storm of protest unleashed by Roosevelt's action echoed throughout the Rocky Mountain West. The attack for dissolution of the monument was led by Representative Frank A. Barrett of Wyoming. "It is unthinkable that this hunters' paradise should be molested in any way," he argued. The only scenery of any consequence was the mountains. "The addition of farm and ranch lands and sagebrush flats is not going to enhance the beauty of the Tetons," Barrett added. That, of course, was the traditional argument—only mountains and canyons should be national parks. As Newton B. Drury, director of the Park Service, testified in rebuttal, the national park idea finally rested on the preservation of wildlife as well as natural wonders. "Visitors to national parks and monuments take great pleasure and obtain valuable education in viewing many species of strange animals living under natural conditions," Drury explained. Given the proximity of Jackson Hole to Grand Teton National Park, its proper role was not, as Representative Barrett argued, simply to allow hunters "to pursue and kill the big game that for so many years roamed our western plains." Rather, Congress must ensure the protection and restoration of all parts "of the wildlife picture" in the valley, including "the largest herd of elk in America."[11]

The mere act of identifying commercial uses still swayed Congress to think twice about a park. With World War II itself unresolved, Barrett at the moment seemed more persuasive. In December 1944, his bill dissolving Jackson Hole National Monument passed both the House and the Senate. Roosevelt simply allowed the bill to die by pocket veto, silently upholding his right to proclaim the monument.[12]

Having come so close, Barrett tried again, but that bill also failed. Finally, after years of bitter controversy, both camps were ready to compromise. It remained for Congress to craft legislation satisfactory to John D. Rockefeller Jr. and the state of Wyoming. Assured that the compromise bill would pass, on December 16, 1949, Rockefeller deeded his property in Jackson Hole to the federal government. On September 14, 1950, President Harry S. Truman signed the legislation abolishing Jackson Hole National Monument, rededicating it as part of Grand Teton National Park.[13]

From an aesthetic standpoint, the addition resounded as a great success. What had rightfully been called the "frame" of the Tetons, the sweeping vistas across Jackson Hole, Jackson Lake, and the Snake River, had forever been spared visual blight. The lingering disappointment was the degree of fragmentation still affecting the natural environment. As the primary illustration, Jackson Hole and the Tetons were not made contiguous with Yellowstone, as first recommended in 1898. A wide corridor between both parks remained, still in the hands of a utilitarian agency, the U.S. Forest Service. As revealing, hunters were still allowed in the park. Now to be called "deputized rangers," they would ostensibly assist the Park Service in maintaining the elk herd at an optimum size. In truth, the "deputies" were private hunters under a less offensive title. Certainly, the void left by the extinction of natural predators would not be filled by sportsmen. Most would continue to shoot the trophy animals rather than cull weak and diseased elk from the herd.[14]

If the elk were no longer threatened with extinction, neither was Grand Teton National Park a self-contained biological unit. The situation was just as frustrating in the Florida Everglades. As stipulated in the bill authorizing the park in 1934, the Everglades could not in fact be dedicated as a national park until the state had purchased and deeded the land. Congressional opponents of the enabling act, further decrying the project as a "snake swamp park," had similarly amended the bill to prohibit any federal aid until 1939.[15]

Efforts to acquire the land also suffered setbacks. The best hope for a viable park was to make speedy purchases before speculators drove up land values. The act of 1934 called for the preservation "of approximately two thousand square miles . . . of Dade, Monroe, and Collier Counties." In fact it was 1957, 10 years after the park was dedicated, before those acquisitions neared completion. Even then, fully 93 percent of the Everglades proper remained outside the park and earmarked for additional farms, water-storage basins, and flood-control projects. To the northwest, another critical aquifer, Big Cypress Swamp, was similarly beyond the park boundaries and thus still subject to intensive development.[16]

Even at 1.4 million acres, Everglades National Park was misleading. Scientists had held from the start that the project should be closer to 2 million acres. In reality, the park included only a portion of the saw grass province, and that with the least potential for development. As much of the park consisted of the mangrove forests, sloughs, and tidelands along the coast. The point remained that even this far south, the park depended on freshwater from the saw grass. Its recharges were essential for maintaining the life cycle of the region. Breeding wood ibis, for example, need high water, allowing fish populations close to the nesting sites. The physical substrata also requires periodic replenishment to prevent salt water intruding from the sea.[17]

It followed that the placement north of the park of new dikes and drainage canals jeopardized the entire preserve. In 1961, a prolonged drought sealed the possibility, ravaging southern Florida. The naturalist Peter Farb then returned to the Everglades to describe the building tragedy. "I found no Eden but rather a waterless hell under a blazing sun," he wrote. "Everywhere I saw Everglades drying up, the last drops of water evaporating from water holes, creeks and sloughs."[18]

The drought by itself was not unusual; what turned this one into a regional crisis was the policy of withholding water from the Everglades. After agricultural needs had been met, water was shunted seaward to check the mere possibility of floods. In an effort to eliminate flooding entirely, in 1962 engineers completed a final link in the system of levees south of Lake Okeechobee. For the first time, drainage into the park could be shut off completely. Three years later, anticipating a normal wet season, engineers actually lowered Lake Okeechobee by flushing more than

280,000 acre feet of water to the sea. Even then, supplying the water-starved Everglades remained impossible. The hydrologist William J. Schneider summed up the reason, noting that "under the existing canal system," excess water could not be moved from Lake Okeechobee to the national park "without also pouring it across the farmlands in-between."[19]

Although obviously prospering at the expense of the park, the farms were not about to be sacrificed in return. Near-record precipitation in 1966 instead allowed the Park Service to work out an interim agreement with the Florida Board of Conservation and the U.S. Army Corps of Engineers. Additional releases of water were scheduled into the park from bordering conservation districts. The extent of damage already done to the Everglades nevertheless haunted preservationists. Would the water be enough, and in time? And what about the future? Only Congress might seal the agreement and guarantee water to the park, the historian Wallace Stegner concluded the following year. "Nobody else can. The most that anyone else can do is slow down the inevitable."[20]

Protecting the Everglades in perpetuity still depended on unified management of the entire ecosystem south of Lake Okeechobee. By now, any hope of acquiring such a vast area—on the order of three to four times the size of Yellowstone—had vanished. Of course, Congress might have condemned the private land; in a nation reaching toward outer space, the cost seemed infinitesimal by comparison. American culture simply did not make that comparison. Not until 1961, with the authorization of Cape Cod National Seashore, Massachusetts, did Congress agree to begin purchasing the land without first relying on the state. The Everglades was many times Cape Cod. Before exercising eminent domain in the Everglades, Congress would have to agree that the national parks demanded a revolutionary reappraisal.

So far, Isle Royale National Park, in Lake Superior, had come closest to the ideal ecological preserve by virtue of its island status and isolation. Nothing surrounded Isle Royale but water, and no farms or industry competed for that. Most of the island was also federal land. Where those conditions did not exist, the protection of an entire ecosystem in a single national park continued to be frustrated. Attention next shifted to the California coast redwoods (*Sequoia sempervirens*). The trees command a narrow range between the ocean and the mountains from the Oregon border south to Monterey Bay. Before settlement, pure and mixed stands of *Sequoia sempervirens* covered approximately 2 million acres, roughly the equivalent of Yellowstone National Park. In river valleys facing the coast, a combination of rich alluvial soil, ocean rains, and blanketing fog propels the largest trees to heights well above 300 feet (the present record is 379.1 feet). As the trees age, they also broaden at the base, commonly attaining diameters of between 15 and 18 feet. Farther inland, the trees grow more modestly and are often interspersed with other species. Yet even here, the groves can be spectacular, if better renowned for their color and grace.[21]

During the last third of the nineteenth century, a similar assessment had won national park status for its Sierra Nevada counterpart, the giant sequoia. The great advantage for the giant sequoias remained their brittleness. Although beautiful when standing upright, the trunks ingloriously shattered as they hit the ground. In marked contrast, *Sequoia sempervirens* was highly durable—in every respect a superior lumber tree. Predicting where that quality would lead, as early as 1852, H. A. Crabb of the California State Assembly called for the withdrawal of "all public lands upon which the Redwood is growing." Not surprisingly, his attempt to forestall its decimation was ignored. In 1879, Interior Secretary Carl Schurz revisited Crabb's proposal with a plan calling for the protection of 46,000 acres of redwoods. Despite its modesty, Schurz's effort also failed. Not until 1901, with the establishment of Big Basin Redwoods State Park near Santa Cruz, were the first significant groves of giants finally spared the logger's ax.[22]

By then, the logging companies—generally employing individuals to file dummy homesteads—had managed to defraud the federal government of nearly all public lands supporting redwoods. Companies individually entitled to 160 acres of land wound up controlling thousands. Parks that previously would have required just a government transfer of property would now have to repurchased at great expense. California had taken the first initiative with the establishment of Big Basin. In 1905, the Bay Area philanthropist William Kent and his wife Elizabeth, acting on what he called an "uncontrollable impulse," purchased 611 acres of redwoods at the base of Mount Tamalpais. Of these, the Kents offered 295 acres to the federal government. Their only preconditions were that the land be managed as a park and named in honor of John Muir. On January 9, 1908, President Theodore Roosevelt gladly complied with both terms by proclaiming the tract Muir Woods National Monument.[23]

Were it not for William Kent's election to Congress in time to support the Hetch Hetchy dam, his reputation among preservationists would have been secure. As matters stood, Congress itself had no intention of repossessing the redwoods, either for parks or for national forests. Reinforced by Muir Woods, the initiative for protecting the trees fell largely to private groups and individuals. The Save-the-Redwoods League, organized in

1918, assumed leadership in the private sector. League members were at first committed to "a National Redwood Park." In the face of persistent congressional indifference, they agreed to make purchases and donations on behalf of California for management as state parks. Big Basin remained the model. By 1964, state park holdings of virgin *Sequoia sempervirens* totaled 50,000 acres, thanks to efforts by the league, John D. Rockefeller Jr., and other philanthropists large and small. In fact, of the $16 million used to establish redwood parks, better than 50 percent had been subscribed by members of the Save-the-Redwoods League.[24]

From north to south, the league gave priority to rounding out five projects—Jedediah Smith, Del Norte Coast, Prairie Creek, Humboldt, and Big Basin state parks. The league at first concentrated on purchasing the low-lying river flats and nearby tablelands, those supporting the largest trees. As more of the giant trees were acquired, the focus shifted to forests upslope and upstream. The league admitted to prospective members that these areas contained fewer of the "cathedral-like groves," those "stretching back into the centuries and forging a noble link with the past." As much as cultural nationalism, the redwoods were about ecology. Logging damage adjacent to the monumental groves underscored the futility of trying to save just the largest trees. Even they depended on adjacent lands; entire watersheds now needed to be acquired. As an example, severe flooding along Bull Creek, part of Humboldt State Park, toppled 300 of the largest redwoods during the winter of 1955–1956. Another 225 trees had been undermined. Although conceding that record rainfall was a major factor, as much of the damage, preservationists maintained, could be laid to the effects of clear-cutting the hillsides adjacent to the park. With the trees removed, the water rushed freely down the slopes, gathering suspended mud and debris. When finally the crest subsided, better than 15 percent of Humboldt Park's primeval, bottomland old growth lay heaped and tangled along the banks of Bull Creek.[25]

Awareness of the need to secure a major watershed in the redwoods reawakened serious discussion about a national park. Left alone to private philanthropy, the costs of such a project were far too great. As secretary of the Save-the-Redwoods League, Newton B. Drury recalled his years as director of the National Park Service to outline the enormity of the task. "It is recognized that even when all the spectacular cathedral-like stands of Redwoods along the river bottoms and the flats have been acquired, the lands surrounding them must be preserved for administrative and protective reasons." Preservationists faced the challenge of "rounding out complete areas, involving basins and watersheds in their entirety."[26]

As justification for this approach, the league profitably recalled the flooding of Bull Creek. Major testimony included that of Russell D. Butcher, a popular writer and environmentalist. "The big lesson from the tragedy," Butcher explained, pleading for Congress to intervene, "is the importance of protecting not only the particular scenic-scientific park features, in this case the unsurpassed stands of coast redwoods, but of bringing under some degree of control the surrounding, ecologically related lands—the upper slopes of the same watershed."[27]

Mill Creek, within and adjacent to Jedediah Smith and Del Norte Coast state parks, had a financial edge. A Mill Creek national park would require $56 million as opposed to a minimum of nearly three times that amount along Redwood Creek, adjoining Prairie Creek Redwoods State Park.[28] In deference to those figures, the Save-the-Redwoods League endorsed the Mill Creek watershed as the preferred site for a national park. Immediately dismayed by the league's alleged conservatism, in 1964 the Sierra Club quoted a study by the National Park Service concluding that Redwood Creek was the superior location. Despite the report, President Lyndon B. Johnson, Interior Secretary Stewart L. Udall, and the National Park Service opted early for Mill Creek as the alternative more likely to receive congressional approval.[29] Disheartened, the Sierra Club took its case to the public in a series of controversial advertisements. "Mr. President," a 1967 example began, "there is one great forest of redwoods left on earth; but the one you are trying to save isn't it. . . . Meanwhile they are cutting down both of them."[30]

The irony of the crisis was the degree to which the popular imagery of redwood trees as "monuments" was now turned against the Sierra Club and the Save-the-Redwoods League. By far the most common rebuttal to either project noted that the best *individual* trees had already been set aside; protection of the watersheds was therefore pointless. The Sierra Club further accused Governor Ronald Reagan of California of berating preservationists with the statement, "If you've seen one redwood, you've seen them all."[31] Such statements continued to imply that Americans wanted only natural "wonders" in their parks. Each phenomenon set off by itself was more than adequate for national parks. Lumber companies and their workers similarly attacked the park proposal by arguing that the area's cool, damp climate discouraged tourism. As for protecting remaining old growth in any watershed, that, too, was best left to industry officials. Surely, they concluded, the industry's long-term investments in mills and other capital improvements proved that it was not about to destroy the redwoods.[32]

There, the point of contention was whether the redwoods would be followed by an entirely different forest. Damage anywhere on a watershed appeared to jeopardize the return of redwoods. Regardless, preservationists found the economic rationales against the park insurmountable. As approved in October 1968, Redwood National Park contained neither the Mill Creek nor the Redwood Creek watersheds in their entirety. Instead forming the three neighboring state parks into a core, Congress added narrow bands of land to their peripheries. Although the state parks had been joined, again, the national park conformed to neither of the larger watersheds. As revealing, of the 30,000 acres acquired to link the state parks, only 10,000 had not been previously logged.[33]

The affected lumber companies received $92 million. Congress further authorized that 14,000 acres of public land—the only redwoods then in federal ownership—be exchanged for corporate holdings within the projected park. As a final stipulation, a ban against logging adjacent to Redwood National Park was described as *possible* but, if enforced, would be limited to a narrow buffer zone no more than 800 feet across.[34]

Well might preservationists have conceded that the lumber companies had won. The allowance of logging anywhere close to the national park defeated its original purpose. Since the tragedy of Bull Creek, the campaign had been all about protecting watersheds. It was argued, of course, that realistically no national park in the twentieth century could include everything its supporters wanted. Nonetheless, the Sierra Club insisted, even higher estimates for the park on Redwood Creek—in the neighborhood of $200 million—were but a fraction of a single moon shot or building a segment of interstate highway. To the Sierra Club, the issue was not whether the United States could afford the redwoods but whether it wanted to afford them. "History will think it most strange," a club circular and advertisement bitterly concluded, "that Americans could afford the Moon and $4 billion airplanes, while a patch of primeval redwoods—not too big for a man to walk through in a day—was considered beyond its means."[35]

The failure of the park as established to guarantee the future of even the world's tallest trees only reinforced that skepticism. In 1963, a team of surveyors enlisted by the National Geographic Society discovered the giants on private land beside Redwood Creek. The inspiration the following year for a lead article in *National Geographic*, news of the trees aroused considerable interest.[36] But although their discovery helped promote the park, the manner of their inclusion was bizarre. Their location in the park was in fact called the "thumb" or "worm." Advancing just far enough up Redwood Creek to include the grove of trees, the sliver of land barely included the streambed, let alone a recognizable forest on either side. The intense gerrymandering involved was clearly to the specifications of the lumber industry. On both sides of the worm, the cutting of redwoods continued unabated. Throughout the 1970s, park officials predicted the worst. With the advent of each rainy season, it appeared that finally the tall trees would be toppled by mudslides off the logging sites.[37]

With even its greatest trees in constant jeopardy, Redwood National Park testified to the entrenchment of those shortcomings identified in 1933 by George M. Wright, Ben H. Thompson, and Joseph S. Dixon in *Fauna of the National Parks of the United States*. In the fate of the "worm" was the latest proof of their assessment that few national parks provided for the broader, more intricate needs of biological conservation. Meanwhile, other scientists had drawn the same conclusion, notably a team chaired in 1963 by A. Starker Leopold, a zoologist with the University of California at Berkeley. Their own report, *Wildlife Management in the National Parks*, became an instant classic. "The major policy change which we would recommend to the National Park Service," the Leopold Committee advised, "is that it recognize the enormous complexity of ecologic communities and the diversity of management procedures required to preserve them." By 1967, two other scientists, F. Fraser Darling and Noel D. Eichhorn, had written in support of the Leopold Committee, publishing *Man and Nature in the National Parks*. "We start from the point of view that the national park idea is a major and unique contribution to world culture by the United States." That said, practically everything new in their evidence merely repeated their predecessors' findings. "We have the uncomfortable feeling," Darling and Eichhorn wrote, concurring with the Leopold Committee, "that such members of the National Park Service as have a high ecological awareness are not taking a significant part in the formulation of policy." If the national parks were to be prepared for the future, that failure needed to be addressed.[38]

Congress was, of course, the responsible party. In constraining the parks from the outset, it only invited their biological failures. From Jackson Hole to the Everglades to the redwoods, park boundaries remained the ultimate proof of the limitations long imposed on the preservation of natural environments. If present-day scientists merely repeated that finding, the fault still lay with Congress. Until Congress itself agreed to respect good science, the hands of management remained largely tied.

Unlike the railroads, the automobile won admission to the national parks and, once inside, was accused of transforming wilderness into a playground. In 1900, Oliver Lippincott, a Los Angeles photographer, drove the first car into Yosemite, posing precariously for this suggestive photograph on the brink of Glacier Point. *Courtesy of the National Park Service*

CHAPTER 8

Schemers and Standard-Bearers

Congress (and the public which elects it) can always be expected to hesitate longer over an appropriation to acquire or protect a national park than over one to build a highway into it. Yet there is nothing which so rapidly turns a wilderness into a reserve and a reserve into a resort.

— JOSEPH WOOD KRUTCH, 1957

THE attempt to round out the national parks as self-sufficient biological units was part of a struggle of equal if not greater magnitude. Despite passage of the National Park Service Act of 1916, the lack of guidance for the reserves had been only partially overcome. Challenged finally by the growing popularity of outdoor recreation, the definition of national parks as both pleasuring grounds and natural sanctuaries seemed a contradiction. Mixed emotions following the completion of the Yosemite Valley Railroad in May 1907 served as an early barometer of the coming debate. "They have built a railroad into the Yosemite," declared Edward H. Hamilton, a correspondent for *Cosmopolitan* magazine. Skeptics had already taken the news "very much as if the Black Cavalry of Commerce has been sent out to trample down the fairy rings." The tracks actually ended at El Portal, 12 miles west of the valley proper. Hamilton was more accurately gauging the fear of development, especially with a railroad now at the gates. "In California and the far West," he noted, "there are people who insist that hereafter the great valley is to be a mere picnic-ground with dancing platforms, beery choruses, and couples contorting in the two-step." He personally dismissed such critics as "nature cranks" and "the athletic rich," those "stout pilgrims with long purses and no ailments." There was now "the railroad into Yosemite," he concluded, "and all the arguments since Adam and Eve will not put it away."[1]

Barely nine years later, however, passenger revenues were in decline. In 1916, more people entered Yosemite Park by automobile than disembarked from the train at El Portal, 14,527 as opposed to 14,251. In 1917, the ratio was nearly three to one and by 1918 almost seven to one, 26,669 in contrast to 4,000.[2] On a positive note, the growing availability of cars to middle-class Americans promised greater support for the national park idea. Although the railroads had "gradually lowered the barrier" between the East and the West, admitted Charles J. Belden, another perceptive journalist, "the subtle influence of the motor-car is bringing them into closer touch than would otherwise be possible." As evidence, on the publication of his article in 1918, there remained only a "few places" in the West, "no matter how remote from the railroad, where fuel and oil may not readily be obtained." Hamilton's so-called nature cranks, politely known as "purists," had already been outvoted. Those with cooler heads embraced the automobile, as they had earlier allied with the railroads, seeing in both an opportunity to bolster the parks' popularity. "Our national parks are far removed from the centers of population," Enos A. Mills of Colorado observed, rejecting purism as impractical. "If visited by people," he stressed, "there must be speedy ways of reaching these places and swift means of covering their long distances, or but a few people will have either time or strength to see the wonders of these parks." Left without convenient transportation, the public would never support scenic preservation. "The traveler wants the automobile with which to see America."[3]

So forewarned that they had no choice, preservationists rapidly made their decision. Much as they had learned to accept the railroad, they now as eagerly promoted the automobile. Its biggest advantage was freedom of mobility. In that vein, Arthur Newton Pack, president of the American Nature Association, observed in 1929, "The greatest of all pleasures open to any automobile owner is travel through the wilder sections of our country . . . with comfort and economy." The motorist "will grow to regard railroads as uncomfortable necessities," another enthusiast affirmed. "He will laugh at himself for believing, before he bought his car, that a real pleasure trip could ever be accomplished by rail." Not only was the car "capable of penetrating into the wilds and bringing its owner into speedy touch with Nature," but it also returned him "before he has dropped any of the necessary threads of civilization."[4] Still another testimonial glorified "this freedom, this independence, this being in the largest possible degree completely master of one's self. . . . That horrible fiend, the railroad time-table, is banished to the far woods." Best of all, another promoter agreed, auto camps could be made "comfortably at a cost of two dollars a day per passenger," one-third the expense of lodging in a luxury hotel. A similar note of prophecy pervaded a succeeding endorsement: "Until this new travel idea developed, costs of travel precluded the average citizen including the whole family."[5]

Popularly known as "sagebrushing," auto camping swept the national parks beginning in the 1920s. "The sagebrusher," a Yellowstone enthusiast defined the term, "is so called to distinguish him from a dude. A dude goes pioneering with the aid of Mr. Pullman's upholstered comforts and carries with him only the impediments ordinary to railroad travel." By contrast, the sagebrusher "cuts loose from all effeteness," bringing "clothes and furniture and house and food—even the family pup—and lets his adventurous, pioneering spirit riot here in the mountain air."[6] "It was in 1915 that the first automobile, an army machine, entered the Yellowstone National Park," a husband and wife team reported. Just four years later, the park "was invaded by more than ten thousand cars, carrying some forty thousand vacationists." By 1919, "nearly ninety-eight thousand machines" had paraded through the national parks, ranking the automobile "as the greatest aid" to their "popularity and usefulness." Rocky Mountain National Park topped the list with 33,638 cars; Yosemite, permanently opened to private motoring since 1913, placed "second with something over twelve thousand." Yellowstone's 10,000 cars matched Mount Rainier National Park; as a result, both ran "a close race" for third in the standings.[7]

Although World War II briefly interrupted the surge, peacetime brought another invasion of motor vehicles. By the mid-1950s, barely 1 to 2 percent of all park visitors were entering the parks using public transportation.[8] Even the most determined proponents of the automobile now faced the sobering realization that cars were the threat to parks. James Bryce, as British ambassador to the United States, predicted the trade-offs as early as 1912. Recalling the close of the American frontier, in a November address before the American Civic Association, he spoke of the agony of growing old. "What Europe is now," he warned, "is that toward which you in America are tending." The nation's population was also rapidly increasing and with it "the number of people who desire to enjoy nature, . . . both absolutely and in proportion." Unfortunately, "the opportunities for enjoying it, except as regards locomotion," were in decline. As in the rest of the "circumscribed" world, the scenery of the

Opened in 1904, Yellowstone's Old Faithful Inn began as a railroad hotel. Although no depot was allowed inside the boundary, practically all visitors came by train. Stagecoaches then met the trains and made the circuit of sights inside the park. By 1922, these women escorted in a Park Service car point to a period of momentous change. *Courtesy of the National Park Service*

United States could no longer be considered "inexhaustible." As a telling example, Bryce chose the ongoing debate "as to whether automobiles should be admitted in the Yosemite." Presently, "the steam-cars stop some twelve miles away from the entrance of the Yosemite Park." Surely, development should come no closer. "There are plenty of roads for the lovers of speed and noise," he maintained, "without intruding on these few places where the wood nymphs and the water nymphs ought to be allowed to have the landscape to themselves." Again, a biblical analogy seemed appropriate. "If Adam had known what harm the serpent was going to work, he would have tried to prevent him from finding lodgment in Eden; and if you were to realize what the result of the automobile will be in that wonderful, that incomparable valley, you will keep it out."[9]

His advice was, of course, ignored. Twenty years later, J. Horace Mc-Farland reminded George Horace Lorimer of the deeper realities of preservation. As editor of the *Saturday Evening Post*, Lorimer was renowned for his coverage of the national parks, spiced with constant editorial support. Yet when he wrote to McFarland in November 1934, he admitted the loss of "some of my early enthusiasm for the National Parks." Lorimer laid his change of heart to the automobile. "Motor roads and other improvements are coming in them so fast," he complained, "that they are gradually beginning to lose some of their attraction for the out-of-door man and the wilderness lover." In fact, he closed, echoing Ambassador Bryce, "if this craze for improvement of the wilderness keeps up, soon there will be little or none of it left."[10]

A sense of wilderness, Lorimer realized, presumed the absence of civilization and its artifacts. The dilemma for preservationists, McFarland reminded him, was that the automobile was needed to protect natural wonders, let alone wilderness. "I am about the last person in this whole wide world to have the nerve to offer you any advice," McFarland began tactfully. "Yet in this matter of the National Park development I am bound to say that we must accept compromises if assaults on the parks from the selfish citizens, of whom we have not a few, are to be repelled." However distasteful, there was no sense bemoaning what could not be changed. "I didn't want automobiles in the parks before any more than I do now," McFarland admitted. Yet what other choice did preservationists have? "[Just] where would the parks have been without this means of getting the 'dear public' to know what the same dear public owns?" He concluded with a personal example. Originally, his summer home at Eagles Mere, Pennsylvania, "included a little bit of pure primeval forest." But that was "more than thirty years ago," he noted soberly. Since then, "I have had to give up much of the primeval relationship in order to have anything at all."[11]

McFarland's sacrifice was not unlike the decision facing preservationists throughout the national park system. Although a prerequisite for public support, development invariably compromised the values they had struggled to save. Nor did park legislation always come to their aid. The closest thing to a common, legislative definition was the National Park Service Act of 1916. To review, the parks in each instance were to be protected "in such manner and by such means as will leave them unimpaired for the enjoyment of future generations."[12] Preservationists at the time were satisfied, indeed almost elated. However, with each new controversy, they began to realize that the clause was itself subjective. Exactly what was meant by "unimpaired"? Who likewise determined whether the term in fact allowed roads, hotels, parking lots, and similar developments? "The law has never clearly defined a national park," Robert Sterling Yard, as executive secretary of the National Parks Association, concluded in 1923. Neither the National Park Service Act "nor other laws," he lamented, "specify in set terms that the conservation of these parks shall be complete conservation."[13]

Much as the automobile threatened solitude, so it accelerated the confrontation between those who viewed the national parks as recreation and those, such as Lorimer and Yard, who saw them as sanctuaries for a primeval state. Although not all preservationists agreed that primeval meant biological, it did mean that the parks should never change. Suddenly, that definition had been put to the test. The automobile far more than the railroad threatened to change the parks from within. People off by themselves need not necessarily believe in either the primeval or the biological. They need only believe in the right of access or, as tourism put it, the inalienable right to play.

"It is the will of the nation," Frederick Law Olmsted wrote, interpreting the Yosemite Park Act of 1864, "that this scenery shall never be private property, but that like certain defensive points upon our coast it shall be held solely for public purposes." With Olmsted's definition, "public purposes," began the never-ending debate what those purposes were. Never did Olmsted doubt for a moment that the word "Yosemite" said it all. It was a national resource, not a common one. Its purposes remained unique. Appointed president of the Yosemite Board of Park Commissioners, he defended that meaning and no other. At present, Olmsted conceded, travelers to the valley and Mariposa Grove totaled but several hundred annually. Yet "before many years," he predicted, "these hundreds will become thousands and in a century the whole number of visitors will be counted by the millions." It followed that laws to prevent Yosemite's defacement "must be made and rigidly enforced." Construction in particular should be limited to "the narrowest limits consistent with the necessary accommodation of visitors." The alternative to imposing standards would be the proliferation of their opposite, activities that "would unnecessarily obscure, distort, or detract from the dignity of the scenery."[14]

A first problem created by Congress was the provision of visitor services by private concessionaires.[15] Olmsted himself did not seek to forbid development but rather insisted that it be channeled creatively. For instance, the completion of an "approach road" would "enable visitors to make a complete circuit of all the broader parts of the valley." Yet while he rejected a rigid, purist philosophy, he left no doubt that his priorities lay with the environment. "The first point to be kept in mind then is the preservation and maintenance exactly as is possible of the natural scenery." No less than a great work of art, Yosemite Valley and the Mariposa Grove belonged to future generations as well as to living Americans. In fact, he claimed, "the millions who are hereafter to benefit by the Yosemite Act have the largest interest in it, and the largest interest should be first and most strenuously guarded."[16]

Regardless, his vision for the future was not as clear-cut to others as Olmsted wished to imply. Indeed, his report, suppressed internally, never made it to the state legislature for review. In November 1865, Olmsted left California and returned to New York City, where the following year he resigned from the Yosemite Park Commission. Gradually, individual commissioners lost touch with his ideals and gladly served other interests. The consequence, much as he had forewarned, was a valley increasingly filled with developments that seemed inappropriate in a public park.[17]

Few better than Olmsted understood the problem as one of perception. No less than at Niagara Falls, where the latest craze, tightrope walkers, competed for the public's attention, Yosemite invited the same urge to capitalize on its scenic grandeur. "There are falls of water elsewhere more finer," Olmsted claimed, "there are more stupendous rocks, more beetling cliffs, there are deeper and more awful chasms."[18] The lingering obstacle to Olmsted's meaning was a country still wrapped up in the opposite. Thus, on entering Yosemite Valley in 1872, the *New York Times* columnist Grace Greenwood protested that "a certain 'cute' Yankee" planned "cutting off the pretty little side cascade of the Nevada [Fall], by means of a dam, and turning all the water into the great cataract. 'Fixing the falls,' he calls this job of tinkering one of God's masterpieces." The commercialization of Niagara Falls again sprang to mind. "Let it not be said by any visitor," she pleaded, "that [Yosemite Valley] is a new Niagara for extortion and impositions—a rocky pitfall for the unwary, a Slough of Despond for the timid and weak." Yosemite unmarred would pay for itself "a hundred-fold." Surely, that statistic, if no other, could be appreciated "even by fools."[19]

Evincing the common side of the profit motive, James McCauley, an early Yosemite pioneer, preferred theatrics over solitude. His two major developments, a trail to Glacier Point and a rustic hotel, were completed in the 1870s. The view of the Sierra from Glacier Point was breathtaking, as was the drop to the valley below—a dizzying 3,214 feet. Adding to the fascination, visitors arrived throughout the day to heft rocks, boxes, and other objects over the side. "An ordinary stone tossed over remained in sight an incredibly long time," one observer recalled, "but finally vanished somewhere about the middle distance." Further experimentation revealed that a "handkerchief with a stone tied in the corner was visible perhaps a thousand feet deeper." Otherwise, "even an empty box, watched by a fieldglass, could not be traced to its concussion with the Valley floor." Carefully timing his opportunity, McCauley then "appeared on the scene, carrying an antique hen under his arm. This, in spite of the terrified ejaculations and entreaties of the ladies, he deliberately threw over the cliff's edge." Their outburst only added to the unfolding drama. "With an ear-piercing cackle that gradually grew fainter as it fell, the poor creature shot downward; now beating the air with ineffectual wings, and now frantically clawing at the very wind, that slanted her first this way and then that; thus the hapless fowl shot down, down, down, until it became a mere fluff of feathers no larger than a quail." Next, "it dwindled to a wren's size," suddenly "disappeared, then again dotted the sight a moment as a pin's point, and then—it was gone!"[20]

With the gods of gravity at last appeased, the visitors allegedly came to their senses. "After drawing a long breath all around, the women folks pitched into the hen's owner with redoubled zest," only to learn, undoubtedly to their embarrassment, that McCauley's chicken went "over that cliff every day during the season. And, sure enough, on our road back we met the old hen about half up the trail, calmly picking her way home!"[21]

McCauley's next invention proved far more durable. One Fourth of July after he had finished his trail, valley residents took up a collection for fireworks (probably dynamite sticks), suggesting he throw them over at Glacier Point. Enchanted, he reciprocated with a scheme of his own. Building a large fire (probably used to light the fireworks), he pushed it off the cliff. The fire was not an original idea; both natives and early settlers had set many fires along the rim. McCauley envisioned a spectacle. From Glacier Point, the embers likely would reach the first outcropping, a ledge some 1,500 feet below. "As time passed," his son later testified, "people wanted fires and were willing to pay for them." When alerted, tourists in the valley scrambled for a ringside seat "to view the performance, shrinking under the ear-splitting detonations of the dynamite that accompanied the fire at intervals."[22]

With the arrival of David and Jennie Curry in 1899, the firefall became a permanent fixture of Yosemite. The founders of the Yosemite Park and Curry Company, they located their namesake, Camp Curry, in the valley directly below Glacier Point. At first, the Currys' guests chipped in "to hire one of [the] porters to go up and gather the necessary fire wood and put the fire over in the evening," E. P. Leavitt, as acting park superintendent, recalled in 1928. Once the event had grown in popularity, Camp Curry assumed the entire expense of displaying the firefall nightly during the summer months. No concessionaire could have wished for a better drawing card, as testified by Camp Curry's colorful brochures. If not on the cover, then somewhere prominent, the firefall was always featured above the darkened campground. "As the embers fall over the cliff, the rush of air makes them glow very brightly," Leavitt explained. And "because of their light weight they fall slowly, which gives the appearance of a fall of living fire." In place of James McCauley, who in retirement had packed his bombs, a violinist played "softly," another observer reported, as the "fairy stars came drifting downwards, . . . floating from sight into some mighty hollow beneath the cliff that was yet fifteen hundred feet above our heads." Thus, "for more than half a century," *Collier's* magazine reported in 1952, "this man-made spectacle has rivaled the natural glories of Yosemite."[23]

Still to mix the two, in Frederick Law Olmsted's words, "fixing the mind on mere matters of wonder or curiosity," was precisely what he had condemned as inappropriate in 1865.[24] Regardless, this costuming of the spectacular only multiplied—in some cases, such as the firefall, persisting long after their inspiration under the auspices of the National Park Service itself. What the firefall was to Yosemite Valley, for example, tunnel trees became for the nearby groves of giant sequoias. In June 1878, a British visitor to the Tuolumne big trees reported another "novelty such as one does not come across every day. This was a tunnel through the stump of one of the largest Wellingtonia in the grove." Beyond enraging his American readers with their British name, he called on everyone to imagine a giant sequoia "through which the road passes and the stagecoach is driven!" Yosemite Park at first did not include the Tuolumne Grove, yet it was not long before the Mariposa Grove had succumbed. Notably in 1881, the Yosemite Stage and Turnpike Company completed a road through that section of the park. Perhaps in honor of the occasion and certainly to attract publicity, the company commissioned a team of workers to carve through the base of the Wawona Tree. The hole should be large enough, the company instructed, for its carriages to pass through. One witness recalled stopping in the center of the cut and standing up to touch the roof of the freshly hewn opening. "Arriving on the other side, I stepped down and the foreman and each of the workers surprised me by shaking hands with me and congratulating me, saying I had the distinction of being the first one to pass through." In 1895, the nearby California Tree was similarly tunneled and the Mariposa Grove asked again to double as a human attraction.[25]

Top: Before being toppled by heavy snowfall in the winter of 1969, the Wawona Tunnel Tree, in the Mariposa Redwood Grove of Yosemite National Park, was the scene of countless snapshots and publicity photos, bridging the era of the stagecoach up through cars. No visiting dignitary was allowed to miss it. *Bottom*: A carriage carrying President Theodore Roosevelt (standing tallest in the carriage) and John Muir (partly hidden, second from left), stops to allow a picture during the president's historic tour in May 1903. *Top: Courtesy of the National Park Service, Henry G. Peabody photograph. Bottom: Courtesy of the National Park Service*

Equally, the campaign to reduce Yosemite National Park, established in 1890, spawned schemes with a decidedly synthetic bent. Chief among them was the so-called restoration of Yosemite waterfalls, sponsored by the park's leading congressional opponent, Representative Anthony Caminetti of California. "The waterfalls of Yosemite Valley are seen at their best in June, and after that rapidly diminish," argued a state forester, Allen Kelley, in smoke-screening Caminetti's actual plan. This was to propose that Congress "pay for surveys of reservoir sites in the mountains surrounding Yosemite Valley, with a view to storing water in the streams that supply the numerous falls." He again underplayed that the water was to be used for irrigation, not just so-called scenic enhancement. His and Kelley's appeal to national pride nonetheless stood to advance their case on the enduring strength of monumentalism. Just "at the time of year when tourists from abroad find it convenient to visit the valley," Kelley noted, Yosemite Falls in reality was "no waterfall, only a discolored streak on the dry face of the cliff." He proposed maintaining the cataract "either by damming the creek or turning a portion of the waters of the Tuolumne River into its bed through a flume about twenty miles long." A similar embankment "100 yards in length . . . would store plenty of water for Nevada and Vernal Falls," while Bridal Veil, in autumn "a merely trickling film over the rocks," would best be augmented "by making a reservoir of the meadows along the creek." In publishing the argument, *Harper's Weekly* lent it special credence, adding before and after woodcuts of the falls and potential dam sites.[26]

Although Caminetti's scheme appropriately died, in 1913 Congress sided with his philosophy by approving the no-less-objectionable Hetch Hetchy reservoir. Again taking their cues from Kelley and Caminetti, Hetch Hetchy's supporters glossed over its damaging features as actual visual improvements. No longer might preservationists ignore the consequences of accepting development in the national parks. Even the most innocent-looking modifications initially could pose serious problems in the future. So with the automobile, the naturalist, Victor H. Cahalane, endorsed the suspicions of its early skeptics. "As more and more visitors flood the parks," he noted in 1940, "demands for all kinds of 'improvements' arise. First and most numerous have been requests for elaborate structures and big-city amusements." If secondary, schemes to dress up the national parks were advanced with equal persistence. "What good is a volcano if it erupts only once in a century or so? inquire the 'efficiency experts.' Since it is futile to ask a mountain to take off its cap and spout lava, they request that tunnels be excavated into Lassen Peak so that they may see how the uneasy giant looks inside." Meanwhile, in Yosemite the Caminetti-Kelley proposal had become an annual petition. Indeed, "each year," Cahalane scoffed, "the administration is asked to build reservoirs above the valley rim where water could be stored and fed to the falls on the Fourth of July and Labor Day," with "special showings" for "the Elks, Kiwanis, Lions and Women's Clubs." At least the National Park Service seemed determined to resist the "Nature-Aiders," he reported, with their "Turkish baths, tunneled volcanoes," and retooled "waterfalls and hot springs."[27]

Like George Horace Lorimer, Cahalane was far less optimistic about the chances of curbing the automobile, by now a part of the Park Service's culture. Most preservationists, still reeling from the loss of Hetch Hetchy, likewise discounted the warnings of Ambassador Bryce and, like Enos Mills, welcomed cars to the national parks with the same enthusiasm previously accorded the railroads. Gradually, the distinctions between cars and trains were lost. Except at Grand Canyon, made a park after the railroad arrived, the railroads stopped outside. Gateway communities then transferred passengers to stagecoaches and motor buses, further controlling visitors' movements inside the parks. As long as public transportation held sway over the visitor, the parks were considered a privilege. In marked contrast, Victor Cahalane observed, the flood of visitors loosed by the automobile defended personal access as a right. "Roads! Roads! Roads! We must have more roads! Bigger and better roads!" he stated, mimicking the "clamor of over-enthusiastic chambers-of-commerce, automobile associations and contractors. Faster roads! Roads into this wilderness. Roads into that wilderness." Apparently, none of "these besiegers" realized, he concluded, echoing Lorimer's lament, "that when processions of automobiles, clumps of filling stations, gasoline smells, restaurants and hot dog stands" invade the parks, "wilderness is gone."[28]

The Park Service itself could be accused of pandering to the public's search for entertainment. In Yellowstone, for example, a searchlight mounted on the roof of Old Faithful Inn periodically illuminated the evening eruption of the fabled geyser. In 1939, the journalist Martelle Trager confessed that she and her family "rushed across the road to a place where we could get a better view of the colored lights playing upon the column of water and steam." As the Tragers further discovered, Yellowstone's sanctioned amusements did not end there. Indeed, "the climax of the trip" was not Old Faithful but rather the Grand Canyon of the Yellowstone, where "the children heard about the Bear Feeding Show." A

Park Service naturalist informed them of two evening performances, "one at six and one at seven." They arrived for the first an hour early, only "to find at least five hundred people already gathered" in the "big amphitheater built on the side of a hill about three miles from the hotel." Considering the entertainment, it was not surprising that the available seats were in the first row, in full view of the "fenced-in pit where the garbage is dumped for the bears each evening." On schedule, the "truck drove through the gate with a ranger-naturalist at the back, his gun loaded and ready to shoot if a bear attempted to attack the men who were emptying the garbage pails." Fortunately, "the Bear Cafeteria" was free of incident, feeding at least 75 of the animals, including black bears and grizzlies.[29]

Popular in Yellowstone, Sequoia, and Yosemite, the bear feedings especially troubled scientists worried about natural balances. Bears behaving normally obviously did not congregate at feeding grounds where they

Despite the concerns of university and Park Service scientists, Yellowstone National Park, among several others, resorted to bear-feeding shows to ensure that visitors got to see the animals. Here grizzlies at the feeding grounds near the Grand Canyon of the Yellowstone hold visitors' fascination sometime in the 1930s. The twilight events were last held in 1945. *Courtesy of the National Park Service, Yellowstone National Park*

got into fights or faced being shot. Over time, this further displacement of natural processes threatened the parks with another unyielding precedent. Visitors expecting the feedings would come to insist on them, and the animals would keep paying the price. An outspoken critic against any theatrics was Henry Baldwin Ward, professor of landscape architecture at the University of Illinois. Tourists seeking pure entertainment "might be wisely diverted to areas of less unique and supreme value," he maintained. The bear feedings especially, however popular, had all "the flavor of a gladiatorial spectacle in Ancient Rome." Instead of people, it was now the animals being reduced to "sadly degenerate representatives of the noble ancestors from which they have sprung." Albert W. Atwood, writing for the *Saturday Evening Post*, further condemned what he termed "the excessive danger of cleaning up, after the manner of city parks; of smoothing, rounding, straightening, manicuring, landscaping. . . . At Grand Canyon," he explained, "roadsides have been graded and the natural growth cut away; walks have been laid out—all with the effect of introducing an element of the artificial, of the smooth and conventional, into what is, perhaps, the supreme primeval landscape of the entire world." Yosemite Valley remained the worst example, with "its dance halls, movies, bear pit shows, studios, baseball, golf, swimming pools, wienie roasts, marshmallow roasts and barbecues—all well advertised in bulletins and printed guides." It was not that most diversions were bad in themselves, he agreed, but simply that none had "any relation whatever to the purpose for which the national parks were established."[30]

Preservationists inevitably kept singling out the automobile as the biggest contributor to the problem. "The majority now come in motors," wrote Robert Sterling Yard, noting the shift from rails to roads as early as 1922. Thus, "while we are fighting for the protection of the national park system from its enemies, we may also have to protect it from its friends." With the surge in park visitation, even the rustic hotels seemed tainted as "resort and amusement-type" features. "The foreground of a picture is of very great importance," Wallace Atwood, as president of the National Parks Association, agreed in 1931. In locating park hotels, there had indeed been errors in judgment, especially "hotels and other buildings too near the objects of interest. Other mistakes have been made in placing hotels or lodges at the choice observation stations." Perhaps visitors "should be brought within easy walking distance of the best outlook points," Atwood conceded. Beyond that, "hotels, lodges or camps should not be allowed to occupy those points." Most important, "no building should be erected in the parks solely for amusement purposes."[31] Although he gave no spe-

The proliferation of automobiles in the 1920s challenged the National Park Service to plan and build aesthetic roads. Here an automobile descends the east side of Logan Pass (Going-to-the-Sun Road) in Glacier National Park. Note the elaborate masonry, a signature of the 1930s, made affordable by the programs of the Great Depression. *Courtesy of the National Park Service, George A. Grant collection*

cific examples, El Tovar, overlooking the South Rim of the Grand Canyon, and Old Faithful Inn, barely several hundred feet from the geyser proper, met his criticism to a fault.

With the growing conviction that the national parks were best seen as natural environments, a change of heart regarding visitation was inevitable. In this vein, Arno B. Cammerer, director of the National Park Service, wrote in 1938, "Our National Parks are wilderness preserves where true natural conditions are to be found." Although the statement still smacked of sentiment, scientists, for one, at least wanted it to be true. "When Americans, in years to come," he continued, "wish to seek out extensive virgin forests, mountain solitudes, deep canyons, or sparsely vegetated deserts, they will be able to find them in the National Parks."[32] The still evident contradictions included transportation policies and visitor facilities in sympathy with the automobile. In 1928 alone, 131,689 cars en-

The dedication of the Going-to-the-Sun Road, July 15, 1933, is a reminder of the power of numbers. Preservationists opposed to the automobile in national parks have obviously been outvoted. *Courtesy of the National Park Service, George A. Grant collection*

tered Yosemite Valley, an 11-fold increase in only nine years.[33] Anyone predicting that the 1929 stock market crash would reverse the trend was just as surprised. Except for a low point in 1933, visitation flourished during even the Great Depression, climbing from approximately 3 million in 1929 to more than 12 million just before World War II. Although several new parks contributed to the increase, the original reserves, led by Yosemite and Yellowstone, averaged between 400,000 and 500,000 visitors annually, an all-time high.[34]

The postwar travel surge was equally unprecedented. By 1955, Frederick Law Olmsted's 1865 prediction for Yosemite Valley—annual visitation "by the millions"—had come true. The point was that the statistic applied not only to Yosemite, with 1,060,000 visitors, but also to Grand Teton (1,063,000), Yellowstone (1,408,000), Rocky Mountain (1,511,000), Shenandoah (1,760,000), and Great Smoky Mountains (2,678,000) national parks. As significant, between 98 and 99 percent of those visitors were motorists. Indeed, as if to signal the end of the railroad era, in 1944 the Yosemite Valley Railroad, reportedly bankrupt, was sold at auction and quickly scrapped.[35] Although quality trains still served the gateway communities at Yellowstone, Glacier, and Grand Canyon, as of 1969 only Glacier's train survived.

"Are the parks doomed in their turn to become mere resorts? Ultimately perhaps." So the respected American naturalist, Joseph Wood Krutch, lamented the growing crowds of the 1950s. Still, his frustration—and that of all preservationists—was the lack of a disciplined park experience. Among the troubling headlines, in June 1955, was one in *U.S. News and World Report.* "This summer 19 million Americans will visit parks that are equipped to handle only 9 million people. Result: Parks overrun like convention cities. Scenery viewed from bumper-to-bumper traffic tie-ups. Vacationing families sleeping in their cars." Krutch's deeper point, like Olmsted's, was the intent behind the numbers. What was each tourist thinking? Had they come to see nature or just to play? If the latter, the numbers obviously made things worse. In Olmsted's lifetime, the expense of traveling and the absence of comforts inside the parks had discouraged the casual visitor. Suddenly, those barriers had come tumbling down. "It is indeed largely a matter of easy accessibility and 'modern facilities,'" Krutch noted. Parks for the first time faced a "considerable number" of motorists who desired nothing more on arrival than "what they can do at home or at the country club." Such frivolous pursuits and visitors needed to be excluded. Then—and only then—might the natural character of the parks be even "fairly well preserved."[36]

It was, of course, ironic that preservationists had come to argue against visitation, having previously argued for it. A sense of the primitive demanded that the parks first be secured. "Even the scenery habit in its most artificial forms," John Muir wrote in 1898, "mixed with spectacles, silliness and kodaks; its devotees arrayed more gorgeously than scarlet tanagers, frightening the wild game with red umbrellas—even this is encouraging, and may well be regarded as a hopeful sign of the times." Behind Muir's rare display of tolerance was his greater intolerance for the designs of dam builders, loggers, and engineers. "The problem is not to discourage amiable diversions," the historian Bernard DeVoto agreed in 1947, "but to scotch every effort, however slight, to convert the parks into summer resorts." Of course, "it would hardly be practicable to examine every visitor . . . to make him prove that he has come for a legitimate purpose," Krutch added. Yet it would be "perfectly possible to make the test automatically" simply "by having the road ask the question: 'Are you willing to take a little trouble to get there?'"[37]

Never comfortable with such proposals, the National Park Service asked instead for road improvements. Fresh on the heels of the postwar travel boom, those ambitions had soon evolved into Mission 66. The even more ambitious, 10-year program looked to expand the entire carrying capacity of the national parks—roads, campgrounds, visitor centers, utilities, employee housing, and overnight accommodations. The $1 billion price tag was justified, Congress agreed, by the now 80 million visitors—most in automobiles—expected to crowd the parks in 1966. As the golden anniversary of the National Park Service (1916–1966), it seemed the perfect target date.[38] In February 1955, the American Automobile Association cosponsored the kickoff dinner, prophetically held in Washington, D.C. No sponsorship or location could have been more convincing evidence that Mission 66 was indeed road- and big-development oriented. When the railroads had met on behalf of parks, they had met in or near the actual parks. Each railroad agreed to prove how its projects fit. The focus of Mission 66 on remaking the parks struck preservationists as entirely political. Again, the beneficiary seemed to be not the parks but rather those commercial ventures with a stake in changing them.

In a prime example, communities west and east of Yosemite National Park had long asked that the Tioga Road across the high country be widened and straightened. As part of Mission 66, the reconstruction had soon raised the ire of preservationists dismayed by its effects on Tenaya Lake. Above the lake to the southwest, an escarpment of brilliant granite had been cut and graded to allow the road. While "the old road in a sense 'tiptoed' across the terrain," Devereux Butcher described, quoting the veteran nature photographer Ansel Adams, "the new one elbows and shoulders its way through the park—it blasts and gouges the landscape." As executive director of the Sierra Club, David Brower's reports were steeped in bitterness. "The rampant bulldozer scrapes, and having scraped ramps on," he declared. "Nor all our piety and wit shall lure it back to cancel half a line, nor all our tears wash out a mark of it." The Tenaya Lake "we knew, the 'Lake of the Shining Rocks' the Indians knew, is dead." On the completion of Mission 66, F. Fraser Darling and Noel D. Eichhorn reached a similar conclusion for the national parks as a whole. "Mission 66 has done comparatively little for the plants and animals," they charged in their 1967 report to the Conservation Foundation. "The enormous increase in drive-in campsites is an example of the very expensive facilities which do nothing at all for the ecological maintenance of a park."[39]

Because Mission 66 had eased the accommodation of tourists, more tourists had inevitably come. Between 1955 and 1974, visitation again more than tripled, from approximately 14 million to 46 million in just the principal national parks. Use of the national monuments also rose proportionally, from roughly 5 million visitors to more than 17 million.[40] To Edward Abbey, another outspoken critic of the National Park Service, the figures evinced the age of "Industrial Tourism." Wherever "trails or primitive dirt roads already exist," he remarked in his popular book *Desert Solitaire*, "the Industry expects—it hardly needs to ask—that these be developed into modern paved highways." However unpopular, there remained only one solution. "No more cars in the national parks. Let the people walk. Or ride horses, bicycles, mules, wild pigs—anything—but keep the automobiles and the motorcycles and all their motorized relatives out." Anticipating the common charge of elitism, Abbey reminded his critics that preservation had always meant making choices. "What about children?" he asked rhetorically. "What about the aged and infirm? Frankly, we need waste little sympathy on these two pressure groups." Children had their entire lives ahead of them; they could afford to wait their turn. The elderly merited "even less sympathy; after all they had the opportunity to see the country when it was still relatively unspoiled."[41]

Few scholars wrote as convincingly in support of Abbey as Garrett Hardin, professor of human ecology at the University of California, Santa Barbara. Partially crippled by polio since the age of four, Hardin reminded his critics what that meant. "I am not fit for the wilderness I praise," he noted. "I cannot pass the test I propose or enter the area I would restrict." Only someone with those limitations might "speak with objectivity" on matters involving wilderness access. For his part, Hardin believed in physical merit. Distributing wilderness "by the marketplace" still obviously favored the wealthy. Similarly, entrance on a "first-come, first-served basis" multiplied waste and fatigue. Holding talented and energetic people in line needlessly sacrificed their contributions while others were given entry. In contrast, restricting access to the "physically vigorous" protected both wilderness and the joy of earning it. In this vein, Yosemite Valley might "be assigned a carrying capacity of about one per acre, which might mean that it could be opened to anyone who could walk ten miles." If "more and more people would be willing to walk such a distance, then the standard should be made more rigorous." Granted, the valley would "be forever closed to people on crutches, to small children, to fat people, to people with heart conditions, and to old people in the usual state of physical disrepair." But "remember, I am a member of this deprived group," Hardin concluded, and also must "give up all claim of right to the wilderness experience."[42]

The possibility that the country would ever accept such a plan was of course remote. "Ours is so much the age of technology and the machine," Joseph Wood Krutch noted, "that machines come to be loved for their own sake rather than used for other ends." Instead "of valuing the automobile because it may take one to a national park, the park comes to be valued because it is a place the automobile may be used to reach."[43] Beyond the entrenchment of auto culture lay the problem of rewording park legislation. The common phraseology, "for the benefit and enjoyment of the people," clearly implied that all citizens, not just the educated, robust, or physically endowed, might freely enter every park. "Certainly," Arno B. Cammerer, as director of the National Park Service, maintained in 1938, "no wilderness lover could selfishly demand that the National Parks be kept only for those who are physically able to travel them on foot or on horseback, for they were definitely set aside for the benefit and enjoyment of all." But "are not the intellectual, aesthetic and emotional rights of a minority just as sacred?" asked Joseph Wood Krutch, himself anticipating Edward Abbey and Garrett Hardin. "Does democracy demand that they be disregarded?"[44] Perhaps not disregarded, critics answered, but certainly there were other minorities besides preservationists. "What of the too-old, the too-young, the timid, the inexperienced, the frail, the hurried, the out-of-shape or just plain lazy?" wrote Eric Julber, a Los Angeles attorney, appointing himself their advocate. They, too, paid taxes to maintain the parks; by what right did the "purist-conservationist" seek to exclude them? Only because "his philosophy is unfair and undemocratic," Julber concluded, deliberately taunting Hardin and Abbey. "His chief characteristic is that he is against everything."[45]

Among the parks, still Yosemite, in particular the valley floor, remained the classic battleground of the debate. Hemmed in by its cliffs, the valley inevitably dramatized every modification, now including smog, noise, litter, congestion, and vandalism. By 1961, the number of summer visitors crowding the park regularly exceeded 70,000 daily.[46] Spread over Yosemite National Park as a whole, 70,000 people would have been little noticed. Because the valley was instead the park's major attraction, it was also where everyone wished to stay. Thus, friends of the park, such as Devereux Butcher, continued to question the wisdom of providing "dancing, pool swimming, golfing," and, in season, "skating on a man-made lake and skiing" in the mountains. By then, the bear feedings had at least been discontinued. But "there is the firefall," he added, "which also draws crowds, and which, like the other artificial amusements, has nothing to do with the beauty and wonders of the park."[47] In 1968, the Park Service finally agreed and abolished the firefall, only to find the problems of overcrowding, crime, and congestion still on the rise. Over the Fourth of July weekend in 1970, matters came to a head. In California, tensions were already high following years of campus protests against the Vietnam War. The confinement of Yosemite Valley only exacerbated the antiestablishment sentiments of student visitors. The uniform of the National Park Service might just as well have been that of the military. A crowd of young people thus gathered in Stoneman Meadow, flinging insults and then rocks at the rangers. Just as suddenly, a group of mounted rangers lost their patience and drove off the crowd by force.[48]

The confrontation was only the latest example of the conflicting demands imposed on the national parks by an urban-based society. Whatever their legitimacy elsewhere, the purely personal aims of park visitors threatened every agenda for preservation. In Yosemite, restoring a sense of the natural environment led to several measures, notably the closure of the eastern third of the valley to motor vehicles. Beginning in 1970, private transportation was prohibited. Visitors might either walk, ride bicycles, or use a new system of free shuttle buses. A new master plan for Yosemite National Park was also shelved in the wake of public opposition. The Park Service then reopened the process to public input. More than 60,000 individuals attended special hearings and mailed in a personalized planning "kit." Following tabulation of the results and further public comment, in 1980 a revised general management plan was approved.[49]

Meanwhile, the issue of Yosemite Valley had been joined on other fronts. In 1974, the Music Corporation of America, successor to the Yosemite Park and Curry Company, unveiled plans for expansion that included not only a new hotel on Glacier Point but also a tramway connecting it to the valley floor. The filming of the short-lived television series *Sierra* immediately enraged the Sierra Club, which noted that production crews, scrambling over the natural formations, had even dyed the rocks to "improve" their color.[50] Preservationists again found themselves rehashing a familiar argument. At what point did commercial pursuits only sharpen the difficulty of protecting the natural environment?

Preservation for the moment had been sustained. Among those still skeptical of the necessity, Eric Julber continued to defend his minorities. "I would install an aerial tramway from the valley floor to Nevada Fall, thence up the backside to the top of Half Dome," he wrote, resurrecting another scheme prominent since the days of McCauley's chicken and the firefall. "The restaurant at the top would be one of the great tourist attractions of the world."[51] Julber's instant notoriety in the pages of *Reader's Digest* only substantiated his credibility. Thus, Joseph Wood Krutch had earlier observed in obvious frustration, "It is only hit or miss that [preservation] questions are being answered."[52] Largely the image of national parks as unmodified areas had become fixed in the American mind. And yet, as demonstrated by the hearing given Julber's proposal, never did the national parks seem fully secure.

As if to vindicate the concerns of preservationists, there remained the example of Niagara Falls. In a 1974 survey conducted by the United States Travel Service, an agency of the Department of Commerce, only Grand Canyon and Yellowstone ranked higher than Niagara in visitor appeal.[53] The troubling significance of the survey was how Niagara had maintained that status. By 1974, everything about the cataract was artificial. During even daylight viewing hours, up to one half the flow of the Niagara River was being diverted entirely around the falls. Between midnight and sunrise, when viewing was minimal, three-fourths of the river made the detour. A major holding reservoir then filled to allow additional releases during periods of peak energy demand. Simply, the original fear that those demands would one day prevail over the natural environment had come true. As of the middle of the twentieth century, Niagara might either be "turned on" for tourists or "turned off" for power. While treaties between the United States and Canada regulated the diversions, modifications to the stream channel were required. These were alleged to preserve the illusion that Niagara Falls was still flowing at its historical volume. For that, a large jetty above the cataract had been needed, equally to speed the water and spread it evenly, maintaining the falls' so-called curtain effect.[54]

As a warning to preservationists, obviously there was still much work to do. If Americans at Niagara overlooked its many changes—and still placed it third in their affection—might they not accept the same changes for the national parks? Thus did the issue of standards enter the

twenty-first century with many questions unresolved. As before, preservationists could only hope that Niagara was the exception. For the national
parks, a majority of Americans would continue to reject things artificial
in the presence of the sublime. In like manner, they would accept limitations on their numbers and behavior in the interest of protecting the
natural environment. There again, it was for the moment just a matter of
hope. In a truthful assessment of the future, every vision of the parks as
immutable landscapes depended on a consensus not yet achieved.

Now defunct, the supersonic transport airplane (SST) was considered an advanced technology of the 1960s. Despite the threat to Everglades National Park, Dade County, Florida, readied the necessary jetport and runways, shown here under construction in December 1969. In 1970, anticipating congressional rejection of an American version of the SST, the Nixon administration dropped funding for the airport. *Courtesy of the National Park Service, Cecil W. Stoughton photograph*

CHAPTER 9

Tradition Triumphant

The "romantic movement" of the early 19th century has long worked itself out as a cultural dominant, yet, for many of their keenest supporters, parks are still viewed as the living embodiment of romantic values. . . . Their delicious dream is proving increasingly hard to reconcile not only with an ever less romantic and more crowded world, but with the realistic tasks of park acquisition and park management.

—E. MAX NICHOLSON, convener, International
Biological Program, British Nature Conservancy, 1972

We can take only momentary pride in the achievements of the national park movement's first 100 years when we realize that in the second 100 years the fate of mankind possibly hangs in the balance.

—NATHANIEL P. REED, assistant secretary of the interior, 1972

GATHERED among a sea of flags at Madison Junction in Yellowstone National Park, delegates to the Second World Conference on National Parks looked forward to a special ceremony. The date was September 19, 1972, also Yellowstone's centennial year. Despite temperatures close to freezing and rain that was turning to sleet, Madison Junction this day was not to be missed. Exactly 102 years ago, on September 19, 1870, members of the celebrated Washburn Expedition had encircled their campfire on this very spot and, according to the diary of Nathaniel Pitt Langford, immediately dedicated themselves to the protection of Yellowstone as a great national park. That even the Park Service was learning to question his claims seemed at the moment immaterial. No story this year—and at an international conference—was ever more primed for resurrection. The honor had gone to Mrs. Richard M. Nixon as First Lady of the United States. Accompanied by Interior Secretary Rogers C. B. Morton, she then paid tribute to the Yellowstone Centennial by relighting, symbolically, the beacon of that renowned encampment. "Regardless of whether or not it is raining," she said, aware of the crowd's discomfort, "this has been a wondrous day for me, and I hope it has been for our delegates from abroad." She then turned and raised a torch. "With the lighting of this torch," Secretary Morton remarked, interpreting her gesture, "we hereby rededicate Yellowstone National Park to a second century of service for the peoples of the world."[1]

Few celebrations during the centennial year did more to link both the past and present of the national park idea. As symbolized by the presence of Mrs. Nixon, the national parks had become revered. From the main street of America to the White House, the United States took pride in the knowledge that it was both the inventor and exporter of the national park idea. The inconsistencies of the Washburn Expedition aside, major newspapers, magazines, television networks, and government reports told and retold its story literally in heroic terms.[2] The explorers "could not have anticipated," one said, "that their idea would flower into a new dimension of the American dream and would capture the imagination of men around the world."[3] Although the roots of Western civilization lay abroad, by the same token the United States was the birthplace of national parks. Every delegate invited to the Yellowstone Conference was somehow a reminder of the same. Mrs. Nixon might generously rededicate Yellowstone to the peoples of the world, but the decision was America's—and America's alone—to make.

The decision in turn forced the United States to admit how romantic nature had failed ecology. Even as the nation celebrated the Yellowstone Centennial, the preceding decade had only reaffirmed the biological limitations imposed on parks. Beginning in 1962, Rachel Carson launched the so-called environmental decade with her powerful exposé *Silent Spring*. Originally serialized in *The New Yorker*, the book then sold 500,000 copies within six months. The continued use of chemical pesticides, Carson warned, spelled possible catastrophe for the natural world. For the first time in history, she noted, "every human being" was being "subjected to contact with dangerous chemicals, from the moment of conception until death." In a series of chilling scenarios, she described the growing concentrations of persistent pesticides found in the bodies of animals higher and higher up the food chain. Already those concentrations had proven lethal to birds and fish. "Man," she argued, "however much he may like to pretend to the contrary, is [also] part of nature. Can he escape a pollution that is now so thoroughly distributed throughout our world?"[4] The startling implications also for the national parks sank gradually into the American mind. If no environment was immune, it followed that even the American wilderness had not escaped toxic substances, no matter how remote its landscapes.

The publication of *Silent Spring* in 1962 coincided with the First World Conference on National Parks, convened at the Seattle World's Fair in July. Sixty-three nations sent delegates; only countries from the communist bloc were conspicuously absent, with the exception of Poland.[5] In keeping with Rachel Carson's message, the theme of the conference was distinctly ecumenical and biological. Indeed, "the problem of conserving nature is not a local matter," the editor of the proceedings later wrote, "because nature does not respect political boundaries. The birds winging their way southward over Europe neither know, nor care, whether they are passing above a Common Market or a group of feudal duchies." Nature paid "no heed" to such "political or social agreements, particularly those that seek to divide the world into compartments. It has been—and always will be—all inclusive."[6]

Its ceremony at Madison Junction aside, the Second World Conference was entirely about ecology. National leaders totally immersed in the wisdom of Rachel Carson included Nathaniel P. Reed, U.S. assistant secretary of the interior in charge of fish, wildlife, and parks. "We would be deluding ourselves," he remarked, "if we did not recognize that with the joy of this occasion there is also sorrow over man's abuse of this lonely planet—and even well-founded foreboding over the future of man." Paul Ehrlich, a professor of biology at Stanford University, had obviously further influenced Reed. In his own best-selling monograph, *The Population Bomb*, Ehrlich predicted in 1968 that unchecked population growth would soon engulf the world with hungry and ignorant people. Out of their desperation just to survive, the remaining naturalness of the planet would be lost. Cooperation among governments to preserve places like the Amazon would become a meaningless gesture. By September 1971, on the eve of the Yellowstone Centennial, *The Population Bomb* was in its twenty-fifth printing. "Nothing could be more misleading to our children than our present affluent society," Ehrlich still argued in his introduction. "They will inherit a totally different world, a world in which the standards, politics, and economics of the past decade are dead."[7]

The effect of expanding human populations on forests, grasslands, and wildlife habitat further testified to the futility of establishing national parks lacking sufficient territory from the outset. Throughout the 1970s, the consequences of overpopulation became a major theme of American environmentalism. The United States itself, noted one panel of scholars, could no longer take refuge in "continental vastness." In another centennial study, *National Parks for the Future*, the Conservation Foundation listed the problems working against biological resources in the establishment of national parks. Heading those problems, Americans had yet to confront the reality of their growth into "an urban nation." The romance of its frontier past aside, the United States was "becoming ever more urbanized." That familiar warning, reminiscent of the Census Report of 1890, was finally sharpened by the realization that earlier predictions were coming true. For the first time, the foundation's panelists agreed, the United States itself had to deal squarely with the same "confinement, lack of opportunity, and environmental insult" caused by the industrial revolution in other countries. Pollution and overcrowding, as the end products of "a specialized, technological age," lent final proof that the United States had also sacrificed its frontier innocence.[8]

The one note of optimism remained America's influence on national parks around the world. In contrast to the 63 nations represented at the First World Conference in 1962, more than 80 attended the Second at Yellowstone 10 years later, including the Soviet Union. Attendees further applauded the number of protected areas worldwide, by 1972 more than 1,200 national parks and "equivalent reserves."[9] That every such area, despite its problems, owed something to the United States only swelled the nation's pride and sense of accomplishment in Yellowstone's centennial year.

The point finally in 1972 was whether the United States would endure as the world's example. Many other nations seemed to have followed America's less resolute path by preserving only marginal tracts of land. Possible exceptions, including Africa's game parks, at second glance owed their establishment and survival to an economic rationale rather than a deep-seated sense of obligation. In the pattern of the "See America First" campaign, the governments behind those parks had also recognized the advantages of attracting wealthy foreign tourists. The protection of wildlife for its own sake, especially wildlife dependent on isolation from tourists, was the last thing those governments wanted. If ever the flow of tourist dollars were to be interrupted, it followed that the parks themselves might be sacrificed, if not intentionally then by neglect.[10]

For the world, as for the United States, the least controversial approach to preservation was the protection of monumental scenery. Itself conceding the limitation, the Second World Conference on National

Parks moved gingerly in addressing the establishment of "world parks" to be recognized by the United Nations. Undoubtedly, the largest and most ambitious would always be controversial. The protection of tropical rain forests in particular imposed the greatest responsibility on poorer countries.[11] It was one thing to suggest that Brazil and the Philippines, for example, owed the world the preservation of their biological diversity and quite another to imply that neither had the right to dispose of its natural resources as each saw fit.

The conference instead endorsed a "safe" environment—Antarctica—as the first international reserve. Unquestionably unique and even rich biologically, it still invited the obvious response: what else could the world do with Antarctica? The underlying advantage was indeed political. Existing treaties already shared Antarctica in the pursuit of science. The contrasting image was one of natural resources hopelessly locked beneath rock and ice. The preservation of Antarctica, no different from Yellowstone, was merely a bigger instance of the decision makers taking a breath, pending a final resolution whether those resources might be tapped.[12]

Mounting threats to the national parks of the United States proved the vulnerability of any resource that became accessible. In the two decades preceding the Yellowstone Centennial, debate turned on the future of the Colorado River basin in the American Southwest. In 1950, the Bureau of Reclamation proposed two high dams across the Colorado River as part of a comprehensive plan to manage water resources the length of the basin. The first dam was to be at Split Mountain, in the northeastern corner of Utah, and the second at Echo Park, just upstream in the northwestern corner of Colorado. The source of the controversy was the location of both reservoirs within Dinosaur National Monument, straddling the boundary between the two states.[13]

Thoroughly alarmed, preservationists joined forces in Washington, D.C., to protest the invasion of another park. A high point of the campaign was the publication in 1955 of *This Is Dinosaur*. Noted contributors to the book of essays included its editor, the historian and novelist Wallace Stegner, and its publisher, Alfred A. Knopf. Stunning illustrations by Philip Hyde, Martin Litton, and other photographers complemented the text of what was later recognized as the first "battle book." Perfected by the Sierra Club during the 1960s, battle books became large format and deliciously lavish, contrasting sharply with before-and-after imagery exactly what the public stood to lose.[14]

In a compromise struck in 1956, Dinosaur National Monument was spared. Not until 1963 and the completion of Glen Canyon dam did preservationists fully appreciate the price of that agreement. Upstream from Grand Canyon National Park and neighboring Marble Canyon, Glen Canyon was the scenery of Dinosaur National Monument many times over. Just as preservationists finally recognized Glen Canyon's own remarkable qualifications for national park status, its redemption from the dam builders was out of the question. The Bureau of Reclamation had merely shifted but had hardly abandoned its dam-building efforts. The cost of saving Dinosaur National Monument was indeed the sacrifice of Glen Canyon. Below it, only Marble Canyon and the Grand Canyon remained untouched, and by 1963 even those monumental landscapes had been threatened with the construction of large reservoirs.[15]

Unlike Glen Canyon, the Grand Canyon was ostensibly protected on its upstream or eastern side as a national park and downstream to the west as a national monument. The establishment of the national park in 1919 had nonetheless reserved to the federal government the prerogative of later water-storage projects. This was the option now exercised by the Bureau of Reclamation in calling for the construction of two large reservoirs in the canyon. The first dam was planned for Bridge Canyon, downstream from the national monument. The flood pool itself would still back up through the monument and well into the park. The second dam site in Marble Canyon would not affect either the national monument or the national park. Nevertheless, preservationists argued, Marble Canyon, as the upstream arm of Grand Canyon, was clearly its ecological partner. Rather than accept the dam, the public should demand that Congress correct its past mistake, finally including Marble Canyon in the adjoining national park.[16]

The ecological argument against the dams sought to demonstrate the interdependence of the Colorado River, its canyons, and its interlocking tributaries. Upstream, the construction of the Glen Canyon dam had already blocked the normal flow of water and suspended silt into the Grand Canyon proper. Gradually, the effects of that blockage could be detected in the erosion of sandbars along the river as well as in the increasing density of shoreline vegetation no longer removed by periodic flooding.[17] The American public meanwhile embraced tradition, responding best to the argument that the pending loss of Grand Canyon was a dagger at the nation's scenic heart.

In that respect, the defeat of the Grand Canyon dams in 1968 occurred on a note of irony. In raising the necessary public outcry against the dams, preservationists appealed to the nation's prejudice for monumental scenery. Indeed, to save the canyon, it seemed that preservationists were often willing to sacrifice everything else. One popular argument suggested that coal-fired or nuclear power plants would more than compensate for the loss of hydroelectricity from the dams.[18] The region's power companies had already obliged, mounting the exploitation of major coal fields. Suddenly, the cost of that trade-off was starkly apparent. Although saved from the dam builders below the rim, above it the Grand Canyon was threatened by smog. With each new power plant that came online, greater emissions drifted into the park.[19] As a monumental landscape, the Grand Canyon had survived; as an ecosystem, its future was still seriously in doubt.

By the mid-1970s, coal-fired emissions, combined with smog drifting in from Los Angeles, had reached into every corner of the Southwest. In February 1975, for example, Philip Fradkin of the *Los Angeles Times* reported reductions in visibility at not only the Grand Canyon but also Zion, Bryce, and Cedar Breaks National Monument. "The view from Inspiration Point in Bryce Canyon was hardly inspiring," he wrote. "To the right of Navajo Mountain was the visible plume from the Navajo power plant at Page, Arizona." Two additional plants planned for the region would only add to the layers "of gray-blue and yellow-brown smog."[20]

Few revelations more pointedly demonstrated the new challenges facing national parks. Never again could preservationists take comfort in the nineteenth-century vision of a boundary separating a park from civilization. Air pollution alone proved the assurance specious. Once believed to be a phenomenon of the city, pollution could no longer be contained. That it now drifted deep into the American wilderness only confirmed the lack of barriers between civilization and the national parks.

Still, the problem of educating the American public to appreciate the futility of boundaries recalled the predicament of defending Grand Canyon as an ecosystem. The changes to the parks caused by air pollution were basically incremental and therefore hard to illustrate. Pollution over a park one day might also blow out the next. Historically, both preservationists and the public had responded with far greater intensity to the prospect of a physical loss. The announcement in mid-1975 of stepped-up mining operations in Death Valley National Monument, extractions allowed under the monument's proclamation of 1933, was another battle cry that aroused the public because the threat was easily understood. "Thank God these same people weren't guarding Michelangelo's *Pieta* or Rembrandt's *Night Watch*," an irate reader of the *Los Angeles Times* wrote, striking the popular chord. "They would still be engaged in some endless discussion on how to limit the damage. . . . I shudder to think," he concluded, summing up a century of preservationists' fears, "that there may be borax or oil in the Grand Canyon."[21]

The strength of the allusion was again simplicity. Nothing about the pending changes to Death Valley was incremental and, as a result, could not be easily discounted in the public mind. In contrast, every environmental issue seemed complex. Merely to understand ecological problems required scientific training beyond that of the average citizen. The admitted lack of solutions for those problems led finally to public apathy. Lacking something specific the public could grasp, preservationists were always at a disadvantage.

The Grand Canyon dams controversy of the 1960s averted public indifference because the entire threat was specific. Preservationists need only appeal to the chasm's symbolic importance rather than its still intangible value as an ecosystem. "If we can't save the Grand Canyon," asked David Brower, executive director of the Sierra Club, "what the hell can we save?"[22] Just as everyone understood what he meant, so by now the standard rebuttal was just as clear. National parks were elitist, charged the Bureau of Reclamation, when enjoyed by the few at the expense of the many. The American Southwest needed more water and power. While providing them, the dams would allow far more visitors, including those in motorboats, to enjoy the scenic beauty of the inner canyon, all this against just a few thousand wilderness enthusiasts floating the river in rubber rafts. There, the Sierra Club, led by David Brower, cleverly reversed the argument, accusing the bureau, just by planning the dams, of ransacking the nation's heritage. A series of full-page newspaper advertisements sealed the image of dam builders run amok. "SHOULD WE ALSO FLOOD THE SISTINE CHAPEL SO TOURISTS CAN GET NEARER THE CEILING?"[23] No more famous headline emerged from the 1960s in the battle for national parks. If indeed the Grand Canyon was America's identity, how could Congress even think of allowing the dams. On July 31, 1968, Congress released its verdict. The bureau and the dams had lost.[24]

The continuing drawback was the lack of a precedent covering every national park. Barely within the decade, mining in Death Valley National Monument served up another reminder that no park was ever "safe." This time the perpetrator and opponent was Tenneco, Death Valley's largest producer of borates and talc. Among the compromises in establishing the monument had been the continued allowance of mining claims. Beginning in 1971, Tenneco stepped up operations on those claims. "The main impact on the monument," Nathaniel P. Reed, as as-

Considered one of the greatest paintings of the Hudson River School, *Kindred Spirits* (1849), by Asher Brown Durand, instructs the viewer that the American experience is defined by nature. Overlooking an idealized Catskill Mountain stream, the artist Thomas Cole (right, with brush and sketchbook) and the poet William Cullen Bryant share its transcendent beauty. Americans defending their cultural identity as nature's purity soon faced enormous and unwanted change. As cities transformed the East, even a minimum exposure to the natural world would henceforth rely on the availability of public parks. Oil on canvas, 44 × 36 inches. *Courtesy of the Crystal Bridges Museum of American Art, Bentonville, Arkansas*

Compiled from personal studies made during the Hayden Expedition of 1871, Thomas Moran's mammoth painting, *The Grand Canyon of the Yellowstone* (1872), was greeted as an artistic tour de force. The "kindred spirits" of earlier American paintings also remain, now to observe a landscape beyond mere words. Probably no painting has been more pop-

ular, and is more reproduced, as a representative example of America's national parks. Oil on canvas mounted on aluminum, 84 × 144¼ inches. *Courtesy of the National Museum of American Art, Smithsonian Institution. Lent by U.S. Department of the Interior, National Park Service*

Route of The **EMPIRE BUILDER**

GREAT NORTHERN

Well into the twentieth century, artists specializing in the national parks received their best commissions from the western railroads, though not all of those commissions were strictly scenic. Featuring the Austrian-born artist Winold Reiss, a colorful series of Blackfeet paintings graced the Great Northern Railway's annual calendar for 30 years, here *The Drummers—Glacier National Park*, the image for 1933. Paper original, 32¾ × 15¾ inches. *Author's collection*

Frustrated that the Grand Canyon of Arizona was not yet a national park, the Santa Fe Railway turned to its artists and a nickname, the Titan of Chasms. A first tourist publication using the title appeared in 1902. For the cover of the 1915 edition, the railroad used a painting by the artist William Robinson Leigh. Original paper edition, 9¼ × 6½ inches. *Author's collection*

Few texts and images of the national parks have been more instructive than the advertising copy of the Union Pacific Railroad. From 1927, note the references in both advertisements to the monumental qualities of Zion (left) and Bryce Canyon (right). At Zion, our "kindred spirits," now on horseback, marvel at the Great White Throne. Visiting Bryce, we

are told to expect "ruined Oriental cities, castles and cathedrals of the Middle Ages." Although subtle, the transition under way is further noted in the promotion of virgin forests and wildlife. Gradually, the vision of the national parks is coming to include the biological and the monumental. Both 9½ × 6½ inches. *Author's collection*

In a poster painting by the California artist Don Perceval (1949), America's kindred spirits have come full circle to stand in the high country of Yosemite National Park. Although the object of their gaze is monumental (Mount Dana), the importance of the surrounding wilderness is equally palpable. As advised by a century of painters beginning with Asher Brown Durand, for nature to remain a timeless vision the nation must pursue its preservation. Paper original, 24 × 18 inches. *Author's collection*

sistant interior secretary, reported to Congress in 1975, "is the use of open pit methods." Before the mining got out of hand, its long-range damage should be addressed. The company's Boraxo pit, Reed noted, "now is some 3,000 feet by 600 feet and is 220 feet deep, while its Sigma pit is 500 by 400 feet, and is more than 75 feet deep." Not only were both mines "being enlarged"; more alarming, "the spoil or waste dumps" had become "highly visible from the scenic road to the Dante's View overlook." Fortunately, he conceded, the biggest deposits of borates "in the same general area of the monument" had "not been developed for production as yet."[25]

As opposition mounted, Congress agreed to consider legislation prohibiting mining claims in the six national parks and monuments, including Death Valley, where such claims could still be filed.[26] On all previous claims, such as Tenneco's Boraxo and Sigma pits in Death Valley, operations would still be allowed. Similarly, Reed hesitated in the case of Glacier Bay National Monument, Alaska, believed to contain major deposits of nickel and copper. Pending a further study of the magnitude of those deposits by the U.S. Bureau of Mines, he recommended that they remain "open" to claims until completion of the study in 1978.[27]

The compromise predictably embittered preservationists as just another postponement of the problem. Representative John F. Seiberling of Ohio, sponsor of the legislation to curb the mining, indeed noted the paradox of telling the public that Death Valley "is to be preserved and even collecting rocks is not allowed" while "at the same time" legally permitting "huge economic interests for their own personal profit to go in and rip it off." Charles Clusen, further testifying on behalf of the Sierra Club, wholeheartedly supported Seiberling's indignation. "[Even] if these were the last borates and talc," Clusen said, "even if there was no substitute for their use, we must still ask if this gives us the right to destroy the one and only Death Valley that we have." Eventually, the United States must "come to grips with the fact that there are finite supplies of minerals, and that we cannot allow the destruction of everything we treasure in the pursuit of those resources."[28]

The affected mining companies, supported by their own champions in Congress, lost no time supporting tradition: why not just eliminate the disputed claims from the monument? Thus, Representative Joe Skubitz of Kansas asked rhetorically whether cutting "that area completely out of the monument" would "do irreparable damage." Representative Philip E. Ruppe of Michigan concurred, observing that the lands currently affected amounted to only 4,000 acres, but .2 percent of the entire monument.

Proclaimed in 1933, Death Valley National Monument had already been compromised by existing mineral claims. Legislation passed in 1976 regulated, but did not abolish outright, operations such as the open-pit mine pictured here. *Courtesy of the National Park Service, Breyne Moskowitz photograph*

"Who cares then if they mine 4,000 acres? . . . If one mined the whole 4,000 acres, does one make an appreciable dent in either the geology or ecology of Death Valley?" Robert E. Kendall, executive vice president of the United States Borax and Chemical Corporation, agreed that the mining was minimal. He nonetheless recommended "a realignment of monument boundaries to exclude areas of low scenic value and high mineral value." Similar adjustments might also "be the most practical approach to easing the adverse reaction to mining within units of the national park system" across the country. At least in Death Valley, Kendall argued, outright removal of the affected claims offered "a better solution" by ensuring that "this highly valuable borate area [is] out of the park, so it is not in conflict with national park objectives."[29]

Kendall then conceded that his company's large mine at Boron, 110 miles southwest of Death Valley, should meet the demand for borates well into the future. The point was the seriousness of his initial attack.

"Does it not destroy the integrity of our park system," Representative Seiberling asked, driving home the inconsistency, "that every time somebody comes up with a new mineral deposit within the park, to say that we will solve the problem, we will just change the boundary?" "I don't think that," Kendall replied, citing the history of Death Valley National Monument. "In 1933 when the park was created, a portion of the eastern border was shifted so as to exclude an existing mining operation."[30]

There was indeed little for preservationists to applaud in the legislation signed by President Gerald R. Ford on September 28, 1976. Ostensibly introduced in Congress to prohibit the mining, the law barely regulated the miners. On all claims worked prior to February 29, 1976, mining might in fact continue. The stipulation in effect sanctioned the open-pit mining that had aroused the public the previous year. The legislation further admonished the secretary of the interior to identify those portions of the monument that might be abolished outright "to exclude significant mineral deposits and to decrease possible acquisition costs."[31] As Robert Kendall and the mining industry had reminded Congress, the historical objective had been to eliminate from Death Valley anything that even might prove controversial.

In the threatened realignment of Death Valley National Monument, there remained the unspoken criterion that national parks could not be justified just on ecology. Even where the United States had come closest to the ideal of biological conservation, as in the Florida Everglades, the reluctance of Congress to protect enough territory threatened the longevity of those areas. During the late 1960s, the Everglades was threatened again, this time by ground breaking for a huge jetport immediately adjacent to the park's northern perimeter. Before the project was halted in 1970, an entire runway had been cleared and graded.[32] The struggle in part led to passage of the Big Cypress National Preserve four years later. With its approval, Congress recognized the legitimacy of fears that Everglades National Park could not survive without protecting its flow of freshwater from the north, particularly from Big Cypress.[33] In denying the jetport and passing the bill to protect Big Cypress, Congress of course had set no precedent. No sooner had the jetport in the Everglades been thwarted than developers advanced a similar scheme in Jackson Hole.[34] As for Big Cypress, mining, hunting, grazing, drainage, agriculture, fishing, trapping, and other traditionally unacceptable uses of the national parks were only to be regulated rather than abolished outright. Ten years later, further invaded by off-road vehicles, Big Cypress seemed not to have been protected at all.[35]

Fulfilling the prophecy that invention drives legitimacy, snowmobiles gained entry to Yellowstone National Park in the 1970s, where they remain controversial to this day. *Courtesy of the National Park Service, Cecil W. Stoughton photograph*

Because Big Cypress was not considered a national park in its own right but more accurately a measure of insurance for one, those compromises were overlooked. In either case, the regulation of incompatible activities was preferable to having no regulation at all. Somewhat the same philosophy lay behind the trend to national recreation areas, scenic rivers, national lakeshores, parkways, and urban preserves. If few were national parks in the traditional sense, they were methods of preserving landscape. It seemed equally desirable to lure purely recreational interests away from places like Yosemite and Yellowstone.

The ecological issues raised between *Silent Spring* and the Yellowstone Conference were still far from being resolved. In what many saw as the final opportunity for the United States to protect a complete ecological record, preservationists next proposed national park status for tens of millions of acres of the public domain in Alaska. Yet even in the forty-ninth state, the Conservation Foundation warned, resource interests were determined to restrict parklands "to lands covered with ice and snow" despite the contention of ecologists that the reserves "should extend to adjacent lowlands as well."[36] No less dramatically, a belated effort to expand Redwood National Park by 48,000 acres further demonstrated how often the national parks had initially been denied the territory they really needed.[37] Even in the biggest parks, led by Yellowstone, Mount McKinley, and Glacier, biologists still feared for the survival of wildlife, as recently exemplified by the grizzly bear.[38]

Preservationists still confronted the paradox of their own beginning. For 100 years, the success of the national parks movement lay in its concentration on natural wonders. Now that preservationists understood ecology, they first had to undo the prevailing image of their founders. Not until the substitution of environmentalism for romanticism would that kind of park system have a chance. This much, at least, seemed certain. Given the sincerity of fears that humans might perish without the knowledge locked up in wilderness, the United States could not afford to wait another 100 years to preserve the land for what it was instead of for what it was not.

From September 1980, a prescribed burn to remove competitive vegetation among the giant sequoias in Giant Forest, Sequoia National Park,
contrasts sharply with earlier images of the big trees as a novelty for
tourists. *Courtesy of the National Park Service, Sequoia National Park,
William Tweed photograph*

CHAPTER 10

The Lesson of the Big Trees

I can remember Dr. A. Starker Leopold, on a zoology class field trip in Lake County, California, in 1951, telling some of his students that before long fire would be restored to national parks. It seemed a startling and revolutionary idea at the time.

— BRUCE M. KILGORE, 1974

MORE visitation, better roads, and improved accommodations—the traditional concerns of national park management—were gradually challenged during the 1960s and early 1970s by the ecological issues summarized at the Second World Conference on National Parks. Meanwhile, America's historical preoccupation with monumentalism masked the nation's failure to establish national parks of unquestionable ecological integrity. The result was renewed interest in the biological significance of the larger, existing national parks and monuments. Granted, these original parks and monuments had been established with cultural rather than ecological ends in mind. Only the larger parks, however, regardless of their imperfections, possessed the diversity of natural features necessary to begin widespread experimentation with the principles of biological management.

Among the Park Service's traditional policies, none seemed more inconsistent with the needs of plants and animals than providing opportunities for mass recreation. Gradually, scientists had begun speaking out against accommodating people at the expense of the natural scene. Scientists achieved special credibility in 1963, when the distinguished Leopold Committee, chaired by A. Starker Leopold of the University of

California at Berkeley, released its sweeping report *Wildlife Management in the National Parks*. A new generation of conservation leaders, further influenced by Rachel Carson's *Silent Spring*, themselves found the Leopold Committee's conclusions too provocative to ignore.[1]

Central to its report, the committee recommended that protection, defined as the strict maintenance of park features, must give way to greater respect for the importance of natural forces. For example, the scientists noted, "It is now an accepted truism that maintenance of suitable habitat is the key to sustaining animal populations, and that protection, though it is important, is not of itself a substitute for habitat." Habitat had less to do with artifacts or physical wonders and more to do with natural processes, such as wind, rain, and fire. It followed that habitat could not be regarded as "a fixed or stable entity that can be set aside and preserved behind a fence, like a cliff dwelling or a petrified tree." Biotic communities evolved by "change through natural stages of succession." Altering the parks biologically itself required the direct "manipulation of plant and animal populations."[2]

How that manipulation might be directed and toward what ends comprised the heart of the Leopold report. "As a primary goal," the committee suggested, "we would recommend that the biotic associations within each park be maintained, or where necessary recreated, as nearly as possible in the condition that prevailed when the area was first visited by the white man." In short, the scientists concluded, "A national park should represent a vignette of primitive America."[3]

The obstacles to achieving "this seemingly simple aspiration are stupendous," the committee wrote, admitting the obvious. "Many of our national parks—in fact most of them—went through periods of indiscriminate logging, burning, livestock grazing, hunting, and predator control." Once those areas became national parks, they again "shifted abruptly to a regime of equally unnatural protection from lightning fires, from insect outbreaks, absence of natural controls of ungulates, and in some areas elimination of normal fluctuations in water levels." Meanwhile, exotic species of plants and animals had "inadvertently been introduced." Finally, the effects of visitation, including "roads and trampling and camp grounds and pack stock," had taken their toll of park environments. It was small wonder that restoring "the primitive scene" would not be "done easily nor can it be done completely," the committee concluded. The point was that the National Park Service needed a new perspective from which to begin a more sensitive management program.[4]

Among practicing scientists in the national parks, these suggestions were hardly new. Restoring the parks to their appearance at the time of European contact had been discussed as early as the 1910s.[5] With the growing popularity of the environmental movement during the 1960s, those ideals had simply found a greater following. Few scientists at the time noted the apparent contradiction in the committee's own conclusions. Having argued that natural forces were dynamic, the committee nonetheless recommended that any restoration approximate the state of the parks 400 years earlier. Obviously, the committee, somewhat like George Catlin in 1832, remained convinced that Europeans were the disruptive force in wilderness. The committee certainly did not condemn the land altering behavior of Native Americans. Rather, the scientists endorsed their manipulation, particularly the Indians' use of fire, as a practice in keeping with the need to restore periodic burning throughout the national parks.[6]

By "natural," in other words, the committee meant "original" to North America before the arrival of Columbus. Put another way, because Native Americans were "original" to North America, their manipulative practices might be excused. Europeans rather than Indians had been responsible for changing the continent ruthlessly and unsystematically. "The goal of managing the national parks and monuments," the committee restated, "should be to preserve, or where necessary recreate, the ecologic scene as viewed by the first European visitors."[7]

If the first Europeans were merely "visitors," it followed that their descendants had overstayed their welcome. Viewed strictly in terms of biology, the uninvited presence in North America was the growth of a European population. As a consequence of the pioneers, wildlife had been greatly reduced in numbers, some species to the point of extinction. Europeans had similarly introduced exotic varieties of plants and animals as well as alien diseases to North America. Every environment had been affected. "All these limitations we fully realize," the committee wrote by way of confession. "Yet, if [our] goal cannot be fully achieved it can be approached." In the absence of perfection, the national parks might at least suggest what North America looked like in the precolonial period. "A reasonable illusion of primitive America could be recreated," the scientists maintained, "using the utmost in skill, judgment, and ecologic sensitivity."[8] Preservationists rushed to agree. At least in the national parks, the ecological damage of European settlement might be reversed, provided that biological management was finally substituted for the historical emphasis on scenery and natural features.[9]

Of all the attractions of the national park system, none more dramatically symbolized what the Leopold Committee meant by its "illusion of primitive America" than the giant sequoias of the High Sierra. Recognition of their cultural symbolism as America's "living antiquity" had presaged their inclusion in the Yosemite Grant of 1864. With such scattered protection, however, had not come an understanding of their life cycle or true fragility. Still in their infancy, the biological sciences were obsessed with cataloging data rather than viewing it comprehensively. Few scientists themselves understood initially that fire was a common occurrence among the groves. Left to government wardens, state or federal, even the periodic ground fires safeguarded by the natives were discouraged and suppressed.[10]

An awareness that fire was not universally destructive grew slowly across the country. As late as 1929, Curtis K. Skinner, a respected conservationist, upheld the popular view that fire "without a doubt" was "the greatest threat against the perpetual *scenic* wealth of our largest National Parks" (emphasis added). Throughout the 1880s and 1890s, Skinner wrote, arguing his point, "a fire might rage in the mountain forests for weeks without exciting any more attention than an occasional remark between ranchers concerning the dryness of the weather." Not until the early 1900s, following greater publicity about the needs of the national parks, did the government fully adopt a policy of "increased vigilance and much careful attention to fire-fighting equipment" that the protection of their forests required.[11]

Given the logic that fire was universally bad, those pointing to its necessity in the natural environment fought an uphill battle against public opinion. Regardless, all forests were not alike, nor did they burn alike, especially when fire was not suppressed. Among the first to identify the benefits from fire was Captain G. H. G. Gale, commandant of the Fourth U.S. Cavalry. Assigned to the patrol of Yosemite in 1894, he believed that fire in the park was vital. "Examination of this subject," he reported in June to the secretary of the interior, "leads me to believe that the absolute prevention of fires in these mountains will eventually lead to disastrous results." Rather than an enemy of the Sierra forest, fire was necessary to its health. Annual fires removed the litter of fallen needles and toppled trees, leaving "the ground ready for the next year's growth." Enough younger trees escaped the flames to replace the forest, "and it is not thought," Gale remarked, appealing to the common wisdom of Sierra natives and pioneers, "that the slight heat of the annual fires will appreciably affect the growth or life of well-grown trees. On the other hand," he concluded with a warning, "if the year's droppings are allowed to accumulate they will increase until the resulting heat, when they do burn, will destroy everything before it."[12]

By 1916 and the establishment of the National Park Service, Gale's recommendations had made little headway. In the normal turnover of custodians and superintendents, those with a sense of continuity were eventually transferred. Gradually, the original forest molded in the presence of fire was transformed by its replacement. By the time scientists revisited the subject of fire suppression during the 1950s, it was a case of not seeing the forest for the trees. So much new vegetation had sprung up among the sequoia groves that current managers considered the density "normal." Not until the Leopold Committee Report—and even some years after that—did the National Park Service seriously reassess whether fire should be returned to its forests as a management tool.[13]

Anticipating the Leopold Committee, a pathbreaking article by H. H. Biswell, professor of forestry at the University of California, noted the consequences of fire suppression in Yosemite's Tuolumne and Mariposa groves. "Two great changes have taken place as a result of fire protection," he wrote in 1961. "First, the more shade-tolerant white fir and incense cedar have developed in dense thickets in the understory of many Big Trees and pines. They greatly add to the fire hazard." Visitors to the park who considered this accumulation "natural" failed "to recognize that fire, too, was a natural and characteristic feature of the environment in earlier times." "The second change of great importance in the Sierra Nevada forests," Biswell noted, "is the large increase in debris on the forest floor." Sierra forests "were relatively clean, open, and park-like in earlier times, and could be easily traveled through." Finally, after decades of fire suppression, most were "so full of dead material and young trees and brush as to be nearly impassable."[14]

By so increasing the fire hazard, such conditions only invited a major conflagration that would wipe out the forest entirely. Fires in the original, primeval forest had been "friendly," limited to the smaller accumulations of "herbs, needles, and leaves on the ground." The giant sequoias themselves, "with their asbestos-like bark," easily resisted the low flames and mild heat. In contrast, a modern fire among the big trees would be enormously destructive, fed by "the development of a solid fuel layer in many places from the tops of the tallest trees to the young saplings and brush and litter on the ground. Is it any wonder," Professor Biswell asked in conclusion, "that the wildfires in such situations are so devastating and difficult to control?"[15]

Additional research in the coming decade further established the importance of fire in providing for the groves' existence. Again, the observations of a few perceptive individuals in the nineteenth century were confirmed. Writing in 1878, John Muir noted that "fire, the great destroyer of Sequoia, also furnishes bare, virgin ground, one of the conditions essential for its growth from seed."[16] Although Muir greatly exaggerated the destructiveness of natural fires, he was nonetheless among the first observers to recognize their significance in the regeneration of giant sequoias.

After 1900, fire suppression throughout the High Sierra undermined Muir's hypothesis well into mid-century. Finally, both private and government scientists admitted the dearth of sequoia seedlings, even in the protected groves. In the first major studies of the sequoia forests that followed, it was confirmed that sequoia seeds simultaneously needed open sunlight and bare, mineral soils. The seeds otherwise failed to germinate. Not only were young sequoias intolerant of shade and competitive vegetation, but their seeds required fire to burn away the forest litter that shielded them from bare ground. Although seedlings also perished in the ground fires that periodically swept the groves, enough of the younger growth had historically survived the flames to replenish the aging sequoias. In contrast, the suppression of all fires over several decades had choked the open areas with cedar and white fir. Along with shading out the forest floor, those competitors contributed increasing amounts of needles and fallen branches to the forest litter. If not stunted by the shade, the sequoia seedlings then strangled in the debris.[17]

"Our great challenge," wrote John L. Vankat, assistant professor of botany at Miami University in Oxford, Ohio, "is to return disturbed ecosystems to the point where natural processes may act as primary management agents." Ideally, the original Sierra forest might be restored, at least in the national parks. Substantiating his conviction, he quoted extensively from the Leopold Committee Report. "When the forty-niners poured over the Sierra Nevada into California, those that kept diaries spoke almost to a man of the wide-spaced columns of mature trees that grew on the lower western slope in gigantic magnificence. The ground was a grass parkland, in springtime carpeted with wildflowers. Deer and bears were abundant." Ground fires were primarily responsible for this pristine environment. With fire suppression began the changes leading to the "dog-hair thicket of young pines, white fir, incense cedar, and mature brush" common along the western slope of the Sierra by 1963.[18]

In September 1967, the Park Service officially reversed its long-standing policy of suppressing all fires in the national parks. "Fires in vegetation resulting from natural causes are recognized as natural phenomena," read the agency's new policy statement. Wherever fires might "be contained within predetermined fire management units" and where burning would "contribute to the accomplishment of approved vegetation and/or wildlife management objectives," natural fires "may be allowed to run their course."[19]

The extensive use of fire by Native Americans was further a way around the dilemma of human intervention. Especially in the giant sequoia groves of Yosemite, Sequoia, and Kings Canyon national parks, intervention was justified by the unnatural accumulation of dead branches, litter, and competitive vegetation. Before naturally occurring fires could be restored, the unnatural debris needed to be removed. First, the competitive vegetation growing among the big trees would have to be cut, stacked by hand, and burned under strict supervision. Afterward, the litter and other accumulated debris on the forest floor might also be burned under carefully monitored conditions. Finally, natural ground fires, obviously from lightning strikes, could again be permitted to burn themselves out in the groves under the watchful eye of park biologists.[20]

In the absence of accumulating fuels, all fires would again be ground fires of lower heat and intensity. Where fire reached the base of mature giant sequoias, they would be protected by their thick, asbestos-like bark. Equally important, enough seedlings would survive any ground fires to perpetuate the forest in coming centuries. If lightning then failed to set enough fires, Park Service managers defining their behavior as "natural" might properly intervene, as had "native" biologists.

The realization of this scenario in the 1970s emerged as the most profound and successful response to the principles of biological management outlined in the Leopold Committee Report of 1963. Unlike the committee's other controversial recommendations, such as the reintroduction of natural predators to park environments, allowing fire to be restored did not depend on the cooperation of other government agencies or private landowners. Predators wandering outside park boundaries were almost certain to be shot by farmers, ranchers, and hunters. At least with the proper precautions, fire could be restricted to areas solely under Park Service control.

Still, the policy had its detractors, including park concessionaires sensitive to canceled reservations. Tourists driving hundreds or thousands of miles to see monumental scenery obviously protested when its features were obscured by smoke. However natural or apparently necessary, fire was not what most tourists had in mind.[21] Other critics saw a contradiction in allowing natural pollution to hang over the parks while at the same time objecting to the smoke and dust of distant cities and coal-fired power plants.[22] Broader still, where should manipulation of the environment begin and end? Were not the pioneers and their descendants now the natural and therefore legitimate presence in the environment? Was it not illogical to suspend the environment at the point of just a native presence? Weighed against those philosophical issues, scenery seemed so simple to understand.

Regardless, no longer were the national parks a simple case of protecting an object without managing for its longevity. Especially when the object was a living entity, it called for special safeguards.[23] Noting the planned restoration of Giant Forest in Sequoia National Park, environmentalists applauded a solution actually advocating the removal of visitor facilities, including cabins and a lodge. Following completion of the restoration in 2006, the National Park Service reported on its Sequoia National Park website, "Over 282 buildings, 24 acres of asphalt, dozens of manholes, a sewage treatment plant and spray field, and all exposed sewer and water pipe, aerial telephone and electric lines, and underground propane and fuel tanks have been removed. Ecological restoration has been conducted on 231 acres."[24]

Thus had an object proved itself an object lesson for every national park. In a broader review of the giant sequoias, the undeniable threats to their longevity had been assessed. Initially viewed as monuments, they had become instructors of the greater relevance of natural environments. Throughout the national park system, there would forever be that new campaign. Certainly, wherever science was now in the ascendancy, the giant sequoias had helped smooth the way.

Characterized by an emphasis on urban settings, the expansion of national parks in the 1970s promised the protection of nature close to home. Here, the Marin Headlands of the Golden Gate National Recreation Area frame the Golden Gate Bridge and San Francisco, California. *Courtesy of the National Park Service, Richard Frear photograph*

CHAPTER 11

Ideals and Controversies
of Expansion

The main flaw in the performance of many existing conservation associations
is that most concentrate on a chosen holy grail, and too few organizations have
entered the fight for the total environment.
— STEWART L. UDALL, 1963

A park, however splendid, has little appeal to a family that cannot reach it. . . .
The new conservation is built on a new promise — to bring parks closer to the
people.
— LYNDON B. JOHNSON, 1968

If you keep standing for perfection, you won't get anything.
— PHILLIP BURTON, 1979

INITIALLY hailed as a milestone of environmental insight, the Leopold
Committee Report of 1963 more accurately reawakened and redi-
rected concerns about the biological health of the national parks evident since the late 1920s. In a similar vein, efforts to expand the national
park system during the 1960s and 1970s merely intensified the long debate over Congress's responsibility to protect so-called national park standards. Again, the issue pitted traditional perceptions of the national parks
against the growing determination to protect all kinds of landscapes,
not just those blessed with outstanding geological wonders. However, the
persuasiveness of monumentalism was not so easily dislodged. "Our
National Parks are much more than recreational resorts and museums of
unaltered nature," wrote Robert Sterling Yard in 1923, defending the national park standards of his own generation; "they are also the Exposition

of the Scenic Supremacy of the United States." Expanding the national park system for expansion's sake openly threatened that reputation. "No other trade-mark," he concluded, "has cost so much to establish and pays such dividends of business, national prestige, and patriotism." Nevertheless, he warned, his concerns now fully obvious, "it is proposed to destroy it."[1]

Especially in the East, calls for "inferior" national parks threatened to distract attention from the world-class landscapes already included in the national park system. Public recreation, Yard charged, not scenic preservation, was the true motivation behind these newer parks. Recreation had its place; similarly, a limited number of areas might qualify for national park status on the basis of their plants, animals, or wilderness alone.[2] In the absence of monumental scenery, however, those needs must be indisputable. The protection of pretty yet uninspiring landscapes was itself secondary to the promotion of scenic wonders. "When Zion National Park was created in 1919," he wrote, offering a recent example, "the whole world knew from the simple announcement of the fact that another stupendous scenic wonderland had been discovered. But when pleasant wooded summits, limestone caves, pretty local ravines, local mountains and gaps between mountains become National Parks, the name 'Zion National Park' will mean nothing at home or abroad to those who have not already seen it." Demeaning the scenic standards of the national parks merely invited "local competition not only for national parks but for national appropriations. If one Congressional District secures its own National Park, why not every other Congressional District in the State, or in many States? . . . What are Congressmen for if not to look out for their districts?" The "increasing dozens of little parks" would undermine financial support for the larger, spectacular, and clearly legitimate reserves. "A National Park Pork Barrel," he bitterly concluded, "would be the final degradation!"[3]

For the next half century, Yard and other purists fought against any use of the term "national park" to describe battlefields, historic sites, parkways, recreation areas, and other federal preserves of limited scenic grandeur.[4] Dr. John C. Merriam, president of the Carnegie Institution, defended Yard's objections to common topography in this vein, writing in 1926 of "the power and order behind nature." "National Parks represent opportunities for worship in which one comes to understand more fully certain of the attributes of nature and its Creator," Merriam said, elaborating on his definition. "They are not objects to be worshipped, but they are altars over which we may worship."[5] A reverence for nature, as exemplified by the existing national parks, would only be eroded by heedless expansion into areas of dubious scenic merit.[6]

In contrast to Yard and Merriam, most preservationists of the succeeding generation—grappling with a deteriorating environment—simply had less in common with the image of national parks as evidence of the country's spiritual commitment and cultural superiority. Certainly by the 1960s, that image had been tempered by the belief that everything in nature was important. National parks, in addition to protecting the "museum pieces" of the American landscape, might also afford protection to land threatened by housing developments, shopping centers, expressways, and similar forms of urban encroachment. Stemming the tide of urban development hinged on educating Americans to appreciate the natural world being sacrificed in their own backyards. The loss of more than a million acres of open space annually indeed alarmed preservationists.[7] Suddenly, Yellowstone's 2 million acres, for example, did not seem very large, what with half as much land being lost every year to housing, highways, parking lots, and other types of urban sprawl.

Equity of access to the national parks was yet another pressing issue for modern preservationists. By virtue of their remoteness, the great western national parks excluded as many Americans as they accommodated. Even in the East, the largest natural areas were too far distant, especially for the urban poor.[8] For Robert Sterling Yard's generation, the quality of park landscapes rather than equity of access had been preservationists' chief concern. Ignoring the fact that states outside the mountain and desert West might deserve national parks, few other regions of the country were comparably scenic. However the United States chose to meet the everyday needs of its citizens for outdoor recreation, the distinctiveness of the national parks should never be compromised. "None but the noblest" national parks, Yard pleaded again, "painstakingly chosen, must be admitted" to the system.[9]

By the early 1960s, Yard's brand of purism had been questioned by all but the most tradition-bound preservationists. Politically and socially, most realized that their movement had changed. If preservationists were to acknowledge the legitimacy of civil rights, for example, it seemed advisable to have more national parks closer to where all Americans lived and worked, not merely where wealthier citizens could afford to spend their summer vacations.[10] Even more to the point, only the federal government had the power and wealth to forestall the degradation of natural environments across the country. What Yard had labeled "pork barrel politics" finally struck preservationists as perhaps their only hope for lending the general environment a proven modicum of protection.[11]

Inevitably, Yard's insistence that recreational needs be addressed apart from scenic preservation was tempered by political realities. Preservationists likewise ignored his warning that bureaucrats and politicians would be tempted to dilute the term "national park." With opportunities for preservation dwindling annually, those seemed to be the concerns of a previous generation. What finally mattered was not what the parks were called or even how they might be used but whether parks—any parks—would be established in the first place.

Across the United States, preservationists had learned the wisdom of championing new parks under a variety of categories, from seashores and lakeshores to urban recreation areas. The new impetus for park expansion reached its peak in 1977 with the appointment of Representative Phillip Burton of California to chair the House Subcommittee on National Parks and Insular Affairs. By the end of the following year, Burton, a strong promoter of local, regional, and urban national parks, had pushed through Congress the largest single legislative package in national park history.[12]

Echoing Robert Sterling Yard, the bill's opponents had tried to derail the measure with the label "Parks Barrel Bill." Such was the reason that it passed—there was something in the bill for everyone. The national park idea had finally reached out to include an urban-based, industrialized society.[13] Finally, among preservationists increasingly calling themselves environmentalists, the Omnibus Bill of 1978 heralded a new era of legitimacy—and success—in the fight for every landscape.

The inevitable controversy over whether to expand the national park system was obviously still influenced by Yellowstone. First applied there, the term "national park" had fixed an indelible image of grandeur and mystery in the public mind. It followed that any national park established subsequently would be measured against Yellowstone's significance in American culture. In that vein, in 1961 the historian John Ise addressed the issue of national park standards. "There were in 1902 six national parks of superlative magnificence; but between 1902 and 1906 three new parks were set aside—Wind Cave, Sullys Hill, and Platt—which did not measure up to this high standard." Ise laid the problem to the absence of a "Congressional policy governing the establishment of national parks," coupled with the lack of a "Park Service to screen park proposals." As a result, these three "inferior" national parks "just happened to be established."[14]

In fact, their preservation marked a subtle rather than accidental shift in the perception of national parks. By the early twentieth century, the

Urban parks also bring urban problems, such as the high rise and abandoned car at Breezy Point, Gateway National Recreation Area, New York and New Jersey. *Courtesy of the National Park Service, Richard Frear photograph*

acceptance of national parks as the embodiment of American romanticism had been joined by a belief in the value of open space for public health. Obviously, the national parks, aside from their natural features, were profound examples of open space. In the pursuit of physical fitness and outdoor recreation, why limit those opportunities to the West? Wind Cave, Sullys Hill, and Platt were but the first examples of this blurring of past and present. Now that the national parks were held to provide something for everyone, areas lesser than Yellowstone were inevitable.

The problem was how to compensate for a scenic focus given that scenery had always been the standard for federal parks. The geological limitations of parks outside the West were obvious. Where equivalent natural features were lacking, it seemed advisable to claim them nonetheless. In this vein, John F. Lacey of Iowa introduced the proposed Wind Cave national park in South Dakota to the House of Representatives as "substantially what the Yellowstone country would be if the geysers should die. It has been excavated by hot water in the same manner that the geyser land is now being excavated in the Yellowstone." Only then did he admit that Wind Cave's dramatic past was obviously not Yellowstone's equal in the present. "The active forces are no longer in operation there," he elaborated; "there is no hot water, and the conditions that formerly prevailed there have ceased." Still, he argued, finally abandoning his extravagant comparison, "a series of very wonderful caves remain, and the Land Department has withdrawn this tract from settlement." The "few claims" of settlers in the area amounted to but "a few hundred acres" of the 9,000 proposed for park status; "I think it is a very meritorious proposition," he concluded, "and that this tract of land ought to be reserved to the American people."[15]

Binger Hermann, as commissioner of the General Land Office, further inflated the reports of his surveyor, who found Wind Cave literally filled with "subterranean wonders." Examples included great caverns and grotesque-looking rooms, "large grottoes," and "tons of specimens." "Those who visited the Yellowstone National Park and the Mammoth Cave of Kentucky," he claimed, "will all accord the Wind Cave only a second place to the Yellowstone Canyon and the geysers of the former and declare the Wind Cave superior, in point of attractiveness, to the Mammoth Cave." The names of Wind Cave's features further betokened its uniqueness and worthiness for national park status—"Pearly Gates," "Fair Grounds," "Garden of Eden," "Castle Garden," and "Blue Grotto," to list but a few.[16] Besides, Congress could hardly find economic reasons to object to the protection of only 9,000 acres. With Yellowstone apparently reborn underground, on January 9, 1903, President Theodore Roosevelt signed the Wind Cave National Park Act into law.[17]

In retrospect, if Wind Cave's critics found scant reason to justify a national park, Congress in 1902 clearly felt otherwise. From the outset, Wind Cave was introduced and discussed as a national park project. Sullys Hill National Park, established by presidential proclamation on June 2, 1904, was obviously not intended as a traditional park. In April 1904, arising from an agreement with the Sioux Indians adjusting the Devils Lake Reservation, North Dakota, Congress authorized the president to establish "a public park" embracing 960 acres at Sullys Hill. Never one to forgo such an opportunity, President Theodore Roosevelt set aside the tract as "Sullys Hill Park."[18]

Neither Congress's authorization nor Roosevelt's proclamation established a national park at Sullys Hill; nevertheless, the term was soon applied. Lacking any monumental significance and only one and a half square miles in area, Sullys Hill later struck its critics as a perfect example of intentionally depreciating national park standards. Not until 1914 did Congress appropriate $5,000 to manage the area; even then, Sullys

Hill was actually to be operated as a game preserve by the U.S. Biological Survey.[19]

The establishment in 1906 of Platt National Park in Oklahoma seemed to invite a further abuse of national park standards. In 1902, Congress purchased 640 acres of spring-fed, rolling hills near the town of Sulphur from the Choctaw and Chickasaw Indians, designating it the Sulphur Springs Reservation. Four years later, seeking a memorial to Orville Hitchcock Platt, the late senator from Connecticut, members of that delegation eyed Sulphur Springs. In June 1906, a resolution passed by the House and Senate made the request official. Henceforth, the Sulphur Springs Reservation would be known as "Platt National Park."[20]

Among Platt, Sullys Hill, and Wind Cave, only the latter, eventually enlarged to 28,000 acres, survived as a national park. Yet the precedent of restricting national parks to monumental landscapes had clearly been broken. Proposals for national parks outside the scenic West continued to escalate every year. Stephen T. Mather, as first director of the National Park Service, defended the scenic reputation of the existing parks by channeling this enthusiasm into the emerging state parks movement. Under Mather's direction, for example, the Park Service was instrumental in the formation of the National Conference on State Parks, which held its first meeting in Des Moines, Iowa, in 1921. Repeatedly throughout the coming decade, he disarmed proponents of so-called unworthy parks by referring them to the conference, noting that state ownership was more appropriate for areas only locally renowned.[21]

Mather's immediate problems with the standard were due in large part to his own reluctance to apply it universally. The Hot Springs Reservation, Arkansas, awarded national park status in 1921, and Mammoth Cave, Kentucky, authorized five years later, were two early examples of his own concession that not every national park could be another Yellowstone.[22] At least Mammoth Cave, like Wind Cave, was a subterranean wonder; in contrast, the Hot Springs Reservation was clearly a resort. Even Mammoth Cave drew objections from the National Parks Association, which pointed to the absence of a study. The Park Service was instead playing "national politics," charged Robert Sterling Yard. "A graver situation cannot be imagined," he concluded, "at a time when a number of southern states are clamoring for National Parks to bring them the tourist business which the fame of the title is supposed to guarantee."[23]

As a purist, Yard would still have Americans go west to visit the national parks. As a government official, on the other hand, Mather could not be insensitive to the needs of the East, regardless of its topographical shortcomings. Concessions to monumentalism could still be made by supporting areas with some semblance of dramatic uplift. In 1919, Acadia National Park, embracing the rugged seacoast of Mount Desert Island, Maine, offered a first example. The park's highest point is Cadillac Mountain, but 1,530 feet above sea level. Yet the standard description of Mount Desert Island as simply "beautiful," the naturalist Freeman Tilden would later write, "utterly fails to do justice to this rock-built natural fortress which thrusts forward into the Atlantic and challenges its power." Where else, Tilden asked, "can you find anything in our country to match these mountains that come down to the ocean, . . . altogether such a sweep of rugged coastline as has no parallel from Florida to the Canadian provinces?" Even Robert Sterling Yard, having dismissed so many other parks as unworthy, defined Acadia in 1923 as "our standard bearer for National Park making in the East." Although conceding that its area covered just 27 square miles, "nevertheless," he agreed, "it includes National Park essentials in full measure."[24]

To reemphasize, that "essential" meant rugged scenery. Next in consideration came uniqueness. Acadia was unarguably one of a kind, the highest and most rugged portion of the Atlantic coast between Maine and Florida. In contrast, the Shenandoah national park project, authorized in 1926, did not win the same endorsement. Although far higher than Cadillac Mountain in Acadia, the Blue Ridge Mountains were not the highest of their type. Only "the impressive massing of lofty mountains," Yard argued, "still covered with primitive forest, in the Great Smoky Mountains between Tennessee and North Carolina," not "the much lesser Shenandoah location," met every existing national park standard of sublime scenery and "primitive quality." Recognizing Shenandoah as a national park, its value for outdoor recreation aside, would in effect condone "the fatal belief that different standards can be maintained in the same system without the destruction of all standards."[25]

Among preservationists as a whole, the growing importance of biological conservation steadily undermined Yard's rigidity. The National Park Service itself finally promoted additions to the system whose significance was distinctly historical or archaeological.[26] Following the retirement of Stephen Mather as director in January 1929, Horace M. Albright personally promoted the National Park Service as the appropriate custodian for all federal historical and archaeological sites. Chief among those areas were the great battlefields of the Civil War, established by Congress beginning in 1890 and placed under direction of the War Department.[27] To Albright's good fortune, he was able to meet personally in April 1933 with the new president, Franklin D. Roosevelt, who enthusiastically allowed Albright to present his case. Roosevelt's executive order of June 10, 1933, then more than doubled the size of the national park system with the transfer of 64 national monuments, military parks, battlefield sites, cemeteries, and memorials from the War Department, Forest Service, and District of Columbia to the National Park Service.[28]

Albright naturally hailed the executive order as an agency milestone, noting that the nation's historic as well as scenic heritage was finally under the direction of a single government agency.[29] Robert Sterling Yard and his supporters were instead incensed, objecting that the transfers only finalized the demeaning of national park standards. "Self-seeking localities," wrote Ovid Butler, editor of *American Forests*, "whose past attempts to obtain national parks in their own interests have been stopped by public opinion, are unquestionably awake to the confused situation and the opportunities it offers for political park making."[30]

As Albright later confessed, he had in fact been influenced by bureaucratic politics. The survival of the National Park Service, not the issue of park standards, had been uppermost on his mind in 1933. "The order of June 10," he wrote, elaborating on this point, "effectively made the Park Service a very strong agency with such a distinctive and independent field of service as to end its possible eligibility for merger or consolidation with another bureau." That "bureau," he maintained, was none other than the U.S. Forest Service, the Park Service's perennial nemesis since Gifford Pinchot. "His associates had opposed the creation of the National Park Service in 1915 and 1916," Albright recalled the history, "and there was rumor current in 1933 that Mr. Pinchot sought to use his influence with President Franklin D. Roosevelt to effect such a transfer." Albright had simply beaten his opponents at getting to the president. Having gained exclusive control over the nation's historical, archaeological, and geological heritage, the Park Service would forever remain independent.[31]

Pinchot's successor, Henry S. Graves, had further given the Park Service good reason to be alarmed. While claiming in public to support the National Park Service, he repeatedly qualified his endorsement by insisting that the new agency, like the Forest Service, should be placed in the Department of Agriculture. Worse for preservation, the Park Service should have no jurisdiction whatsoever over timbered lands, not even forests within the parks.[32]

In this vein, the debate about national park standards had proved troubling to the Park Service by playing into the hands of its critics. In February 1927, Henry Graves, now dean of forestry at Yale University, again wrote menacingly about "the problem of the National Parks." The "problem," he remarked, "arose when with the extension of the system the original standards were departed from when areas of mediocre character were incorporated in the Park system." His specific objection remained—the inclusion within national parks of commercial stands of timber, not simply geological wonders of "special," "unusual," or "exceptional" interest. "There is," he wrote, underscoring his bias for worthless lands, "the serious problem of including in their boundaries natural resources of great economic value." He then added the standard subterfuge that removing resources was also best for the national parks. "The presence of extensive natural resources in the Parks will constitute a standing menace to the system," he warned. "Economic pressure will force the restriction of the boundaries, . . . or will jeopardize the very existence of the Parks."[33] "If I am right," Graves added, "it will be the character of the *natural features only* [emphasis added] that should determine the location of National Parks, and there should not be an effort to develop a chain of National Parks primarily to secure a distribution of them in all sections of the country or in the majority of the states." National Parks, after all, were "designed to preserve certain extraordinary features of national as distinguished from local interest, regardless of where they may be located."[34]

Unlike Robert Sterling Yard, who ostensibly accepted Graves's assessment, Horace Albright recognized the forester's appeal for park standards as the self-serving logic of the Forest Service. In the long run, Albright further realized, by restricting the national parks to world-class, monumental scenery, only the West would have parks within convenient access of its residents. The problem with that limitation was its obvious failure to enhance either public or political support for the national park system. However much Robert Sterling Yard and his associates decried the thought, outdoor recreation was not a by-product of the national park experience. All Americans did not, in John C. Merriam's words, seek out the national parks to "worship" nature. The appropriate forms of recreation were, of course, still open to debate. The point was that the American political system, with its emphasis on equity, spelled inevitable changes for the national park idea once other regions of the country objected to their lack of parks.

Outside the West, population growth alone made the call for parks inevitable. By 1920, the population of the country had surpassed 100 mil-

lion, nearly three and a half times the 30 million when Yellowstone became the first national park in 1872. As revealing, half the population in
1920 lived in cities and towns with 2,500 or more residents, up from only
one in four Americans living in urban areas in 1870.[35]

At its first meeting in Washington, D.C., in May 1924, the National
Conference on Outdoor Recreation formally recognized the trend. The
importance of the conference was further revealed in the 128 organizations providing delegates. The influence of the National Parks Association and its executive secretary, Robert Sterling Yard, surfaced in the
summary of resolutions. As distinct from local, state, and city parks, national parks "should represent features of national importance as distinguished from sectional or local significance." Nevertheless, the conferees
remained convinced that something in every part of the country qualified, recommending for immediate study the White Mountains in New
Hampshire, the Appalachian highlands, and the headwaters of the Mississippi River.[36]

Although the conference dissolved in 1929 because of a lack of funding, its recommendations advanced under other venues. Notably, in
1936, Congress and the president approved the Park, Parkway, and
Recreational Area Study Act, authorizing the Park Service to plan and coordinate all federal activities in outdoor recreation. The Park Service responded in 1941 with the publication of *A Study of the Park and
Recreation Problem in the United States*, which, among other contributions, contained an extensive inventory of recreation sites throughout the
country.[37]

After World War II, the determination of other federal agencies to
protect their interests effectively undermined the report. Meanwhile, the
surge in visitation was to provide an important catalyst for expanding the
national parks. No less influential, the rising concern about biological resources also tipped the scales of preservation farther eastward. Preservationists, gradually referred to as "environmentalists," annually viewed
with alarm the loss of accessible fields, woodlands, and marshes on the
urban fringe. Most state and local governments protested a lack of money
to protect those lands on their own. Only the federal government, preservationists concluded, had both the tax base and the expertise to tackle
what the nation now termed "urban sprawl."

Cape Cod, Massachusetts, as the second national seashore, set the all-
important precedent in 1961 for the expansion of nontraditional parks.
The first national seashore had been Cape Hatteras, North Carolina, authorized in 1937. However, no federal funds could be used to purchase

the land. As in the Everglades, Congress expected North Carolina, in co-operation with private individuals, to actually buy the park. Only then might the Park Service accept and administer it.[38] Although Congress occasionally authorized small appropriations, the basic purchase of eastern parks was left to others. At Cape Cod, Congress recognized, literally for the first time, that areas found worthy for authorization as parks should also be purchased with federal funds.

In the West, parks were still easily established by a simple transfer of public lands. Cape Cod National Seashore had to be fashioned from lands both previously owned and largely occupied. Homes, businesses, and cottages dotted the cape; six separate towns lay within or adjacent to the park project. Considering the number of people involved, condemning those lands outright was hardly a viable option. For the National Park Service, Cape Cod foretold a new era of learning to accommodate the reality of people actually living inside a park.[39]

Still the deeper problem raised by Cape Cod was entirely philosophical. Simply, for what reasons did it qualify as a national park, or, conceding that it would be called a seashore, why should the Park Service still be the manager? In the Everglades, where similar questions had arisen in the 1930s, its unquestionable uniqueness had saved the project. Even its detractors had to admit that the Everglades was the nation's only subtropical wilderness. Cape Hatteras and Cape Cod were hardly one-of-a-kind national parks. Little about either could be called pristine, and now Cape Cod was to be carved from a mixture of lands and properties already claimed for development.

As with Everglades National Park, a redefinition of the term "significance" proved the key in winning passage for Cape Cod National Seashore. Its rarity lay not in pristine lands but rather in its status as a threatened landscape. In that vein, Senator Alan Bible of Nevada, as chairman of the Senate Subcommittee on the Public Lands, asked his colleagues to consider the bill authorizing the park as a measure "of tremendous importance." During "the last 15 years," he noted, "there has been a great impetus to buy seashore property for commercial and private uses. Extensive and costly developments now line mile after mile of seashore which before World War II was uninhabited." As a result, more Americans, especially in the most populated regions of the country, were being denied unrestricted access to coastal beaches.[40]

Indeed, the bill was "unique," Bible remarked, "in that it is the first attempt to develop a unit of the national park system in an area which is highly urbanized, by comparison with other areas of the country in which substantial acreage has been set aside for national park purposes." Cape Cod would truly be a park for all Americans, one-third of whom lived "within a day's drive of the area." "Cape Cod as a national seashore," Senator Leverett Saltonstall of Massachusetts agreed, would be "dedicated to the spiritual replenishment of American families increasingly locked in by urbanization and commercialization who seek the refreshing beauty and natural grandeur of the clean, open spaces." The uniqueness of Cape Cod lay in suspending development at a point where people and the landscape might coexist. "Favorable action by Congress on this proposal," Saltonstall concluded, addressing precedent, "would give encouragement to other efforts to preserve our rapidly vanishing natural shoreline in such areas as Padre Island, Texas, the Oregon Dunes, and Point Reyes, California."[41]

Authorized August 7, 1961, Cape Cod National Seashore was indeed the precedent for eight additional seashores over the next 15 years. In another important series of nontraditional parks, Congress further recognized the desirability of protecting the shorelines of the Great Lakes. The first of four national lakeshores—Pictured Rocks, Michigan, along the southeastern edge of Lake Superior—received authorization on October 15, 1966.[42] Close behind came Indiana Dunes, where in fact the movement for the preservation of the Great Lakes had originated a half century before. As early as 1916, Stephen T. Mather had suggested that the "monumental" grandeur of the great dunes between Chicago, Illinois, and Gary, Indiana, warranted their possible inclusion in a dunelands national park. Simultaneously, the pioneer ecologists John Merle Coulter and Henry Chandler Cowles drew attention to the Indiana Dunes as a heartland of biological uniqueness, one worthy of protection exclusive of its scenic qualities. In 1927, a state park of approximately 2,000 acres realized those early hopes that urban encroachment might be contained. Itself acknowledging that greater need, on November 5, 1966, Congress authorized roughly 6,500 acres of windswept sand, prairie, woodlands, and marsh as the Indiana Dunes National Lakeshore.[43]

A related concern for landscape offered an opportunity to preserve America's wild and scenic rivers. Like seashores and lakeshores, the linear nature of a riverfront park was ideal for an urban setting. For the cost of several hundred yards of territory on either side of the streambed, river enthusiasts could enjoy boating, swimming, or walking beside the waterway without being reminded that civilization lay close at hand.

In rural areas, both wild and scenic rivers added incentive for the protection of the neighboring landscape. As the first, Ozark National Scenic

Riverways, Missouri, authorized in 1964, inspired the conviction that America's rural character deserved the same attention as threatened wilderness.[44] Approved in 1968, the Wild and Scenic Rivers Act formally established a national system through the designation of eight additional sites.[45] Park Service management was initially limited to the Ozark National Scenic Riverways and the St. Croix National Scenic Riverway in Wisconsin and Minnesota. Both the U.S. Forest Service and Bureau of Land Management successfully defended their right to administer their affected waterways.[46] In the future, when principally private lands were acquired, such as along the St. Croix River, those parks would customarily fall to the Park Service for maintenance and protection.

Overcoming their lack of monumental significance, national seashores, lakeshores, and rivers were justified for their rarity as unblemished landscapes. All spoke to the issue of encroachment from commercial, industrial, and residential development. Most of America's great rivers had been dammed; most of its ocean beaches and lakeshores forever altered by roads, breakwaters, and vacation homes. Outside of existing parks, the conclusion seemed reasonable that few of the nation's free-flowing rivers or unmarred shorelines would survive into the twenty-first century.

A similar justification for federal intervention was applied to the open space surrounding the nation's cities, including New York, Cleveland, Atlanta, San Francisco, and Los Angeles. Opponents restated that urban recreation areas, like other nontraditional parks, would strain Park Service budgets, diluting the agency's effectiveness in managing its wilderness preserves.[47] Established simultaneously on October 27, 1972, Gateway National Recreation Area, on the outskirts of New York City, and its West Coast counterpart, Golden Gate in San Francisco, proved that those objections could be overcome.[48] As previously authorized, national recreation areas had been confined almost exclusively to large reservoirs in the West and South.[49] Accordingly, each exacerbated the problem of affluent Americans winning exclusive access to distant parks. With the establishment of Gateway and Golden Gate national recreation areas, the National Park Service had further been asked to bring the national parks within a bus or subway ride of the nation's poor.

Regardless, such an expanding mission inevitably renewed the complaint that national park standards had been diluted. Already geologically deficient, most of the new parks also suffered the absence of biological resources of pristine quality. Itself the model for biological management, Everglades National Park proved the difficulty of preserving anything constrained by boundaries. At least Everglades National Park was a block of land. In contrast, most seashores, lakeshores, and scenic rivers lacked a biological core. Practically all such units came pockmarked with residential and industrial developments. The question then remained: should areas lacking the geological uniqueness, territorial integrity, and natural qualities of their predecessors be national parks in the first place?

Funding was also an obstacle. Hamstrung perennially by limited budgets, the National Park Service obviously could not meet the purchasing requirements of so much private land. A first proposal to address the problem was the Land and Water Conservation Fund Act of 1964. Entrance and user fees at federal recreation sites, coupled with the sale of surplus federal properties and a federal tax on motor fuel, were to be applied to purchasing parks. A later amendment added revenues from the sale of oil and gas leases on the continental shelf.[50]

By the late 1960s, however, the limitations of the fund were apparent in the spiraling pace of park expansion. Despite the expectation that hundreds of millions of dollars would be raised, the fund could not keep up. Where the best lands were largely private, the moment purchasing fell behind, speculators drove up prices. The fund's companion emphasis on recreation, as distinct from limiting purchases to just natural parks, further compromised the success of the largest and most ambitious environmental projects.[51]

The lack of funding only confirmed the common charge that most of these new parks drained the system. In each case, preservationists felt obligated to justify that their park somehow met the standards of the past. The result was a tendency to inflate both the range and the quality of the natural features present. The strategy was not deliberately dishonest; the problem was rather that preservationists, having discovered the importance of habitat, still worked in the shadow of their initial crusade.

Every insistence that the national park system should encompass general landscapes therefore relied on a biological perspective. Crucial was the ability to show that these latest parks contained a multiplicity of biological resources, ideally commingling in combinations found nowhere else in the United States. Thus, Stewart Udall, as secretary of the interior, testified in 1961 before Congress that the proposed Cape Cod National Seashore contained "not only the most extensive natural seashore area in New England but also one of the finest on the North American coast." Acknowledging the standards of the western parks, Udall assured Congress that the Cape Cod region also possessed evidence of "continental glaciation," "erosion," and "deposition," all providing "important opportunities for geologic study." Still, the biota of the park was unquestionably its greatest natural resource. "The plants and wildlife that mingle on Cape Cod in unusual variety give the area outstanding biological significance," he remarked. It was simply a matter of considering the seashore in its totality rather than strictly as a scenic resource. "From the highland on Griffin Island," he stated, noting that some uplift was also present, "one can get magnificent views of scenic upland and marsh typical of the cape." Yet beyond scenery, scientists had observed "four general types" of "glacial kettle hole ponds," each with "a distinct association of plant and animal life." Morris Island further contained not only "a rare white cedar bog and a stand of beech forest, but also, . . . one of the most important bird resting and feeding grounds, acre for acre, in New England—and one of the two or three most important such habitats on the entire Atlantic seaboard."[52]

Following Udall, every nontraditional park typically grew into a "biological crossroads." In 1963, for example, Leonard Hall, as director of the Ozark National Rivers Association, argued before the House Subcommittee on Public Lands that the proposed national river in Missouri possessed "one of the richest floras of any area of its size on this continent. We have Kansas plants there. We have Michigan plants. We have plants from the South and others which have developed there." James Carver Jr., assistant interior secretary, likewise endorsed the proposed Indiana Dunes National Lakeshore on the basis of its "outstanding" flora. Carver's objective, like Hall's, was again to demonstrate both the diversity and the commingling of the species present in the Indiana Dunes. "Following the slow retreat of the Wisconsin ice," he wrote, briefly tracing the impact of the Ice Age, "the plants which are now characteristic of the northern forests moved through the dunes area northward." Where soil, moisture, and temperatures were favorable, "isolated colonies of northern species held on." For example, "moderating breezes" off Lake Michigan allowed both "jack pine and white pine . . . to hang on south of their normal range." In low swamps and bogs, more northern plants lay "cloistered within the larger world of central forest and prairie species. Tamarack, buckthorn, leather leaf, checkerberry, orchids, and other unusual plants characterize these special environments," he added. Elsewhere, the botanical mosaic included plants of the "central forests and there are occurrences of flora of both the Prairie Peninsula and the Atlantic Coastal Plain species." "The result," he concluded, "is a natural scientific and scenic asset so diverse that it is difficult to equal anywhere in this country."[53]

Even the national recreation areas were similarly obligated to present some outstanding feature. In 1972, Interior Secretary Rogers C. B. Morton thus noted that the proposed Gateway National Recreation Area in New York City "would contain ten miles of ocean beach and natural and historic features of great significance." Granted, portions of the Jamaica Bay Unit, with "14,000 acres of land and water," had been previously developed. "Despite the inroads of civilization," Morton still argued, "Jamaica Bay remains an ecological treasure." Twenty-nine species of waterfowl and 70 of wading, shore, and marsh birds still used the area for nesting, feeding, and refuge. In a similar vein, Representative John F. Seiberling of Ohio defined the proposed Cuyahoga River National Recreation Area between Cleveland and Akron as "a pastoral wonder, a quiet haven away from the nearby bustling cities." Yet beyond its potential for outdoor recreation, the region had great value as a "unique meeting ground for plant life." A single 100-acre tract in the valley, Seiberling elaborated, had been found to contain "over 400 species of plants, including some usually found only in the far West, some only in the deep South, and some only at higher altitudes or northern latitudes." Surely, Cuyahoga Valley should be recognized as a park "for the people of the entire country, not just residents of the Cleveland-Akron metropolitan area."[54]

The presence of an unusual human history comprised the final element in justifying modern parks. Like appealing to a region's biological uniqueness, most historical arguments consisted of an inventory, again, lest the history appear too weak. Several pioneer cabins were obviously better than one—the same for old farmhouses and Indian burial sites. Few such inventories, as a result, dispelled the notion that urban parks, whatever their ecological or historical assets, were not in fact still meant for recreation.[55]

The alternative, preservationists conceded, would forever mean fewer parks. By the 1970s, few supported the viewpoint of Robert Sterling Yard, an opinion a half century old, that parks other than primeval wilderness were either pointless or inappropriate. Only affluent Americans might visit wilderness parks. Thus, Senator Alan Cranston of California spoke on behalf of his disadvantaged constituency, noting that "only a relatively small number of Americans have the opportunity to enjoy the wide range of natural wonders [the national park system] protects and preserves. Those fortunate enough to visit distant units of the National Park System," he declared, "are most likely white, educated, relatively well-off economically, young, and suburban. More than 90 percent of the National Park visitors in 1968 were white." America now had "a responsibility to 'bring the parks to the people,' especially to the residents of the inner-city who have had virtually no opportunity to enjoy the marvelous and varied recreation benefits of our national parks."[56]

It remained for Phillip Burton, a crusading representative to Congress from San Francisco, to orchestrate the grand finale to nearly two decades of park making involving nontraditional sites. As chairman of the House Subcommittee on National Parks and Insular Affairs, Burton proved instrumental in winning passage of the National Parks and Recreation Act of 1978. In essence, the bill combined under one piece of legislation a host of national park projects of special concern to Congress, among them increased appropriations and acquisition ceilings for existing parks, boundary changes, wilderness designations, and final authorization for new parks, historic sites, and wild and scenic rivers. Benchmark additions to the national park system included authorization of the Santa Monica Mountains National Recreation Area near Los Angeles and the New River Gorge National River in West Virginia. All told, the bill added 15 units to the national park system, appropriated $725 million over five years to renovate recreational facilities in urban areas, established eight new wild and scenic rivers, and designated 17 additional rivers for study and possible inclusion in the wild and scenic rivers system.[57]

The bill further established a system of national historic trails, designating four—the Oregon Trail, Mormon Pioneer Trail, Lewis and Clark Trail, and Iditarod Trail (Alaska)—as initial components. Similarly, Congress added the Continental Divide Trail to the national system of scenic trails already in existence, this to span the length of the Rocky Mountains between the Canadian border in Montana and the Mexican border in New Mexico.[58] With few exceptions, in other words, the new parks remained basically linear sites, slices of landscape rather than major blocks of territory whose management might conflict with neighboring development.

However, seen in terms of the number of areas affected, the legislation was both impressive and unprecedented. Higher development ceilings were authorized for no fewer than 34 existing units of the national park system; similarly, 39 units received boundary adjustments ranging from a few acres to several thousand acres of land.[59] Even the bill's supporters, as a result, occasionally agreed with critics that the measure might be termed the "parks barrel bill." Those critics had simply been outvoted in Congress, where more than 200 congressional districts would somehow share in the final financial package.[60]

If less mercenary in their reasoning, most preservationists themselves hailed rather than questioned the National Parks and Recreation Act. By 1978, the deeper issue was apparent: every year, a rise to 2 million acres in the loss of land to highways, airports, shopping centers, and subdivisions. Their scenic limitations aside, properties protected under the act secured an urban future in which open space mattered close to home. Perhaps Robert Sterling Yard had been correct. Parks with any other emphasis would in fact dilute the financial base and international fame of the original parks. Now given the threat to landscape and wilderness, preservationists simply thought it advisable to take the risk. Ignoring the doubts of history, promoting open space as the equivalent of wilderness finally seemed the best chance for saving both.

Pursuing ecological values, preservationists hoped that new national parks in Alaska would recognize more than rugged terrain. Established in 1917, Mount McKinley National Park, shown here, reminded preservationists of the topography park opponents most preferred. *Courtesy of the National Park Service, William S. Keller photograph*

CHAPTER 12

Decision in Alaska

If you think that Alaska is a long way to go for a national park, so was Yellowstone in 1872. Now Yellowstone is irreplaceable. So is Alaska and so are its unspoiled wildlands and magnificent wildlife.

—ALASKA COALITION BROCHURE, 1977

Our decisions on the designation of Alaska lands for conservation will shape the Nation's future as surely as our decisions on questions of energy, taxes, or the national budget. . . . In making that determination, we are confronting probably for the last time an opportunity which we have missed so many times before as our Nation's civilization has spread from coast to coast and border to border.

—JOHN F. SEIBERLING, 1977

Alaska is more than an environmental treasure, it is a resource storehouse.

—DON YOUNG, 1977

BORN of romanticism and cultural nationalism, the first great national parks of the United States were clearly the result of nineteenth-century perceptions of the American landscape. Outside the continental United States, only Alaska offered preservationists of the twentieth century a final opportunity to have national parks in keeping with the principles of biological management. In preservationists' own words, Alaska was "our last chance to do it right," to design national parks around entire watersheds, animal migration routes, and similar ecological rather than political boundaries.[1] "This will require the largest possible blocks of land to be set aside as national-interest lands," wrote Peggy

Wayburn, arguing the case for expansive parks on behalf of the Sierra Club. "This alone can prevent the loss of perhaps the greatest remaining wildlife, wilderness, and scenic resources on earth."[2]

Even the largest national parks in the lower 48 states, among them Yellowstone, Yosemite, and the Everglades, were but pieces of far larger biological wholes. Alaska, in contrast, offered the best of both the monumental and the biological in nature. Scenically, its mountains, glaciers, and volcanic areas were unsurpassed on the North American continent. In short, preservationists need not contradict their own traditions in their quest for Alaskan parks. As important, Alaska's immensity and near complete ownership by the federal government made the realization of biological parks no less attainable. With the public still its principal owner, Alaska heartened preservationists with the prospect that finally no compromises need be made.

Such optimism was quickly dispelled. As previously in the West, the opposition proved no less organized and demanding in reaffirming its right to exploit the public domain. For industrialists, Alaska's importance lay beyond its heralded role as the last great refuge for plants and animals. Rather, the nation's last major repository of timber, minerals, oil, natural gas, freshwater, and hydroelectric power seemed to be at stake. "I think we are all acutely aware," noted John H. LaGrange, representing the Kennecott Copper Corporation, "that our Nation and, indeed the world, is passing from an era of surplus to an era of shortage in many mineral and energy commodities." If there were to be new national parks in Alaska, it followed that they should again be restricted to monumental topography, areas rich in scenery but poor from the standpoint of natural resources. "National park and critical habitat withdrawals should not contain more than 15 million acres," LaGrange argued. National parks would otherwise conflict with the nation's pressing need to find more oil and, in the meantime, to exploit its vast deposits of coal and other minerals. Alaska had all those resources in abundance. Unfortunately, alone between 40 and 80 percent of its richest copper deposits were located where preservationists wished to have national parks.[3]

For preservationists, the opposition of resource interests to the establishment of national parks—as typified by LaGrange's remarks—was nothing new. The problem in Alaska was rather that the resource issue frequently overlapped the question of Native American rights. Unlike the continental United States, where Indians had been forced onto reservations generally before the parks themselves had been established, Alaska was still largely inhabited by groups of native peoples. In Alaska, any designation of national parks could not be divorced from the issue of civil rights. Drawing the boundaries of each new park demanded simultaneous respect for native traditions, cultures, and means of subsistence—customs deeply intertwined with national park lands. "If we are to err," argued Elvis J. Stahr, president of the National Audubon Society, "let us not err on the side of destroying a truly unique culture."[4]

It was as if the national park idea had come back full circle to 1832 and George Catlin's plea for "A *nation's Park,* containing man and beast, in all the wild and freshness of their nature's beauty!" On the plains of South Dakota, the artist had called for precisely the kind of sensitivity that planning for parks in Alaska now demanded.[5] Native Americans would obviously wish to continue using their ancestral hunting grounds. Although Catlin's perspective had been tinged with romanticism, Alaska was indeed the final opportunity not only to establish national parks with expansive natural environments but also to have parks that did not—as Catlin himself would have opposed—drive out or exclude native cultures in the process.

With the establishment of Yellowstone National Park in 1872, Catlin's revolutionary point of view was rejected. By preservation was meant the protection of scenery rather than the historical relationships between landscapes and people. Not until the 1960s was the policy of protecting natural features exclusive of natural processes widely criticized for national parks. Biologists at last acknowledged the role of Indians in changing park landscapes through the use of fire. Alaska proved again that native peoples throughout North America had long influenced the biological composition of the continent.

It followed that Native Americans were themselves "part of nature," a key link in the chain of natural processes biologists hoped to reintroduce to park environments. At least in Alaska, preservationists conceded, the chain had not been broken. "Indeed," argued Anthony Wayne Smith, president of the National Parks and Conservation Association, "the practice of subsistence hunting, as understood by the Native cultures, can well be looked upon as part of *a natural ecosystem* which has sustained itself in Alaska for something like 10,000 years and which has proved itself compatible with the stability and diversity of both wildlife and human population" (emphasis added). The historical opposition of the National Parks and Conservation Association to hunting, Smith said, elaborating on his point, dealt "only with sports hunting, and if the distinction is kept quite clear along the lines of the pending legislation, no violence can be done to established traditions of national park management."[6]

The naïveté in such assumptions was that native cultures, much like park environments, could be maintained at a fixed approximation of some earlier and more ideal appearance. Catlin's romanticism might not be dead, but neither were the technological forces inevitably bringing change to native cultures. Preservationists could only hope that in honoring the civil rights of the natives, they in turn would not overwhelm the parks. "No conservation group of which I am aware," remarked Louis S. Clapper, representing the National Wildlife Federation, "would deny a Native the right to take whatever fish and wildlife he needs for his own family's welfare." That said, so-called subsistence hunting was often "a much abused practice," a "subterfuge" for "the recreational practices" of "employed and 'modernized' natives."[7]

Clapper's comments were compromised by the National Wildlife Federation's own defense of sport hunting among its members. Yet even the most ardent proponents of subsistence hunting could not dismiss the influence of modern weapons and motor vehicles. Ideally, Alaskan natives would resist those temptations and continue hunting in moderation. It was just as likely, however, that the marketplace would corrupt the practice, eroding the national parks from within.

The resource at stake was wilderness—remote, pristine, and teeming with wild animals. Before World War II, the natives of Alaska had hardly made a dent in either its wildness or its wildlife. Modern firearms and the introduction of airplanes rapidly shrank the boundaries of the Alaskan wilderness.[8] Preservationists in the 1970s still legitimately compared Alaska to Yellowstone 100 years before. Much as Yellowstone had been America's frontier in the nineteenth century, so Alaska was its frontier in the twentieth. The striking difference was the end of the public domain. Alaska would be America's last wilderness, at least with respect to wilderness on earth. "What we save now is all we will ever save," declared another popular slogan of the period.[9] Especially in the forty-ninth state, no statement seemed to be a more appropriate—or compelling—call to action.

The wilderness movement, as distinct from the campaign for national parks, won its most important victory on September 3, 1964, when President Lyndon B. Johnson signed the Wilderness Act into law. Over much of the preceding decade, wilderness enthusiasts had argued the need for roadless areas, whether in the national parks or in the national forests. The bill immediately focused on the national forests, identifying 9 million acres as protected wilderness. Although allowed more time for study, the National Park Service was also to recommend to Congress which of its holdings should be managed in a wild and undeveloped state.[10]

For a variety of reasons, the study and establishment of wilderness areas in the national parks moved slowly. The largest parks were already wilderness, at least in the public mind. Preservationists themselves were far more concerned about the public lands controlled by the U.S. Forest Service, the U.S. Fish and Wildlife Service, and the Bureau of Land Management. In contrast to the Park Service, those were the agencies historically renowned for their determination to open the public domain to multiple use. For the moment, the Wilderness Act itself excluded the Bureau of Land Management. If the National Park Service could be accused of overdevelopment, the areas developed were still quasi wilderness. Preservationists feared most for the future of public lands outside the agency, where scenery still was vulnerable.[11]

Even the Park Service, however, resented the threat that wilderness posed to the agency's bureaucratic autonomy. In managing wilderness, the Wilderness Act of 1964 superseded the Park Service's Organic Act of August 25, 1916. A prohibition against motorized access, not to mention roads, clearly restricted the Park Service's discretion in managing its backcountry zones. Formal wilderness designations would also forfeit using those areas for visitor overflows. In a final defense of tradition, park concessionaires also strongly opposed the idea of wilderness as antithetical to the expansion of visitor services.[12]

Not until October 23, 1970, six years after the passage of the Wilderness Act, did Congress designate portions of Petrified Forest National Park, Arizona, and Craters of the Moon National Monument, Idaho, as wilderness. In October 1972, portions of Lassen Volcanic National Park and Lava Beds National Monument, both in California, also received wilderness status. Truly major additions to wilderness in national parks awaited congressional approval in 1976. On September 22 and October 1, the House and Senate, respectively, approved legislation designating wilderness in portions of 13 existing parks and monuments—Badlands National Monument, Bandelier National Monument, Black Canyon of the Gunnison National Monument, Chiricahua National Monument, Great Sand Dunes National Monument, Haleakala National Park, Isle Royale National Park, Joshua Tree National Monument, Mesa Verde National Park, Pinnacles National Monument, Point Reyes National Seashore, Saguaro National Monument, and Shenandoah National Park. President Gerald R. Ford then approved the legislation on October 20, 1976.[13]

The Omnibus Park Bill of 1978, also known as the National Park and Recreation Act, further designated 1,854,424 acres of wilderness in eight additional units of the national park system—Buffalo National River,

Carlsbad Caverns National Park, Everglades National Park, Guadalupe Mountains National Park, Gulf Islands National Seashore, Hawaii Volcanoes National Park, Organ Pipe Cactus National Monument, and Theodore Roosevelt National Park. Among those parks, the bill declared another 119,581 acres as "potential" wilderness, bringing the grand total to nearly 2 million acres. Congressional supporters of the legislation, eager to draw attention to their achievement, quickly noted that the figure exceeded "the total acreage of all lands previously designated as wilderness in the National Park System."[14]

In most of the largest parks, however, among them Yellowstone, Yosemite, Glacier, and Grand Canyon, wilderness had not been approved. Those proposals remained controversial. Although the Park Service endorsed wilderness in public, many ranking officials privately expressed their doubts. Declared wilderness precluded the opportunity for expanding visitor services. As existing facilities filled, wilderness would mean restricting visitors to already developed portions of the parks. For an agency used to measuring its success by greater visitation, such restrictions seemed politically unwise. Besides, even where the Park Service favored wilderness, concessionaires generally remained opposed.[15]

With each frustrated attempt to establish wilderness in the continental United States, preservationists had looked on Alaska with even greater favor. If national parks in particular were to be managed as biological sanctuaries, wilderness loomed as the crucial prerequisite. The management of fragmented pieces of habitat could accomplish only so much. That definition still best explained the national park system outside Alaska. The alternative to constantly manipulating plants and animals was to provide the parks with sufficient territory in the first place.

For a land with equivalent economic promise, the history of Alaska as an American possession began on a distinct note of irony. Ratification of the treaty in 1867 authorizing the purchase of Alaska from Russia passed the Senate over strong objections. Opponents denounced the territory as nothing but a worthless repository of snow, rocks, and icebergs. Popular images of Alaska as the frozen north held well into the twentieth century. Although an occasional gold rush and travelogue challenged those perceptions, it was not until World War II, following completion of the Alaska Military Highway through Canada, that Americans finally began to appreciate the true richness and diversity of what was to become the forty-ninth state.[16]

Statehood, which came in 1959, did not end the opinion among many Alaskans that they had still been treated as second-class citizens.

Living in a territory of roughly 365 million acres, Alaskans believed that federal officials had been far too conservative in allowing the exploitation of its natural resources. In either case, residents were eager to get on with development, not only logging, fishing, and trapping—the state's traditional economy—but also the opening of oil and gas fields and the extraction of precious metals. The legislation granting statehood allowed Alaska to select approximately 104 million acres of federal lands; similarly, the federal government relinquished title to tens of millions of acres of submerged lands along the continental shelf. The unforeseen obstacle was straight out of history—Native Americans also claimed the public domain. In 1966, as Aleuts, Eskimos, and Indian tribes prepared to take their grievances to court, Interior Secretary Stewart Udall froze the state selections pending congressional consideration of the case.[17]

The ensuing stalemate ended in October 1971 with passage of the Native Claims Settlement Act. All told, 40 million acres and $1 billion were awarded the native groups. The point is that during the five-year interval, preservationists themselves became acutely aware of the opportunity the bill presented to voice their case. Although most sympathized with the demands of the natives for a secure land base, native selections, in addition to the selections already guaranteed the state, conceivably might undercut the establishment of wilderness parks even before the best areas had been identified. Alaska, to reemphasize, represented the final opportunity to establish national parks, wilderness areas, and wildlife refuges of irrefutable ecological significance and integrity. Without simultaneously addressing that need, preservationists argued, all hope of coordinating the development of Alaska with the protection of wilderness would be lost for good.[18]

With the environmental movement, like the civil rights movement, at the peak of its influence, Congress was in little mood to ignore the concerns of preservationists any more than the grievances of Native Americans. Accordingly, section 17 (d)(2) of the Alaska Native Claims Settlement Act further recognized the desirability of designating up to 80 million acres of the public domain in Alaska as national parks, national forests, wildlife refuges, and wild and scenic rivers. The secretary of the interior would have nine months to make those withdrawals and, by December 19, 1973, was to make his final recommendations to Congress concerning which of those lands should in fact be protected in perpetuity.[19]

Yet another opportunity for preservation was provided by section 17 (d)(1) of the Alaska Native Claims Settlement Act. Under its provisions, the secretary of the interior was allowed 90 days after enactment to select additional "public interest" lands for withdrawal. Although the provision apparently did not affect state selections or native selections close to villages, it did take precedence over all other state and native selections elsewhere on the unreserved public domain. In the confusion over that interpretation, however, the state of Alaska, in January 1972, proclaimed the selection of its entire remaining allotment of 77 million acres under the Statehood Act of 1958.[20]

By September of 1972, Interior Secretary Rogers C. B. Morton had withdrawn 79 million acres of the public domain under subsection (d)(2) of the Native Claims Settlement Act, in addition to 47 million acres under subsection (d)(1). The state of Alaska immediately protested that the withdrawals conflicted with many of its own selections and, as a result, filed suit in federal court to have Secretary Morton's disputed choices summarily revoked. In an out-of-court settlement, Alaska won concessions affecting some 14 million acres of the (d)(1) and (d)(2) withdrawals. As its part of the compromise, the state agreed to relinquish claims to 35 million of the 77 million acres it had selected in January.[21]

In the end, Secretary Morton's own final recommendations for parks, wilderness areas, and wildlife refuges pleased no one. The state of Alaska again filed suit; meanwhile, preservationists further protested his proposal to include over 18 million acres of the (d)(2) lands in national forests rather than wilderness. The objective of the (d)(2) designation, preservationists insisted, was land protection rather than development, even on a sustained-yield basis. Adding urgency to their concerns, Congress's established deadline for a resolution was December 18, 1978. Preservationists had but seven years to make their case, and already two of those years had slipped by without appreciable progress on the issues.[22]

As a first priority, preservationists recognized the need for a united front. The so-called Alaska Coalition, representing the National Audubon Society, Wilderness Society, Sierra Club, National Parks and Conservation Association, and Defenders of Wildlife, officially organized in 1971 during the debate about native claims. By January 1977, as Congress took up the final debate, that informal coalition had become a powerhouse. Under the circumstances, its members agreed, pooling their staffs and financial resources was the best approach to "the most important conservation issue of the century."[23]

The battle was finally joined on January 4, 1977, when Representative Morris Udall of Arizona introduced his bill, H.R. 39, to the 95th Congress. By early April, H.R. 39 was accompanied by a host of similar bills; numerous cosponsors had also attached their names to Udall's original. To sift through the proposals and assess public opinion, the House Committee on Interior and Insular Affairs, with Udall as chairman, approved the creation of a special Subcommittee on General Oversight and Alaska Lands. On April 21 and 22, Representative John F. Seiberling of Ohio, chairman of the subcommittee and a cosponsor of H.R. 39, convened the first public hearings on the Alaska lands issue in Washington, D.C.[24]

Five months and 16 volumes of testimony later, the Subcommittee on General Oversight and Alaska Lands concluded its work. In addition to its hearings in Washington, D.C., the committee had taken testimony in Chicago, Atlanta, Denver, and Seattle. Afterward, the committee moved to Alaska, where it heard the residents of 16 separate towns and cities, including Sitka, Juneau, Ketchikan, Anchorage, and Fairbanks.[25] Never before in national park history had any issue sparked so much public interest and discussion. Even in noted controversies of the recent past, such as the campaign to preserve the redwood groves of the California coast, there had been no comparable insistence that the general public, as well as the renowned adversaries, should be heard by a major congressional panel.

By itself, however, the sheer number of people who participated still had little effect on the opposing arguments. To be sure, although many people took the opportunity to testify, their positions were both traditional and predictable. The hearings, in other words, contained no real surprises. Again, those with a personal stake in the economy of Alaska pushed for smaller parks and greater development of the state's natural resources. Likewise, those who looked to Alaska as the last American wilderness wanted desperately to have larger parks of indisputable ecological significance.

It followed that support for wilderness parks in Alaska was greatest outside the state. Indeed, much as people living on the Alaskan frontier universally opposed the parks, so citizens in the lower 48 states overwhelmingly endorsed H.R. 39.[26] Not surprisingly, supporters and opponents of the legislation lined up similarly in the halls of Congress. Senators Ted Stevens and Mike Gravel of Alaska, in addition to the state's lone member of the House, Don Young, strongly opposed H.R. 39 in its original form. After all, their constituents believed that they had the most to lose if the bill were enacted. In contrast, Representatives Udall and Seiberling, among the 72 other sponsors of H.R. 39, spoke out for preservation with the obvious assurance that their own political futures would not be determined in Alaska.

As if to rationalize their immunity from the Alaskan electorate, the sponsors of H.R. 39 noted repeatedly that their bill was of national rather than local importance. "Obviously, this is a national issue, not just a regional or sectional one," said Representative Seiberling, setting the environmental agenda for the hearings and congressional debates. "The lands involved are public lands, the property of all the American people." Granted, the residents of Alaska deserved the protection of their interests. "But they must also be harmonized with the interests of the other 220 million Americans," he maintained. "As Members of the Congress of the United States, we must act in the interests of all the people."[27]

By definition, that meant preservation as well as economic development, Representative Udall agreed. "If you go to Europe," he noted, "you don't participate in making new national parks. In the Lower 48 States, we are rounding out the system." Only Alaska still offered Americans "a chance to display some vision" and "some foresight" in national park planning. Since the establishment of Yellowstone in 1872, approximately 25 million acres of land had been set aside as national parks. For the first time in history, Americans had the opportunity in Alaska to double or perhaps even triple that figure. "So I am looking forward to participating in this endeavor," Udall concluded. "I don't know of any major piece of legislation that will have more far-reaching consequences in the country in the future than this one will."[28]

Predictably, opponents of H.R. 39 took precisely the opposite stance, that of stressing Alaska's significance for the United States as a storehouse of natural resources. "D-2 lands are obviously critical to the State of Alaska," remarked Representative Don Young, admitting the biases of the Alaska delegation, "but, more importantly, they are critical to the Nation as a whole." Congress must consider what the United States stood to lose if preservation of the state got "out of hand." Alaskan oil alone would soon "comprise 20 percent of our domestic oil supply," Young noted; "another natural treasure" of the state was "critical metals." The national parks and wilderness areas as proposed were simply too large to allow adequate exploitation of those resources. "The key issue is how much needs to be set aside to provide appropriate protection without going overboard," he said, invoking a century of park history. "I trust that the subcommittee will act to set aside those unique areas which everyone agrees need preserving but place other lands in less restrictive management systems where diversified uses will be permitted."[29]

Supporting Young, Senator Mike Gravel of Alaska proposed the protection of no more than 25 million acres of land in national parks, wilderness areas, wildlife refuges, and wild and scenic rivers. "Let me just say," he remarked, justifying his figure, "there is a body of land in Alaska where there is no question, no dispute, that should be preserved in the four conservation Systems." The figure of 25 million acres, as opposed to the more than 100 million acres requested by preservationists, was the more "balanced," "moderate," and "reasonable position." Gravel did not need to admit the obvious; the 25 million acres he had in mind clearly contained nothing of economic value to the state. Only with that assurance did he freely concede that preservation "is the highest and best use of the land."[30]

On lands where natural resources might in fact be abundant, Gravel further proposed a delay in decision making pending the formation of a joint federal–state commission, "a legislative body, or, as the press has characterized it, in Alaska, a beefed-up zoning commission for the entire State." The object of the commission "would be the development of policy" with respect to all state and federal lands outside the parks. Deposits of oil, gas, and coal, for example, had "not even been scratched." A federal–state commission to protect access to those resources would ensure flexibility in future management decisions. "It would be a terrible tragedy in our human existence," he concluded, again revealing his bias for development, "to foreclose the possibility of making an intelligent adjudication when the time came to do it."[31]

Gravel's Senate colleague, Ted Stevens, as well as Governor Jay Hammond and Representative Don Young, equally endorsed the commission. Meeting with Alaska residents the previous fall, the four had basically agreed to accept a limit of 25 million acres for parks, refuges, and wilderness areas. The key objection to those lands among preservationists was their undeniable focus on monumental topography at the expense of territory with greater biological significance. In that respect, national park history again played into the hands of Senator Stevens and the Alaska delegation. "I view the process that we are in now of trying to determine which of our lands have national significance in the true sense that the Grand Canyon and Yosemite and Yellowstone and the other areas that have been made national parks had," he stated, quoting precedent. As that precedent implied, the preservation of similar natural wonders, areas both rugged and devoid of natural resources, certainly would arouse little opposition among residents of the forty-ninth state. Their concern remained— a decision by Congress "which may well impede future generations of Alaskans from having the ability to utilize the land bank that Congress wisely gave us as an economic floor for the future of our State."[32]

Arrigetch Peaks, Gates of the Arctic National Park and Preserve (*top*), and Ruth Glacier, Denali National Park and Preserve (*bottom*), thrilled preservationists for their beauty while assuring Alaska that its economy had not been threatened. *Top: Courtesy of the National Park Service. Bottom: Courtesy of the National Park Service, Norman Herkenham photograph*

Its legislative complexity aside, the Alaska lands issue was basically another manifestation of the traditional struggle between preservation and use. Only the object of the debate had changed. Just as resource interests worked to thwart a comprehensive protection bill, so preservationists campaigned diligently to effect a parks and wilderness package of both biological substance and legislative permanence. Advocates of greater development and fewer parks invariably relied on the Alaska delegation to espouse their views in Congress. Similarly, preservation groups, rallying under the banner of the Alaska Coalition, looked to Representatives Udall and Seiberling, among other concerned members of Congress, for their own leadership on Capitol Hill.

Much to their advantage, by 1977 and the introduction of H.R. 39, preservationists knew a great deal about Alaska, certainly more than their predecessors a century earlier had known about the West. By the late 1960s, the major conservation magazines were sending writers throughout the state, informing readers and memberships of the areas most worthy of protection. The discovery of oil at Prudhoe Bay in 1968, coupled with the completion of the controversial Trans-Alaska Pipeline in 1977, lent further credence to preservationists' claims that Alaska, much like the lower 48 states, was in danger of being subdivided into economic spheres of influence. In all probability, the search for oil and construction of the pipeline would destroy the Alaska tundra and decimate the great herds of migrating caribou. Proposals to dam the largest rivers in Alaska and then shunt their water southward through Canada into the thirsty American West also struck preservationists as the epitome of utilitarian arrogance and callousness toward the natural world.[33]

Preservationists asked that none of that history be repeated. "In Alaska we have the opportunity to learn from our past mistakes," remarked Edgar Wayburn, chairman of the Sierra Club's Alaska Task Force. "We have given away the Redwoods of California, the Big Thicket in Texas, and the Big Cypress Swamp in Florida, just to name a few, and we have had to buy them back at exorbitant prices." Large parks in Alaska would still be "free as far as the exchange of cash is concerned."[34] David Brower, now president of Friends of the Earth, likewise emphasized the unique opportunity offered by federal ownership of so much of the state. "Alaska, as a late maturing child in the society's scheme of things," he said, "is still richly endowed, as youth always is, and we should think carefully before we let qualities that only Alaska still possesses be made as ordinary, or even as repugnant, as too many other places have been driven to become." As examples, he was "mind-ful" of California, "my native State, not to mention Texas." The unre-strained development of Alaska would only turn an extraordinary environment into another common one, undermining all hope of sus-taining "Alaska's appeal, productivity, and creativity for centuries."[35]

Although such statements buoyed the movement's resolve, the en-tirety of 1977 passed without any action on H.R. 39, with the exception of the public hearings conducted by the House Subcommittee on Gen-eral Oversight and Alaska Lands. As preservationists feared, the delay worked to the advantage of their opponents, especially Representative Don Young, who succeeded in adding a whopping 85 amendments to the original bill once the subcommittee reconvened in 1978 to draft the final version. Not until April 7, 1978, was the Interior Committee pre-pared to report to Congress as a whole. By then, only eight months re-mained until December 18, 1978, the deadline established for resolving the Alaska lands issue under the Native Claims Settlement Act. If not re-solved by that date, technically all the lands withdrawn from entry would revert to the unreserved public domain, there to be subject again to both state and native selections.[36]

Under the circumstances, preservationists were indeed fortunate to have the support of the new administration. Granted, President Jimmy Carter and his secretary of the interior, Cecil Andrus, proposed a ceiling of only 92 million acres of parks and wilderness, that as distinct from the 115 million acres sought by the Alaska Coalition and originally specified in H.R. 39. Still, with Senators Mike Gravel and Ted Stevens threatening delay in the Senate and in light of their claim that 25 million acres was sufficient, the endorsement of the White House was crucial. On May 17, 1978, the House of Representatives began debate on H.R. 39, approving the bill two days later by a vote of 277 to 31. Preservationists were jubi-lant not only because the House proposed to protect more than 120 mil-lion acres as national parks, wildlife refuges, and wild and scenic rivers but also because passage of the bill had been won by such a stunning, lopsided margin.[37]

The celebration proved to be premature. In the Senate, Mike Gravel successfully thwarted the bill throughout the summer and into fall. Al-though his delaying tactics grew unpopular, even with Senator Stevens, they nonetheless had the desired effect of preventing final action on H.R. 39 in 1978.[38]

In other words, the December 18 deadline would not be met. Preser-vationists were again extremely fortunate to have the support of the

Carter administration. Even as the 95th Congress prepared to disband, President Carter and Interior Secretary Andrus considered their options. On October 11, Andrus informed the public in a signed editorial, "If Congress is unable to act, President Carter and I will."[39] On November 16, Andrus made good the promise, sealing 110 million acres under authority of the Fish and Wildlife Act of 1956 and the Federal Land Management Act of 1976. Each allowed the secretary of the interior broad discretion in the protection of wildlife and wilderness areas on the public domain. Finally, on December 1, further invoking the Antiquities Act of 1906, President Carter doubled the protection on 56 million of the 110 million acres by proclaiming them national monuments. Although Andrus's total withdrawals would eventually expire, by law within three years, anything Carter had proclaimed a national monument would be permanent until Congress finally agreed to budge.[40]

Carter in fact hoped to force a decision from Congress. Like President Franklin D. Roosevelt in 1943, upholding Jackson Hole National Monument, Carter believed with Andrus that the protection of Alaska transcended local prejudices and special interests. A few legislators manipulating the political process should never forestall the nation's will. Regardless, 1979 was another year of postponement. The political season indeed began as another of frustration and disappointment, with still more amendments threatening the integrity of the legislation passed by the House of Representatives the previous year. In the second House vote, taken May 16, 1979, preservationists held off the opposition by a tally of 268 to 157, only to lose ground again in the Senate. After considerably weakening the House's management safeguards, the Senate version of the bill actually granted protection to 26 million fewer acres.[41]

Ironically, the fate of parks in Alaska was sealed in 1980 by compromise and intimidation. On August 19, 1980, the Senate finally passed a considerably less protective Alaska lands bill. In the past, preservationists would have worked for another postponement, carrying the bill into the coming year. However, on November 4, Ronald Reagan defeated Jimmy Carter's bid for reelection as president of the United States. Unlike Carter, Reagan was openly hostile to environmentalists, and Alaska certainly would be no different. Fearing that he might kill the Alaska lands legislation entirely, preservationists both within and outside the Congress saw no choice but to make their peace with the Senate version of H.R. 39. "Political realities dictate that we act promptly on the Senate-passed bill," Representative Morris Udall said, issuing a personal warning. "We must accept the fact that Reagan is here for four years."[42] On November

12, the House agreed to concur with the Senate, and on December 2, 1980, President Jimmy Carter signed the compromise package into law. Although a disappointment for preservationists, the legislation did, in Udall's words, "accomplish 85–90 percent of the things the House wanted."[43] The penalty of delaying until the Reagan administration took office might well have meant a total loss.

Considering that prospect, preservationists understandably celebrated what they had won in Alaska as a milestone of American conservation. "Never has so much been done on conservation for future generations with one stroke of the pen," wrote Charles Clusen, chairman of the Alaska Coalition. The acreages protected were indeed impressive, a total of more than 100 million acres, or 28 percent of the state, including 43.6 million acres of new national parks, 53.8 million acres of new wildlife refuges, and 1.2 million acres for the national wild and scenic rivers system. Of those lands, 56.7 million acres were to receive further protection as wilderness, subject only to accessibility by foot, horseback, raft, or canoe. "Not since the days of Theodore Roosevelt's large public land withdrawals," Clusen concluded, "have we seen such boldness, dynamism, and leadership for the protection of our land heritage. The Alaska "victory' also shows that the American people believe in a conservation ethic and support environmental protection more than at any previous time in history."[44]

Only on reflection did preservationists concede that perhaps the battle for Alaska had just begun. In park after park, critical wildlife habitat had been either fragmented to accommodate resource extraction or excluded entirely. As a concession to copper mining interests, for example, approximately 1 million acres in Gates of the Arctic National Park were denied wilderness protection. Similarly, state selections threatened grizzly bear habitat, salmon streams, and caribou breeding grounds bordering Mount McKinley National Park. The Alaska Lands Act renamed the park Denali and expanded it by a whopping 3.7 million acres. The point again was that size by itself was no guarantee that wildlife, especially migrating populations such as caribou, could be sustained without further extending protection to their lowland breeding grounds.[45]

Other preservationists sensed a troublesome precedent in using the term "preserve" to describe wilderness that in the past outright would have been labeled "national parks" or "national monuments." The management principles of parks and monuments were defined by precedent, but what was a "national preserve"? An unsettling answer could be gleaned from the legislative histories of Big Thicket National Preserve, Texas, and Big Cypress National Freshwater Preserve in Florida. In each instance, the secretary of the interior possessed wide discretion to allow mining, oil drilling, grazing, hunting, trapping, and other extractive uses both within and adjacent to the parks.[46] On the roughly 20 million acres designated as "preserves" in Alaska, the same discretion largely prevailed. The management of a preserve, in other words, could be swayed by local concerns. Ideally, the preserves in Alaska would act as buffers for the most sensitive wilderness areas. In fact, however, often the preserves needed greater protection. If the landscape had economic potential, it was likely on the periphery of a park—in the preserve. Although the national parks of Alaska were significantly larger, the history of the lower 48 states had also repeated itself. Outside Alaska's mountainous terrain, especially in the rich forests of the southeastern panhandle, entrenched commercial interests, both native and nonnative, successfully resisted long-range efforts to effect preservation over use.

In defense of that choice, Alaskans argued that all pioneer Americans had enjoyed the freedom to exploit the land as they saw fit. Now that the rest of the country had been developed, the lower 48 states had no right dictating to Alaska that it alone must make commercial sacrifices. Besides, Alaskans loved the frontier way of life and themselves wished to preserve the land base and wilderness supporting it.[47]

Preservationists asked again whether Alaskans could in fact resist unwanted change. "Big, outside corporations are looking all over the world for resources," noted Representative John F. Seiberling, warning Alaskans to support H.R. 39. "And with the kind of machinery and airplanes and the kind of money that people have in the outside, they are going to come in here and each one is going to take a cut of the salami and when he gets through, there will not be much left for the people of Alaska unless we set aside certain areas."[48] Persistent opposition to H.R. 39 as an affront to personal freedom led to the allowance of subsistence hunting. Gradually, however, even preservationists supporting the practice came to recognize the potential for its abuse, especially since the snowmobile, airplane, and high-powered rifle had replaced the dogsled, spear, and hunting knife as tools of the chase.[49]

Alaska, it seemed, eventually would change much as the rest of America had changed. Writing on behalf of the Alaska Coalition, an anonymous preservationist was among those who conceded the point. "For a land which is expected to give so much material wealth to the nation, we only ask in return that the nation seek to protect certain lands and wildlife so that this priceless natural heritage will survive for future generations."[50] Margaret Murie, the noted author and longtime Alaskan adventurer, personally rose to eloquence. "My prayer is that Alaska will not lose the heart-nourishing friendliness of her youth, . . . that her great wild places will remain great, and wild, and free, where wolf and caribou, wolverine and grizzly bear, and all the Arctic blossoms may live in the delicate balance which supported them long before impetuous man appeared in the north. This is the great gift Alaska can give to the harassed world."[51]

On a scale unique in American history, the Alaska National Interest Lands Conservation Act of 1980 realized this fondest of preservationists' dreams. But could the dream be sustained?[52] Indeed, even in the vastness of Alaska, one fundamental accomplishment still eluded the movement— effecting its dreams in perpetuity, in physical reality as well as in transitory laws.

July 25, 1983 / $1.50

Newsweek

Battle Over The Wilderness

Uncle Sam owns one-third of the country, and Americans are fighting over every acre.

Interior Secretary James Watt at Glacier National Park

Appointed Secretary of the Interior in 1981, James Watt poses in Glacier National Park for the cover of *Newsweek* magazine. A religious fundamentalist, Watt epitomized the growing backlash against the national parks from conservative interests in the West. *Author's collection*

CHAPTER 13

Into the Twenty-First Century: Encirclement and Uncertainty

The results of this study indicate that no parks of the System are immune to external and internal threats, and that these threats are causing significant and demonstrable damage.

— STATE OF THE PARKS REPORT, 1980

I will err on the side of public use versus preservation.

— JAMES WATT, 1981

TRUE to precedent, the jubilation of preservationists following their achievements in Alaska proved to be short lived. On January 20, 1981, Ronald Reagan took the oath as president, promising a platform of fiscal conservatism and government restraint. In keeping with those principles, his appointee as secretary of the interior, James Watt, openly admitted that he disapproved of expanding the national parks. Nor should the existing parks be managed principally as biological sanctuaries. In Watt's view, the problem was rather the number of visitors turned away by poor facilities. Any additional funding for parks should be invested in their deteriorating physical plant. To be sure, that wilderness should be protected for its own sake was the last thing on either the president or the secretary's agenda.[1]

By itself, Watt's preference for development over protection was enough to arouse preservationists nationwide. It was nonetheless his outspoken disdain for everything environmental that assured him a place in history. Within months, historians had likened Watt to Albert B. Fall, the nation's last infamous interior secretary. In 1922, Fall had attempted

Numerous political cartoons parodied James Watt's conviction that God intended the earth to be exploited. In this example, David Horsey of the *Seattle Post-Intelligencer* depicts Watt as the serpent in the Garden of Eden. *Courtesy of David Horsey and the* Seattle Post-Intelligencer

giving away the nation's petroleum reserve at Teapot Dome, Wyoming, to the Sinclair Oil Company.[2] Watt's chilling indifference to the fate of the public lands now suggested the same potential for the national parks. Certainly, not in decades had their detractors seemed in greater control of the federal bureaucracy.[3]

Watt as shrewdly made it appear that he at least supported preservation. The key in delaying parks was to uphold tradition—focusing on the glory of worthless lands. But for a sharp rise in external threats to the national parks, his strategy might have worked. Led by air pollution and land development, even the "crown jewels" were clearly in jeopardy. Delaying land acquisitions, among other policies of retrenchment, merely ensured the escalation of those threats.[4] Particularly in the Southwest, pollution experts noted the deterioration of visibility over Grand Canyon, Bryce, Zion, Canyonlands, and neighboring national monuments. At stake was the sense of a limitless horizon that those areas had long evoked. On a clear day, visitors to one park might see mesas and mountain ranges in another park more than 100 miles away. Nowhere was that sensation more pronounced and, accordingly, more in danger of being lost to air pollution. By 1980, scientists reported that "pristine" air over the desert was down to one day out of every three, largely because of the spread of smelters and coal-fired power plants feeding the region's spiraling urbanization.[5]

The conclusions seemed inescapable. In its own report to the Congress, *State of the Parks—1980*, the National Park Service agreed that external threats to the national parks posed the gravest danger to their future. "The 63 National Park natural areas greater than 30,000 acres in size reported an average number of threats nearly double that of the Service-wide norm," the document opened soberly. As premier examples, the reported identified "Yellowstone, Yosemite, Great Smoky Mountains, Everglades, and Glacier." Noting how each had changed, "these great parks were at one time pristine areas surrounded and protected by vast wilderness regions," the report continued. "Today, with their surrounding buffer zones gradually disappearing, many of these parks are experiencing significant and widespread adverse effects associated with external encroachment."[6]

Preservationists were immediately alarmed by a proposal to lease portions of the Targhee National Forest, bordering Yellowstone, for a large geothermal power project. In a direct line, the core of the project would be located only 15 miles west of the Upper Geyser Basin and Old Faithful Geyser. At issue was whether the geothermal systems underlying the park and forest were related. If so, using those in the forest might deplete those in the park. Released in 1980, an environmental impact statement prepared by the U.S. Forest Service admitted that Yellowstone's geysers might in fact be lost. "The exact boundaries of the Yellowstone geothermal reservoir(s) are uncertain," the Forest Service concluded. "Thus, it is difficult to say how much of a connection—if any—there is between the possible geothermal resource . . . and thermal areas inside the park, or if any adverse effects might result."[7]

The reminder about parks central to a broader ecosystem was the insecurity of their outlying parts. Yellowstone National Park itself depended on "greater Yellowstone," that territory including the millions of acres of national forests, wilderness areas, and private property surrounding it. As a concept, "greater Yellowstone" was especially relevant to wildlife populations. If the grizzly bear in particular were to survive in the continental United States, regulations governing the lands adjacent to Yellowstone and Glacier national parks would have to accommodate the bears' need to wander freely.[8]

Symbolically, the administration of James Watt suggested the pitfalls for making that case anywhere in the West. Respect for grizzly bears and other potentially dangerous animals called for a level of tolerance generally absent among their human neighbors. The American public itself remained ambivalent. To be sure, when Watt himself was forced to resign in 1983, a prejudicial joke reflecting on disabled Americans and minorities, not his disdain for the environment, was the actual basis for his fall from grace. William Clark, as Watt's successor, simply pursued the same agenda with greater diplomacy. Certainly, with respect to national park policy, little at the Department of the Interior was to change.[9]

Preservationists knowledgeable about American culture still viewed materialism as the silent threat. Finally, no national park, whatever its size or makeup, could accommodate every public whim. Population alone had diminished the luxury of decisions based on individual preferences. The country setting aside Yellowstone in 1872 had held just 30 million people. As late as 1915, barely 50,000 people visited Yellowstone, still the nation's most popular park. The country carrying the national parks into the twenty-first century had 10 times the population. Visitation to Yellowstone, both domestic and foreign, finally exceeded 3 million people every year. Increasingly besieged by such numbers, the parks were constantly importuned, providing digression, but hardly sanctuary, from the complexities of the modern world.[10]

Even in the most expansive parks, biologists doubted that wilderness would survive. Offering an especially dramatic example, during the summer and fall of 1988, Yellowstone was swept by a series of unprecedented wildfires. Although their intensities widely varied, virtually all of the park was affected by drifting smoke and ash, and approximately one-third of its forests burned. In late August and early September, flames literally raced across the park, forcing firefighters into heroic "last stands" around Yellowstone's historic buildings. Other contingents battled to protect popular overlooks surrounding the primary scenic wonders. By October, the costs of firefighting had surpassed $100 million to maintain an assault force still numbering several thousand people, including rangers, military personnel, and members of the National Guard.[11]

Even then, not until a few inches of snow had blanketed the park were the last of the flames snuffed out. Taking final stock of the landscape, many in the media pronounced it hopelessly burned. However, as in the giant sequoias, the biological value of fire had its defenders. For them, the talk of tragedy had been grossly overstated. Granted, the fires had been serious and their intensity unforeseen. Too late, the Park Service had moved to suppress backcountry burns worsened by lengthening weeks of heat and drought. Even so, Yellowstone would recover. Over time, fire was less an enemy of the landscape than human abuse and manipulation.[12]

As the latest pivotal event, the Yellowstone fires refocused the debate regarding when to intervene in the management of natural environments. For a majority of Americans, Yellowstone's obvious appeal was still as the nation's distant, fabled "wonderland." Much relieved, visitors applauded that its geyser basins, canyon, and waterfalls had survived the flames intact. Still the proper measure of wilderness, scientists maintained, was the integrity of the natural environment. In Yellowstone, the wolf had been exterminated and the grizzly bear long threatened with extinction. If the term "wilderness" were in fact to apply, all wild animals deserved a sanctuary.

Originally coupled with the biological sciences, that awareness governing national parks had also crept into history, where a new field, environmental history, inevitably began with preservation. Relevant books included *Yellowstone: A Wilderness Besieged* (1985), by the historian Richard A. Bartlett, and *Olympic Battleground: The Power Politics of Timber Preservation*, by a former park ranger, Carsten Lien.[13] Too often, development, these historians agreed, influenced what the National Park Service wished to protect. With specific reference to the Yellowstone fires, the historian Stephen J. Pyne further criticized the agency for masking a mistake as science. Yellowstone had in fact survived only because the park was big enough to absorb a 750,000-acre holocaust. Even if fire were a natural occurrence, allowing those fires to get out of control in the first place had only made things worse.[14]

However, within months of the fires, efforts to assess their long-term damage evinced a dwindling air of certainty. Over the winter and into spring, precipitation returned to normal. A minor percentage of park soils sterilized by the flames showed no signs of imminent recovery. Elsewhere, in 1989 Yellowstone came alive in a sea of grass and wildflowers. It was, even skeptics admitted, one of the most glorious springs on record. Past the skeletons of blackened trees, long-forgotten vistas had reopened while, underfoot, millions of new seedlings were taking root. Granted, the forest would take decades to recover. Then again, if fire had historically thinned the forest, who was to say what "original" meant? Certainly, the density that many had thought "natural" before the fires had been deceptive in its own right. Absent human preference, Yellowstone's "recovery" biologically had in fact occurred. It was the same forest, just starter trees. Cleansed of the old trees that were no longer viable, a seedling forest was as original as one full grown.[15]

Thus did the drama of the Yellowstone fires play into the hands of the broader argument. Wherever the national parks had been carelessly altered, authenticity required that they be restored. Yellowstone was again asked to set an example through reintroduction of the wolf. After eliminating large predators from the national parks in the 1920s, the Park Service needed to make amends. In a move no less controversial than prescribing fire, the wolf returned in 1995. Biologists who were prepared for a difficult recovery were instead elated as the population rapidly grew and thrived. Only local opinion held steadfast to the assumption that predators killed indiscriminately. And undoubtedly, some livestock would be lost. While agreeing to compensate for those incursions, the Park Service asked Yellowstone's neighbors to see the larger point. The wolf could hardly know Yellowstone's boundaries and at times would hunt beyond them. Greater Yellowstone, not just the park, should feel privileged to set the example for how to make biological management work.[16]

Still hoping to further that mandate across the country, preservationists also reviewed their maps. Obviously, the last substantive opportunity for biological parks was the desert Southwest. Fortuitously spurned by settlers a century earlier, much of southern California, Nevada, and Arizona also survived as public land. In California, the popularity of the Mojave Desert for long-distance motorcycle rallies sounded the alarm in the 1970s. Energized by the example in Alaska, citizen activists banded together to campaign for desert parks and wilderness. The coalition awaited a sympathetic majority in Congress, which was finally achieved in the elections of 1992. As passed in 1994, the California Desert Protection Act curbed off-road vehicles and greatly expanded preservation. Yellowstone itself suddenly lost its historical preeminence as the largest national park in the continental United States. Death Valley National Monument, expanded and renamed Death Valley National Park, now surpassed Yellowstone by more than a million acres.[17]

Of course, the unyielding perception of Death Valley as worthless land helped significantly in the effort. Similarly, the monumental outcroppings of Joshua Tree National Monument, simultaneously expanded and renamed a national park, suggested the absence of a habitable environment. Weeks earlier, Saguaro National Monument in southern Arizona as easily transitioned into a national park. Elsewhere, even in the desert, the rules of commerce still applied. Principally in California's East Mojave Desert, mining and grazing were still pursued. Hunting was also popular. Hence, its preservation, beginning with the weaker title national preserve, was appropriately delayed and qualified.[18] In a subse-

Preservationists working in the 1930s for the establishment of Olympic National Park, Washington, encountered stiff opposition from commercial loggers determined that the park boundary should hug the mountains. The loggers lost, and the Hoh River Valley, pictured here from High Divide, was included in the national park. Today, rich in lowland forests holding 35 billion board feet of timber, Olympic remains a true exception and a test case whether extractive interests can forever be contained. *Courtesy of the National Park Service, Jack Boucher photograph*

quent act of Congress, the Timbisha Shoshone, pleading subsistence, actually received title to several thousand acres in Death Valley as compensation for the tribe's ancestral claims.[19]

That all such claims remained daggers at the heart of the national parks was again dramatically proved in Yellowstone. In 1994, Noranda Minerals Inc., a Canadian conglomerate, asked final approval for a large gold and silver mine near Cooke City, Montana. The mine proper would be barely two miles outside Yellowstone's northeastern boundary. For obvious reasons, every prior conviction that the region should be added to Yellowstone National Park had summarily been dismissed, even though mining, first advanced in the 1880s, had suggested only a modest strike. Over the years, existing mines were occasionally reworked and other mountainsides freshly scarred, little of which, it was argued, had spilled over into the park. Technology finally overtook preservation with the invention of new extractive options. One technique, using cyanide as a leaching agent, coaxed as little as an ounce of gold from several tons of low-yield ore. Suddenly, what had once been accepted as a marginal deposit was hailed as a new bonanza. The problem was that the mounds of tailings and a reservoir of toxic wastes would loom over a watershed feeding directly into Yellowstone.[20]

If still outside the park, the so-called New World Mine was clearly part of Greater Yellowstone. No matter the precautions taken, what happened at the mine would affect the whole. Accordingly, even if the company were forced to retreat, it had positioned itself handsomely for compensation. In August 1996, President Bill Clinton announced an agreement with Noranda to abandon the New World Mine. On payment of $65 million and in exchange for other federal properties yet to be determined, Noranda pledged to relinquish its historical claims to the Yellowstone site.[21]

Recalling the situation in the nineteenth century, the nation's mining laws still trumped preservation. As ominous, replicating the custodianship of national monuments before 1933, new monuments were again retained by the agency originally in charge of the land. At 1.9 million acres, Grand Staircase-Escalante National Monument, Utah, set the precedent in 1996, remaining with the Bureau of Land Management. The possibility that extractive interests would pressure the bureau for access could hardly be ignored. Indeed, of the 21 national monuments proclaimed or expanded by President Clinton (1993–2001), only seven involved the Park Service, and three of those were historical sites.[22] Although presaged by the need to make compromises in Alaska, leading to passage of the Alaska National Interest Lands Conservation Act, the pattern in the lower 48 states proved troubling. In the view of preservationists, all monuments should still go to the Park Service rather than agencies internally committed to multiple use.

At least, allowing for precedent, the establishment of any monument advanced the likelihood that it would eventually become a national park. In time, the National Park Service should prevail. A less certain future seemed to await preservation itself. In 2007, scientists studying global warming in Glacier National Park, Montana, conceded that its namesake formations had nearly disappeared. "The last official count—in 1998— pegged the number of glaciers here at 27, down from 150 a century ago," reported USA Today. "Grinnell Glacier has lost 14 acres—9% of its total coverage—just in the past 24 months." By 2030, likely every glacier would be gone.[23] It followed that Everglades National Park would suffer from rising sea levels and over several centuries might be entirely lost.

However caused, global warming is changing the face of many national parks, notably Glacier in Montana. Although this photograph, taken in the 1940s, suggests nothing about the threat, in fact Glacier's namesakes were already shrinking. *Courtesy of the National Archives, Ansel Adams photograph*

Further inviting thoughts of Armageddon, American television reminded viewers that Yellowstone was a giant caldera whose next eruption might be imminent. If and when a catastrophe of that magnitude happened, the end of civilization need not wait for global warming.[24]

A more optimistic assessment began with the assurance that the national parks were an enduring achievement. Although the country had finally exhausted its geographical surprises, those magisterial landscapes still remained. One could only hope that the threats of the twenty-first century would not undo every past success. If so, the original convictions of American nationalism would obviously have to hold. The glory of the United States lay in territory consistently suggestive of opportunity. It was important that Americans, searching for their national horizon, find nothing to mar the view in between. In landscape, that horizon was the national parks. Certainly, if ever the American psyche survived losing the parks, the United States would be a very different country indeed.

Purchased by the Boticário Foundation for Nature Protection, the Salto Morato Nature Preserve, in the Atlantic rain forest of Paraná state, southern Brazil, symbolizes the adoption of national parks and equivalent reserves around the world. Reminiscent of the Florida Everglades, critical remnants of the Atlantic rain forest need intervention to survive, and again, owe much to private philanthropy for motivating the use of parks. *Courtesy of the Fundação O Boticário de Proteção à Natureza, José Luiz Martins Paiva photograph*

The Future of National Parks

Perhaps the most serious obstacle impeding the evolution of a land ethic is the fact that our educational and economic system is headed away from, rather than toward, an intense consciousness of land.

     —ALDO LEOPOLD, A *Sand County Almanac*, 1949

T HE point at which history is solicited for predications has always been a slippery slope. To date, the enduring consensus about the national parks is the perception they are unique. Land everywhere else remains an object. Even as the United States advanced preservation, land was principally valued for use and settlement. Well into the nation's history, little of the natural world was exempt from change. The prediction still to be gleaned from experience is that the national parks will always be subject to human whim.

As if to test that preservation is legitimate, a visible undercurrent of postmodern opinion suggests that the founders of parks had it wrong. Because Native Americans had no need for parks, for example, why should we? By demanding a line between civilization and wilderness, parks in fact deny the historical intimacy between people and the land. What Americans think they know as wilderness was once inhabited and widely used. As it was for the original inhabitants of North America, all thought of a boundary should be unimaginable. Insisting that only boundaries can protect the parks, the nation perpetuates the idea of exclusion. For that matter, in reviewing the history of civilization, the growth of cities and the development of agriculture are far more important examples of how people and the land interact.[1]

Advancing a similar faith in economics, others insist that market forces should prevail. The market rather than government is a better predictor of the need for public parks. Unfettered by government bureaucrats, private entrepreneurs would gladly establish and manage parks. The only requirement would be the chance to profit. Nor should environmentalists worry that the market would fail to clarify what areas should be saved. Parks such as Yellowstone, Yosemite, and Grand Canyon would obviously still head the list. Once Americans learned to accept market efficiencies, government could sell the parks to private enterprise.[2]

The point is that neither model, the market nor the garden, is a truthful test of history. No society has ever been so altruistic that its motives were always "right." Although nature has evolved in flux, the flux imposed by humans is entirely different. Despite the popular perception of Native Americans as ecologists, for example, their practices could just as easily be called good luck. The world in either case has drastically changed. Overcoming the spread of industry and the growth of population, only parks allow nature some measure of permanence. Without preservation that is legally as well as morally binding, the land would have no future. Certainly, as the first claimants to the floor of Yosemite Valley, James Mason Hutchings and James Lamon did not see beyond their lives. Only when the promise of restraint is backed by permanence does it elevate into a public good.

Government is that permanence. The best quote is still John Muir's. "Any fool can destroy trees. They cannot run away; and if they could, they would still be destroyed,—chased and hunted down as long as fun or a dollar could be got out of their bark hides, branching horns, or magnificent bole backbones." Left to the forces of nature, the trees of the Sierra had learned to adapt. Finally faced with the inroads of civilization, their survival was in doubt. "Through all the wonderful, eventful centuries since Christ's time—and long before that—God has cared for these trees, saved them from drought, disease, avalanches, and a thousand straining, leveling tempests and floods; but he cannot save them from fools,—only Uncle Sam can do that."[3]

Although emotionally he wished it otherwise, Muir had honestly read the history. Civilization is the problem parks solve. The point they clarify—the point of having them—is that civilization is here to stay. It makes no difference what might have happened had civilization not evolved. It did evolve—and today with a population of 7 billion people reaching into every corner of the earth. That every country is still exploiting wilderness disproves what might have been. No doubt, the establishment of parks is artificial when the greater landscape is ignored. The people directly affected by the loss of lands and opportunities also become casualties of the process. The point is that the world has lost the luxury of preserving nature as if 7 billion people did not exist. No highway, dam, or airport indulges individuals, and the enormity of those displacements the world accepts. Without reserving a similar claim for nature, little in nature would be secure.

Worldwide, the telling statistic is 102,102—the number of national parks, equivalent reserves, and "protected sites" last recognized by the United Nations in 2003.[4] Following America's lead, practically every country faced with the loss of landscape has embraced the principle of national parks. Despite significant variations in managing parks, notably the allowance of inhabited reserves, the protecting hand of government is still essential. It is only when government agrees that restraint is formal, again permanent, that preservation has expanded and endured.

Ultimately, the future demands what the country started. A first genuine commitment to the good of nature began with the invention of public parks. They may be as imperfect as they are exceptional, but they are all we will ever have. After restraint, only our humility can uphold their integrity, ensuring the timelessness of the national parks as the best idea that America—and the world—ever shared.

NOTES

PROLOGUE: PARADISE LOST

1. Before the availability of this volume, critical studies of the national parks began with Hans Huth, *Nature and the American: Three Centuries of Changing Attitudes* (Berkeley: University of California Press, 1957), and Roderick Nash, *Wilderness and the American Mind* (New Haven, CT: Yale University Press, 1967). However, as their titles imply, neither remains specific to the national parks. A pathbreaking article is Roderick Nash, "The American Invention of National Parks," *American Quarterly* 22 (Fall 1970): 726–35. See also Alfred Runte, "The National Park Idea: Origins and Paradox of the American Experience," *Journal of Forest History* (April 1977): 64–75. In large part because of its quotable title, one of the most cited articles is Wallace Stegner, "The Best Idea We Ever Had," *Wilderness* 46 (Spring 1983): 4–13. Although dated, the standard administrative history remains John Ise, *Our National Park Policy: A Critical History* (Baltimore: The Johns Hopkins Press, 1961). An important history of the national monuments as a precursor to national parks is Hal Rothman, *Preserving Different Pasts: The American National Monuments* (Urbana: University of Illinois Press, 1989). An illustrated history and companion to the public television series of the same title is Dayton Duncan and Ken Burns, *The National Parks: America's Best Idea* (New York: Knopf, 2009).

2. George B. Tobey, *A History of Landscape Architecture: The Relationship of People to Environment* (New York: American Elsevier, 1973), 25–52. Also relevant are Charles E. Doell and Gerald B. Fitzgerald, *A Brief History of Parks and Recreation in the United States* (Chicago: Athletic Institute, 1954), 12–15, and Norman T. Newton, *Design on the Land: The Development of Landscape Architecture* (Cambridge, MA: Harvard University Press, Belknap Press, 1971), 1–20.

3. A concise history of environmental change in the ancient world is J. Donald Hughes, *Ecology in Ancient Civilizations* (Albuquerque: University of New Mexico Press, 1975).

4. *Webster's New Collegiate Dictionary* (Springfield, MA: G. and C. Merriam Co., 1961), 611.

5. More detailed discussions of romanticism, deism, and primitivism may be found in Nash, *Wilderness and the American Mind*, 44–66, and Huth, *Nature and the American*, 1–53.

6. Doell and Fitzgerald, *A Brief History of Parks and Recreation in the United States*, 19; Newton, *Design on the Land*, 221–32; Frederick Law Olmsted, *Walks and Talks of an American Farmer in England* (New York: George P. Putnam, 1852), 81.

7. The definitive biography of Olmsted is Laura Wood Roper, *FLO: A Biography of Frederick Law Olmsted* (Baltimore: Johns Hopkins University Press, 1973). Also relevant is Elizabeth Stevenson, *Park Maker: A Life of Frederick Law Olmsted* (New York: Macmillan, 1977). Important studies of Olmsted's influence further include Witold Rybczynski, *A Clearing in the Distance: Frederick Law Olmsted and America in the Nineteenth Century* (New York: Scribner, 1999); Charles E. Beveridge and Paul Rocheleau, *Frederick Law Olmsted: Designing the American Landscape* (New York: Rizolli, 1996); David Schuyler, *The New Urban Landscape: The Redefinition of City Form in Nineteenth-Century America* (Baltimore: Johns Hopkins University Press, 1986); and Albert Fein, *Frederick Law Olmsted and the American Environmental Tradition* (New York: George Braziller, 1972).

8. John F. Sears, *Sacred Places: American Tourist Attractions in the Nineteenth Century* (New York: Oxford University Press, 1989), 99–116; Huth, *Nature and the American*, 66–67; Thomas Bender, "The 'Rural' Cemetery Movement: Urban Travail and the Appeal of Nature," *New England Quarterly* 47 (June 1974): 196–211.

9. Roper, *FLO*, 126–28; Newton, *Design on the Land*, 267–73; Doell and Fitzgerald, *A Brief History of Parks and Recreation in the United States*, 23–41.

10. There is no question that Central Park was also a real-estate enterprise, expected to enhance the value of neighboring properties. See Roy Rozenzweig and Elizabeth Blackmar, *The Park and the People: A History of Central Park* (Ithaca, NY: Cornell University Press, 1992). Also relevant are Sara Cedar Miller, *Central Park, an American Masterpiece: A Comprehensive History of the Nation's First Urban Park* (New York: Harry N. Abrams, 2003), and Morrison H. Heckscher, "Creating Central Park," *The Metropolitan Museum of Art Bulletin* 65 (Winter 2008): 1–75.

11. Roper, *FLO*, 339–435, passim.

12. The standard history of the public lands is Roy M. Robbins, *Our Landed Heritage: The Public Domain, 1776–1936* (Lincoln: University of Nebraska Press, 1962). See also Marion Clawson, *The Land System of the United States: An Introduction to the History and Practice of Land Use and Land Tenure* (Lincoln: University of Nebraska Press, 1968).

13. A critical history is Elizabeth McKinsey, *Niagara Falls: Icon of the American Sublime* (Cambridge, MA: Cambridge University Press, 1985). See also Jeremy Elwell Adamson et al., *Niagara: Two Centuries of Changing Attitudes, 1697–1901* (Washington, DC: Corcoran Gallery of Art, 1985).

14. As quoted from George Wilson Pierson, *Tocqueville in America*, abridged by Dudley C. Lunt from "Tocqueville and Beaumont in America" (New York: Doubleday and Co., 1959), 210; Charles M. Dow, ed., *Anthology and Bibliography of Niagara Falls*, 2 vols. (Albany, NY: J. B. Lyon Co., 1921), 2:1059.

15. Dow, *Anthology and Bibliography of Niagara Falls*, 2:1059–62.

16. Dow, *Anthology and Bibliography of Niagara Falls*, 2:1070–71.

17. Dow, *Anthology and Bibliography of Niagara Falls*, 2:1075–76.

CHAPTER 1: THE AMERICAN WEST

1. Thomas Jefferson, *Notes on the State of Virginia*, ed. William Peden (Chapel Hill: University of North Carolina Press, 1982), xi–xxv.

2. Jefferson, *Notes on the State of Virginia*, 19.

3. Jefferson, *Notes on the State of Virginia*, 25.

4. Jefferson's obvious dislike for these two great scholars is further noted by William Peden. See pp. 274–76 of Jefferson, *Notes on the State of Virginia*. A revered French naturalist, the Comte de Buffon (George-Lewis Leclerc) angered Jefferson with his theories of New World inferiority, as did the French historian the Abbé Raynal (Guillaume Thomas Francois Raynal) with his direct attacks on American arts and letters.

5. Jefferson, *Notes on the State of Virginia*, 64–65.

6. As quoted in Roderick Frazier Nash, *Wilderness and the American Mind*, 4th ed. (New Haven, CT: Yale University Press, 2001), 68.

7. Washington Irving, *Ten Selections from the Sketch-Book* (New York: American Book Company, 1892), 14–15.

8. The impact of the quote is discussed in Merle Curti, *The Growth of American Thought*, 3rd ed. (New York: Harper and Row, 1964), 237–38.

9. James Fenimore Cooper, "American and European Scenery Compared," chapter 3 of Washington Irving et al., *The Home Book of the Picturesque: Or, American Scenery, Art, and Literature* (New York: G. P. Putnam, 1852), 52, 61, 66, 69.

10. Susan Fenimore Cooper, "A Dissolving View," chapter 5 of Irving, *The Home Book of the Picturesque*, 81–82, 88–94.

11. Irving, *The Home Book of the Picturesque*, 52. Continuing his analysis, Cooper referred to the Atlantic coast, noting, "[it] is, with scarcely an exception, low, monotonous and tame. It wants Alpine rocks, bold promontories, visible heights inland, and all those other glorious accessories of the sort that render the coast of the Mediterranean the wonder of the world." Similarly, Washington Irving

bemoaned that the mountains of the East "might have given our country a name, and a poetical one, had not the all-controlling powers of common-place determined otherwise." Irving, *The Home Book of the Picturesque*, 54, 72. European writers also picked up the theme; see, e.g., Alexis de Tocqueville's impressions of the East in George Wilson Pierson, *Tocqueville in America*, abridged by Dudley C. Lunt from "Tocqueville and Beaumont in America" (New York: Doubleday and Co., 1959), 122, 178–79.

12. Still definitive is Barbara Novak, *Nature and Culture: American Landscape and Painting, 1825–1875* (New York: Oxford University Press, 1980), 3–134. For added interpretations, see James Thomas Flexner, *That Wilder Image* (New York: Bonanza Books, 1962).

13. As quoted in Roderick Frazier Nash, *American Environmentalism: Readings in Conservation History* (New York: McGraw-Hill, 1990), 36–39.

14. As quoted in Elizabeth McKinsey, *Niagara Falls: Icon of the American Sublime* (Cambridge, MA: Cambridge University Press, 1985), 244. Church's painting is meticulously reproduced in Jeremy Elwell Adamson et al., *Niagara: Two Centuries of Changing Attitudes, 1697–1901* (Washington, DC: Corcoran Gallery of Art, 1985), 12–13.

15. Quoted from *Special Report of New York State Survey on the Preservation of the Scenery of Niagara Falls, and Fourth Annual Report on the Triangulation of the State for the Year 1879* (Albany, NY: Charles Van Benthuysen and Sons, 1880).

16. Jefferson, *Notes on the State of Virginia*, 43–48. The standard history of American exploration remains William H. Goetzmann, *Exploration and Empire: The Explorer and the Scientist in the Winning of the American West* (New York: Alfred A. Knopf, 1966). On Jefferson's instructions to Meriwether Lewis, see pp. 4–6. A popular history of the Lewis and Clark expedition is Stephen E. Ambrose, *Undaunted Courage: Meriwether Lewis, Thomas Jefferson, and the Opening of the American West* (New York: Simon and Schuster, 1996).

17. Referring to the miners' invasion, the word is actually believed to mean "some among them are killers." See Alfred Runte, *Yosemite: The Embattled Wilderness* (Lincoln: University of Nebraska Press, 1990), 12, and Elizabeth Godfrey, *Yosemite Indians*, rev. James Synder and Craig Bates (Yosemite National Park, CA: Yosemite Natural History Association in cooperation with the National Park Service, 1977), 3–4, 35.

18. J. M. Hutchings, *Scenes of Wonder and Curiosity in California: A Tourist's Guide to the Yo-Semite Valley* (New York: A. Roman and Company, 1875), 161; William Henry Brewer, *Up and Down California in 1860–1864: The Journal of William H. Brewer*, ed. Francis P. Farquhar (New Haven, CT: Yale University Press, 1930), 404–5.

19. Horace Greeley, *An Overland Journey from New York to San Francisco in the Summer of 1859* (New York: C. M. Saxton, Barker and Co., 1860), 306–7.

20. Thomas Starr King, "A Vacation among the Sierras," *Boston Evening Transcript*, January 26, 1861, 1.

21. Greeley, *An Overland Journey from New York to San Francisco in the Summer of 1859*, 311–12.

22. Clarence King, *Mountaineering in the Sierra Nevada* (Boston: James R. Osgood and Co., 1872), 41–43.

23. Major studies of the artist include Gordon Hendricks, *Albert Bierstadt: Painter of the American West* (New York: Harry N. Abrams, 1974), and Nancy K. Anderson and Linda S. Ferber, *Albert Bierstadt: Art and Enterprise* (New York: Hudson Hills Press in association with the Brooklyn Museum, 1990). See also Patricia Trenton and Peter H. Hassrick, *The Rocky Mountains: A Vision for Artists in the Nineteenth Century* (Norman: University of Oklahoma Press in association with the Buffalo Bill Historical Center, 1983), 116–49; Flexner, *That Wilder Image*, 135–36, 293–302; and Novak, *Nature and Culture*, 24–27. Relevant articles include Gordon Hendricks, "The First Three Western Journeys of Albert Bierstadt," *The Art Bulletin* 46 (September 1964): 333–65; David W. Scott, "American Landscape: A Changing Frontier," *Living Wilderness* 33 (Winter 1969): 3–13; and William S. Talbot, "American Visions of Wilderness," *Living Wilderness* (Winter 1969): 14–25.

24. A contemporary account is Fitz Hugh Ludlow, "Seven Weeks in the Great Yo-Semite," *Atlantic Monthly* 13 (June 1864): 744–45.

25. Hendricks, *Albert Bierstadt*, 130–35, 154–65.

26. On Watkins, see Hans Huth, *Nature and the American: Three Centuries of Changing Attitudes* (Berkeley: University of California Press, 1957), 145, 149–51, and Brewer, *Up and Down California in 1860–1864*, 406, 413. An important catalog is Peter E. Palmquist, *Carleton E. Watkins: Photographer of the American West* (Albuquerque: University of New Mexico Press and Amon Carter Museum, 1983).

27. A brief analysis and reproduction of Catlin's lithograph appears in Adamson et al., *Niagara*, 38, 116.

28. George Catlin, *Illustrations of the Manners, Customs, and Conditions of the North American Indians*, 2 vols. (London: H. G. Bohn, 1851), 1:262.

29. Based on Catlin, recent scholarship has critically focused on national parks as a loss to the first Americans. See especially Mark David Spence, *Dispossessing the Wilderness: Indian Removal and the Making of the National Parks* (New York: Oxford University Press, 2000); Philip Burnham, *Indian Country, God's Country: Native Americans and the National Parks* (Washington, DC: Island Press, 2000); and Robert H. Keller and Michael F. Turek, *American Indians and National Parks* (Tucson: University of Arizona Press, 1999).

30. As quoted in Francis P. Farquhar, *History of the Sierra Nevada* (Berkeley: University of California Press in collaboration with the Sierra Club, 1965), 87.

31. Jefferson, *Notes on the State of Virginia*, 64; Farquhar, *History of the Sierra Nevada*, 87.

32. The best analysis of the discovery and naming of the big trees remains Farquhar, *History of the Sierra Nevada*, 83–91.

33. Farquhar, *History of the Sierra Nevada*, 84–85.

34. As quoted in Joseph H. Engbeck Jr., *The Enduring Giants* (Berkeley: University Extension, University of California, in cooperation with the California Department of Parks and Recreation, Save-the-Redwoods League, and the Calaveras Grove Association, 1973), 77.

35. For a more detailed account of these claims, see Runte, *Yosemite*, 22–27.

36. The complexities and inconsistencies of frontier land law are best followed in Roy M. Robbins, *Our Landed Heritage: The Public Domain, 1776–1936* (Lincoln: University of Nebraska Press, 1962).

37. Raymond to Conness, February 20, 1864, Yosemite—Legislation, file 979.447, Y-7, Yosemite National Park Research Library. This is a copy of the original in the National Archives, Records of the General Land Office, Miscellaneous Letters Received, G33572.

38. Olmsted's probable role in the legislation is best summarized in Laura Wood Roper, *FLO: A Biography of Frederick Law Olmsted* (Baltimore: Johns Hopkins University Press, 1973), 268.

39. Runte, *Yosemite*, 19. Other important accounts include Hans Huth, "Yosemite: The Story of an Idea," *Sierra Club Bulletin* 33 (March 1948): 63–76, and Holway R. Jones, *John Muir and the Sierra Club: The Battle for Yosemite* (San Francisco: Sierra Club, 1965), 28–29.

40. *Congressional Globe*, 38th Cong., 1st sess., May 17, 1864, 2300–2301; United States, *Statutes at Large* 13 (1864): 325.

41. Runte, *Yosemite*, 46; United States, *Statutes at Large* 13 (1864): 325.

42. *Congressional Globe*, 40th Cong., 2nd sess., June 3, 1868, 2816–17; U.S. Congress, Senate, Committee on Private Land Claims, S. *Rept. 185 to Accompany H.R. 1118*, 40th Cong., 2nd sess., July 23, 1868, 1–2. See also Runte, *Yosemite*, 23–26.

43. Frederick Law Olmsted, "The Yosemite Valley and the Mariposa Big Trees," ed. Laura Wood Roper, *Landscape Architecture* 43 (October 1952): 16–17. The public's failure to appreciate pastoral scenery was a perennial theme with Olmsted. See also "Governmental Preservation of Natural Scenery," March 8, 1890, printed circular, Library of Congress, Washington, DC, Olmsted Papers, box 32.

44. John Muir, "Flood-Storm in the Sierra," *Overland Monthly* 14 (June 1875): 496. Major biographies of John Muir include Linnie Marsh Wolfe, *Son of the Wilderness: The Life of John Muir* (New York: Alfred A. Knopf, 1945); Stephen Fox, *John Muir and His Legacy: The American Conservation Movement* (Boston: Little, Brown, 1981); Michael P. Cohen, *The Pathless Way: John Muir and American Wilderness* (Madison: University of Wisconsin Press, 1984); and Donald Worster, *A Passion for Nature: The Life of John Muir* (New York: Oxford

University Press, 2008). See also William F. Bade, ed., *The Life and Letters of John Muir*, 2 vols. (Boston: Houghton Mifflin, 1924).

45. Samuel Bowles, *Our New West* (Hartford, CT: Hartford Publishing Company, 1869), v–viii.

46. Samuel Bowles, *Across the Continent* (Springfield, MA: Samuel Bowles and Company, 1865), 226–27.

47. Albert D. Richardson, *Beyond the Mississippi* (Hartford, CT: American Publishing Company, 1867), 426.

48. Bowles, *Across the Continent*, 231.

CHAPTER 2: YELLOWSTONE

1. The scholarship on Yellowstone is large. Original historical works include Louis C. Cramton, *Early History of Yellowstone National Park and Its Relation to National Park Policies* (Washington, DC: U.S. Government Printing Office and National Park Service, 1932); Richard A. Bartlett, *Nature's Yellowstone* (Albuquerque: University of New Mexico Press, 1974); Aubrey L. Haines, *Yellowstone National Park: Its Exploration and Establishment* (Washington, DC: U.S. Government Printing Office and National Park Service, 1974); Aubrey L. Haines, *The Yellowstone Story*, 2 vols. (Yellowstone National Park, WY: Yellowstone Library and Museum Association in cooperation with Colorado Associated University Press, 1977); and Richard A. Bartlett, *Yellowstone: A Wilderness Besieged* (Tucson: University of Arizona Press, 1985). Economic interpretations of Yellowstone include Chris J. Magoc, *Yellowstone: The Creation and Selling of an American Landscape, 1870–1903* (Albuquerque: University of New Mexico Press; Helena: Montana Historical Society Press, 1999), and Mark Daniel Barringer, *Selling Yellowstone: Capitalism and the Construction of Nature* (Lawrence: University Press of Kansas, 2002).

2. A summary of Yellowstone during the fur-trade era is Bartlett, *Nature's Yellowstone*, 93–116.

3. A detailed account of miners' explorations in and near Yellowstone is Haines, *The Yellowstone Story*, 1:60–83.

4. Charles W. Cook, David E. Folsom, and William Peterson, *The Valley of the Upper Yellowstone*, ed. Aubrey L. Haines (Norman: University of Oklahoma Press, 1965), 3–7; W. Turrentine Jackson, "The Cook-Folsom Exploration of the Upper Yellowstone, 1869," *Pacific Northwest Quarterly* 32 (July 1941): 307–12; Bartlett, *Nature's Yellowstone*, 117–21, 147–51.

5. Suggestive of their cultural baggage, Cook and Folsom were from New England, respectively, Maine and New Hampshire. Peterson, a Dane, may have been less susceptible to cultural anxiety but obviously supported his colleagues in describing Yellowstone as superior scenery. Biographical accounts of Yellowstone's early explorers may be found in Haines, *Yellowstone National Park*, 133–52.

6. Charles W. Cook, "The Valley of the Upper Yellowstone," *Western Monthly* 4 (July 1870): 61.

7. Cook, "The Valley of the Upper Yellowstone," 64.

8. Cited above, the article was initially rejected by the *New York Tribune*, *Scribner's*, and *Harper's*, which considered it fictitious or unreliable. Jackson, "The Cook-Folsom Exploration of the Upper Yellowstone, 1869," 316–17.

9. Cramton, *Early History of Yellowstone National Park and Its Relation to National Park Policies*, 12–13; W. Turrentine Jackson, "The Washburn-Doane Expedition into the Upper Yellowstone," *Pacific Historical Review* 10 (June 1941): 189–91; Nathaniel Pitt Langford, *Diary of the Washburn Expedition to the Yellowstone and Firehole Rivers in the Year 1870*, reprinted as *The Discovery of Yellowstone National Park: Journal of the Washburn Expedition to the Yellowstone and Firehole Rivers in the Year 1870*, ed. Aubrey L. Haines (Lincoln: University of Nebraska Press, 1972), vii–xvii.

10. There is no standard title to the expedition; subsequently, only Washburn will be used.

11. Nathaniel P. Langford, "The Wonders of the Yellowstone," pt. 1, *Scribner's Monthly* 2 (May 1871): 13.

12. Everts's personal account appeared the following year as "Thirty-Seven Days of Peril," *Scribner's Monthly* 3 (November 1871): 1–17.

13. *Letter from the Secretary of War communicating the Report of Lieutenant Gustavus C. Doane upon the so-called Yellowstone Expedition of 1870*, S. Ex. Doc. 51, 41st Cong., 3rd sess., March 3, 1871, 32; Nathaniel P. Langford, "The Wonders of the Yellowstone," pt. 2, *Scribner's Monthly* 2 (June 1871): 127.

14. Several are reprinted in Cramton, *Early History of Yellowstone National Park and Its Relation to National Park Policies*, 90–110.

15. The explorers named the stream Tower Creek and its cataract Tower Fall. Langford, *Diary of the Washburn Expedition to the Yellowstone and Firehole Rivers in the Year 1870*, 21–22.

16. "The Yellowstone Expedition," *New York Times*, October 14, 1870, 4.

17. W. Turrentine Jackson, "Governmental Exploration of the Upper Yellowstone, 1871," *Pacific Historical Review* 11 (June 1942): 189–90; Bartlett, *Nature's Yellowstone*, 188–89; Richard A. Bartlett, *Great Surveys of the American West* (Norman: University of Oklahoma Press, 1962), 40–56; William H. Goetzmann, *Exploration and Empire: The Explorer and the Scientist in the Winning of the American West* (New York: Alfred A. Knopf, 1966), 504–8.

18. Bartlett, *Great Surveys of the American West*, 40–41; Bartlett, *Nature's Yellowstone*, 189.

19. W. H. Jackson's autobiography, *Time Exposure* (New York: G. P. Putnam's Sons, 1940), 186–203, is a very descriptive account of his work on the Hayden Survey. Important interpretations of Moran include Thurman Wilkins, *Thomas Moran: Artist of the Mountains* (Norman: University of Oklahoma Press,

1966); Joni Louise Kinsey, *Thomas Moran and the Surveying of the American West* (Washington, DC: Smithsonian Institution Press, 1992); and Nancy K. Anderson et al., *Thomas Moran* (Washington, DC: National Gallery of Art; New Haven, CT: Yale University Press, 1997).

20. Wilkins, *Thomas Moran*, 3–5, 68–70.

21. Apparently, the springs were already known to miners and invalids. See Jackson, *Time Exposure*, 198.

22. Haines, *The Yellowstone Story*, 1:142–46.

23. *Preliminary Report of the United States Geological Survey of Montana and Portions of Adjacent Territories; Being a Fifth Annual Report*, by F. V. Hayden (Washington, DC: U.S. Government Printing Office, 1872), 83–84. Moran's painting, meticulously restored, hangs in the National Museum of American Art, Smithsonian Institution, Washington, D.C.

24. Bartlett, *Great Surveys of the American West*, 49–56; Jackson, "Governmental Exploration of the Upper Yellowstone, 1871," 194–97.

25. The so-called Yellowstone creation myth has been exhaustively treated in Paul Schullery and Lee Whittlesey, *Myth and History in the Creation of Yellowstone National Park* (Lincoln: University of Nebraska Press, 2003). See also Paul Schullery, *Searching for Yellowstone: Ecology and Wonder in the Last Wilderness* (Boston: Houghton Mifflin, 1997), 56–64. Earlier treatments of the debate include Haines, *Yellowstone National Park*, 111–12; Hans Huth, "Yosemite: The Story of an Idea," *Sierra Club Bulletin* 33 (March 1948): 72–76; and Holway R. Jones, *John Muir and the Sierra Club: The Battle for Yosemite* (San Francisco: Sierra Club, 1965), 26–28.

26. Langford, *Diary of the Washburn Expedition to the Yellowstone and Firehole Rivers in the Year 1870*, 117–18.

27. United States, *Statutes at Large* 17 (1872): 32–33.

28. Langford, *Diary of the Washburn Expedition to the Yellowstone and Firehole Rivers in the Year 1870*, 96–97.

29. Cornelius Hedges, "The Great Falls of the Yellowstone: A Graphic Picture of Their Grandeur and Beauty," *Helena Daily Herald*, October 15, 1871, reprinted in Cramton, *Early History of Yellowstone National Park and Its Relation to National Park Policies*, 100.

30. Langford, "The Wonders of the Yellowstone," pt. 1, 7, 8, 12; pt. 2, 124.

31. Revelations of cultural anxiety continue in Ferdinand V. Hayden, "The Wonders of the West—II: More about the Yellowstone," *Scribner's Monthly* 3 (February 1872): 388–96; Ferdinand V. Hayden, "The Hot Springs and Geysers of the Yellowstone and Firehole Rivers," *The American Journal of Science and Arts* 103 (February 1872): 105–15; (March 1872): 161–76; and Walter Trumbull, "The Washburn Yellowstone Expedition," *Overland Monthly* 6 (May 1871): 431–37; (June 1871): 489–96.

32. W. Turrentine Jackson, "The Creation of Yellowstone National Park," *Mississippi Valley Historical Review* 29 (September 1942): 192–93. Similarly, at

Mammoth Hot Springs, Hayden noted that "two men have already pre-empted 320 acres of land covering most of the surface occupied by the active springs, with the expectation that upon the completion of the Northern Pacific Railroad this will become a famous place of resort for invalids and pleasure-seekers." Hayden, "The Wonders of the West—II," 390–91.

33. State of California, Geological Survey, J. D. Whitney, State Geologist, *The Yosemite Book; A Description of the Yosemite Valley and the Adjacent Region of the Sierra Nevada, and of the Big Trees of California* (New York: Julius Bien, 1868), 9.

34. U.S. Congress, House, *Congressional Globe*, 40th Cong., 2nd sess., June 3, 1868, 2816–17; U.S. Congress, Senate, Committee on Private Land Claims, *S. Rept. 185 to Accompany H.R. 1118*, 40th Cong., 2nd sess., July 23, 1868; U.S. Congress, House, Committee on the Public Lands, *J. M. Hutchings, J. C. Lamon*, H. Rept. 2 to accompany H.R. 184, 41st Cong., 2nd sess., January 18, 1870; U.S. Congress, Senate, Committee on Public Lands, *Memorial of J. M. Hutchings Praying a Grant of Lands in the Yosemite Valley, California*, S. Misc. Doc. 72, 41st Cong., 3rd sess., February 21, 1871. In *Hutchings v. Low* (December 1872), the Supreme Court irrevocably denied Hutchings and Lamon's claims.

35. As quoted in Haines, *Yellowstone Story*, 1:155. Nettleton himself was quoting Judge William D. Kelley, a prominent Philadelphia congressman with strong ties to Jay Cooke and the Northern Pacific.

36. U.S. Congress, House, Committee on the Public Lands, *The Yellowstone Park*, H. Rept. 26 to accompany H.R. 764, 42nd Cong., 2nd sess., February 27, 1872, 1–2.

37. As quoted in Haines, *The Yellowstone Story*, 1:169.

38. With slight variations, there are several good accounts of what proponents did to promote the bill, including Haines, *The Yellowstone Story*, 1:166–69; Hiram Martin Chittenden, *The Yellowstone National Park* (Cincinnati: Robert Clarke Company, 1895), 93–95; Haines, *Yellowstone National Park*; and Bartlett, *Nature's Yellowstone*, chap. 9.

39. *Congressional Globe*, January 30, 1872, 697.

40. United States, *Statutes at Large* 17 (1872): 32–33.

41. United States, *Statutes at Large* 17 (1872): 32–33.

42. These interpretations are further gleaned from the bill's Senate sponsor, Samuel Pomeroy of Kansas, who introduced the legislation "as the result of the exploration, made by Professor Hayden. . . . With a party he explored the headwaters of the Yellowstone and found it to be a great natural curiosity, great geysers, as they are termed, water spouts, and hot springs, and having platted the ground himself, and having given me the dimensions of it, the bill was drawn up, as it was thought best to consecrate and set apart this great place of national resort, as it may be in the future, for the purposes of public enjoyment." U.S. Congress, Senate, *Congressional Globe*, 42nd Cong., 2nd sess., January 23, 1872, 520.

CHAPTER 3: WORTHLESS LANDS

1. U.S. Congress, Senate, *Congressional Globe*, 38th Cong., 1st sess., May 17, 1864, 2300–2301.

2. Initial expressions of this thesis include Alfred Runte, "Yellowstone: It's Useless, So Why Not a Park?" *National Parks and Conservation Magazine: The Environmental Journal* 46 (March 1972): 4–7, and "'Worthless' Lands: Our National Parks," *American West* 10 (May 1973): 4–11. A critical debate is Richard W. Sellars, Alfred Runte, et al., "The National Parks: A Forum on the 'Worthless Lands' Thesis," *Journal of Forest History* 27 (July 1983): 130–45.

3. U.S. Congress, House, Committee on the Public Lands, *The Yellowstone Park*, H. Rept. 26 to accompany H.R. 764, 42nd Cong., 2nd sess., February 27, 1872, 1–2. William H. Goetzmann, in *Exploration and Empire: The Explorer and the Scientist in the Winning of the American West* (New York: Alfred A. Knopf, 1966), 498, refers to Hayden as "par excellence the businessman's geologist."

4. U.S. Congress, Senate, *Congressional Globe*, 42nd Cong., 2nd sess., January 30, 1872, 697.

5. *Congressional Globe*, January 30, 1872, 697.

6. U.S. Congress, House, *Congressional Globe*, 42nd Cong., 2nd sess., February 27, 1872, 1243.

7. *Congressional Globe*, February 27, 1872, 1243.

8. John Ise, *Our National Park Policy: A Critical History* (Baltimore: The Johns Hopkins Press, 1961), 20–22; Aubrey L. Haines, *The Yellowstone Story*, vol. 1 (Yellowstone National Park, WY: Yellowstone Library and Museum Association in cooperation with Colorado Associated University Press, 1977), 216–39.

9. U.S. Congress, Senate, *Congressional Record*, 48th Cong., 1st sess., May 27, 1884, 4547–53; Ise, *Our National Park Policy*, 42–43; Richard A. Bartlett, *Nature's Yellowstone* (Albuquerque: University of New Mexico Press, 1974), 141–42.

10. United States, *Statutes at Large* 18 (1875): 517–18. The park was actually superimposed over a military site. Section 3 of the enabling act, for example, provided that "any part of the park hereby created shall be at all times available for military purposes, either as a parade ground or drill ground, in time of peace, or for complete occupation in time of war." The reserve might "also be used for the erection of any public buildings or works." Michigan took over the park in 1895.

11. Important analyses of the anxiety aroused by the close of the frontier are Earl Pomeroy, *In Search of the Golden West: The Tourist in Western America* (New York: Alfred A. Knopf, 1957), 93–103, 152–58, and Roderick Frazier Nash, *Wilderness and the American Mind*, 4th ed. (New Haven, CT: Yale University Press, 2001), 143–47.

12. George B. Tobey Jr., *A History of Landscape Architecture: The Relationship of People to Environment* (New York: American Elsevier, 1973), 271.

13. As quoted in Kermit Vanderbilt, *Charles Eliot Norton: Apostle of Culture in a Democracy* (Cambridge, MA: Harvard University Press, Belknap Press, 1959), 190.

14. A definitive account of the movement to preserve Niagara is Alfred Runte, "Beyond the Spectacular: The Niagara Falls Preservation Campaign," *New-York Historical Society Quarterly* 57 (January 1973): 30–50. Olmsted's quotes appear in *Special Report of New York State Survey on the Preservation of the Scenery of Niagara Falls, and Fourth Annual Report on the Triangulation of the State for the Year 1879* (Albany, NY: Charles Van Benthuysen and Sons, 1880), 27.

15. Charles M. Dow, *The State Reservation at Niagara: A History* (Albany, NY: J. B. Lyon Co., 1914), 39–41. The total removals came to 150 buildings, including flour, paper, pulp, and brick mills.

16. State of New York, State Land Survey, *Report on the Adirondack State Land Surveys to the Year 1886*, by Verplanck Colvin (Albany, NY: Weed, Parsons and Co., 1886), 5–7. A definitive summary of the movement to preserve the Adirondacks is Nash, *Wilderness and the American Mind*, 116–21. See also Philip G. Terrie, *Forever Wild: A Cultural History of Wilderness in the Adirondacks* (Syracuse, NY: Syracuse University Press, 1994).

17. John Muir, "Studies in the Sierra: Mountain Building," *Overland Monthly* 14 (January 1875): 65; William Frederick Bade, ed., *The Life and Letters of John Muir*, 2 vols. (Boston: Houghton Mifflin, 1924), 2:237.

18. State of California, Geological Survey, *The Yosemite Guide-Book*, by J. D. Whitney (Cambridge, MA: University Press, 1869), 21; Robert Underwood Johnson, "The Case for Yosemite Valley," *Century Magazine* 39 (January 1890): 478.

19. Ise, *Our National Park Policy*, 100–104; Douglas Hillman Strong, "A History of Sequoia National Park" (PhD diss., Syracuse University, 1964), 61–62.

20. A complete history of the movement to protect the giant sequoias is Lary M. Dilsaver and William C. Tweed, *Challenge of the Big Trees: A Resource History of Sequoia and Kings Canyon National Parks* (Three Rivers, CA: Sequoia Natural History Association, Inc., 1990). On George W. Stewart and the origins of Sequoia National Park, see pp. 61–73.

21. Robert Underwood Johnson, *Remembered Yesterdays* (Boston: Little, Brown, 1923), 279–80, 287–88; Holway R. Jones, *John Muir and the Sierra Club: The Battle for Yosemite* (San Francisco: Sierra Club, 1965), 43.

22. John Muir, "The Treasures of the Yosemite," *Century Magazine* 40 (August 1890): 487–88.

23. John Muir, "Features of the Proposed Yosemite National Park," *Century Magazine* 40 (September 1890): 666–67; Muir, "The Treasures of the Yosemite," 483.

24. The long-debated importance of the Southern Pacific Railroad to the establishment of Sequoia, General Grant, and Yosemite national parks has been richly verified in Richard J. Orsi, *Sunset Limited: The Southern Pacific Railroad*

and the Development of the American West, 1850–1930 (Berkeley: University of California Press, 2005), 358–71. See also Orsi's article, "'Wilderness Saint' and 'Robber Baron': The Anomalous Partnership of John Muir and the Southern Pacific Company for Preservation of Yosemite National Park," *Pacific Historian* 29 (Summer/Fall 1985): 136–56. California's early fear about losing its Sierra watersheds is graphically portrayed in Robert L. Kelley, *Gold vs. Grain: The Hydraulic Mining Controversy in California's Sacramento Valley: A Chapter in the Decline of the Concept of Laissez Faire* (Glendale, CA: A. H. Clark Co., 1959).

25. Bade, *The Life and Letters of John Muir*, 2:244–45.

26. United States, *Statutes at Large* 26 (1890): 478, 650–52; U.S. Congress, House, *Congressional Record*, 51st Cong., 1st sess., August 23, 1890, 9072–73; U.S. Congress, Senate, *Congressional Record*, 51st Cong., 1st sess., September 8, 1890, 9829; U.S. Congress, House, *Congressional Record*, 51st Cong., 1st sess., September 30, 1890, 10751–52; U.S. Congress, Senate, *Congressional Record*, 51st Cong., 1st sess., September 30, 1890, 10740; Orsi, "'Wilderness Saint' and 'Robber Baron,'" 147–48.

27. U.S. Department of the Interior, *Annual Report of the Secretary of the Interior for the Year 1890* (Washington, DC: U.S. Government Printing Office, 1890), 123–26. Noble also named the parks since Congress had merely set forth their boundaries.

28. "Proceedings of the Sierra Club," *Sierra Club Bulletin* 1 (January 1896): 275.

CHAPTER 4: THE MARCH OF MONUMENTALISM

1. Carl Snyder, "Our New National Wonderland," *Review of Reviews* 9 (February 1894): 164, 169, 171.

2. John Muir, "The Wild Parks and Forest Reservations of the West," *Atlantic Monthly* 81 (January 1898): 26–28.

3. U.S. Congress, Senate, 53rd Cong., 2nd sess., "Memorial from the Geological Society of America Favoring the Establishment of a National Park in the State of Washington," *Misc. Doc. No. 247*, 1894, 4, as quoted in Theodore Catton, *Wonderland: An Administrative History of Mount Rainier National Park* (Seattle: National Park Service, Cultural Resources Program, 1996), chap. 3.

4. A first interpretation of the Northern Pacific's role in Mount Rainier National Park is John Ise, *Our National Park Policy: A Critical History* (Baltimore: The Johns Hopkins Press, 1961), 121–22. Now standard and far more detailed is Carsten Lien, *Olympic Battleground: The Power Politics of Timber Preservation*, 2nd ed. (Seattle: The Mountaineers Books, 2000), 1–15. Environmental histories of the park include Arthur D. Martinson, *Wilderness above the Sound: The Story of Mount Rainier National Park* (Niwot, CO: Roberts Rinehart Publishers, 1994), and Theodore Catton, *National Park, City Playground: Mount Rainier in the Twentieth Century* (Seattle: University of Washington Press, 2006).

5. United States, *Statutes at Large* 30 (1899): 993–95.

6. Rick Harmon, *Crater Lake National Park: A History* (Corvallis: Oregon State University Press, 2002), 10–11; W. G. Steel, *The Mountains of Oregon* (Portland, OR: David Steel, 1890), 32–33. Steel first visited Crater Lake in 1885.

7. U.S. Congress, House, *Congressional Record*, 57th Cong., 1st sess., April 19, 1902, 4450.

8. *Congressional Record*, April 19, 1902, 4450, 4453; United States, *Statutes at Large* 32 (1902): 202–3.

9. U.S. Congress, House, *Protection of Game in Yellowstone National Park*, H. Rept. 658 to accompany H.R. 6442, 53rd Cong., 2nd sess., April 4, 1894, 1–2. The poaching incident made national headlines. See, for example, "Save the Park Buffalo," *Forest and Stream* 42 (April 14, 1894): 1.

10. United States, *Statutes at Large* 28 (1894): 73–75.

11. U.S. Congress, Senate, *Report of the Yosemite Park Commission*, S. Doc. 34, 58th Cong., 3rd sess., December 13, 1904, 1–20, 51.

12. United States, *Statutes at Large* 33 (1905): 702–3. A detailed summary of the withdrawals is Alfred Runte, *Yosemite: The Embattled Wilderness* (Lincoln: University of Nebraska Press, 1990), 72–76.

13. The standard history of the origins of utilitarian conservation is Samuel P. Hays, *Conservation and the Gospel of Efficiency: The Progressive Conservation Movement, 1890–1920* (Cambridge, MA: Harvard University Press, 1959).

14. Of the nation's population in 1910 (91,972,266), just 2,633,517 lived in the Rocky Mountain states and only 4,192,304 in all of Washington, Oregon, and California. U.S. Bureau of the Census, *Thirteenth Census of the United States, 1910*, 13 vols. (Washington, DC: U.S. Government Printing Office, 1913), 1:30.

15. John Ise, *The United States Forest Policy* (New Haven, CT: Yale University Press, 1920), 109–18, 120; Hays, *Conservation and the Gospel of Efficiency*, 47.

16. Theodore Roosevelt, *An Autobiography* (New York: Macmillan, 1913), 17–18, 35–36.

17. Roosevelt, *An Autobiography*, 103. The definitive biography of Roosevelt as a conservationist is Douglas Brinkley, *The Wilderness Warrior: Theodore Roosevelt and the Crusade for America* (New York: Harper, 2009).

18. Hays, *Conservation and the Gospel of Efficiency*, 14–15, 122–46; Ise, *The United States Forest Policy*, 143–63; Roderick Frazier Nash, *Wilderness and the American Mind*, 4th ed. (New Haven, CT: Yale University Press, 2001), 149–53.

19. "Mr. Roosevelt Sees the Grand Canyon," *New York Times*, May 7, 1903, 2. Roosevelt's 1903 trip is described in Edmund Morris, *Theodore Rex* (New York: Random House, 2001), 218–31, and Brinkley, *The Wilderness Warrior*, 502–53.

20. Gifford Pinchot, *The Fight for Conservation* (New York: Doubleday, Page and Co., 1910), 45. Pinchot, an 1889 graduate of Yale University, immediately studied forestry in England, France, and Germany, there being no equivalent

training in the United States at that time. He describes his life and career in *Breaking New Ground* (New York: Harcourt Brace Jovanovich, 1947). On his early relationship with President Roosevelt, see pp. 188–97. Two important biographies of Pinchot are M. Nelson McGeary, *Gifford Pinchot* (Princeton, NJ: Princeton University Press, 1960), and Harold T. Pinkett, *Gifford Pinchot: Public and Private Forester* (Urbana: University of Illinois Press, 1970). The relationship between Roosevelt and Pinchot in the establishment of the U.S. Forest Service is critically detailed in Harold K. Steen, *The U.S. Forest Service: A History* (Seattle: University of Washington Press, 1976), 69–78.

21. U.S. Congress, House, 59th Cong., 1st sess., *Preservation of American Antiquities*, H. Rept. 2224 to accompany H.R. 11016, March 12, 1906, 1.

22. United States, *Statutes at Large* 34 (1906): 225.

23. United States, *Statutes at Large* 34 (1906): 3236–37.

24. United States, *Statutes at Large* 34 (1906): 3266–67. An early chronology of the national monuments and their establishment may be found in Ise, *Our National Park Policy*, 143–62. However, he largely ignores their cultural motivation.

25. A history of the region is George M. Lubick, *Petrified Forest National Park: A Wilderness Bound in Time* (Tucson: University of Arizona Press, 1996).

26. United States, *Statutes at Large* 34, pt. 1 (1906): 616–17. A basic history of Mesa Verde is Duane A. Smith, *Mesa Verde National Park: Shadows of the Centuries* (Boulder: University Press of Colorado, 2002).

27. United States, *Statutes at Large* 35 (1908): 2175–76.

28. United States, *Statutes at Large* 35 (1908): 2175–76, and *Statutes at Large* 35 (1909): 2247–48.

29. Roosevelt, *An Autobiography*, 459.

30. A detailed account of the opposition and events leading to the reduction of Mount Olympus National Monument is Lien, *Olympic Battleground*, 32–52.

31. A definitive reexamination of this interpretation is Hal Rothman, *Preserving Different Pasts: The American National Monuments* (Urbana: University of Illinois Press, 1989).

32. United States, *Statutes at Large* 34 (1906): 831–32.

33. Grinnell's early career is summarized in Gerald A. Diettert, *Grinnell's Glacier: George Bird Grinnell and Glacier National Park* (Missoula, MT: Mountain Press Publishing Company, 1992), 5–17. On Grinnell as a sportsman-conservationist, see John F. Reiger, ed., *The Passing of the Great West: Selected Papers of George Bird Grinnell* (New York: Winchester Press, 1972), and John F. Reiger, *American Sportsmen and the Origins of Conservation*, rev. ed. (Norman: University of Oklahoma Press, 1986), 114–51. An important history of Glacier's early years is Curt W. Buchholtz, *Man in Glacier* (West Glacier, MT: Glacier Natural History Association, 1976).

34. George Bird Grinnell, "The Crown of the Continent," *The Century Magazine* 62 (September 1901): 660.

35. George Bird Grinnell, "Protection of the National Park," *New York Times*, January 29, 1885, 6.

36. Grinnell, "The Crown of the Continent," 660; W. B. Rhoades to Theodore Roosevelt, February 11, 1909, United States, National Archives and Records Administration, Record Group 79, Central Files, file 12-14-1, pt. 1, "Legislation Creating [Glacier] Park," box 25; "Glacier National Park," *Forest and Stream* 70 (March 7, 1908): 366.

37. U.S. Congress, Senate, *Congressional Record*, 61st Cong., 2nd sess., January 25, 1910, 958–60; *Congressional Record*, February 9, 1910, 1639–41.

38. "The Glacier National Park," *Forest and Stream* 74 (March 5, 1910): 367.

39. U.S. Congress, House, *Congressional Record*, 61st Cong., 2nd sess., April 14, 1910, 4669.

40. United States, *Statutes at Large* 36 (1910): 354–55.

41. "The Glacier National Park," *Forest and Stream* 74 (May 21, 1910): 807.

42. John Muir, "Hetch Hetchy Valley: The Lower Tuolumne Yosemite," *Overland Monthly* 2 (June 1873): 42–50; Nash, *Wilderness and the American Mind*, 161–62.

43. The definitive history of the Hetch Hetchy controversy is Robert W. Righter, *The Battle over Hetch Hetchy: America's Most Controversial Dam and the Birth of Modern Environmentalism* (New York: Oxford University Press, 2005). See also Holway R. Jones, *John Muir and the Sierra Club: The Battle for Yosemite* (San Francisco: Sierra Club, 1965), 85–169, and Nash, *Wilderness and the American Mind*, chap. 10.

44. U.S. Department of the Interior, *Report of the Secretary of the Interior for the Fiscal Year Ending June 30, 1903* (Washington, DC: U.S. Government Printing Office, 1903), 156; Righter, *The Battle over Hetch Hetchy*, 47–54.

45. Righter, *The Battle over Hetch Hetchy*, 55–71; Jones, *John Muir and the Sierra Club*, 95–100.

46. The House vote was 183 to 43, with 194 absent. U.S. Congress, House, *Congressional Record*, 63rd Cong., 1st sess., September 3, 1913, 4151. In the Senate, the tally was 43 for, 25 against, and 27 either absent or not voting. U.S. Congress, Senate, *Congressional Record*, 63rd Cong., 2nd sess., December 6, 1913, 385–86.

47. John P. Young, "The Hetch Hetchy Problem," *Sunset Magazine* 22 (June 1909): 606.

48. The photograph is reproduced in Jones, *John Muir and the Sierra Club*, opposite p. 112. It originally appeared as part of a series in San Francisco, California, Board of Supervisors, *On the Proposed Use of a Portion of the Hetch-Hetchy, Eleanor and Cherry Valleys . . . for the Water Supply of San Francisco, Calif., and Neighboring Cities*, by John R. Freeman (San Francisco: Rincon Publishing Co., 1912), 5–56.

49. J. Horace McFarland to Robert Underwood Johnson, October 31, 1913, University of California, Berkeley, Bancroft Library, Robert Underwood Johnson Papers, box 3.

50. United States, *Statutes at Large* 38 (1913): 242–51.

CHAPTER 5: SEE AMERICA FIRST

1. John Muir, "The Wild Parks and Forest Reservations of the West," *Atlantic Monthly* 81 (January 1898): 15; Allen Chamberlain, "Scenery as a National Asset," *The Outlook* 95 (May 28, 1910): 169.

2. A history of railroad development of the national parks is Alfred Runte, *Trains of Discovery: Western Railroads and the National Parks*, 4th ed. (Boulder, CO: Roberts Rinehart Publishers, 1998). See also Alfred Runte, *Allies of the Earth: Railroads and the Soul of Preservation* (Kirksville, MO: Truman State University Press, 2006).

3. United States, *Statutes at Large* 26 (1890): 651.

4. An alleged confrontation between John Muir and Gifford Pinchot over development of the national forests is recounted in Linnie Marsh Wolfe, *Son of the Wilderness: The Life of John Muir* (New York: Alfred A. Knopf, 1945), 275–76. The emerging split between preservationists and resource professionals is best documented in Samuel P. Hays, *Conservation and the Gospel of Efficiency: The Progressive Conservation Movement, 1890–1920* (Cambridge, MA: Harvard University Press, 1959), 189–98.

5. Holway R. Jones provides a complete listing of these groups in *John Muir and the Sierra Club: The Battle for Yosemite* (San Francisco: Sierra Club, 1965), 4–5, n. 5.

6. The role of nature in the development of suburbia is discussed in Peter J. Schmidt, *Back to Nature: The Arcadian Myth in Urban America* (New York: Oxford University Press, 1969), 1–32.

7. J. Horace McFarland, "Why Billboard Advertising as at Present Conducted Is Doomed," *Chautauquan* 51 (June 1908): 19, 32. There is one full-length biography by Ernest Morrison, *J. Horace McFarland: A Thorn for Beauty* (Harrisburg: Pennsylvania Historical and Museum Commission, 1995). My principal source remains the J. Horace McFarland Papers, William Penn Memorial Museum, Pennsylvania Historical and Museum Commission, Division of Archives and Manuscripts, Harrisburg.

8. J. Horace McFarland, "Shall We Make a Coal-Pile of Niagara?" *Ladies' Home Journal* 22 (September 1905): 19. See also McFarland's follow-up column, "How the Power Companies Beautify Niagara," *Ladies' Home Journal* 23 (October 1906): 39.

9. McFarland, "Shall We Make a Coal-Pile of Niagara?" 19.

10. Allen Chamberlain to McFarland, April 22, 1908, McFarland Papers, box 16; William E. Colby to Allen Chamberlain, April 16, 1908, McFarland Papers, box 16.

11. Colby to Pinchot, April 20, 1908, McFarland Papers, box 16.

12. McFarland to Pinchot, November 26, 1909, McFarland Papers, box 16.

13. See, e.g., James D. Phelan, "Why Congress Should Pass the Hetch Hetchy Bill," *The Outlook* 91 (February 13, 1909): 340–41. A complete inventory of each side's arguments throughout the debate is contained in Robert W. Righter, *The Battle over Hetch Hetchy: America's Most Controversial Dam and the Birth of Modern Environmentalism* (New York: Oxford University Press, 2005).

14. For example, William Frederick Bade, a director of the Sierra Club and vice-president of the Western Branch of the Society for the Preservation of National Parks, wrote, "As soon as a good road is built to Hetch-Hetchy and transportation facilities provided, hotels will spring up, and the tide of tourist travel . . . will turn to Hetch-Hetchy in both winter and summer." Bade to Richard A. Ballinger, undated, McFarland Papers, box 16.

15. J. Horace McFarland, "Shall We Have Ugly Conservation?" *The Outlook* 91 (March 13, 1909): 595; Chamberlain to McFarland, March 18, 1909, McFarland Papers, box 16.

16. Chamberlain, "Scenery as a National Asset," 162–64.

17. Roderick Frazier Nash, in *Wilderness and the American Mind*, 4th ed. (New Haven, CT: Yale University Press, 2001), 170, maintains that preservationists should have mentioned wilderness more. The "tactical error" cost them "considerable support." The question remains whether the support for wilderness was there. All the principal arguments for the national parks were based on scenery—America had the greatest spectacles, not the finest solitude. Wilderness "was not an issue in the Hetch Hetchy fight," agrees Robert Righter. "The defenders of the valley consistently advocated development, including roads, hotels, winter sports amenities, and the infrastructure to support legions of visitors. The land use battle joined over one question: Would the valley be used for water storage or nature tourism?" Righter, *The Battle over Hetch Hetchy*, 5–6.

18. Chamberlain, "Scenery as a National Asset," 165.

19. Watrous to McFarland, August 18, 1911; Watrous to McFarland, September 6, 1911, McFarland Papers, box 17.

20. U.S. Department of the Interior, *Proceedings of the National Park Conference Held at Yellowstone National Park September 11 and 12, 1911* (Washington, DC: U.S. Government Printing Office, 1912), 4.

21. *Proceedings of the National Park Conference, 1911*, 4–17.

22. U.S. Congress, Senate, *Congressional Record*, 61st Cong., 2nd sess., January 25, 1910, 961; U.S. Congress, House, *Congressional Record*, 63rd Cong., 3rd sess., January 18, 1915, 1790.

23. U.S. Congress, House, *Congressional Record*, 63rd Cong., 3rd sess., January 18, 1915, 1790.

24. U.S. Congress, House, *Congressional Record*, 63rd Cong., 3rd sess., January 18, 1915, 1789–91; United States, *Statutes at Large* 38 (1915): 798–800. A full-length study of the park is C. W. Buchholtz, *Rocky Mountain National Park: A History* (Boulder: Colorado Associated University Press, 1983).

25. Mary Roberts Rinehart, "Through Glacier National Park with Howard Eaton," *Collier's* 57, pt. I (April 22, 1916): 11, and pt. II (April 29, 1916): 26.

26. Typed transcript, R. B. Marshall, "Our National Parks," March 6, 1911, McFarland Papers, box 22.

27. George Otis Smith, "The Nation's Playgrounds," *American Review of Reviews* 40 (July 1909): 44; Marshall, "Our National Parks."

28. McFarland to C. R. Miller, November 24, 1911, McFarland Papers, box 19.

29. McFarland to C. R. Miller, November 24, 1911, McFarland Papers, box 19.

30. H. Duane Hampton, *How the United States Cavalry Saved the National Parks* (Bloomington: Indiana University Press, 1971). See also Harvey Meyerson, *Nature's Army: When Soldiers Fought for Yosemite* (Lawrence: University Press of Kansas, 2001).

31. John Ise, *Our National Park Policy: A Critical History* (Baltimore: The Johns Hopkins Press, 1961), 27, 133.

32. Frederick Law Olmsted Jr. to John Olmsted, December 19, 1910, McFarland Papers, box 20.

33. *Proceedings of the National Park Conference, Held at Yellowstone National Park September 11 and 12, 1911*, 19.

34. *The American Civic Association's Movement for a Bureau of National Parks, Proceedings*, National Parks Session of the American Civic Association, Seventh Annual Convention, December 13, 1911 (Washington, DC: American Civic Association, 1912), 4, 9.

35. McFarland to Overton W. Price, October 30, 1911, McFarland Papers, box 20; McFarland to Olmsted, April 17, 1916, McFarland Papers, box 20.

36. Pinchot to McFarland, March 4, 1911, McFarland Papers, box 20; McFarland to Chamberlain, April 2, 1914, McFarland Papers, box 18; Harold J. Howland to Richard B. Watrous, January 9, 1912, McFarland Papers, box 21. For a summary of the circumstances surrounding Pinchot's removal as chief forester, see Hays, *Conservation and the Gospel of Efficiency*, 165–74.

37. In the House, John E. Raker and William Kent were sponsors, both from California. Important histories of the bill include Donald C. Swain, "The Passage of the National Park Service Act of 1916," *Wisconsin Magazine of History* 50 (Autumn 1966): 4–17, and Robin W. Winks, "The National Park Service Act of 1916: 'A Contradictory Mandate'?" *Denver University Law Review* 74 (1997): 575–623. The best primary source remains the McFarland Papers.

38. Harold J. Howland to Richard B. Watrous, January 9, 1912, McFarland Papers, box 21; "A National Park Service," *The Outlook* 100 (February 3, 1912): 246.

39. McFarland to Olmsted, April 17, 1916, McFarland Papers, box 20; Pinchot to McFarland, March 4, 1911, McFarland Papers, box 20.

40. U.S. Congress, House, Committee on the Public Lands, *Establishment of a National Park Service*, Hearings on H.R. 22995, 62nd Cong., 2nd sess., 1912, 7.

41. U.S. Congress, House, Committee on the Public Lands, *National Park Service*, Hearings on H.R. 434 and H.R. 8668, 64th Cong., 1st sess., 1916, 55–56.

42. A visual and factual history of the exposition is Robert A. Reid, *The Blue Book: A Comprehensive Official Souvenir View Book of the Panama-Pacific International Exposition at San Francisco 1915* (San Francisco: Panama-Pacific International Exposition Company, 1915).

43. Union Pacific System, "Yellowstone National Park: Exhibit of Union Pacific System at Panama-Pacific International Exposition," *California and the Expositions* (Omaha, NE: Union Pacific System, 1915), 13.

44. Union Pacific, "Yellowstone National Park," 14–15.

45. Atchison, Topeka & Santa Fe Railway, "Grand Canyon at the Panama-Pacific International Exposition, San Francisco," *Coast Lines Time Tables, Corrected to 1915* (Chicago: Atchison, Topeka & Santa Fe Railway, 1915), n.p.

46. Reid, *The Blue Book*, 100, 311–26; Great Northern Railway, "Great Northern Railway Exhibit Building, Panama-Pacific International Exposition, San Francisco, California," promotional postcard, 1915.

47. Western Pacific; Denver & Rio Grande; Missouri Pacific; St. Louis, Iron Mountain & Southern [Railroads], *The Globe at the San Francisco Exposition*, souvenir pamphlet, 1915.

48. Mather's principal biographer is Robert Shankland, *Steve Mather of the National Parks*, 3rd ed. (New York: Alfred A. Knopf, 1970).

49. Shankland, *Steve Mather of the National Parks*, 7. Albright's biographer is Donald C. Swain, *Wilderness Defender: Horace M. Albright and Conservation* (Chicago: University of Chicago Press, 1970).

50. U.S. Department of the Interior, *Proceedings of the National Park Conference Held at the Yosemite National Park, October 14, 15, and 16, 1912* (Washington, DC: U.S. Government Printing Office, 1913), 8–11, 44–58; U.S. Department of the Interior, *Proceedings of the National Park Conference Held at Berkeley, California, March 11, 12, and 13, 1915* (Washington, DC: U.S. Government Printing Office, 1915), 138–39.

51. The best account of the Mather mountain party is Shankland, *Steve Mather of the National Parks*, 68–73.

52. Stephen T. Mather, "The National Parks on a Business Basis," *American Review of Reviews* 51 (April 1915): 429–30.

53. United States, *Statutes at Large* 39 (1916): 535.

54. United States, *Statutes at Large* 39 (1916): 535. Olmsted's role in guiding the preparation of this paragraph is exhaustively credited in the correspondence of the J. Horace McFarland collection. See also Winks, "The National Park Service Act of 1916."

55. An early example of building the Mather tradition is Horace M. Albright and Frank J. Taylor, *"Oh, Ranger!" A Book about the National Parks* (Stanford,

CA: Stanford University Press, 1928). See also Horace M. Albright as told to Robert Cahn, *The Birth of the National Park Service: The Founding Years, 1913–1933* (Salt Lake City, UT: Howe Brothers, 1985).

56. U.S. Department of the Interior, National Park Service, *Proceedings of the National Parks Conference Held in the Auditorium of the New National Museum, January 2–6, 1917* (Washington, DC: U.S. Government Printing Office, 1917), 17, 20.

CHAPTER 6: COMPLETE CONSERVATION

1. Mary Roberts Rinehart, "The Sleeping Giant," *Ladies' Home Journal* 38 (May 1921): 21.

2. Rinehart, "The Sleeping Giant," 21.

3. Joseph Grinnell and Tracy Storer, "Animal Life as an Asset of National Parks," *Science* 44 (September 15, 1916): 377.

4. Rinehart, "The Sleeping Giant," 21.

5. Relevant contemporary articles include Stephen T. Mather, "Do You Want to Lose Your Parks?" *Independent* 104 (November 13, 1920): 220–21, 238–39; Frank A. Waugh, "The Market Price on Landscape," *The Outlook* 127 (March 16, 1921): 428–29; and William C. Gregg, "The Cascade Corner of Yellowstone Park," *The Outlook* 129 (November 23, 1921): 469–76.

6. United States, *Statutes at Large* 17 (1872): 33.

7. The Glacier Park debates of 1910 were among the first to recognize wildlife as a companion justification for national parks. For example, Senator Thomas H. Carter of Montana sparked brief discussion with a reminder that the proposed reserve would also save the mountain sheep. U.S. Congress, Senate, *Congressional Record*, 61st Cong., 2nd sess., January 25, 1910, 960.

8. Robert Sterling Yard, *National Parks Portfolio* (New York: Charles Scribner's Sons, 1916), 3–6.

9. Robert Sterling Yard, "The People and the National Parks," *The Survey* 48 (August 1, 1922): 547; Rinehart, "The Sleeping Giant," 21; Grinnell and Storer, "Animal Life as an Asset of National Parks," 377; Stephen T. Mather, "National Parks Are Field Laboratories for the Study of Nature," *School Life* 12 (November 1926): 41; Robert Sterling Yard, "Economic Aspects of Our National Parks Policy," *Scientific Monthly* 16 (April 1923): 384–85. Contemporary articles further include Charles C. Adams, "The Relation of Wild Life to Recreation in Forests and Parks," *Playground* 18 (July 1924): 208–9; John C. Merriam, "Scientific, Economic, and Recreational Values of Wild Life," *Playground* 18 (July 1924): 203–4; and Horace M. Albright, "Our National Parks as Wildlife Sanctuaries, *American Forests and Forest Life* 35 (August 1929): 505–7, 536.

10. U.S. Department of the Interior, *Annual Report of the Director of the National Park Service, June 30, 1920* (Washington, DC: U.S. Government Printing Office, 1920), 66.

11. Grinnell and Storer, "Animal Life as an Asset of National Parks," 378. Grinnell's strategy for seeding the Park Service with skilled naturalists is detailed in Alfred Runte, "Joseph Grinnell and Yosemite: Rediscovering the Legacy of a California Conservationist," *California History* 69 (Summer 1990): 170–81. See also Alfred Runte, *Yosemite: The Embattled Wilderness* (Lincoln: University of Nebraska Press, 1990), chaps. 8–11.

12. John Burroughs, "The Grand Canyon of the Colorado," *Century* 81 (January 1911): 425, 428.

13. John Ise, *Our National Park Policy: A Critical History* (Baltimore: The Johns Hopkins Press, 1961), 241–48; Robert Shankland, *Steve Mather of the National Parks*, 3rd ed. (New York: Alfred A. Knopf, 1970), 136–39.

14. Rufus Steele, "The Celestial Circuit," *Sunset Magazine* 56 (May 1926): 24–25.

15. *Nature Magazine* 13 (June 1929): end piece; *Nature Magazine* 13 (April 1929): 277; *Nature Magazine* 13 (May 1929): 353. Similar Union Pacific advertisements appeared throughout the 1920s in *National Geographic*, *Golden Book*, *The Literary Digest*, and *Sunset Magazine*. Additional examples of monumental perceptions of the Southwest include Paul C. Phillips, "The Trail of the Painted Parks," *Country Life* 55 (April 1929): 65–66; Charles G. Plummer, "Utah's Zion National Park," *Overland Monthly* 81 (June 1923): 27–28; Stephen T. Mather, "The New Bryce Canyon National Park," *American Forests and Forest Life* 35 (January 1929): 37–38; and Atchison, Topeka & Santa Fe Railway, Passenger Department, *The Grand Canyon of Arizona* (Chicago: Santa Fe Railway, 1902).

16. United States, *Statutes at Large* 39 (1916): 432–34; United States, *Statutes at Large* 39 (1917): 938–39. A history of Lassen is Douglas H. Strong, *Footprints in Time: A History of Lassen Volcanic National Park* (Red Bluff, CA: Lassen Loomis Museum Association, 1998).

17. Ise, *Our National Park Policy*, 238–41, 251; United States, *Statutes at Large* 40 (1919): 1178–79.

18. Copy, H. W. Temple et al. to Hubert Work, December 12, 1924, McFarland Papers, box 18.

19. Isabelle F. Story, "The Park of the Smoking Mountains," *Home Geographic Monthly* 2 (August 1932): 45; Robert Sterling Yard, "Great Smokies: Mountain Throne of the East," *American Forests* 39 (January 1933): 32.

20. William C. Gregg, "Two New National Parks?" *The Outlook* 141 (December 30, 1925): 667; U.S. Department of the Interior, *Report of the Director of the National Park Service, June 30, 1925* (Washington, DC: U.S. Government Printing Office, 1925), 3.

21. United States, *Statutes at Large* 44 (1926): 616–17. With the establishment of national parks from private instead of public property, it becomes necessary to distinguish between the date a park was authorized and when it was actually dedicated. The interval was often a decade or more.

22. Shenandoah National Park awaits a full-length, published history. Portions of the park campaign are chronicled in Darwin Lambert, *The Earth-Man Story* (New York: Exposition Press, 1972), chap. 5. and Ise, *Our National Park Policy*, 248–58, 262–64. See also Dennis E. Simmons, "Conservation, Cooperation, and Controversy: The Establishment of the Shenandoah National Park, 1924–1936," *Virginia Magazine of History and Biography* 89 (October 1981): 387–404. A natural and human history of the Great Smoky Mountains, including the park, is Michael Frome, *Strangers in High Places: The Story of the Great Smoky Mountains* (Knoxville: University of Tennessee Press, 1994). See also Daniel S. Pierce, *The Great Smokies: From Natural Habitat to National Park* (Knoxville: University of Tennessee Press, 2000). A participant in the park campaign, Carlos C. Campbell, leaves another important account in *Birth of a National Park in the Great Smoky Mountains* (Knoxville: University of Tennessee Press, 1960). A sampling of contemporary publications would include Plummer F. Jones, "The Shenandoah National Park in Virginia," *American Review of Reviews* 72 (July 1925): 63–70; Laura Thornborough, "A New National Park in the East: The Great Smokies," *American Forests and Forest Life* 36 (March 1930): 137–40, 190; and Charles Peter Rarich, "Development of the Great Smoky Mountains National Park," *Appalachia* 21 (December 1936): 199–210.

23. Yard, "The People and the National Parks," 550.

24. Among the mountain men who first penetrated the region, the term "hole" defined a valley encircled by peaks. "Jackson Hole" derived from David E. Jackson, a trapper of the 1820s. A definitive geological history of the region is J. D. Love and John C. Reed Jr., *Creation of the Teton Landscape* (Moose, WY: Grand Teton Natural History Association, 1971). See also F. M. Fryxell, *The Tetons: Interpretations of a Mountain Landscape* (Berkeley: University of California Press, 1938). The Tetons, French for "breasts," were also named by fur trappers around 1810. On the early history of the region, see David J. Saylor, *Jackson Hole, Wyoming: In the Shadow of the Grand Tetons* (Norman: University of Oklahoma Press, 1970), 54. The definitive history is Robert W. Righter, *Crucible for Conservation: The Struggle for Grand Teton National Park* (Moose, WY: Grand Teton Natural History Association, 1982).

25. Saylor, *Jackson Hole, Wyoming*, 117–23.

26. Dillon Wallace, "Saddle and Camp Life in the Rockies: The Tragedy of the Elk," *Outing* 58 (March 1911): 187–201; Saylor, *Jackson Hole, Wyoming*, 159–63.

27. U.S. Congress, Senate, *Region South of and Adjoining Yellowstone National Park*, Sen. Doc. 39, 55th Cong., 3rd sess., 1898, 4–32.

28. Saylor, *Jackson Hole, Wyoming*, 161.

29. As quoted in U.S. Congress, Senate, Subcommittee of the Committee on Public Lands and Surveys, *Enlarging Grand Teton National Park in Wyoming*, Hearings on Sen. Res. 250, 75th Cong., 3rd sess., August 8–10, 1938, 6, hereafter cited as Sen. Res. 250, Hearings.

30. U.S. Department of the Interior, *Report of the Director of the National Park Service to the Secretary of the Interior, June 30, 1918* (Washington, DC: U.S. Government Printing Office, 1918), 40; U.S. Department of the Interior, *Report of the Director of the National Park Service to the Secretary of the Interior, June 30, 1919* (Washington, DC: U.S. Government Printing Office, 1919), 48.

31. U.S. Congress, Senate, *Congressional Record*, 65th Cong., 3rd sess., February 18, 1919, 3646. The measure had passed the House the previous day, where its sponsor, Representative Frank Mondell of Wyoming, had convinced his colleagues of Mather's sincerity. On Mather's internal assurances to Wyoming, see the National Park Service, Record Group 79, National Archives, Washington, D.C., file 602, Yellowstone National Park Boundaries, box 460.

32. Sen. Res. 250, Hearings, 7.

33. See, e.g., Mather to George Bird Grinnell, December 11, 1919, Yellowstone Park Boundaries, Record Group 79, box 460.

34. Sen. Res. 250, Hearings, 7.

35. Albright to Mather, October 16, 1919, Yellowstone Park Boundaries, Record Group 79, box 460.

36. U.S. Department of the Interior, *Annual Report of the Director of the National Park Service, June 30, 1920* (Washington, DC: U.S. Government Printing Office, 1920), 104.

37. U.S. Department of the Interior, *Annual Report of the Director of the National Park Service, June 30, 1920*, 112.

38. U.S. Congress, House, *Congressional Record*, 69th Cong., 1st sess., May 26, 1926, 10143; United States, *Statutes at Large* 44 (1926): 820.

39. Sen. Res. 250, Hearings, 9–10.

40. Sen. Res. 250, Hearings, 10; Struthers Burt, "The Battle of Jackson's Hole," *The Nation* 122 (March 3, 1926): 226.

41. Sen. Res. 250, Hearings, 10–11.

42. Sen. Res. 250, Hearings, 13–14. A revealing look into the Rockefeller–Albright relationship, drawn from their personal letters, is Joseph W. Ernst, ed., *Worthwhile Places: Correspondence of John D. Rockefeller, Jr. and Horace M. Albright* (New York: Fordham University Press, 1991). For their early Teton correspondence, see pp. 50–74.

43. U.S. Congress, Senate, Subcommittee of the Committee on Public Lands and Surveys, *Investigation of Proposed Enlargement of the Yellowstone and Grand Teton National Parks*, Hearings on Sen. Res. 226, 73rd Cong., 2nd sess., August 7–10, 1933, 49–80.

44. Sen. Res. 250, Hearings, 15.

45. Fritiof M. Fryxell, "The Grand Tetons: Our National Park of Matterhorns," *American Forests and Forest Life* 35 (August 1929): 455.

46. The characteristics of the reserve are detailed in Ise, *Our National Park Policy*, 338–40.

47. U.S. Congress, Senate, *Congressional Record*, 70th Cong., 2nd sess., February 7, 1929, 2982–83; U.S. Congress, House, *Congressional Record*, 70th Cong., 2nd sess., February 18, 1929, 3699; U.S. Congress, Senate, *Congressional Record*, 70th Cong., 2nd sess., February 20, 1929, 3810; United States, *Statutes at Large* 45 (1929): 1314–16.

48. Struthers Burt, "The Jackson Hole Plan," *Outdoor America* (November–December 1944), reprint, J. Horace McFarland Papers, box 22.

49. United States, *Statutes at Large* 46 (1931): 1514; Albert Stoll Jr., "Isle Royale: An Unspoiled and Little Known Wonderland of the North," *American Forests and Forest Life* 32 (August 1926): 457–59, 512; Arthur Newton Pack, "Isle Royale National Park," *Nature Magazine* 26 (September 1935): 176–77; Ben East, "Park to the North," *American Forests* 47 (June 1941): 274–76, 300–301.

50. Original histories of the region include Marjory Stoneman Douglas, *The Everglades: River of Grass* (New York: Rinehart and Co., 1947), and Charlton W. Tebeau, *Man in the Everglades: 2000 Years of Human History in the Everglades National Park* (Miami: University of Miami Press and Everglades Natural History Association, 1968). Patricia Caulfield, *Everglades* (San Francisco: Sierra Club, 1970), is a readable study by an environmental activist, while Luther J. Carter provides a detailed, scholarly treatment of the ecology of the Everglades in *The Florida Experience: Land and Water Policy in a Growth State* (Baltimore: Johns Hopkins University Press and Resources for the Future, 1974), 86–88. Recent studies include David McCallym, *The Everglades: An Environmental History* (Gainesville: University Press of Florida, 2000), although McCallym virtually ignores the park. The superior volume is Michael Grunwald, *The Swamp: The Everglades, Florida, and the Politics of Paradise* (New York: Simon and Schuster, 2006).

51. William J. Schneider, "Water and the Everglades," *Natural History* 75 (November 1966): 32–40; Mark Derr, "Redeeming the Everglades," *Audubon* 95 (September–October 1993): 50–51.

52. Caulfield, *Everglades*, 48–49; Schneider, "Water and the Everglades," 32–36; Carter, *The Florida Experience*, 83–84; Derr, "Redeeming the Everglades," 52.

53. Van Name to Ernest F. Coe, October 6, 1932, United States, National Archives and Records Administration, Records of the National Park Service, Record Group 79, file 101, "Proposed Everglades National Park, History and Legislation"; Grosvenor to David Fairchild, January 24, 1929, file 101, "Proposed Everglades National Park, History and Legislation," Record Group 79.

54. Fairchild to National Park Service, January 21, 1929, file 101, "Proposed Everglades National Park, History and Legislation," Record Group 79; Ernest F. Coe, "The Land of the Fountain of Youth," *American Forests and Forest Life* 35 (March 1929): 158–62.

55. Marjory Stoneman Douglas, *Voice of the River: An Autobiography with John Rothchild* (Sarasota, FL: Pineapple Press, 1987), 135. A comprehensive biography of Douglas, also with much on Ernest F. Coe, is Jack E. Davis, *An Everglades Providence: Marjory Stoneman Douglas and the American Environmental Century* (Athens: University of Georgia Press, 2009).

56. Hornaday to John K. Small, December 30, 1932, file 129, "Proposed Everglades National Park, Legislation," Record Group 79.

57. Albright to Ray Lyman Wilbur, May 10, 1930, file 204-020, "Proposed Everglades National Park, Inspections and Investigations," Record Group 79.

58. A commissioned history of the association is John C. Miles, *Guardians of the Parks: A History of the National Parks and Conservation Association* (Washington, DC: Taylor & Francis in cooperation with National Parks and Conservation Association, 1995).

59. For example, in 1931, Yard wrote to the secretary of the interior, "This is a promoter's proposition. It has scarcely been touched by competent specialists. . . . What's the hurry? Nobody wants the Everglades." Yard to Ray Lyman Wilbur, January 7, 1931, file 101, "Proposed Everglades National Park, History and Legislation," Record Group 79.

60. Yard publicly opposed the inclusion of Jackson Hole in Grand Teton National Park in "Jackson Hole National Monument Borrows Its Grandeur from Surrounding Mountains," *Living Wilderness* 8 (October 1943): 3–13.

61. Frederick Law Olmsted and William P. Wharton, "The Florida Everglades," *American Forests* 38 (March 1932): 143, 147. Senator Duncan U. Fletcher of Florida further presented the investigation to Congress as U.S. Congress, Senate, *The Proposed Everglades National Park*, Sen. Doc. 54, 72nd Cong., 1st sess., January 22, 1932.

62. Olmsted and Wharton, "The Florida Everglades," 143–47.

63. Olmsted and Wharton, "The Florida Everglades," 143–47, 192.

64. Arno B. Cammerer, memorandum, April 2, 1934; Ickes to Louis B. DeRouen, April 9, 1934, file 120, "Proposed Everglades National Park, Legislation," Record Group 79.

65. Ernest F. Coe, "America's Tropical Frontier: A Park," *Landscape Architecture* 27 (October 1936): 6–10. However, Coe was not above cultural nationalism, either, insisting early in the park campaign that the Everglades were "a veritable natural Venice." Coe, "The Land of the Fountain of Youth," 159.

66. United States, *Statutes at Large* 48 (1934): 817; Coe, "America's Tropical Frontier," 6–7; Small to William T. Hornaday, February 28, 1933, file 120, "Proposed Everglades National Park, Legislation," Record Group 79.

67. United States, *Statutes at Large* 50 (1937): 670. As in the Florida Everglades, North Carolina was required to buy the property. This delayed the official dedication of the seashore until 1953.

CHAPTER 7: ECOLOGY DENIED

1. Their careers are briefly described in John Ise, *Our National Park Policy: A Critical History* (Baltimore: The Johns Hopkins Press, 1961), 593–96; Carl P. Russell, *One Hundred Years in Yosemite: The Story of a Great Park and Its Friends* (Yosemite National Park, CA: Yosemite Natural History Association, 1968), 134–36, 143; and Robert Shankland, *Steve Mather of the National Parks*, 3rd ed. (New York: Alfred A. Knopf, 1970), 274–75, 314, 331. A more comprehensive treatment of national park science would include Alfred Runte, *Yosemite: The Embattled Wilderness* (Lincoln: University of Nebraska Press, 1990), and Richard West Sellars, *Preserving Nature in the National Parks: A History*, rev ed. (New Haven, CT: Yale University Press, 2009).

2. U.S. Department of the Interior, National Park Service, *Fauna of the National Parks of the United States: A Preliminary Survey of Faunal Relations in National Parks*, by George M. Wright, Joseph S. Dixon, and Ben H. Thompson (Washington, DC: U.S. Government Printing Office, 1933), 37–39.

3. Wright, *Fauna of the National Parks of the United States*, 37–39. The second volume appeared as U.S. Department of the Interior, National Park Service, *Fauna of the National Parks of the United States: Wildlife Management in the National Parks*, by George M. Wright and Ben H. Thompson (Washington, DC: U.S. Government Printing Office, 1935). Partly in anticipation of the findings of both reports, in 1931 the National Park Service reevaluated its long-standing predator-control program. In noting its endurance, the scientists concluded, "There is sometimes a tendency in men in the field to hold any predator in the same disreputable position as any human criminal. It seems well to comment that no moral status should be attached to any animal. It is just as natural (just as much a part of nature) for [predators] to prey upon other animal life as it is for trees to grow from the soil, and nobody questions the morality of the latter." Wright, *Fauna of the National Parks of the United States*, I:48.

4. A comprehensive history is John Jameson, *The Story of Big Bend National Park* (Austin: University of Texas Press, 1996). See also Ise, *Our National Park Policy*, 379–82.

5. John B. Yeon, "The Issue of the Olympics," *American Forests* 42 (June 1936): 255. For the opposing point of view, see Asahel Curtis, "The Proposed Mount Olympus National Park," *American Forests* 42 (April 1936): 166–69, 195–96.

6. The definitive history remains Carsten Lien, *Olympic Battleground: The Power Politics of Timber Preservation*, 2nd ed. (Seattle: The Mountaineers Books, 2000). Dyana Z. Furmansky, *Rosalie Edge, Hawk of Mercy: The Activist Who Saved Nature from the Conservationists* (Athens: University of Georgia Press, 2009), also includes much on Irving Brant and Willard Van Name.

7. The secrecy, effects, and extent of the logging are exhaustively documented in Lien, *Olympic Battleground*, 254–98. Contemporary accounts in opposition to

park reductions include Herb Crisler, "Our Olympic National Park—Let's Keep All of It," *Nature Magazine* 40 (November 1947): 457–60, 496; Fred H. McNeil, "The Olympic Park Problem," *Mazama* 29 (December 1947): 42–46; Herb Crisler, "Our Heritage—Wilderness or Sawdust?" *Appalachia* 27 (December 1948): 171–77; Weldon F. Heald, "Shall We Auction Olympic National Park?" *Natural History* 63 (September 1954): 311–20, 336; E. T. Clark and Irving Clark Jr., "Is Olympic National Park Too Big?" *American Forests* 60 (September 1954): 30–31, 89, 98; "Olympic Park Viewpoints" (editorial), *Nature Magazine* 49 (August–September 1956): 369–70, 374; and Anthony Wayne Smith, "Hands Off Olympic Park!," *National Parks Magazine* 40 (November 1966): 2.

8. John Muir, "A Rival of Yosemite: The Cañon of the South Fork of King's River, California," *Century Magazine* 43 (November 1891): 77–97; Ben H. Thompson, "The Proposed Kings Canyon National Park" *Bird-Lore* 37 (July–August 1935): 239–44; "Proposed John Muir-Kings Canyon National Park," *Planning and Civic Comment* 5 (January–March 1939), 17–34; United States, *Statutes at Large* 54 (1940): 44.

9. However, significant private lands, totaling 47,000 acres, were later added to Olympic National Park, including land obtained by condemnation. Purchased lands included major portions of the Queets River corridor and a strip along the Pacific coast. Ise, *Our National Park Policy*, 390. Carsten Lien discusses the continuing vulnerability of these areas in *Olympic Battleground*, 299–392.

10. U.S. Congress, House, Committee on the Public Lands, *To Abolish the Jackson Hole National Monument, Wyoming,* Hearings on H.R. 2241, 78th Cong., 1st sess., May–June 1943, 81; Donald C. Swain, *Wilderness Defender: Horace M. Albright and Conservation* (Chicago: University of Chicago Press, 1970), 262–64.

11. H.R. 2241, Hearings, 17–18, 68.

12. U.S. Congress, House, *Congressional Record,* 78th Cong., 2nd sess., December 11, 1944, 9183–96; U.S. Congress, Senate, *Congressional Record,* 78th Cong., 2nd sess., December 19, 1944, 9769, 9807–8.

13. Ise, *Our National Park Policy,* 506–8; United States, *Statutes at Large* 64 (1950): 849.

14. United States, *Statutes at Large* 64 (1950), 849; Ise, *Our National Park Policy,* 508. For example, in 1933, George M. Wright, Joseph S. Dixon, and Ben H. Thompson opposed recreational hunting as a means of reducing overpopulated wildlife species. "Shooting for sport is unsatisfactory," they noted, "because it is selective of the finest specimens instead of the poor ones which, by rights, should be removed first." Wright, *Fauna of the National Parks of the United States,* I:35.

15. U.S. Congress, House, *Congressional Record,* 73rd Cong., 2nd sess., May 24, 1934, 9497; United States, *Statutes at Large* 48 (1934): 817.

16. United States, *Statutes at Large* 48 (1934): 816; William J. Schneider, "Water and the Everglades," *Natural History* 75 (November 1966): 35; Patricia Caulfield, *Everglades* (San Francisco: Sierra Club, 1970), 53.

17. Luther J. Carter provides a comprehensive analysis of the south Florida ecosystem in *The Florida Experience: Land and Water Policy in a Growth State* (Baltimore: Johns Hopkins University Press and Resources for the Future, 1974). See especially chaps. 7 and 8.

18. Peter Farb, "Disaster Threatens the Everglades," *Audubon* 67 (September 1965): 303. Also of relevance are Verne O. Williams, "Man-Made Drought Threatens Everglades National Park," *Audubon* 65 (September 1963): 290–94, and Joan Browder, "Don't Pull the Plug on the Everglades," *American Forests* 73 (September 1967): 12–15, 53–55.

19. Schneider, "Water and the Everglades," 39.

20. Wallace Stegner, "Last Chance for the Everglades," *Saturday Review* 50 (May 6, 1967): 23, 73.

21. The coast redwood is also generally younger than the Sierra species (*Sequoiadendron giganteum*). Scientific comparisons contemporary with the effort to establish Redwood National Park include Edward C. Stone and Richard B. Vasey, "Preservation of Coast Redwood on Alluvial Flats," *Science* 159 (January 12, 1968): 157–60; Samuel T. Dana and Kenneth B. Pomeroy, "Redwoods and Parks," *American Forests* 71 (May 1965): 1–32; and Emanuel Fritz, "A Redwood Forester's View," *Journal of Forestry*, May 1967, 312–19.

22. Dana and Pomeroy, "Redwoods and Parks," 5.

23. United States, *Statutes at Large* 35 (1908): 2174–75; Charles Mulford Robinson, "Muir Woods—A National Park," *The Survey* 20 (May 2, 1908): 181–83; Robert W. Righter, *The Battle over Hetch Hetchy: America's Most Controversial Dam and the Birth of Modern Environmentalism* (New York: Oxford University Press, 2005), 123–24. An interesting footnote to the careers of Muir and Kent is Roderick Nash, "John Muir, William Kent and the Conservation Schism," *Pacific Historical Review* 34 (November 1967): 423–33.

24. Dana and Pomeroy, "Redwoods and Parks," 9–10. Including cutover lands and second growth, the state parks made up nearly 103,000 acres.

25. Promotional circular, Save-the-Redwoods League, 1967; Stone and Vasey, "Preservation of Coast Redwood on Alluvial Flats," 157.

26. As quoted in Dana and Pomeroy, "Redwoods and Parks," 11.

27. Russell D. Butcher, "Redwoods and the Fragile Web of Nature," *Audubon* 66 (May–June 1964): 174.

28. The discrepancy was in large part due to size, approximately 43,000 acres for Mill Creek as opposed to 90,000 for Redwood Creek.

29. The particulars of the various proposals were exhaustively argued in Congress. See, e.g., U.S. Congress, House, Subcommittee on National Parks and Recreation of the Committee on Interior and Insular Affairs, *Redwood National Park* (three parts), Hearings on H.R. 1311 and Related Bills, June–July 1967, May 1968, passim. A revealing history of the philosophical differences between the Save-the-Redwoods League and the Sierra Club is Susan R. Schrepfer, *The*

Fight to Save the Redwoods: A History of Environmental Reform, 1917–1978 (Madison: University of Wisconsin Press, 1983).

30. Promotional circular, Sierra Club, 1967.

31. Lou Cannon analyzes Reagan's opposition to the park in *Governor Reagan: His Rise to Power* (New York: Public Affairs, 2003), 300–303. His more likely quote was, "A tree is a tree—how many more do you need to look at?"

32. H.R. 1311, Hearings, 439–509, passim.

33. The effect of these provisions on the failure to establish Redwood National Park as a self-contained ecosystem is detailed in John Graves, "Redwood National Park: Controversy and Compromise," *National Parks and Conservation Magazine: The Environmental Journal* 48 (October 1974): 14–19.

34. Graves, "Redwood National Park," 14–19.

35. Promotional circular, Sierra Club, undated.

36. Paul A. Zahl, "Finding the Mt. Everest of All Living Things," *National Geographic* 126 (July 1964): 10–51.

37. "Logging Practices Still Ravaging State's Forests," *Los Angeles Times*, August 24, 1975, pt. 2, 1; "Curb on Logging of Redwoods Rejected," *Los Angeles Times*, September 13, 1975, pt. 2, 1; "Redwood Grove Periled: State Moves to Save World's Tallest Tree," *Los Angeles Times*, August 29, 1975, pt. 1, 3; "State Asks Expansion of U.S. Redwood Park," *Los Angeles Times*, September 19, 1976, pt. 1, 3.

38. A. Starker Leopold et al., "Wildlife Management in the National Parks," *National Parks Magazine* 37 (April 1963): iii; F. Fraser Darling and Noel D. Eichhorn, "Man and Nature in the National Parks: Reflections on Policy," *National Parks Magazine* 43 (April 1969): 14, 17. Darling, an ecologist, and Eichhorn, a geographer, were sponsored by the Conservation Foundation of Washington, D.C. The Leopold Committee report, originally published by the Interior Department, was widely reprinted in conservation journals.

CHAPTER 8: SCHEMERS AND STANDARD-BEARERS

1. Edward H. Hamilton, "The New Yosemite Railroad," *Cosmopolitan* 43 (September 1907): 569–70. See also Lanier Bartlett, "By Rail to the Yosemite," *Pacific Monthly* 17 (June 1907): 730–38. A history of railroad development of the national parks is Alfred Runte, *Trains of Discovery: Western Railroads and the National Parks*, 4th ed. (Boulder, CO: Roberts Rinehart Publishers, 1998).

2. United States, National Archives and Records Administration, Records of the National Park Service, Record Group 79, Yosemite National Park, "Travel," pt. 1, box 727. An entertaining departure on the admission of automobiles into Yosemite Valley is Richard Lillard, "The Siege and Conquest of a National Park," *American West* 5 (January 1968): 28–31, 67, 69–71. Recent histories include Paul S. Sutter, *Driven Wild: How the Fight against Automobiles Launched the Modern Wilderness Movement* (Seattle: University of Washington Press,

2002), and Hal K. Rothman, *Devil's Bargains: Tourism in the Twentieth-Century American West* (Lawrence: University Press of Kansas, 1998).

3. Charles J. Belden, "The Motor in Yellowstone," *Scribner's Magazine* 63 (June 1918): 673; Enos A. Mills, "Touring in Our National Parks," *Country Life in America* 23 (January 1913): 36. Mills was a leading proponent of Rocky Mountain National Park.

4. Arthur Newton Pack, "Hunting Nature on Wheels," *Nature Magazine* 13 (June 1929): 388; Robert Sloss, "Camping in an Automobile," *Outing* 56 (May 1910): 236.

5. H. P. Burchell, "The Automobile as a Means of Country Travel," *Outing* 46 (August 1905): 536; Frank E. Brimmer, "Autocamping—the Fastest Growing Sport," *The Outlook* 137 (July 16, 1924): 439; Gilbert Irwin, "Nature Ways by Car and Camp," *Nature Magazine* 10 (July 1927): 27. A modern history of transportation in Yellowstone is Lee H. Whittlesey, *Storytelling in Yellowstone: Horse and Buggy Tour Guides* (Albuquerque: University of New Mexico Press, 2007).

6. Anonymous, "Neighbors for a Night in Yellowstone Park" *Literary Digest* 82 (August 30, 1924): 45.

7. Ethel and James Dorrance, "Motoring in the Yellowstone," *Munsey's Magazine* 70 (July 1920): 268–70. A sampling of other relevant articles would include W. A. Babson, "Motor in the Wilderness," *Country Life in America* 8 (June 1905): 247–48; Hrolf Wisby, "Camping Out with an Automobile," *Outing* 45 (March 1905): 739–45; Samuel M. Evans, "Forty Gallons of Gasoline to Forty Miles of Water: Recipe for a Motor Trip to Crater Lake, Oregon," *Sunset Magazine: The Pacific Monthly* 27 (October 1911): 393–99; Arthur E. Demaray, "Our National Parks and How to Reach Them," *American Forestry* 27 (June 1921): 360–70; Ronne C. Shelse, "The Pageant Highway: A 6,000-Mile Ride from Park to Park," *Mentor World Traveler* 12 (July 1924): 29–45; Hazel R. Langdale, "To the Yellowstone," *Woman's Home Companion* 56 (May 1929): 120–21; and Anonymous, "Seeing the Western National Parks by Motor," *American Forests and Forest Life* 35 (August 1929): 508–9.

8. The implications of the statistic for rail passenger service are noted in George W. Long, "Many-Splendored Glacierland," *National Geographic Magazine* 160 (May 1956): 589–90.

9. James Bryce, "National Parks—The Need of the Future," *The Outlook* 102 (December 14, 1912): 811–13.

10. Lorimer to McFarland, November 12, 1934, Pennsylvania Historical and Museum Commission, Division of Archives and Manuscripts, McFarland Papers, box 18.

11. McFarland to Lorimer, November 13, 1934, McFarland Papers, box 18.

12. United States, *Statutes at Large* 39 (1916): 535.

13. Robert Sterling Yard, "Economic Aspects of Our National Parks Policy," *Scientific Monthly* 16 (April 1923): 381.

14. Frederick Law Olmsted, "The Yosemite Valley and the Mariposa Big Trees," ed. Laura Wood Roper, *Landscape Architecture* 43 (October 1952): 17, 22.

15. A history of the contradictions emanating from this policy is Alfred Runte, *Yosemite: The Embattled Wilderness* (Lincoln: University of Nebraska Press, 1990). See also John Ise, *Our National Park Policy: A Critical History* (Baltimore: The Johns Hopkins Press, 1961), especially pp. 606–18.

16. Olmsted, "The Yosemite Valley and the Mariposa Big Trees," 22–24.

17. Laura Wood Roper, *FLO: A Biography of Frederick Law Olmsted* (Baltimore: Johns Hopkins University Press, 1973), 287.

18. Olmsted, "The Yosemite Valley and the Mariposa Big Trees," 16.

19. Grace Greenwood, *New Life in New Lands* (New York: J. B. Ford and Co., 1873), 358–60. Grace Greenwood was the pen name of Mrs. Sara Jane Clarke Lippincott (1823–1904).

20. As quoted in Carl P. Russell, *One Hundred Years in Yosemite: The Story of a Great Park and Its Friends* (Yosemite National Park, CA: Yosemite Natural History Association, 1968), 108–9.

21. Russell, *One Hundred Years in Yosemite*, 109.

22. Laurence V. Degnan to Douglas H. Hubbard, January 24, 1959, U.S. National Park Service, Yosemite National Park Research Library, Firefall Collection, Y-22. The firefall may also have been accidental. After the revelers had finished lighting their sticks of dynamite from the bonfire, they may simply have pushed the coals off the cliff.

23. E. P. Leavitt to Agnes L. Scott, September 20, 1928, Yosemite National Park Research Library, Firefall Collection, Y-22; G. B. MacKenzie, "The Flaming Wonder of the Sierras," *Travel* 45 (June 1925): 15, 44; Anonymous, "Let the Fire Fall!" *Collier's* 130 (August 16, 1952): 66.

24. Olmsted, "The Yosemite Valley and the Mariposa Big Trees," 17.

25. W. G. Marshall, *Through America; or, Nine Months in the United States* (London: H. G. Bohn, 1881), 340–41; Frank Strauser to Ansel F. Hall, July 27, 1925, Yosemite National Park Research Library, Y-21a.

26. Allen Kelley, "Restoration of Yosemite Waterfalls," *Harper's Weekly* 36 (July 16, 1892): 678. A similar plea is Hiram Martin Chittenden, "Sentiment versus Utility in the Treatment of Natural Scenery," *Pacific Monthly* 23 (January 1910): 29–38. Chittenden further included Hetch Hetchy and Niagara Falls as scenic wonders whose beauty could be both preserved and developed. Other schemes afoot included an elaborate cable-car system in the Grand Canyon and an elevator beside the Lower Falls of the Yellowstone River in Yellowstone National Park. Although neither again succeeded, their promoters indeed were serious. See U.S. Congress, House, Committee on the Public Lands, *Granting Right of Way Over Certain Sections of the Grand Canyon National Monument Reserve in Arizona to the Grand Canyon Scenic Railroad Company*, Hearings on H.R. 2258, 61st Cong., 2nd sess., 1910; and U.S. Congress, Senate, *David B. May*, S. Doc. 151, 54th Cong., 2nd sess., 1897.

27. Victor H. Cahalane, "Your National Parks—and You," *Nature Magazine* 33 (May 1940): 264–65.

28. Cahalane, "Your National Parks—and You," 264.

29. Martelle W. Trager, *National Parks of the Northwest* (New York: Dodd and Mead, 1939), 31–33, 45–48. Less elaborate bear feedings were noted years earlier, originally popularized by Yellowstone's camps and hotels. See, e.g., Thomas D. Murphy, *Three Wonderlands of the American West* (Boston: L. C. Page and Co., 1912), 15–16.

30. Henry Baldwin Ward, "What Is Happening to Our National Parks?" *Nature Magazine* 31 (December 1938): 614; Albert W. Atwood, "Can the National Parks Be Kept Unspoiled?" *Saturday Evening Post* 208 (May 16, 1936): 18–19.

31. Robert Sterling Yard, "The People and the National Parks," *The Survey* 48 (August 1, 1922): 552; Yard, "Economic Aspects of Our National Parks Policy," 387; Wallace W. Atwood, "What Are National Parks?" *American Forests* 37 (September 1931): 543.

32. Arno B. Cammerer, "Maintenance of the Primeval in National Parks," *Appalachia* 22 (December 1938): 207.

33. Robert Sterling Yard, "Historical Basis of National Park Standards," *National Parks Bulletin* 10 (November 1929): 4.

34. U.S. Bureau of the Census, *Historical Statistics of the United States: Colonial Times to 1957* (Washington, DC: U.S. Government Printing Office, 1960), 222.

35. "U.S. Is Outgrowing Its Parks," *U.S. News and World Report* 38 (June 10, 1955): 79; Runte, *Trains of Discovery*, 59.

36. Joseph Wood Krutch, "Which Men? What Needs?" *American Forests* 63 (April 1957): 23, 46; "U.S. Is Outgrowing Its Parks," 78. A macabre look at the underside of tourism is Lee H. Whittlesey, *Death in Yellowstone: Accidents and Foolhardiness in the First National Park* (Boulder, CO: Roberts Rinehart Publishers, 1995).

37. John Muir, "The Wild Parks and Forest Reservations of the West," *Atlantic Monthly* 81 (January 1898): 16; Bernard DeVoto, "The National Parks," *Fortune* 35 (June 1947): 120–21; Krutch, "Which Men? What Needs?" 22–23. Bernard DeVoto, an outspoken defender of the national parks, has his biographer in Wallace Stegner, *The Uneasy Chair: A Biography of Bernard DeVoto* (New York: Doubleday, 1974). See especially pp. 301–22. DeVoto's most famous commentary is "Let's Close the National Parks," *Harper's Magazine* 207 (October 1953): 49–52.

38. A history of the program is Ethan Carr, *Mission 66: Modernism and the National Park Dilemma* (Amherst: University of Massachusetts Press in association with Library of American Landscape History, 2007). Practices Mission 66 displaced are treated in Linda Flint McClelland, *Building the National Parks: Historic Landscape Design and Construction* (Baltimore: Johns Hopkins University Press, 1998).

39. Devereux Butcher, "Resorts or Wilderness?" *Atlantic* 207 (February 1961): 47, 51; Brower to Alexander Hildebrand, July 23, 1958, and "The Sierra Club's National Park Road Policy—and Tenaya Lake," in Confidential Memorandum, July 25, 1958, both in Wayburn Files, Records of the Sierra Club, Bancroft Library, University of California, Berkeley; F. Fraser Darling and Noel D. Eichhorn, "Man and Nature in the National Parks: Reflections on Policy," *National Parks Magazine* 43 (April 1969): 17.

40. U.S. Bureau of the Census, *Statistical Abstract of the United States: 1974*, 95th ed. (Washington, DC: U.S. Government Printing Office, 1974), 204.

41. Edward Abbey, *Desert Solitaire: A Season in the Wilderness* (New York: Ballantine Books, 1968), 57–61.

42. Garrett Hardin, "The Economics of Wilderness," *Natural History* 78 (June–July 1969): 20–27.

43. Krutch, "Which Men? What Needs?" 23.

44. Cammerer, "Maintenance of the Primeval in National Parks," 210–11; Krutch, "Which Men? What Needs?" 23.

45. Eric Julber, "Let's Open Up Our Wilderness Areas," *Reader's Digest* 100 (May 1972): 126; Julber, "The Wilderness: Just How Wild Should It Be?" reprinted in cooperation with the Western Wood Products Laboratory (n.d.), 1.

46. Butcher, "Resorts or Wilderness?" 50.

47. Butcher, "Resorts or Wilderness?" 50. Similar contemporary arguments include Paul Brooks, "The Pressure of Numbers," *Atlantic* 207 (February 1961): 54–56; Benton MacKaye, "If This Be Snobbery," *Living Wilderness* 77 (Summer 1961): 3–4; and Jerome B. Wood, "National Parks: Tomorrow's Slums?" *Travel* 101 (April 1954): 14–16.

48. Jack Hope, "Hassles in the Park," *Natural History* 80 (May 1971): 22–23; "Yosemite: Better Way to Run a Park?" *U.S. News and World Report* 72 (January 24, 1972): 56.

49. George B. Hartzog Jr., "Changing the National Parks to Cope with People—and Cars," *U.S. News and World Report* 72 (January 24, 1972): 52; U.S. Department of the Interior, National Park Service, *Yosemite Master Plan Workbook* (Washington, DC: U.S. Government Printing Office, 1975); U.S. Department of the Interior, National Park Service, *Yosemite Master Plan: Update* (Washington, DC: U.S. Government Printing Office, June 1976); U.S. Department of the Interior, National Park Service, *Yosemite: Summary of the Draft General Management Plan* (Washington, DC: U.S. Government Printing Office, August 1978); U.S. Department of the Interior, National Park Service, "Final Yosemite General Management Plan Released," news release, October 30, 1980 (all Yosemite National Park Research Library).

50. Jack Anderson, "Yosemite: Another Disneyland?" *Washington Post*, September 15, 1974, reprint; Philip Fradkin, "Sierra Club Sees Damage in Yosemite Filming," *Los Angeles Times*, August 28, 1974, pt. 1, 22; "Yosemite National

Convention Center Proposed by New Concessionaire," *Sierra Club Bulletin* 59 (September 1974): 29.

51. Julber, "The Wilderness: Just How Wild Should It Be?" 5.

52. Krutch, "Which Men? What Needs?" 23.

53. "America's 'Magnificent Seven,'" *U.S. News and World Report* 78 (April 21, 1975): 56–57. In order, the public voted as follows: Grand Canyon, Yellowstone, Niagara Falls, Mount McKinley, California's "big trees"—the sequoias and redwoods—the Hawaii volcanoes, and the Everglades.

54. The belief that the flow of Niagara Falls can be reduced even further is discussed in B. F. Friesen and J. C. Day, "Hydroelectric Power and Scenic Provisions of the 1950 Niagara Treaty," *Water Resources Bulletin* 13 (December 1977): 1175–89.

CHAPTER 9: TRADITION TRIUMPHANT

1. As quoted in U.S. National Parks Centennial Commission, *Preserving a Heritage* (Washington, DC: U.S. Government Printing Office, 1973), 79–80.

2. An inventory of major publicity may be found in National Parks Centennial Commission, *Preserving a Heritage*, 52–61.

3. Conservation Foundation, *National Parks for the Future* (Washington, DC: Conservation Foundation, 1972), 31. For a discussion of the national park idea abroad, see Roderick Nash, *Nature in World Development: Patterns in the Preservation of Scenic and Outdoor Recreation Resources* (New York: The Rockefeller Foundation, 1978), and Jeremy Harrison et al., "The World Coverage of Protected Areas: Development Goals and Environmental Needs," *Ambio* 11, no. 5 (1982): 238–45. Also pertinent but now dated is John Ise, *Our National Park Policy: A Critical History* (Baltimore: The Johns Hopkins Press, 1961), chap. 31.

4. Rachel Carson, *Silent Spring* (New York: Fawcett Crest, [1962] 1964), 24, 169.

5. U.S. Department of the Interior, National Park Service, *First World Conference on National Parks, Proceedings* (Washington, DC: U.S. Government Printing Office, 1962), 433–47.

6. U.S. Department of the Interior, National Park Service, *First World Conference on National Parks, Proceedings*, xxxi.

7. International Union for Conservation of Nature and Natural Resources et al., *Second World Conference on National Parks, Proceedings* (Morges, Switzerland: International Union, U.S. National Parks Centennial Commission, 1974), 38; Paul R. Ehrlich, *The Population Bomb*, rev. ed. (New York: Sierra Club/Ballantine Books, 1971), xi.

8. Conservation Foundation, *National Parks for the Future*, 9.

9. International Union for Conservation of Nature and Natural Resources et al., *Second World Conference, Proceedings*, 15.

10. See, e.g., Norman Myers, "National Parks in Savannah Africa," *Science* 178 (December 22, 1972): 1255–63; Norman Myers, "Wildlife Parks in Emergent Africa: The Outlook for Their Survival," *Chicago Field Museum of Natural History Bulletin* 45 (February 1974): 8–14; and David Western, "Amboseli National Park: Enlisting Landowners to Conserve Migratory Wildlife," *Ambio* 11, no. 5 (1982): 302–8. Persistent threats to the African parks is also a common theme in the proceedings of the world national parks conferences.

11. See, e.g., Paul W. Richards, "National Parks in Wet Tropical Areas," in International Union for Conservation of Nature and Natural Resources et al., *Second World Conference, Proceedings*, 219–27.

12. International Union for Conservation of Nature and Natural Resources et al., *Second World Conference, Proceedings*, 443–44. Regarding potential threats to Antarctica from the assessment of its economic potential, see P. H. C. Lucas, "International Agreement on Conserving the Antarctic Environment," *Ambio* 11, no. 5 (1982): 292–95.

13. A detailed overview of the struggles for the Colorado River is Roderick Nash, "Conservation and the Colorado," chap. 9 of T. H. Watkins et al., *The Grand Colorado: The Story of a River and Its Canyons* (Palo Alto, CA: American West Publishing Co., 1969). Also relevant is Roderick Frazier Nash, *Wilderness and the American Mind*, 4th ed. (New Haven, CT: Yale University Press, 2001), 209–20.

14. Wallace Stegner, ed., *This Is Dinosaur: Echo Park Country and Its Magic Rivers* (New York: Alfred A. Knopf, 1955). The definitive modern history is Mark W. T. Harvey, *A Symbol of Wilderness: Echo Park and the American Conservation Movement* (Albuquerque: University of New Mexico Press, 1994). Also relevant is Mark W. T. Harvey, *Wilderness Forever: Howard Zahniser and the Path to the Wilderness Act* (Seattle: University of Washington Press, 2005).

15. The loss of Glen Canyon is featured in Eliot Porter, *The Place No One Knew: Glen Canyon on the Colorado* (San Francisco: Sierra Club Press, 1963).

16. Preservationists' arguments for a "greater" Grand Canyon National Park are summarized in Roderick Nash, ed., *Grand Canyon of the Living Colorado* (San Francisco: Sierra Club/Ballantine Books, 1970), 106–7.

17. Robert Dolan et al., "Man's Impact on the Colorado River in the Grand Canyon," *American Scientist* 62 (July–August 1974): 392–401.

18. Nash, "Conservation and the Colorado," 269; Laurence I. Moss, "The Grand Canyon Subsidy Machine," *Sierra Club Bulletin* 52 (April 1967): 89–94.

19. The issue of air pollution is summarized in Jerome Ostrov, "Visibility Protection under the Clean Air Act: Preserving Scenic and Parkland Areas in the Southwest," *Ecology Law Quarterly* 10, no. 3 (1982): 397–453.

20. Philip Fradkin, "Smog from Power Plants Threatens Utah 'Color Country,'" *Los Angeles Times*, February 9, 1975, pt. 2, 1.

21. *Los Angeles Times*, December 28, 1975, pt. 7, 2.

22. As quoted in Nash, *Wilderness and the American Mind*, 230. A further analysis of the canyon's hold on the American imagination is Stephen J. Pyne, *How the Canyon Became Grand: A Short History* (New York: Viking, 1998).

23. The advertisement is reprinted in Watkins et al., *The Grand Colorado*, 270.

24. Nash, *Wilderness and the American Mind*, 234.

25. U.S. Congress, House, Subcommittee on National Parks and Recreation of the Committee on Interior and Insular Affairs, *To Prohibit Certain Incompatible Activities within Any Area of the National Park System*, Hearing on H.R. 9799, 94th Cong., 1st sess., October 6, 1975, 5.

26. In addition to Death Valley National Monument, these included Glacier Bay National Monument and Mount McKinley National Park, Alaska; Crater Lake National Park, Oregon; and Organ Pipe Cactus National Monument and Coronado National Memorial, Arizona. H.R. 9799, Hearing, 4–5.

27. H.R. 9799, Hearing, 38.

28. H.R. 9799, Hearing, 66–68.

29. H.R. 9799, Hearing, 45, 52, 101–3.

30. H.R. 9799, Hearing, 103–4.

31. United States, *Statutes at Large* 90 (1976): 1342–44.

32. "Jetport and the Everglades—Life or Runway?" *Living Wilderness* 33 (Spring 1969): 13–20; "Jets vs. the Call of the Wild," *Business Week*, August 30, 1969, 76–77; "The Newest Trouble on Everglades Waters," *Business Week*, June 5, 1971, 45–46.

33. Melvin A. Finn, "Fahkahatchee: Endangered Gem of the Big Cypress Country," *Living Wilderness* 35 (Autumn 1971): 11–18; George Reiger, "The Choice for Big Cypress: Bulldozers or Butterflies," *National Wildlife* 10 (October–November 1972): 5–10; Luther J. Carter, *The Florida Experience: Land and Water Policy in a Growth State* (Baltimore: Johns Hopkins University Press and Resources for the Future, 1974), chap. 8; Nelson M. Blake, *Land into Water— Water into Land: A History of Water Management in Florida* (Tallahassee: University Press of Florida, 1980), 231–35.

34. Robert Belous, "Hello, Jet Age; Goodbye, Wilderness," *Living Wilderness* 37 (Spring 1973): 40–49.

35. United States, *Statutes at Large* 88 (1974): 1258–61; Michael J. Duever et al., *The Big Cypress National Preserve* (New York: National Audubon Society, 1986).

36. Conservation Foundation, *National Parks for the Future*, 19; Robert Cahn, "Alaska: A Matter of 80,000,000 Acres," *Audubon* 76 (July 1974): 2–13, 66–81.

37. Efforts leading to the expansion of Redwood National Park in 1978 are discussed in Susan R. Schrepfer, *The Fight to Save the Redwoods: A History of Environmental Reform, 1917–1978* (Madison: University of Wisconsin Press, 1983), 186–244.

38. George H. Harrison and Frank C. Craighead Jr., "They're Killing Yellowstone's Grizzlies," *National Wildlife* 11 (October–November 1973): 4–8, 17; Christopher Cauble, "The Great Grizzly Grapple," *Natural History* 86 (August–September 1977): 74–81.

CHAPTER 10: THE LESSON OF THE BIG TREES

1. U.S. Department of the Interior, Advisory Board on Wildlife Management, *Wildlife Management in the National Parks*, by A. S. Leopold et al., Report to the Secretary, March 4, 1963 (hereafter cited as Leopold Committee, *Report*). As testimony to its importance, it was reprinted in its entirety in *Living Wilderness, Audubon, National Parks Magazine*, and *American Forests*.

2. Leopold Committee, *Report*, 1–2.

3. Leopold Committee, *Report*, 4.

4. Leopold Committee, *Report*, 5.

5. The classic example remains Joseph Grinnell and Tracy Storer, "Animal Life as an Asset of National Parks," *Science* 44 (September 15, 1916): 377. Important histories of the evolution of science in the national parks include Alfred Runte, *Yosemite: The Embattled Wilderness* (Lincoln: University of Nebraska Press, 1990); Richard West Sellars, *Preserving Nature in the National Parks: A History*, rev. ed. (New Haven, CT: Yale University Press, 2009); and James A. Pritchard, *Preserving Yellowstone's Natural Conditions: Science and the Perception of Nature* (Lincoln: University of Nebraska Press, 1999).

6. Leopold Committee, *Report*, passim.

7. Leopold Committee, *Report*, 21.

8. Leopold Committee, *Report*, 5.

9. "Leopold Report Appraised," *Living Wilderness* 83 (Spring 1963): 20–24; Anthony Wayne Smith, "Editorial Comment on the Leopold Report," *National Parks Magazine* 37 (April 1963): I.

10. An overview of this history is Richard J. Hartesveldt, "Effects of Human Impact upon *Sequoia gigantea* and Its Environment in the Mariposa Grove, Yosemite National Park, California" (PhD diss., University of Michigan, 1962).

11. Curtis K. Skinner, "Fire, the Enemy of Our National Parks," *American Forests and Forest Life* 35 (August 1929): 519–20. With special emphasis on the public lands, the standard history of fire and fire management is Stephen J. Pyne, *Fire in America: A Cultural History of Wildland and Rural Fire* (Princeton, NJ: Princeton University Press, 1982). On the early debate over the advantages of light burning, see pp. 100–122.

12. U.S. Department of the Interior, *Report of the Acting Superintendent of the Yosemite National Park for the Fiscal Year Ended June 30, 1894*, H. Exec. Doc. 1, pt. 5, vol. 3, 53rd Cong., 3rd sess., 1894, 675–76. Gale further elaborated, "It is a well-known fact that the Indians burned the forests annually." J. W.

Zevely, acting superintendent of Yosemite in 1898, was among those who later endorsed the light burning theory. See U.S. Department of the Interior, *Report of the Acting Superintendent of the Yosemite National Park for the Fiscal Year Ended June 30, 1898*, H. Doc. 5, 55th Cong., 3rd sess., 1898, 1056–57. An influential opponent of proposals to reintroduce fire to the giant sequoia groves was Colonel S. B. M. Young, acting superintendent of the park in 1896. See U.S. Department of the Interior, *Report of the Acting Superintendent of Yosemite National Park*, August 15, 1896, in H. Doc. 5, vol. 3, 54th Cong., 2nd sess., 1896, 736–37.

13. A relevant bibliography of the scientific literature is provided in U.S. Department of the Interior, National Park Service, *Giant Sequoia Ecology: Fire and Reproduction*, by H. Thomas Harvey et al., Scientific Monograph Series No. 12 (Washington, DC: U.S. Government Printing Office, 1980), 163–68.

14. H. H. Biswell, "The Big Trees and Fire," *National Parks Magazine* 35 (April 1961): 13–14.

15. Biswell, "Big Trees and Fire," 14.

16. Quoted in R. J. Hartesveldt and H. T. Harvey, "The Fire Ecology of Sequoia Regeneration," *California Tall Timbers Fire Ecology Conference, November 9–10, 1967, Proceedings* (Tallahassee, FL: Tall Timbers Research Station, 1968), 65.

17. Hartesveldt and Harvey, "Fire Ecology of Sequoia Regeneration," 65–76. The scientific literature grew voluminously throughout the late 1960s and 1970s. See also H. H. Biswell, "Forest Fire in Perspective," *California Tall Timbers Fire Ecology Conference, November 9–10, 1967, Proceedings* (Tallahassee, FL: Tall Timbers Research Station, 1968), 43–63; Bruce M. Kilgore, "Impact of Prescribed Burning on a Sequoia–Mixed Conifer Forest," *Annual Tall Timbers Fire Ecology Conference, June 8–9, 1972, Proceedings* (Tallahassee, FL: Tall Timbers Research Station, 1973), 345–75; Peter H. Schuft, "A Prescribed Burning Program for Sequoia and Kings Canyon National Parks," *Annual Tall Timbers Fire Ecology Conference, June 8–9, 1972, Proceedings* (Tallahassee, FL: Tall Timbers Research Station, 1973), 377–89; John McLaughlin, "Restoring Fire to the Environment in Sequoia and Kings Canyon National Parks," *Annual Tall Timbers Fire Ecology Conference, June 8–9, 1972, Proceedings* (Tallahassee, FL: Tall Timbers Research Station, 1973), 391–95; Bruce M. Kilgore, "Fire Management in the National Parks: An Overview," *Tall Timbers Fire Ecology Conference and Fire and Land Management Symposium, October 8–10, 1974, Proceedings* (Tallahassee, FL: Tall Timbers Research Station, 1976), 45–57; John L. Vankat, "Fire and Man in Sequoia National Park," *Annals of the Association of American Geographers* 67 (March 1977): 17–27; and Bruce M. Kilgore and Dan Taylor, "Fire History of a Sequoia–Mixed Conifer Forest," *Ecology* 60 (February 1979): 129–42.

18. Vankat, "Fire and Man in Sequoia National Park," 17, 25; Leopold Committee, *Report*, 6.

19. Vankat, "Fire and Man in Sequoia National Park," 26; U.S. Department of the Interior, National Park Service, *Compilation of the Administrative Policies . . . of the National Park System* (Washington, DC: U.S. Government Printing Office, 1968), 20.

20. A detailed justification for this approach is Kilgore, "Impact of Prescribed Burning on a Sequoia–Mixed Conifer Forest," 366–72.

21. As one example from 1974, a fire set by lightning burned 3,500 acres in the Tetons, periodically obscuring the mountains between July and November. In the Park Service's own words, allowing the fire to burn "was quite controversial." U.S. National Park Service, Grand Teton National Park, Wyoming, "Natural Resources Management Plan and Environmental Assessment," bound typescript, March 1985, 72–73. The incident is also mentioned in Pyne, *Fire in America*, 304.

22. Pyne, *Fire in America*, 122; McLaughlin, "Restoring Fire to the Environment in Sequoia and Kings Canyon National Parks," 394.

23. Beyond fire ecology, a survey of the literature includes Robert Dolan, Bruce P. Hayden, and Gary Soucie, "Environmental Dynamics and Resource Management in the U.S. National Parks," *Environmental Management* 2, no. 3 (1978): 249–58; Thomas M. Bonnicksen and Edward C. Stone, "Managing Vegetation within U.S. National Parks: A Policy Analysis," *Environmental Management* 6 (March 1982): 109–22; Robert Dolan and Bruce Hayden, "Adjusting to Nature in Our National Seashores," *National Parks and Conservation Magazine: The Environmental Journal* 48 (June 1974): 9–14; Robert Dolan et al., "Man's Impact on the Barrier Islands of North Carolina," *American Scientist* 61 (March–April 1973): 151–62; and James K. Agee, "Issues and Impacts of Redwood National Park Expansion," *Environmental Management* 4 (September 1980): 407–23. The Leopold Committee Report should further be supplemented with the National Academy of Sciences, National Research Council, Advisory Committee to the National Park Service on Research, "Report to the Secretary of the Interior," by William J. Robbins et al., bound typescript, August 1, 1963.

24. U.S. National Park Service, Sequoia and Kings Canyon National Parks, *Giant Forest Restoration Overview (Demolition)*, http://www.nps.gov/seki/history culture/gfdemover.htm (accessed May 11, 2009).

CHAPTER 11: IDEALS AND
CONTROVERSIES OF EXPANSION

1. Robert Sterling Yard, "Gift-Parks the Coming National Park Danger," *National Parks Bulletin* 4 (October 9, 1923): 4.

2. Robert Sterling Yard, *National Parks Portfolio* (New York: Charles Scribner's Sons, 1916), 3–6.

3. Yard, "Gift-Parks the Coming National Park Danger," 4.

4. Robert Sterling Yard, "To Double Our National *Military* Parks System—But Let Us Not Mix Systems," *National Parks Bulletin* 5 (January 21, 1924): 8.

5. John C. Merriam, "Our National Parks," *American Forests and Forest Life* 32 (August 1926): 478. Merriam's views on landscape are the focus of Stephen R. Mark, *Preserving the Living Past: John C. Merriam's Legacy in the State and National Parks* (Berkeley: University of California Press, 2005). The John C. Merriam Papers, Library of Congress, Washington, D.C., offer additional insights into the concerns of Merriam, Robert Sterling Yard, and their contemporaries.

6. A major analysis of these emotions is Susan R. Schrepfer, *The Fight to Save the Redwoods: A History of Environmental Reform, 1917–1978* (Madison: University of Wisconsin Press, 1983). See especially chaps. 3–6.

7. A seminal analysis of the period is Samuel P. Hays in collaboration with Barbara D. Hays, *Beauty, Health, and Permanence: Environmental Politics in the United States, 1955–1985* (New York: Cambridge University Press, 1987).

8. Urban concerns are summarized in Peter Marcuse, "Is the National Parks Movement Anti-Urban?" *Parks and Recreation* 6 (July 1971): 17–21, 48.

9. Yard, "Gift-Parks the Coming National Park Danger," 5.

10. Marcuse, "Is the National Parks Movement Anti-Urban?" passim.

11. A primary example of this thinking is "NPCA Interviews Phillip Burton: Meeting the Needs of Tomorrow Today," *National Parks and Conservation Magazine: The Environmental Journal* 53 (May 1979): 22–26.

12. U.S. Congress, House, Committee on Interior and Insular Affairs, Subcommittee on National Parks and Insular Affairs, *Legislative History of the National Parks and Recreation Act of 1978*, Committee Print No. 11, 95th Cong., 2nd sess., December 1978 (hereafter cited as *Legislative History*).

13. "NPCA Interviews Phillip Burton," 22.

14. John Ise, *Our National Park Policy: A Critical History* (Baltimore: The Johns Hopkins Press, 1961), 136.

15. U.S. Congress, House, *Congressional Record*, 57th Cong., 2nd sess., December 6, 1902, 81.

16. U.S. Congress, Senate, *Wind Cave National Park*, S. Rept. 1944 to accompany S. 6138, 57th Cong., 1st sess., June 17, 1902, 2–3.

17. U.S. Congress, Senate, *Congressional Record*, 57th Cong., 2nd sess., January 12, 1903, 666; United States, *Statutes at Large* 32 (1903): 765–66.

18. United States, *Statutes at Large* 33 (1904): 2368–72.

19. United States, Congress, House, *Congressional Record*, 71st Cong., 3rd sess., January 14, 1931, 2163–65.

20. Ise, *Our National Park Policy*, 140–42; U.S. Congress, House, *Sulphur Springs Reservation to Be Known as Platt National Park*, H. Rept. 5016 to accompany H. J. Res. 181, 59th Cong., 1st sess., June 26, 1906; United States, *Statutes at Large* 34 (1906): 837.

21. U.S. Department of the Interior, National Park Service, *Report of the Director for the Fiscal Year Ended June 30, 1921* (Washington, DC: U.S. Government Printing Office, 1921), 32–33. Mather's role in the state parks movement is further treated in Robert Shankland, *Steve Mather of the National Parks*, 3rd ed. (New York: Alfred A. Knopf, 1970), chap. 14.

22. U.S. Department of the Interior, National Park Service, *Report of the Director for the Fiscal Year Ended June 30, 1921*, 60. Mather at least rationalized that Hot Springs National Park had national popularity, inasmuch as park visitors came "heavily from the South and Southwest."

23. Robert Sterling Yard, "Politics in Our National Parks," *American Forests and Forest Life* 32 (August 1926): 485.

24. Freeman Tilden, *The National Parks* (New York: Alfred A. Knopf, 1970), 257–58; Yard, "Gift-Parks the Coming National Park Danger," 5.

25. Yard, "Politics in Our National Parks," 486, 489.

26. The origins of historic preservation are exhaustively documented in Charles B. Hosmer Jr., *Preservation Comes of Age: From Williamsburg to the National Trust, 1926–1949*, 2 vols. (Charlottesville: University of Virginia Press, 1981). A contemporary assessment is Carl P. Russell, "The Conservation of Historic Values," *National Parks Bulletin* 14 (December 1938): 16–19. Also relevant is F. Ross Holland Jr., "The Park Service as Curator," *National Parks and Conservation Magazine: The Environmental Journal* 53 (August 1979): 10–15.

27. See Ronald F. Lee, *The Origin and Evolution of the National Military Park Idea* (Washington, DC: Office of Park Historic Preservation, National Park Service, 1973).

28. Horace M. Albright, *Origins of National Park Service Administration of Historic Sites* (Philadelphia: Eastern National Park and Monument Association, 1971), 17–23.

29. Albright, *Origins of National Park Service Administration of Historic Sites*, 24.

30. Ovid Butler, "The New National Park Emergency," *American Forests* 40 (January 1934): 21.

31. Albright, *Origins of National Park Service Administration of Historic Sites*, 23.

32. See, e.g., "Remarks by Mr. H. S. Graves," in U.S. Department of the Interior, *Proceedings of the National Park Conference Held at the Yellowstone National Park, September 11 and 12, 1911* (Washington, DC: U.S. Government Printing Office, 1912), 66–68, and U.S. Department of the Interior, *Proceedings of the National Park Conference Held at Berkeley, California, March 11, 12, and 13, 1915* (Washington, DC: U.S. Government Printing Office, 1915), 142–46. See also the J. Horace McFarland Papers, Pennsylvania Historical and Museum Commission, Division of Archives and Manuscripts, Harrisburg, box 18, especially Graves to McFarland, March 30, 1916. "My own view has always been that the National Park Service should be in the Department of Agriculture. I ex-

pressed my views on this subject to [the secretary of the interior] in 1911 in various conferences and also in official correspondence."

33. Henry S. Graves, "National and State Parks," *American Forests and Forest Life* 33 (February 1927): 97–100.

34. Henry S. Graves, "National and State Parks, Part II," *American Forests and Forest Life* 33 (March 1927): 150.

35. U.S. Department of Commerce, Bureau of the Census, *1980 Census of Population: Characteristics*, vol. 1, pt. 1 (Washington, DC: U.S. Government Printing Office, 1983), 35–37.

36. "Summary of Resolutions Adopted by President's National Conference on Outdoor Recreation," *Playground* 18 (July 1924): 247.

37. U.S. Department of the Interior, National Park Service, *A Study of the Park and Recreation Problem of the United States* (Washington, DC: U.S. Government Printing Office, 1941), 90.

38. United States, *Statutes at Large* 50 (1937): 670.

39. U.S. Congress, Senate, Committee on Interior and Insular Affairs, Subcommittee on the Public Lands, *Cape Cod National Seashore Park*, Hearing on S. 857, 87th Cong., 1st sess., March 9, 1961. For proposed methods of acquiring the land, see the testimony of Interior Secretary Stewart Udall (p. 10). Section 4 (a)(1) of the bill further provided (p. 5), "The beneficial owner or owners of improved property which the Secretary acquires by condemnation may elect, as a condition to such acquisition, to retain the right of use and occupancy of the said property for noncommercial residential purposes for a term of twenty-five years, or for such lesser time as the said owner or owners may elect at the time of such acquisition."

40. U.S. Congress, Senate, *Congressional Record*, 87th Cong., 1st sess., June 27, 1961, 11391.

41. *Congressional Record*, June 27, 1961, 11391–92.

42. Significant facts and the dates of establishment for all the national parks are provided in Office of Public Affairs and Harpers Ferry Center, National Park Service, *The National Parks: Index 2005–2007* (Washington, DC: U.S. Department of the Interior, 2005).

43. R. M. Strong, "Indiana's Unspoiled Dunes," *National Parks Magazine* 33 (August 1959): 6–7. A social, cultural, and intellectual history of the region is J. Ronald Engel, *Sacred Sands: The Struggle for Community in the Indiana Dunes* (Middletown, CT: Wesleyan University Press, 1983). The standard political history is Kay Franklin and Norma Schaeffer, *Duel for the Dunes: Land Use Conflict on the Shores of Lake Michigan* (Urbana: University of Illinois Press, 1983).

44. Office of Public Affairs and Harpers Ferry Center, National Park Service, *The National Parks*, 58. Hearings on the park were first held in 1961. See U.S. Congress, Senate, Committee on Interior and Insular Affairs, Subcommittee on Public Lands, *Ozark Rivers National Monument*, Hearing on S. 1381, 87th Cong., 1st sess., July 6, 1961.

45. U.S. Congress, Senate, Committee on Interior and Insular Affairs, *Wild and Scenic Rivers*, Hearings on S. 119 and S. 1092, 90th Cong., 1st sess., April 13–14, 1967; U.S. Congress, House, *Providing for a National Scenic Rivers System*, H. Rept. 1623 to accompany H.R. 18260, 90th Cong., 2nd sess., July 3, 1968.

46. In all federal hearings, competitive management agencies were consistently opposed to seashores, lakeshores, and wild and scenic rivers. A revealing example of those pressures, limiting Ozark National Scenic Riverways through the elimination of 20,000 acres along the Eleven Point River, is U.S. Congress, Senate, Committee on Interior and Insular Affairs, Subcommittee on Public Lands, *The Ozark National Rivers*, Hearings on S. 16, 88th Cong., 1st sess., April 8–9 and May 22, 1963.

47. A policy analysis of this argument and its implications is Ronald A. Foresta, *America's National Parks and Their Keepers* (Washington, DC: Resources for the Future, 1984), 46–47, 218–22.

48. Office of Public Affairs and Harpers Ferry Center, National Park Service, *The National Parks*, 27, 66.

49. Lake Mead National Recreation Area, including Hoover Dam on the Colorado River, bordering Arizona and Nevada, was the first. Office of Public Affairs and Harpers Ferry Center, National Park Service, *The National Parks*, 61.

50. United States, *Statutes at Large* 78 (1964): 897–904; United States, *Statutes at Large* 82 (1968): 354–56.

51. Foresta, *America's National Parks and Their Keepers*, 237–40.

52. S. 857, Hearing, 11, 34–35.

53. U.S. Congress, House, Committee on Interior and Insular Affairs, Subcommittee on National Parks, *Ozark National Rivers, Missouri*, Hearings on H.R. 1803, H.R. 2884, and S. 16, 88th Cong., 1st sess., April 9 and May 6, 1963, 22, 27; U.S. Congress, Senate, Committee on Interior and Insular Affairs, Subcommittee on Public Lands, *Indiana Dunes National Lakeshore*, Hearings on S. 2249, 88th Cong., 2nd sess., March 5–7, 1964, 5. For similar arguments, see also U.S. Congress, Senate, Committee on Interior and Insular Affairs, Subcommittee on Public Lands, *Sleeping Bear Dunes National Recreation Area*, Hearing on S. 2153, 87th Cong., 1st sess., November 13, 1961, 11–13, and U.S. Congress, Senate, Committee on Interior and Insular Affairs, Subcommittee on Public Lands, *Pictured Rocks National Lakeshore*, Hearing on S. 1143, 88th Cong., 2nd sess., July 20, 1964, 8–11.

54. U.S. Congress, House, Committee on Interior and Insular Affairs, Subcommittee on National Parks and Recreation, *Gateway Area Proposals*, Hearings on H.R. 1370, H.R. 1121, and Related Bills, 92nd Cong., 1st sess., June 26 and July 19–20, 1971, 55; U.S. Congress, House, Committee on Interior and Insular Affairs, Subcommittee on National Parks and Recreation, *Proposed Cuyahoga Valley National Historical Park and Recreation Area, Part I*, Hearing on H.R. 7167 and Related Bills, 93rd Cong., 2nd sess., March 1, 1974, 9.

55. See, for example, Representative Seiberling's continuing remarks in Hearing on H.R. 7167, 9–10.

56. U.S. Congress, Senate, Committee on Interior and Insular Affairs, Subcommittee on Parks and Recreation, *Golden Gate National Recreation Area*, Hearings on S. 2342, S. 3174, and H.R. 16444, 92nd Cong., 2nd sess., September 22 and 27, 1972, 74. See also U.S. Congress, Senate, Committee on Interior and Insular Affairs, Subcommittee on Parks and Recreation, *Santa Monica Mountain and Seashore National Urban Park*, Hearings on S. 1270, 93rd Cong., 2nd sess., June 15 and August 1, 1974, passim.

57. *Legislative History*, 978–86.

58. *Legislative History*, 985.

59. *Legislative History*, 981.

60. "NPCA Interviews Phillip Burton," 22.

CHAPTER 12: DECISION IN ALASKA

1. Robert A. Jones, "Alaska Parks: Battle Lines Form around Last Frontier," *Los Angeles Times*, September 5, 1977, pt. 1, 1.

2. Peggy Wayburn, "Great Stakes in the Great Land: Alaska Lands for Public Good," *Sierra Club Bulletin* 59 (September 1974): 17–18.

3. U.S. Congress, House, Committee on Interior and Insular Affairs, Subcommittee on General Oversight and Alaska Lands, *Inclusion of Alaska Lands in National Park, Forest, Wildlife Refuge, and Wild and Scenic Rivers Systems*, Hearings on H.R. 39, H.R. 1974, H.R. 2876, H.R. 5505, et al., 95th Cong., 1st sess., April 21–September 21, 1977, pt. 1, 184, 188 (hereafter cited as H.R. 39, Hearings).

4. H.R. 39, Hearings, pt. 1, 162.

5. George Catlin, *Illustrations of the Manners, Customs, and Conditions of the North American Indians*, 2 vols. (London: H. G. Bohn, 1851), 1:262.

6. H.R. 39, Hearings, pt. 1, 635.

7. H.R. 39, Hearings, pt. 1, 944–45.

8. See Morgan Sherwood, *Big Game in Alaska: A History of Wildlife and People* (New Haven, CT: Yale University Press, 1981). A history sympathetic to the natives' perspective is Theodore Catton, *Inhabited Wilderness: Indians, Eskimos, and National Parks in Alaska* (Albuquerque: University of New Mexico Press, 1997).

9. The quote is attributed to Allen H. Morgan, former executive vice president of the Massachusetts Audubon Society. Les Line, ed., *What We Save Now: An Audubon Primer of Defense* (Boston: Houghton Mifflin, in cooperation with the National Audubon Society, 1973), vii.

10. I have avoided duplicating the history of the wilderness movement and parklands in Alaska as previously treated in Roderick Frazier Nash, *Wilderness and the American Mind*, 4th ed. (New Haven, CT: Yale University Press, 2001); Michael Frome, *Battle for the Wilderness* (New York: Praeger, 1974); and Craig W. Allin,

The Politics of Wilderness Preservation (Westport, CT: Greenwood Press, 1982). Allin should be supplemented with G. Frank Williss, *"Do Things Right the First Time": The National Park Service and the Alaska National Interest Lands Conservation Act of 1980* (Washington, DC: U.S. Department of the Interior, National Park Service, 1985). Daniel Nelson focuses on the bill's environmental activists in *Northern Landscapes: The Struggle for Wilderness Alaska* (Washington, DC: RFF Press, 2004).

11. See Allin, *Politics of Wilderness Preservation*, chap. 5, and Ronald A. Foresta, *America's National Parks and Their Keepers* (Washington, DC: Resources for the Future, 1984), 69–70.

12. Conrad L. Wirth, as director of the Park Service between 1951 and 1964, is an example of management hostility to wilderness because it precluded building roads. See Wirth, *Parks, Politics, and the People* (Norman: University of Oklahoma Press, 1980), 358–61, and Ethan Carr, *Mission 66: Modernism and the National Park Dilemma* (Amherst: University of Massachusetts Press in association with Library of American Landscape History, 2007), chap. 9.

13. United States, *Statutes at Large 84* (1970–1971): 1105–6; Office of Public Affairs and Harpers Ferry Center, National Park Service, *The National Parks: Index 2005–2007* (Washington, DC: U.S. Department of the Interior, 2005), 27; U.S. Congress, House, *Congressional Record*, 94th Cong., 2nd sess., September 26, 1976, 31888–91; United States, *Statutes at Large 90* (1976): 2692–96. The controversial side of national park wilderness is also revealed in U.S. Congress, House, Committee on Interior and Insular Affairs, Subcommittee on National Parks and Recreation, *Designation of Wilderness Areas, Part IV*, Hearings on H.R. 13562 and H.R. 13563, 93rd Cong., 2nd sess., March 22, 25, and 26, 1974, and U.S. Congress, House, Committee on Interior and Insular Affairs, *Designating Certain Lands within Units of the National Park System as Wilderness . . . and for Other Purposes*, H. Rept. 94-1427 to accompany H.R. 13160, 94th Cong., 2nd sess., August 13, 1976.

14. U.S. Congress, House, Committee on Interior and Insular Affairs, Subcommittee on National Parks and Insular Affairs, *Legislative History of the National Parks and Recreation Act of 1978*, Committee Print No. 11, 95th Cong., 2nd sess., December 1978, 982.

15. A sample of general opposition to wilderness is U.S. Congress, Senate, Committee on Energy and Natural Resources, Subcommittee on Parks, Recreation, and Renewable Resources, *National Park Service Concessions Policy*, Hearings on Oversight—the Concessions Policy Act of 1965, 96th Cong., 1st sess., March 29 and April 23 and 27, 1979.

16. Nash, *Wilderness and the American Mind*, 281–88.

17. Allin, *Politics of Wilderness Preservation*, chap. 7.

18. An important summary of these arguments is Eugenia Horstman Connally, ed., *Wilderness Parklands in Alaska* (Washington, DC: National Parks and Conservation Association, 1978).

19. United States, *Statutes at Large* 85 (1971): 708–9.

20. United States, *Statutes at Large* 85 (1971): 708–9; Allin, *Politics of Wilderness Preservation*, 216–18.

21. Allin, *Politics of Wilderness Preservation*, 218–19.

22. Allin, *Politics of Wilderness Preservation*, 219.

23. As quoted in Allin, *Politics of Wilderness Preservation*, 221.

24. H.R. 39, Hearings, pt. 1, 1–8.

25. H.R. 39, Hearings, pts. 2–13.

26. For a breakdown of public support, see Allin, *Politics of Wilderness Preservation*, 223.

27. H.R. 39, Hearings, pt. 1, 2.

28. H.R. 39, Hearings, pt. 1, 3–4.

29. H.R. 39, Hearings, pt. 1, 4–5.

30. H.R. 39, Hearings, pt. 1, 103–6.

31. H.R. 39, Hearings, pt. 1, 104, 107.

32. H.R. 39, Hearings, pt. 1, 118–19.

33. Sierra Club Alaska Task Force, *Alaska Report* 3 (September 1976): 1–8; Robert A. Jones, "Development or Parks? Wild Alaska to Change; Only Direction Is in Doubt," *Los Angeles Times*, September 6, 1977, pt. 1, 1, 3, 16–17. An important history of the Trans-Alaska Pipeline is Peter A. Coates, *The Trans-Alaska Pipeline Controversy: Technology, Conservation, and the Frontier* (Bethlehem, PA: Lehigh University Press, 1991).

34. H.R. 39, Hearings, pt. 1, 624.

35. H.R. 39, Hearings, pt. 1, 156.

36. Allin, *Politics of Wilderness Preservation*, 226.

37. U.S. Congress, House, *Congressional Record*, 95th Cong., 2nd sess., May 17, 1978, 14146–73; May 18, 1978, 14391–470; May 19, 1978, 14660–95.

38. Nash, *Wilderness and the American Mind*, 298.

39. Cecil D. Andrus, "Guarding Alaska's Crown Jewels," *Los Angeles Times*, October 11, 1978, pt. 2, 7.

40. Nash, *Wilderness and the American Mind*, 298; Allin, *Politics of Wilderness Preservation*, 236; United States, *Statutes at Large* 93 (1978–1979): 1446–75.

41. U.S. Congress, House, *Congressional Record*, 96th Cong., 1st sess., May 16, 1979, 11457–59. There were actually two votes on May 16; the first, 268 to 157, was the important vote upholding Udall. After that, substitutes to his bill were easily defeated. Consequently, the final vote, 360 to 65, reflected his opponents shrewdly switching sides. Further machinations in the Senate are discussed in Allin, *Politics of Wilderness Preservation*, 244–55.

42. As quoted in Julius Duscha, "How the Alaska Act Was Won," *Living Wilderness* 44 (Spring 1981): 9.

43. As quoted in Nash, *Wilderness and the American Mind*, 301.

44. Charles M. Clusen, "Viewpoint," *Living Wilderness* 44 (Spring 1981): 3. Acreages, details, and descriptions of the protected lands are to be found in

Charles R. Miller, "The New National Interest Lands," *Living Wilderness* 44 (Spring 1981): 10–13, and Celia Hunter and Ginny Wood, "Alaska National Interest Lands: The D-2 Lands," *Alaska Geographic* 8, no. 4 (1981): 1–240.

45. On preservationists' concerns and disappointments, see Rebecca Wodder, "The Alaska Challenge Ahead," *Living Wilderness* 44 (Spring 1981): 13–19; Clusen, "Viewpoint," 3; Bill Curry, "Alaska Land Battle Far from Settled," *Los Angeles Times*, July 25, 1983, pt. 1, 1, 11; and Jim Doherty, "Alaska: The Real National Lands Battle Is Just Getting Under Way," *Audubon* 85 (January 1983): 114–16.

46. The hearings are especially instructive. See U.S. Congress, House, Committee on Interior and Insular Affairs, Subcommittee on National Parks and Recreation, *Proposed Big Thicket National Reserve, Texas*, Hearings on H.R. 4270, et al., 93rd Cong., 1st sess., July 16 and 17, 1973, and *Proposed Big Cypress Reserve, Florida*, Hearings on H.R. 46 and H.R. 4866, 93rd Cong., 1st sess., May 10 and 11, 1973.

47. The theme is prevalent throughout the hearings, especially H.R. 39, Hearings, pts. 8–13.

48. H.R. 39, Hearings, pt. 13, 215.

49. Edgar Wayburn, "Hunters Take Aim at Alaska's National Parks," *Sierra* 68 (May–June 1983): 16–19.

50. Alaska Coalition, "Alaska: Imperiled Heritage," undated leaflet.

51. Margaret Murie, *Two in the Far North*, 2nd ed. (Anchorage: Alaska Northwest Publishing Co., 1978), preface.

52. By preservationists' own admission, the issue of resource extraction was still unresolved. An important document portending the fate of commercially productive lands within or adjacent to national parks, wilderness areas, and wildlife refuges is U.S. Congress, Senate, Committee on Interior and Insular Affairs, *An Assessment of Mineral Resources in Alaska*, prepared by the U.S. Geological Survey, the Bureau of Mines, and the Bureau of Land Management, Committee Print, 93rd Cong., 2nd sess., July 1974.

CHAPTER 13: INTO THE TWENTY-FIRST CENTURY: ENCIRCLEMENT AND UNCERTAINTY

1. Peter Steinhart, "Interior Motives: Will Watt Get His Way in the Parks?" *Los Angeles Times*, May 3, 1981, pt. 5, 2; Michael Frome, "Park Concessions and Concessioners," *National Parks* 55 (June 1981): 16–18; Peter Steinhart, "The Park Service Feels an Early Winter Chill from Watt's Interior," *Los Angeles Times*, November 8, 1981, pt. 5, 1–2.

2. Then known as the Mammoth Oil Company. See Burl Noggle, *Teapot Dome: Oil and Politics in the 1920's* (Baton Rouge: Louisiana State University Press, 1962), and Morris Robert Werner and John Starr, *Teapot Dome* (New York: Viking, 1959).

3. For an inventory of objections to Watt's policies, see "Watt's Wrongs," *Living Wilderness* 45 (Fall 1981): 40–41.

4. Watt, of course, counted on the support of conservative managers within the National Park Service itself who generally agreed with him that urban parks in particular distracted from the Park Service's original and legitimate mission. See Ronald A. Foresta, *America's National Parks and Their Keepers* (Washington, DC: Resources for the Future, 1983), 77–82, 175–76. For further analyses of Watt's policies, see T. H. Watkins, "James Gaius Watt: An Idea Whose Time Has Gone," *Living Wilderness* 45 (Winter 1981): 34–38; Chuck Williams, "The Park Rebellion: Charles Cushman, James Watt, and the Attack on the National Parks," *Not Man Apart* 12 (June 1982): 11–26; "Battle over the Wilderness: Special Report," *Newsweek* 102 (July 25, 1983): 22–29; and Bil Gilbert and Robert Sullivan, "Inside Interior: An Abrupt Turn," *Sports Illustrated* 59 (September 26, 1983): 66–80 and (October 3, 1983): 96–112.

5. Gordon Anderson, "Coal: Threat to the Canyonlands," *Living Wilderness* (December 1980): 4–11; John J. Kearney, "Is the Air Visibility of Our National Parks Being Adequately Protected?" *EPA Journal* 7 (May 1981): 2–6; Jeff Radford, "Stripmining Arid Navajo Lands in the U.S.: Threats to Health and Heritage," *Ambio* 11, no. 1 (1982): 9–14; Jerome Ostrov, "Visibility Protection under the Clean Air Act: Preserving Scenic and Parkland Areas in the Southwest," *Ecology Law Quarterly* 10, no. 3 (1982): 397–453.

6. U.S. Department of the Interior, National Park Service, *State of the Parks—1980: A Report to the Congress*, prepared by the Office of Science and Technology, May 1980, viii.

7. U.S. Department of Agriculture, Forest Service, *Final Environmental Impact Statement of the Island Park Geothermal Area, Idaho-Montana-Wyoming*, January 15, 1980, 112.

8. Rick Reese, *Greater Yellowstone: The National Park and Adjacent Wild Lands*, Montana Geographic Series No. 6 (Helena: Montana Magazine, Inc., 1984); Dave Alt et al., *Glacier Country: Montana's Glacier National Park*, Montana Geographic Series No. 4 (Helena: Montana Magazine, Inc., 1983). Wildlife issues have been exhaustively debated in Warren Hanna, *The Grizzlies of Glacier* (Missoula, MT: Mountain Press, 1978); Frank C. Craighead Jr., *Track of the Grizzly* (San Francisco: Sierra Club Books, 1979); Paul Schullery, *The Bears of Yellowstone* (Yellowstone National Park, WY: Yellowstone Library and Museum Association, 1980); Thomas McNamee, *The Grizzly Bear* (New York: Knopf, 1984); and Alston Chase, "The Last Bears of Yellowstone, *Atlantic Monthly* 251 (February 1983): 63–73.

9. Vic Ostrowidzki, "Clark Will Keep Environmentalists Active," *Seattle Post-Intelligencer*, October 24, 1983, pt. A, 9.

10. Recent population and development pressures are treated in Michael Frome, *Regreening the National Parks* (Tucson: University of Arizona Press, 1992).

11. The literature generated by the Yellowstone fires is exceptionally large if highly repetitious. A critical review of the initial titles is Alfred Runte, "Man Bites Dog in Yellowstone: The Fire Books of 1989," *Montana: The Magazine of Western History* 39 (Autumn 1989): 86–87.

12. See, e.g., Richard A. Bartlett, "Nature Is the Least of Yellowstone's Adversaries," *Los Angeles Times*, September 26, 1988, pt. 2, 5.

13. Richard A. Bartlett, *Yellowstone: A Wilderness Besieged* (Tucson: University of Arizona Press, 1985); Carsten Lien, *Olympic Battleground: The Power Politics of Timber Preservation*, 2nd ed. (Seattle: The Mountaineers Books, 2000).

14. Stephen J. Pyne, "The Summer We Let Wild Fire Loose," *Natural History* (August 1989): 45–49. See also Stephen J. Pyne, "Letting Wild Fire Loose: The Fires of '88," *Montana: The Magazine of Western History* 39 (Summer 1989): 76–79, and Alston Chase, "Greater Yellowstone and the Death and Rebirth of the National Parks Ideal," *Orion Nature Quarterly* 8 (Summer 1989): 44–55. A further criticism of national park management is Joseph L. Sax, *Mountains without Handrails: Reflections on the National Parks* (Ann Arbor: University of Michigan Press, 1980). See also William C. Everhart, *The National Park Service*, 2nd ed. (Boulder, CO: Westview Press, 1983).

15. An early analysis of the recovery is George Wuerthner, "The Flames of '88," *Wilderness* 52 (Summer 1989): 41–54.

16. Jim Robbins, "Return of Wolves to West Brings Back Fear and Anger," *New York Times*, December 29, 1995, 7. U.S. Department of the Interior, National Park Service, Yellowstone National Park, *Yellowstone Today*, Autumn 1995, 6. Important studies of American wildlife include Thomas R. Dunlap, *Saving America's Wildlife* (Princeton, NJ: Princeton University Press, 1988), and Lisa Mighetto, *Wild Animals and American Environmental Ethics* (Tucson: University of Arizona Press, 1991).

17. Marc Reisner, "A Decision for the Desert," *Wilderness* 50 (Winter 1986): 33–53; California Desert Protection League, *The California Desert: A Time to Protect Our Western Heritage*, printed brochure, May 1993; Katharine Q. Seelye, "House Approves Desert Preserve in a Vast Expanse of California," *New York Times*, July 28, 1994, 1, 10. The first definitive history of the California Desert Protection Act is Frank Wheat, *California Desert Miracle: The Fight for Desert Parks and Wilderness* (San Diego, CA: Sunbelt Publications, 1999). See also Elisabeth M. Hamin, *Mojave Lands: Interpretive Planning and the National Preserve* (Baltimore: Johns Hopkins University Press, 2003).

18. Timothy Egan, "New Parks Mix Public and Private, Uneasily," *New York Times*, December 26, 1994, 1, 9.

19. United States, *Statutes at Large* 114 (2000): 1875–82.

20. Timothy Egan, "New Gold Rush Stirs Fears of Exploitation," *New York Times*, August 14, 1994, 1, 11; Todd Wilkinson, "Fool's Gold," *National Parks* 68 (July–August 1994): 31–35; Greater Yellowstone Coalition, *"Mine from Hell"*

Threatens Yellowstone, undated brochure, c. 1994; James Brooke, "Montana Mining Town Fights Gold Rush Plan," *New York Times*, January 7, 1996, 8.

21. John M. Broder, "Clinton Unveils Deal to Stop Yellowstone Mine," *Los Angeles Times*, August 13, 1996, 1.

22. U.S. Department of the Interior, National Park Service, "National Monument Proclamations under the Antiquities Act (William J. Clinton)," http://www.nps.gov/history/history/hisnps/npshistory/monuments.htm (accessed January 27, 2009).

23. Michael Jamison, "Warming Climate Shrinking Glacier Park's Glaciers," *USA Today*, October 11, 2007, http://www.usatoday.com/weather/climate/global warming/2007-10-11-glacier-park_N.htm (accessed January 27, 2009). See also Daniel B. Fagre, "Global Environmental Effects on the Mountain Ecosystem at Glacier National Park," in U.S. Department of the Interior, National Park Service, J. Selleck, ed., *National Park Service Natural Resource Year in Review—2002* (Washington, DC: National Park Service, 2003), 24–25.

24. Discovery Channel, "Supervolcano: What's under Yellowstone? America's Explosive Park," http://dsc.discovery.com/convergence/supervolcano/under/under.html (accessed January 27, 2009). With constant reference to the national parks, Daniel B. Botkin challenges traditional assumptions about macroforces and the so-called balance of nature in *Discordant Harmonies: A New Ecology for the Twenty-First Century* (New York: Oxford University Press, 1990). See also Daniel B. Botkin, *No Man's Garden: Thoreau and a New Vision for Civilization and Nature* (Washington, DC: Island Press, 2001), and Daniel B. Botkin, *Beyond the Stony Mountains: Nature in the American West from Lewis and Clark to Today* (New York: Oxford University Press, 2004).

EPILOGUE: THE FUTURE OF NATIONAL PARKS

1. Representative examples of these ideas and undertones may be found in William Cronon, "The Trouble with Wilderness; or, Getting Back to the Wrong Nature," *Environmental History* 1 (January 1996): 7–28, and William Cronon, ed., *Uncommon Ground: Toward Reinventing Nature* (New York: W. W. Norton, 1995). A statement of rebuttal is Alfred Runte, "Right for the World: Preservation in Historical Perspective," *Natureza & Conservação* 1 (April 2003): 67–70.

2. An influential promoter of these viewpoints is the Property and Environment Research Center, headquartered in Bozeman, Montana. See especially its quarterly publication, *PERC News*.

3. John Muir, "The American Forests," *Atlantic Monthly* 80 (August 1897): 156–57. The article and quote reappear in Muir's anthology, *Our National Parks* (Boston: Houghton Mifflin, 1901), 364–65.

4. *2003 United Nations List of Protected Areas* (Gland: International Union for Conservation of Nature and Natural Resources, 2003), vii.

BIBLIOGRAPHICAL NOTE

T HE notes provide a detailed listing and evaluation of the major
works used in this study. The following is to summarize briefly
some of the sources and studies that stand apart.

Relevant manuscript collections on the national parks are widely scattered across the country. The definitive finding aids to these collections
continue to be maintained by the Forest History Society in Durham,
North Carolina. Collections opened before 1977 are listed in Richard C.
Davis, *North American Forest History: A Guide to Archives and Manuscripts in the United States and Canada* (Santa Barbara, CA: Forest History Society, Inc., and Clio Books, 1977). Now the *Guide to Environmental
History Archival Collections*, updates appear online at http://www.foresthistory
.org/Research/archguid.html. Current listings disclose more than 7,000
record groups in 450 repositories in North America and around the world.
For the beginning years of conservation, the Library of Congress offers *The
Evolution of the Conservation Movement, 1850–1920* at http://memory
.loc.gov/ammem/amrvhtml/conshome.html. In addition to manuscripts,
the site is an excellent source for locating the founding publications of
American conservation, beginning with the principal books, pamphlets,
and government documents maintained in the collections of the library.

Library of Congress manuscript collections consulted for this study
include the Frederick Law Olmsted and John C. Merriam papers. The
sources of the Bancroft Library of the University of California at Berkeley
are especially rich, highlighted by the William E. Colby, Francis P. Farquhar, Robert Underwood Johnson, John Muir, Robert Bradford Marshall, and Sierra Club records. The J. Horace McFarland collection,
located in the archives building of the Pennsylvania Museum and Historical Commission, Harrisburg, proved invaluable for its coverage of the

Progressive era and the formation of the National Park Service (1900–1920). By far, the most voluminous repository of primary materials is Record Group 79, the Records of the National Park Service maintained by the National Archives in College Park, Maryland. Despite its size, Record Group 79 is well cataloged and easy to use. Generally, for records produced in the parks since the 1960s, the relevant regional repository of the National Archives is the holder of all recent files. However, most of the larger, original parks, including Yosemite, Yellowstone, Glacier, and Grand Canyon, maintain their own libraries and specialty archives. For Yellowstone, there is a magnificent new facility at Gardiner, Montana, the Yellowstone Heritage and Research Center, with 5.3 million cataloged items. Meanwhile, library departments around the country, such as the Conservation Library Center of the Denver Public Library, continue to acquire private papers on environmental history subjects.

Government documents are the most important printed sources. Especially useful are the House and Senate debates published in the *Congressional Globe* and *Congressional Record*. Most of the major parks were also the subject of congressional hearings, reports, and investigations, most of which are printed. The annual reports of the secretary of the interior and director of the National Park Service are invaluable additions to the congressional literature, as are the annual reports of the U.S. Forest Service and other agencies closely tied to the parks. Squaring the congressional debates with what Congress actually approved, it is always advisable to consult *Statutes at Large* for the final wording of the respective park acts.

No examination of national park history is complete without extensive use of the primary source materials also to be found in major newspapers, periodicals, and conservation journals. *Poole's Index* and *Reader's Guide* list hundreds of relevant articles. Researchers should be aware, however, that many popular magazines and specialty journals, among them *National Parks Magazine*, the *Sierra Club Bulletin*, and *American Forests and Forest Life*, were not always indexed during their initial years of publication. For maximum coverage, collections of the more important journals should be examined off the shelf. Although time consuming, the procedure often yields unexpected dividends, including period advertisements and letters-to-the-editor columns.

Predictably, most of the secondary literature is characterized largely by histories of the individual national parks. Again, for the period prior to 1977, the Forest History Society has published the standard guide,

Ronald J. Fahl, *North American Forest and Conservation History: A Bibliography* (Santa Barbara, CA: Forest History Society, Inc., and A. B. C.—Clio Press, 1977). For secondary literature published since the 1980s, there is the society's searchable database, the *Environmental History Bibliography*, at http://www.foresthistory.org/Research/biblio.html. As a legislative and administrative history of the national parks to 1960, John Ise, *Our National Park Policy: A Critical History* (Baltimore: The Johns Hopkins Press, 1961), is still definitive but increasingly dated. Henry Nash Smith, *Virgin Land: The American West as Symbol and Myth* (Cambridge, MA: Harvard University Press, 1950); Leo Marx, *The Machine in the Garden: Technology and the Pastoral Ideal in America* (New York: Oxford University Press, 1964); Roderick Frazier Nash, *Wilderness and the American Mind*, 4th ed. (New Haven, CT: Yale University Press, 2001); Hans Huth, *Nature and the American: Three Centuries of Changing Attitudes* (Berkeley: University of California Press, 1957); and Barbara Novak, *Nature and Culture: American Landscape and Painting, 1825–1875* (New York: Oxford University Press, 1980) are still the leading intellectual studies suggesting why Americans invariably looked to landscape as a cultural resource.

The ability to cast a single park in a broader light remains the distinguishing feature of the best management histories. A noteworthy example is Carsten Lien, *Olympic Battleground: The Power Politics of Timber Preservation*, 2nd ed. (Seattle: The Mountaineers Books, 2000). The Carsten Lien Papers, in the University of Washington Archives, Special Collections, Seattle, add immeasurably to the printed volume. Alfred Runte, *Yosemite: The Embattled Wilderness* (Lincoln: University of Nebraska Press, 1990), traces the evolution of national park science in perhaps the system's most controversial park. Similarly, Mark W. T. Harvey, *A Symbol of Wilderness: Echo Park and the American Conservation Movement* (Albuquerque: University of New Mexico Press, 1994), demonstrates that the water development issues of Dinosaur National Monument, although a single park, had troubling implications for the park system as a whole. By Richard A. Bartlett, *Yellowstone: A Wilderness Besieged* (Tucson: University of Arizona Press, 1985) equally broadens the Yellowstone story, contrasting the behavior of visitors, managers, and concessionaires as they affected the park's physical and biological resources. The same insights and inclusiveness characterize Susan R. Schrepfer, *The Fight to Save the Redwoods: A History of Environmental Reform, 1917–1978* (Madison: University of Wisconsin Press, 1983). Noting that preservationists were often divided, Schrepfer points out the penalty of those ideological differences, in the instance of the redwoods costing the smaller national park favored by conservative preservationists the biological integrity it deserved. A comprehensive look at science in the national parks is Richard West Sellars, *Preserving Nature in the National Parks: A History*, rev. ed. (New Haven, CT: Yale University Press, 2009).

Biographies add significantly to the secondary literature, especially when the biographer again values the broader history. In that regard, a truly exceptional volume is Douglas Brinkley, *The Wilderness Warrior: Theodore Roosevelt and the Crusade for America* (New York: Harper, 2009). Robert Shankland, *Steve Mather of the National Parks*, 3rd ed. (New York: Alfred A. Knopf, 1970), and Donald C. Swain, *Wilderness Defender: Horace M. Albright and Conservation* (Chicago: University of Chicago Press, 1970), are as much about the formative years of the National Park Service as they are biographies of Mather and Albright. Stephen Fox, *John Muir and His Legacy: The American Conservation Movement* (Boston: Little, Brown, 1981), adds immeasurably to the life of John Muir by developing the contributions of his distinguished successors. Dyana Z. Furmansky, *Rosalie Edge, Hawk of Mercy: The Activist Who Saved Nature from the Conservationists* (Athens: University of Georgia Press, 2009), and Jack E. Davis, *An Everglades Providence: Marjory Stoneman Douglas and the American Environmental Century* (Athens: University of Georgia Press, 2009), are similar reminders that few national parks have ever been established without the persistence of dedicated individuals.

INDEX

ABOUT THE AUTHOR

A LFRED RUNTE lives in Seattle, Washington, where he continues to write about the national parks and their relationship with American culture. One of the country's leading environmental historians, he received his Ph.D. in 1976 from the University of California, Santa Barbara, and came to specialize in public history. He was recently an adviser to the Ken Burns PBS documentary *The National Parks: America's Best Idea* and appeared in all six episodes. He speaks frequently on environmental and transportation matters, including invited appearances on *Nightline, The Today Show, 48 Hours,* and The History Channel. In addition to *National Parks: The American Experience,* his other acclaimed books include *Yosemite: The Embattled Wilderness, Trains of Discovery: Western Railroads and the National Parks,* and *Allies of the Earth: Railroads and the Soul of Preservation.*